INTERNATIONAL STUDIES OF THE

COMMITTEE ON INTERNATIONAL RELATIONS

UNIVERSITY OF NOTRE DAME

The Limits of Hegemony

The Limits of Hegemony

United States Relations with
Argentina and Chile during
World War II

MICHAEL J. FRANCIS

UNIVERSITY OF NOTRE DAME PRESS

NOTRE DAME ~ LONDON

Library of Congress Cataloging in Publication Data

Francis, Michael J.
    The limits of hegemony.

    Includes bibliographical references and index.
    1. United States—Foreign relations—Chile.
2. Chile—Foreign relations—United States. 3. United
States—Foreign relations—Argentine Republic.
4. Argentine Republic—Foreign relations—United States.
5. Pan-Americanism. 6. World War, 1939–1945—Diplomatic
history. I. Title.
E183.8.C4F7   327.73'082   77-89754
ISBN 0-268-01260-1

Manufactured in the United States of America

CONTENTS

ACKNOWLEDGEMENTS

One pleasurable aspect of publishing a book is that it offers the opportunity to acknowledge some of the people who have assisted in the research and writing of the manuscript.

In the case of this manuscript, the critical first shove toward working on this topic came when the Social Science Research Council funded me for a summer in the United States National Archives. Later support from the Institute of International Studies of the University of Notre Dame (then headed by Professor Stephen D. Kertesz) allowed me to travel to Chile and Argentina on other projects, but with enough spare time to gather materials for this volume. The Institute, currently headed by Professor George Brinkley, also helped support publication of the manuscript. During his eight years as chairman of my department, George was unfailingly considerate of my problems—even when they were of my own making. I did the final revision while a visiting scholar at the University of Michigan on a Consortium for a World Order Studies fellowship. That stay was made extremely pleasant by the thoughtfulness of Professor Harold Jacobson.

Of the many libraries I used during the course of this project, two were particularly helpful. They were the National Archives (with special thanks to Patricia Dowling) and the library of the Centro Bellarmino in Santiago (with thanks to Marta Zanelli).

So many individuals gave me advice on all or parts of this manuscript that it is difficult to list them all. I would particularly mention Peter G. Snow, Juan Carlos Puig, Hernan Vera-Godoy, H. E. Bicheno, John J. Kennedy, and Michael Potashnik. A number of "my" graduate students read the text and gave me helpful ideas—in particular Walter Sánchez González, David Landry, Frank Kessler, Lloyd Wagner, Ronald Deziel, Tony O'Brien, and Lee Berry. I benefited greatly from the editing skills of Frances Burdette.

Norman Armour, who appears often as a figure in this book and a man for whom I have enormous admiration, carefully read the manuscript and provided interesting insights.

My intellectual *patrón* has been Professor Kennedy, who directed my dissertation at the University of Virginia and then, after his coming to Notre

Dame as chairman of the Department of Government and International Studies, was instrumental in my hiring. *Patrones* in Latin America kept their peasants in line by lending them more than they could repay. Likewise I owe Professor Kennedy far more than can ever be repaid. However, he differs from the traditional *patrón* in that he has never made the slightest effort to draw on that account.

Professor Kertesz has been another continuing source of encouragement to me. He has treated me with a kindness and generosity which I have always appreciated.

Portions of chapters two, four, and five have previously appeared as articles in the *Journal of Latin American Studies* (May 1974 and May 1977). Professor Harold Blakemore, co-editor of the journal, has kindly allowed me permission to incorporate those articles into this volume.

My wife Deanna and my two indefatigable children have been willing to pack up and go to Latin America with me. Without this I would never have been able to produce the research I have. I apologize to the three of them for all the times my mind was more on dependency (and other such topics) than on their problems.

Because I chose to preserve many of the idiosyncracies in this manuscript, it is more than usually necessary to absolve any of the above-mentioned individuals of responsibility for the shortcomings of the book.

INTRODUCTION

Almost from the beginning of World War II, United States foreign policy-makers were dissatisfied with Argentina's and Chile's support for the Allied war effort. Compared to other questions confronting the United States government during the period, this problem was not a paramount issue in the White House or Department of State. Still, attempts by the United States to force a change in the policies of these two South American countries, and the impact these attempts had on Chile and Argentina, are worth examining. The confrontation casts light on a number of problems connected with United States foreign policy and international relations generally, and besides tells us something about the domestic politics of Latin American countries.

It may help to clarify the discussion if we begin by defining the three basic subjects or questions this book examines.

First, the author hopes to help define the nature of Pan-American relations. The hemispheric system has at times been interpreted as a special, almost spiritual, relationship, one setting the countries of the western hemisphere apart from the corruption of the old world.[1] The opposite interpretation is that Pan-Americanism is rhetoric pushed by Washington to justify its hegemony in Latin America; in other words, that Pan-Americanism is simply a smoke screen for the satellite position of the countries of Latin America. Gordon Connell-Smith's examination of the situation favors the latter interpretation when he concludes:

> Clearly, the inter-American system has served the interests of the United States much more than it has those of the Latin American countries. . . . The inter-American system has helped the United States to maintain her hegemony and safeguard her interests in the hemisphere with the minimum of intervention from extracontinental powers and influence.[2]

Because inter-American cooperation in its almost mystical sense was cited as a justification for actions during the period under consideration, the author hopes that what follows will help explore beneath the surface into the realities of the western hemisphere idea as it stood in the mid-twentieth century.

1

Linked to the first question is the second, which concerns the magnitude and operation of United States power in the hemisphere. The present study was originally undertaken because the author was curious about the various forms this power takes, the way it is used, and the limits of its influence.

One of the concepts which students of international relations have begun to use to help explain when influence is effective and when it is not is that of the "penetrated political system." This is defined as a system in which "nonmembers of a national society participate directly and authoritatively, in either the allocation of its values or the mobilization of support on behalf of its goals."[3] Norman Bailey puts the idea in a more systematic and mechanistic sense when he states that "the countries of Latin America are now, and have always been, client-states, members of a sub-hierarchical structure within the over-all international hierarchy."[4] He sees the "paramount" (the United States) as setting forth

> parameters of international action, beyond which the client may not stray without the risk of enforcement action (reprisal) by the paramount. The paramounts supply their clients with protection and assistance and the clients supply the paramounts with foreign policy support.[5]

One of the explanations for the workings of penetrated or paramountcy/client relationships is the idea of the clientele elite which is emphasized in dependency theorizing. Although the primary interest of most dependency writers is in the area of economic development,[6] the theory is also a concept of international relations.[7] Important to the workings of the dependency analysis is the existence of a clientele elite in the dependent country. This group owes its position to the workings of international capitalism and consequently benefits from actions which strengthen the existing divisions of labor in international capitalism. Thus the elite favors keeping the developing country open to foreign capital, by offering their country's primary products while in turn, serving as a market for manufactured goods from the developed world. The vagueness of the theory makes the testing of the international relations aspects of dependency difficult. But a case study of two dependent countries facing the same kind of pressure and reacting in different manners suggests some of the strengths and shortcomings of the dependency explanation.

So by using the interrelated concepts of dependency and penetration, this study has as its second major consideration the analysis of the degree of United States influence over Latin American states in bilateral and multilateral relations. It examines the instruments of coercion available, and in the cases cited outlines the limits of power (or hegemony) and the costs of using that power.

The third subject is the impact the United States pressure had on the domestic politics of the countries involved and the effect their domestic political systems had on their ability or determination to resist the wishes of Washington. Although it has become rather commonplace to allude to this, the reader should be reminded that in the discipline of political science an unfortunate division has arisen between the study of international relations and the study of comparative politics. In the former, national states are often seen as reacting mechanically to the international environment. In the latter external inputs are ignored and the culture, society, politics, and legal system are emphasized as major determinants of governmental policy. Surely foreign policy is a policy emanating from the same system as domestic policy, even if the elites involved differ somewhat according to the issue.[8]

This division has led to the infant (perhaps perpetually infant) field of the comparative study of foreign policy,[9] which attempts to explore the research gap between the mechanistic international systems or power approaches and the domestic emphasis of comparative politics scholars. In some senses this study thus becomes a comparative study of foreign policies (Argentina's and Chile's), but the author has not attempted to utilize the major theories[10] or pre-theories of foreign policy in order to render the raw materials of the study "comparative and ready for theorizing."[11] At this stage in their development, the theories are too poorly developed to lend themselves to successful application to case studies as narrowly bounded by time as are the cases presented here.

What this study does, is look at the domestic politics of Argentina and Chile in order to help explain the successes and failures of United States foreign policy. Thus the researcher, dissatisfied with existing theories, and of the opinion that additional theories based on narrow case studies are not the answer, has resisted a mild model-building urge and has approached the subject in a relatively traditional manner with only a few attempts to fit the findings into any single framework. Far too much of the analysis of United States relations with Latin America has been dominated by attempts to explain the relations as being solely one of containment,[12] dependency,[13] or what have you. This is not to argue that these approaches do not provide valuable insights but, rather, to criticize them on the grounds that the theory often obscures the events or processes it claims to explain. Put in the form of an analogy, if the approach of this book is seen by some as missing the forest for the trees, it does so as a reaction to the tendency to declare that a few isolated saplings are a forest.

With these primary considerations outlined, some explanation should be made for the approach (or methodology) used in the study. Essentially, the book is a decision-making study on the United States side of the relationship. On the Chilean and Argentine side, the emphasis is on the domestic politics of those countries as the key to understanding their foreign policies.

Even the most superficial scanning of Argentine history during World
War II will show that foreign policy was an important political issue both
among civilian power contenders and then, after they took control in June
of 1943, among the military officers. Thus, to understand Argentina's international position, one must start with its domestic political situation. In the
case of Chile, this starting point is less obvious. But this study argues that
the delicate balance of the Chilean political system largely accounts for that
peculiar foot-dragging form of resistance to Washington's initiatives that
Chile demonstrated throughout 1942.

On the United States side, this approach is justified by the fact that
domestic political considerations had little influence on policy toward Latin
America during World War II. All eyes were on the war in Europe and the
Pacific, thereby leaving the President, the Department of State, and other
agencies free to handle Latin American affairs without reference to public
opinion (up to a point, of course). The only real exception to the American
public's lack of interest in Latin America during this period may have been
in regard to Argentina during 1944-45; but even there there is little evidence
to suggest that public opinion had much impact on policy.[14]

This is not, however, a study of the impact of bureaucratic politics on
United States foreign policy. Graham Allison's models for analyzing the
policy process are not used.[15] There has been a preliminary attempt by
historian Ernest May to look at United States–Argentine relations from 1942
to 1947 utilizing Allison's models.[16] The analysis is an interesting one, but
the paradigm interferes with its effectiveness by not differentiating between
what was important and what was marginal. Perhaps more importantly, the
Allison analysis tends to ignore the mind-set and general perceptions of
decisionmakers.[17] These images set the boundaries on possible actions and
help to explain why one decision was made and another was not.[18]

Thus, to understand the policy process one should have some listing of
the shared global (or hemispheric, in this case) images of American officials
who were making foreign policy at the time. Unfortunately, the stating of
these images is far from being a science. Selective marshaling of information
can lend support to almost any set of images one can conceive.[19] The list
below is based on the author's reading of governmental despatches and
memos, on Morton Halperin's listing of shared images of the postwar period,[20] and on a previous attempt to formulate the U.S. government's "basic
beliefs" vis-á-vis Latin America for the World War II period.[21]

In descending order of priority, the major images of the foreign policy decisionmakers dealing with Latin America during World War II can be said to be:

(1) *Germany, Japan, and Italy ought to be defeated at all costs.*

This perception is significant in that it reflects the high degree of international responsibility the United States had assumed. Had the United States not felt itself capable, with the assistance of its allies, of defeating the Axis Powers, presumably the image would have been different. And, if the war had gone badly enough (England occupied, etc.), the facts of international power might have altered this belief into a fall-back position regarding the terms of a stalemate or accord with the Axis. It should be noted that the Latin American countries generally did not feel themselves to have much of a capability to change the course of events in Europe or the Far East and thus had a different perception of their national interest in terms of World War II.

(2) *Fascist movements and governments ought to be eliminated.*

David Green argues that the fascist scare in Latin America was manipulated by Washington in order to put down any potentially disruptive nationalists[22] in the same way that the threat of communism was later used to justify intervention against nationalist reformers. Obviously, the fear of fascism helped to justify United States meddling in the domestic politics of Latin American countries; but, at least during the war, the image had a life of its own flowing from events in Europe, and it was not just an excuse to protect U.S. investment.

(3) *Except as altered by the exigencies of the war effort, free trade of exports and capital is good for all countries.*

This general perception was commonly held in Washington, but with Secretary of State Cordell Hull it reached new heights. He believed world peace could emerge from freer world trade. But, as one author states, the philosophy of liberal trade "engendered the rhetoric of idealism and the diplomacy of imperialism."[23] Based on a study of the Good Neighbor Policy and reciprocal trade, he goes on to observe:

> Although Hull was perhaps a gratuitous moralist, his imperial objectives were tempered by a profound belief that freer trade, to a large degree untested in the United States' experience, could promote recovery for economies as diverse as Guatemala and the United States.[24]

(4) *The interests of the United States and Latin America are the same.*

Part of the support for the belief that U.S. and Latin American interests are the same stemmed from the rhetoric of Pan-Americanism. This idea was also persistent in academic circles, where the idea that those interests might be in conflict was not normally given serious attention.[25] The significance of this shared image is that it meant that what was good for the United States normally was good for Latin America. Thus one could press one's interests without much worry about those of the Latin Americans.

(5) *Idealistic goals such as the promotion of hemispheric cooperation and economic development should be pursued.*

That this perception ranks as the least important is indicative of the general belief among scholars of international relations that national interest will prevail over ideology and morality in foreign policy.[26]

Thus we have the intellectual boundaries of United States foreign policy-makers—or at least one suggested ordering of them. Perhaps the individual interested simply in diplomatic history will find this and the other concerns stated in this introduction too theoretical and vague. But it is well for the reader to realize that although this study reads at times as a very detailed diplomatic history, the author is not so much concerned with touching all the historical bases as he is with examining the problems of United States pressure on Latin America via a case study of an admittedly extreme situation. The concern is the limits of hegemony.

1: PREWAR CHILE

The standard description of Chile is something along the lines of its being a geographic absurdity clinging desperately to the western slope of the Andes hoping to avoid slipping into the Pacific.[1] In 1940 approximately five million people were living in this long (2,600 miles) and narrow (average 110 miles) country. Although the boundary lines of Chile may seem illogical when viewed on a flat map (or by a Peruvian or Bolivian still smarting from Chile's imperialistic moves in the late nineteenth century), there is a logic to the borders when one considers the almost impenetrable barrier presented by the snow-capped mountains that form much of Chile's eastern boundary. Only the beginning of air transportation did much to soften the effect these harsh peaks have had on Chile's trade and communication.

Chile's mineral-rich northern regions are only semi-habitable and the ruggedly beautiful south gradually becomes so sparsely populated that Germany was supposedly able to anchor ships there undetected for days during World War I.[2] Thus, over half of Chile's population lives in the mild climate of the central, or Mediterranean, portion of the country, and it is here that the industrialization of prewar Chile began. Also in this region, which comprises only one-eighth of the total area, the bulk of the farming took place and the capital city of Santiago—more European than Latin American—rested surrounded by beautiful mountains. The city, always the focal point of Chilean life, had between a fourth and a fifth of the population of Chile before the war and a much larger share of the nation's commerce. Its economy (and the nation's) was greatly dependent on the nitrate and copper mines of the north, the products of which could be traded for valuable foreign exchange. The country's major port, Valparaíso, was the primary channel for the export of ores and the import of goods. The farms of the region were rich, large, and paternalistic.

Chile has never been a poor country by Latin American standards, but neither has it been continually prosperous. Its fragile economy has been beset by earthquakes, poor income distribution, bad housing conditions, and a vulnerability to events outside its national borders. A child born in 1940 had a life expectancy of less than forty years.[3] The per capita annual income in 1940 was a little less than $185 in terms of 1950 U.S. dollars.[4]

7

The War of the Pacific (1879–83) and the healthy international market for nitrates caused by the tensions leading up to World War I gave the vigorous Chileans a position of leadership in South America almost on a par with Brazil and Argentina. However, the discovery of methods for producing nitrates artificially and a generally lopsided economy pushed Chile back from a role as a hemispheric power. This seemed to produce an awareness of the facts of international life, almost a defeatist mood, behind the rhetoric of Chilean nationalism.[5]

Although the society and economy of Chile was dominated by a few families with strong linkages among themselves,[6] the politics in Chile have traditionally been more democratic and more stable than in most of Latin America. This is not to say that this elite did not dominate the political process, but the formal democratic procedures were generally observed and were pointed to as a symbol of the country's sophistication. The turning point, for the purposes of this study, came with the 1938 Chilean presidential election.

Before discussing that event, a few comments are needed on the man who dominated Chilean politics during much of the 1930s—Arturo Alessandri. Under the weight of the Depression, the political processes of Chile had largely collapsed, but the country staggered to the polls in 1932 to elect Alessandri, who had managed to find the middle position in a field of five candidates. As President from 1920 to 1925 he had been a dynamic, outspoken reformer until the pressures of the election campaign began to fragment political cohesion. When Alessandri returned to office he was expected to continue his previous efforts to turn the country away from the traditional oligarchical domination. However, in his 1932 to 1938 term he moved to the right even though his Congress was relatively evenly balanced between right and left. The multi-party system was in the process of moving toward the form it would have for twenty years.[7] In mid-1937 the two largest parties were the Conservatives (36 of the 146 seats in the Chamber of Deputies) and the Liberals (34 seats).[8] Both parties were instruments of the traditional ruling elites divided by historical rivalries and issues that were becoming increasingly less significant. Coupled with four other rightist deputies, these conservative interests could claim 74 seats. Another ten seats were held by essentially center parties. On the left were 62 seats, half of which were held by the Radical Party. The second most powerful party of the left—although it was much weaker than the Liberal, Conservative or Radical organizations—was the Socialist Party with 17 seats. The other 14 positions were divided among the Communists (6) and several small parties plus some independents.

Although the strongest party of the left, the Radicals lacked ideological coherence. Also Radical Party support of Masonry and its criticism of the

Catholic Church in Chile had caused bitter feelings on the part of the Conservatives. The Liberals were upset by the Radical advocacy of state intervention in the economy, a position counter to the Liberal belief in laissez-faire economics. The Radicals were split between groups which seemed to be advocating programs that were acceptable to the rightist parties and those which apparently took the reformist rhetoric of the party seriously.

Although such factors as age and changes in circumstances may have caused Alessandri to move to the right during his second term of office,[9] there were two other, rather obvious forces at work. The first of these was his refusal to allow the Radical Party ministers to alternate offices under the direction of the party. He felt that in view of the problems this switching had caused in the past, it would detract seriously from the unity of the Cabinet if he allowed the parties to change their representatives at will as the Radicals desired.[10] This was symptomatic of a crisis in which the Radicals withdrew their support of the government and refused to serve. For all practical purposes Alessandri found himself by 1934, two years after his election, with a government that was based primarily on the Liberal and Conservative groups and with no Radicals in the Cabinet. The second factor was the unpopularity among liberal elements of Gustavo Ross, the President's confidant and Finance Minister.[11] The cold arrogance of the Minister, who seemed to relish insulting the Radicals and their leaders, caused much of the hard feeling which developed—enough, in fact, to be one of the major reasons for the cooperation of the moderate, if not conservative, Radical Party in the Popular Front.

By some standards Alessandri was a successful President in view of the fact that he served during the Depression. Exports increased more than three times from 1932 to 1937, while imports doubled. Industrialization increased and unemployment was cut. The treasury managed to show a surplus of sorts from 1934 on; however, it was accomplished by devaluations of currency and by efforts designed to keep wages and salaries down despite an inflationary situation. These combined to make the stability and prosperity a burden to be carried by the common man.[12]

United States relations with Chile were generally good during Alessandri's second term. The most important points of contact during this period were economic. Although the flow of United States economic influence was definitely on the rise, Chile's foreign trade was not completely dominated by the United States.[13] Exports to England and Europe during the period 1935 to 1939 composed slightly over 45 percent of Chile's shipments. The United States share of the export market was about 18 percent. Almost half of Chile's imports came from Europe, with the United States accounting for another 30 percent. Under the trade policies of Nazi Germany, in 1938 the German share of Chile's imports was approaching that of the United States.

On the other hand, in the field of foreign investment the United States had been the dominant force in Chile since World War I. In 1936, for example, North American investment totaled $484 million, with $383 million in mining and smelting.[14] About $5 million was in manufacturing, $12 million in trade, and $84 million fell into the miscellaneous category, which included public utilities. The pattern of United States investment helps to explain some of Chile's resentment toward it. Most of the U.S. money was in extractive industries with only about 1 percent devoted to manufacturing, the field Chile was most anxious to bolster.

In terms of actual citizens living in Chile, the United States was far behind several other countries. According to the 1940 census, only 1,514 U.S. citizens lived in Chile, there were more than twice that many British citizens, 13,933 Germans, 10,619 Italians, 23,323 Spaniards, and 10,860 Argentines.[15]

BONDS AND TRADE

Chile's large indebtedness in the form of bonds held by United States investors was a source of irritation in the relations between the two countries. The official Department of State position was to allow this problem to be handled by the Foreign Bondholders Protective Association (FBPA)—a private group which in its formative stages in 1933, the Department had unofficially helped to become an organized spokesman for U.S. investors having problems during the Great Depression. The formal Department of State position, as expressed in a more-or-less form letter that was sent out to citizens protesting treatment on questions of bonds, was:

> It is the long-established policy of this Government to consider difficulties in regard to foreign securities as primarily matters for negotiation and settlement between the parties directly in interest, acting through agencies of their own. The Department of State, within its function of protecting all American interests in foreign countries, is glad to facilitate such discussions when it appropriately can and to take such other action, usually informal, as it finds proper and advisable in the varying circumstances to assist in obtaining due consideration of the interests of American investors.[16]

The reply would then refer the complainant—who often claimed to be a widow dependent upon bond interest payments for her survival—to the Foreign Bondholders Protective Association.

Although its formation had certainly been encouraged in order to take the onus for negotiating payment on defaulted bonds off the Department of State, the Association served another purpose. It was an effective bargaining device because it allowed the Department to appear as a mediator between the two sides. The Association usually initially took a belligerent position demanding full repayment of the face value and interest payments on the bonds—a much more militant position than the United States government could have taken under the circumstances. When the Association and the foreign government found their negotiations deadlocked, the Department of State was able to step into the discussion and make suggestions that seemed moderate to the foreign government in comparison to the position taken by the Association. At times, however, the Department had trouble convincing the Association to accept the settlement it suggested.

The Chilean bond question was particularly serious due to the enormous sums involved. During Carlos Ibáñez's term as President in the late 1920s he had found credit easy to obtain through North American banking institutions. In the period 1915-30 Chilean dollar bonds amounting to $295,-592,000 were floated from North American banks.[17] This was partially a response to the United States prosperity of the 1920s, but it also represented a movement by North American investors into the void left by the withdrawal of European economic interests from South America during World War I. These bonds were usually heavily discounted and then passed on to individual investors (who should have realized they were speculating), thereby removing the bank from responsibility for collection after making a healthy profit. Ibáñez's prosperous presidency had left Chile with one of the highest per capita debt totals in the world.

Historically, the Chilean debt record had been good. Then in July of 1931 the government declared a partial moratorium and in August a complete moratorium. As a result of a truly catastrophic drop in foreign exchange receipts during the Depression, Chile was forced to default on both interest and sinking fund payments. In 1935 the Alessandri government, with the leadership of Finance Minister Gustavo Ross, passed a law aimed at trying to restore Chile's credit. It set aside the government's share of the profits from the Chilean Nitrate and Iodine Sales Corporation, income taxes paid by copper companies, and tariff duties received from petroleum imports to the foreign-dominated nitrate and copper industries, for a fund designed to service the long-term foreign indebtedness of the country. This measure served to transfer responsibility for repayment, at least in the eyes of Chileans, back to the United States, who controlled the prices. One of the interesting features of the plan was that almost half of the receipts were to be used for the retirement of bonds by direct purchase below par on the open market. Although this idea was not considered ethical by some, it proved to be effective. With the bond market for Chilean securities justifiably depressed, Gustavo Ross was able to purchase large amounts at relatively low market prices. As a result, the total external debt in the form of state bonds fell from $449 million in 1934 to $295 million by 1939.[18]

This did little to placate the Protective Association. The approach of the 1938 Chilean election served to bring the problem to a crisis. One reason for this was that it would have bolstered the Ross campaign for the presidency to have negotiated a settlement advantageous to Chile prior to the election. For another reason, the opposing Popular Front candidate appeared to be considerably less interested in meeting the obligations, thereby scaring the Protective Association leadership. This gave Ross, who was the model of international capitalist responsibility, a lever in his negotiations by allowing him to tacitly bargain from a position that, if no settlement were reached soon, the next negotiator would be much less reasonable.

The U.S. Embassy in Santiago felt the Association should settle more or less on Ross's terms. One despatch pointed out that although Ross was certainly not going to negotiate a capitulation to the Association, the Popular Front seemed unwilling to even continue the servicing of the debt.[19] Particularly when it appeared that Ibáñez might be the candidate of the Popular Front, the Embassy suggested that the acceptance of the Ross A-bond settlement plan, (which had been announced in August of 1937) would be a good idea because it would help the Finance Minister to win his race for the presidency and that "it would appear that a Ross administration would offer more guarantees of stability and conservatism in the management of the economic affairs of Chile."[20] Incidentally, this was the only time that a despatch suggested any action on the part of Washington to defeat the Popular Front, and the remark was made at a time when Ibáñez, who was reputed to be pro-German, had a good chance to be the candidate, according to some observers. During the actual campaign, the Embassy went to lengths to try to keep the United States business community from becoming involved in the election.

The Ross plan essentially called for a partial cut in the total size of the debt and the renegotiation of the debt at a lower interest rate. The English had already accepted a similar solution. Ross argued that bankers had taken advantage of Ibáñez and had forced the loans on him at a time when the peso was several times more valuable, in relation to the dollar, and at an interest rate which was higher than the rate in the 1920s. Another complaint of Chile was that the high Smoot-Hawley tariff barriers the United States had erected made dollars very difficult to earn and therefore made repayment impossible. The Council of the Bondholders Association advised its members in January of 1938 to reject the plan.[21] The FBPA Council complained that since the Ross plan tied repayment to the nitrate and copper revenues, the bondholders were vulnerable to fluctuations of the international market.[22] It also must have occurred to the Chilean government that, if accepted, such a plan would create a pressure group in the United States anxious to keep the price and flow of Chilean nitrates and copper high. Despite the sympathy of the Embassy in Santiago for the proposal, the Bondholders Association combined with some unsympathetic elements of the Department of State to reject the Ross plan and leave the question unsolved,[23] a situation that continued until after World War II.

Of the numerous problems plaguing trade between the United States and Chile prior to World War II one of the most persistent and trying was that of exchange restrictions instituted by Chile. The country had a strong tendency to import more than it exported—a particularly dangerous situation in view of the tremendous lack of liquidity in the international monetary market. The crisis was largely the result of an incredible 88 percent drop in exports between 1929 and 1932.[24] In response, Chile initiated a number of measures, all basically within a free enterprise context, to stop the gold outflow caused by the inability of the country to cut its imports by a corresponding figure. The exchange rate for money earned in Chile to be sent abroad in the form of dollars was set artificially high, and this caused some funds which desired to return to the United States to be delayed several years waiting for acceptable exchange rates or, at times, the availability of dollars at any price. United States diplomats consistently protested this treatment but were generally only given illusionary assurances of changes in the situation. It may be that the long-run impact was greatly to the detriment of Chile if it wanted foreign capital for development. One North American economist has argued that the "hoard of legislation discriminating against the foreign sector and in favor of import-competing industries" during the 1932–37 period (much of which was triggered by the United States Congress's copper tariff of 1932) led to an artificial restructuring of the Chilean economy. This discouraged "investment in the foreign sector, and, ultimately, restricted the nation's capacity to import and its gains from trade."[25] This criticism, however, ignores the extreme political difficulties involved in removing the discriminatory legislation and the possible benefits of industrialization with domestic capital.

There were several other questions complicating trade relations between the United States and Chile. One was the fact that Chile had historically granted concessions to other Latin American countries beyond any most-favored-nation agreement—an idea the United States rejected.[26] There also was the fact that Chile had a series of compensation trade agreements with Germany which were counter to Hull's reciprocal trade agreements principle. The Embassy in Santiago expressed some sympathy regarding Chile's compensation trade with Europe;[27] but the Department of State in trade talks with Chile[28] rejected the idea as simply ignoring the question, and thereby helped to prevent the signing of any trade agreement prior to Chile's 1938 presidential election.

THE 1938 PRESIDENTIAL ELECTION

The early developments pointing toward the 1938 Chilean presidential election initially did not worry the Conservatives and Liberals who were rallying behind Gustavo Ross. As Minister of Finance, Ross's record had been enviable prior to his March 1937 resignation to begin preparing for the campaign. He had sufficient money to help underwrite a major campaign both in terms of propagandizing and in terms of buying votes (a more-or-less accepted custom at the time). There were some problems however. Alessandri had not made many friends with his strong repression of dissident labor elements during his term of office, nor with his harassment of opposition publications.[29] Then in May of 1938 the leftist congressmen began to file out during the President's annual message to the Congress in protest to an alleged slight by Alessandri. In the confusion the leader of the Nazi Party, González von Marées, shot a revolver and the police descended on the chamber and began clubbing González and numerous leftist congressmen, including the President of the Radical Party.[30] But Ross also proved to be an unappealing candidate, since he made no effort to hide his distaste for the democratic process. His strong views on this subject, and his generally aristocratic outlook, were partly responsible for his extreme distaste for the Radical leaders, whom he considered to be petty politicians pursuing votes among the grubby masses.

It is of some importance to the later understanding of relations with Chile to comprehend the background of the Popular Front. The opposition to Alessandri had been making serious attempts to organize a popular front movement composed of Radicals, Socialists, Communists, and other center and left groups since 1936. This was acceptable to the Communists as a result of the decision of the Seventh World Congress of the Comintern in 1935 which had approved the strategy of popular frontism. Whether the actual impetus for the Front in Chile came from the Communists is debatable;[31] however, the sight of popular front governments in Spain and France—two countries with close cultural ties to Chile—made it a logical course of action for consideration. As the movement toward a front developed, it became obvious that the major reason for the adoption of the popular front strategy in Europe, essentially the threat of fascism, was not the prime motivation in Chile. Ernst Halperin writes in his book *Nationalism and Communism in Chile:* "That the Popular Front formula proved successful in Chile . . . is to be attributed to purely Chilean causes that had little to do with ideology and nothing whatsoever to do with the international situation."[32] The major reasons for the Front's initial cohesion were the unpopularity of Ross and his bitter unwillingness to compromise with even the more conservative Radicals. This, plus the fact that a Ross victory seemed inevitable, made such a coalition the logical instrument for defeating the Conservative-Liberal alliance.

Nonetheless, what may have been logical was not always obvious to those involved. The Radicals and the Socialists were not enthused about cooperation with the Communists. The Socialists were engaged in a struggle with the Communists for control of the union organizations of Chile.[33] The competition between the Socialists and the Radicals was also bitter because they were competing for influence among white-collar workers and school teachers, and even in the non-Marxist labor movement where the Radicals retained some influence.[34] Additionally, as Halperin has pointed out, "the Radicals were very strong and an immensely power-and-patronage-hungry party; it was most unlikely that after victory they would afford the Socialists a fair share of the spoils."[35] Until late 1937 the Radicals kept their neutrality in regard to the up-coming presidential election, keeping one foot in the popular front movement and one foot in the Alessandri government.[36] The fact that the government coalition appeared to win in the March 1937 congressional elections strengthened the Ross supporters in their belief that the Radicals' support was not necessary for victory.

With the presidential election scheduled for October, the Chilean voters went to the polls on April 3, 1938, for municipal elections. Although these contests are for positions of little importance and may well be influenced by local issues and personalities, they are somewhat of a barometer of public sentiment.[37] The Conservatives and Liberals each captured approximately 19 percent of the vote, and their allies, the Democrats, picked up another 4 percent to give the three parties 42.2 percent of the vote. The candidates of the potential popular front won 41.7 percent of the vote, with the Radicals taking 21.1 percent, the Socialists 11.1, the Democrats 2.7 and the Communists 6.8 percent. The remainder went to parties not identified with either faction. The Agrarians took 2.1 percent, the Republic Action 1.5, the Nazis 5.5, and the independents the remaining 7 percent.[38] Although the results cheered the hopes of the Popular Front adherents, the United States Ambassador at the time, Norman Armour, still felt that Ross had the best chance to win the October election.[39]

The convention of the Popular Front later in April was a dramatic event. The Radicals were the dominant group but this was not clearly reflected in the allocation of delegate strength which gave the Radicals 400, the Socialists 300, Communists 130, Democrats 120, and the labor movement 120. The Socialist candidate was Marmaduke Grove, a prominent and dynamic political leader.[40] He had the support of the 300 Socialists and half of the labor vote. This total of 360 was enough to prevent the

election of anyone else under the rules of the convention.[41] The Radical
candidate was Pedro Aguirre Cerda, a millionaire farmer and educator with
considerably less political experience than Grove. However, Aguirre Cerda's
fatherly image and the potential voting strength of the Radicals, plus the
antagonism the Communists felt toward the Socialists, brought most of
the convention strength behind him after several ballots. The Ross supporters, who had seen the left divided previously by internal quarrels, predicted that the Popular Front would never be able to agree on a candidate
and took pleasure from the deadlock. However, on the final day Grove
spoke to the convention and declared that he was stepping down in favor
of the candidacy of Aguirre Cerda in the name of Popular Front unity. In
purely pragmatic terms it was obvious that the Popular Front, in order to
win, would have to hold back defections from the Radical Party and that
this could best be done by nominating a Radical for the presidency. The
parties to the left of the Radicals, while perhaps not initially enthusiastic
about Aguirre Cerda, certainly found him much more acceptable than Gustavo Ross. As a North American student of the movement wrote, "actually,
the Popular Front was nothing more or less than a political alliance of the
Left, and its organization in Chile was, in truth, more of a defensive than
an offensive maneuver."[42] Nowhere was this more evident than at the convention.

Even this turn of events did not discourage the right. A third candidate,
former President Carlos Ibáñez, entered the race after being allowed to return to Chile in May of 1937. At that time he was making statements designed to appeal to the Socialists[43] and evidently hoped for a Popular Front
nomination. The Radicals, however, had made it clear when they began to
move into the Front that they would not accept Ibáñez as a candidate. Thus
the former President ended up running under the Popular Liberating Alliance
which was supposedly anti-oligarchical, anti-fascist, and anti-imperialist.[44]
Although his main source of support was the small Nazi Party, it was generally felt by the rightist politicians that Ibáñez could attract enough leftist
votes to ensure the election of Ross. This view was fortified as it became
obvious that few conservatives were rallying behind Ibáñez.

On September 5, 1938, seven weeks before the election, with Ibáñez
running behind Aguirre Cerda and Ross, a group of young Chilean Nazis
seized a government building in hopes of triggering a military uprising in
support of Ibáñez. When the policemen moved in and captured those who
had taken possession of the building, which was across the street from the
President's office, the sixty-two young Nazis were killed on the spot, under
somewhat mysterious circumstances. The coup had an interesting impact because Chilean public opinion regarded (and still regards) the attempted coup
"as a pardonable expression of youthful high spirits, whereas the killing of

the perpetrators caused a wave of indignation to sweep the country."[45] As Alessandri moved to arrest the head of the Chilean Nazi Party (Jorge González von Marées) and Ibáñez, increasingly severe criticism descended upon the President. The word then went out to Ibáñez followers to swing their support to Aguirre Cerda. The rightists tried to prevent this by releasing Ibáñez from prison two days before the election, and the conservative newspapers continued to discuss the election race in terms of three candidates. The leftist press, however, retaliated by publishing a picture of Aguirre Cerda and Ibáñez taken immediately after Ibáñez was released from prison.[46]

With Ibáñez out of the race and with widespread Radical support for the candidacy of Aguirre Cerda, the Popular Front candidate managed to win a very narrow victory—by about 4,000 votes out of more than 400,000 cast. The difference came in the cities, where the urban proletariat managed to almost double the Ross total, and in the nitrate and copper areas, where the labor union influence through the Socialists and Communists was strong. Ross did pile up large majorities where the conservatives had always done it—in the rural areas where corruption was widespread and the freedom of the *campensinos* to vote against the wishes of the landlord was limited by both the degree to which they were politically aware and by pressure. Although Ross initially protested the results, Alessandri, who had always been fiercely dedicated to the democratic process, and the military made way for the inauguration of the new government. The election was a definite turning point in Chilean political history and initiated fourteen years of Radical presidents. The Conservatives, who had been fanatically bitter towards Aguirre Cerda (to some extent on the grounds that he was a traitor to his upper-class origins) restrained their criticism a little after he assumed office, but they never trusted the new coalition and continued to feel that there was something vaguely "un-Chilean" about it. Undoubtedly there was some of this same distrust in the United States Department of State (particularly since the Nazis had supported the coalition) and among North American businessmen in Chile who identified with the upper classes.

President Aguirre Cerda had scarcely gotten settled into office when a typically Chilean disaster struck. On January 24, 1939, a savage earthquake rocked the area near Concepción and Chillan, about 250 miles south of Santiago. Villages were destroyed and between 15,000 and 20,000 people lost their lives. The United States Red Cross responded with a gift of $10,000 to the local Red Cross, and North American diplomats did what they could to alleviate the short-term problems connected with the disaster.

The quake also had its impact on economic relations between the United States and Chile. It was soon obvious that the rebuilding of the area would take more governmental economic planning and mobilization than Chile had done previously, and the Popular Front was more willing than the Conservative-

Liberal coalition might have been to move into this realm. However, the ambitious programs envisioned by the executive were expensive and the needed funds were lacking. Almost all the potential sources of funds involved the United States to one degree or another. The government could supplement its income by halting the bond payments which Ross had worked so hard to arrange. It could borrow abroad, with the United States and Germany being the most likely prospects. It could increase taxes, with the most obvious candidate for increased taxation, both for reasons of nationalism and for reasons of their lack of political influence, being the North American investors in the country.

Initially, Ambassador Armour in Santiago emphasized in his long-distance telephone talks with Washington that the United States should respond promptly to Chile's needs rather than allow any other nation to appear more generous and that he hoped that United States assistance would not be merely symbolic. Specifically, he suggested large credits arranged through the Export-Import Bank.[47] However, it soon developed that Chile was expecting a great deal of assistance from the United States in the rebuilding process, and that there were numerous difficulties confronting the State Department in supplying this help. Not the least of the problems was a series of obstacles which were being faced at the time in getting the charter of the Export-Import Bank renewed. Also, there was the fear in Washington that if Chile sought to alleviate the situation by taking some steps against properties owned by United States citizens in Chile, it might be interpreted as an unfriendly gesture. With Congress still irritated by Mexico's expropriation of oil interests, the legislature was sensitive to protests from businessmen abroad who felt they were being ill-treated. Without congressional authorizations, no money could go to Chile regardless of the sentiments of the Department of State and the President.

Ambassador Armour visited Washington in early February and brought with him Chile's ideas for reconstruction. These included a comprehensive plan covering projects stemming from the earthquake damage and also a general development plan which would cost $100 million over five years. Armour called the need for the plan "self-evident" and approved if the plan could be properly executed.[48] Obviously there were questions as to whether or not the new government could actually execute the policies, but Armour argued that the plan could help to raise the standard of living of the poor in Chile and that it could turn Chile away from Germany.[49]

Upon returning to Chile, Armour talked to the Minister of Hacienda, Roberto Wachholtz, who was very interested in the progress of the Ambassador's talks in Washington. Armour told him that until the Export-Import Bank charter was reapproved by the Congress, it was difficult to secure or promise loans. He also warned the Minister that Chile's plan would need to

be scaled down and concentrated on measures to alleviate problems growing directly from the earthquake. Any financing of the general economic development plan would have to be delayed. Washington was not of a mood
to support general far-reaching national planning for economic development.
Wachholtz told Armour that the Chilean plan now called for expenditures
of about $80 million over a five-year period and that this would have to be
about 70 percent materials and the other 30 percent in the form of direct
cash.[50] United States support for these kinds of projections was also made
difficult because the Export-Import Bank's goals were relatively narrow and
closely tied to the promotion of United States foreign trade. According to
Armour's despatch, he admonished Wachholtz that

> a determination by the Chilean Government to continue with the main-
> tenance of the present plan and a moderate attitude toward American
> companies and investments in Chile would do more in my opinion to
> secure favorable consideration of the various projects he had in mind
> than any other fact. Not unnaturally, perhaps, I said New York and even
> Washington were looking with some apprehension as to what the new
> Government's attitude might be in these directions, and I felt it my duty
> to state quite frankly that drastic action against the American companies
> would make it very difficult, if not impossible, for our Government or
> one of its agencies, e.g., the Export-Import Bank, to consider favorably
> or with the same sympathetic approach the plans the Minister was put-
> ting forth.[51]

Less than two weeks later Armour repeated his views to President Aguirre
Cerda. However, the new President said, according to Armour's account,

> After all, we must have money and if we can't get it in the form of a
> loan or abroad, then we must secure it from the companies or from
> other sources through taxation. However, . . . I hope that we can work
> these things out, but in any case nothing could be done until after our
> international legislation has been passed.[52]

Thus the classic diplomatic confrontation emerged: The diplomat asserts
the friendliness of his country to country X; but says that if such-and-such
action takes place, public opinion and the congress in the diplomat's country would make favorable action toward X difficult even though the diplomat's government is friendly. And, on the other hand, the spokesman for X
says that circumstances will force it to take such-and-such an action detrimental to the diplomat's country unless the diplomat's country takes certain actions. The threats are not actually made and both executive branches
can acclaim their friendship while pressuring each other. In reality, Chile
wanted money in support of its plans. On the other side, the President of
the United States was unwilling to push hard for money from Congress. He

wanted to preserve his popularity in Congress for trials that would soon come, and he was not ready to embark on massive aid programs.

The Department of State's position on the matter, as set forth by Undersecretary Sumner Welles, was flexible on the question of continued full payments on external debts. Wells recognized that although "the maintenance of such payments would make any action by [the United States] . . . easier to carry through and a complete suspension would [make] . . . assistance difficult," the Department was "not prepared to take a rigid stand in this matter and if, as a part of a general program, the Chilean Government should reduce debt payments for a limited period, it might be" that the United States "would not assume a critical position."[53] On the subject of nondiscriminatory treatment of United States business, Welles was somewhat less flexible. He also suggested that the $80-million request, of which four-fifths was to be raised abroad, was overly ambitious, particularly in regard to the construction of housing which was not directly to replace housing destroyed in the earthquake.

The decision on how much the United States would be able to give was not immediately soluable. Chile was slow in bringing forth a scaled-down, detailed plan, and the Congress of the United States found itself faced with a number of issues that seemed to deserve more immediate attention than the refinancing of the Export-Import Bank. There were also elements of opposition among the Chilean right which hoped that the United States would not make loans to the Aguirre Cerda regime, particularly in view of the United States failure to prop up the Alessandri regime during its final year.[54] The Popular Front hoped that the loans would help give the new government an air of respectability. The government did not hesitate to point out that it had credit offers from Germany which it might be forced to take if Washington was unwilling to provide the needed assistance.[55]

Minister of Hacienda Wachholtz finally asked for credits of $10 to $15 million, primarily for electrical machinery, roadmaking equipment, and agricultural tools.[56] He hoped to have the money spread over three years. In late August the United States decided to extend $5 million over a six-month period to facilitate imports. Even this was difficult since Congress had failed to expand the lending power of the Export-Import Bank. The credit, as was customary, was an indirect one and could only be used to finance imports from the United States.[57] As finally agreed upon, the notes carried 4 percent interest and were amortized over an eight-year period.[58] These notes were contingent on favorable consideration of individual requests from American exporters. In the minds of some Chileans, this clause put a veto over the Chilean Development Corporation's plans in the hands of the United States.[59] In operation this did not prove to be the case since the credit was handled in the usual manner by Washington.

Chile hoped that the agreement would be the first of a series of efforts to assist Chile's development. Wachholtz planned to visit the United States to help coordinate these efforts. However, Washington made it clear that under existing Export-Import Bank authorizations and appropriations, no further aid could be extended and discouraged the Minister from visiting, since he could not return to Chile with anything to show for his journey.[60]

Complicating the situation was United States uneasiness about the programs and reliability of the Popular Front, and the fear of the Aguirre Cerda government that Washington would attempt to undermine its operation. Chilean officials were particularly sensitive over the question of the Development Corporation (FOMENTO) as an alternative to development via private investment. There were United States business interests in Chile which felt that the FOMENTO should be spurned—although this was not the position of the Department of State.

When the Export-Import Bank was re-funded the following year (1940), negotiations with Chile opened again. Chile was seeking a credit for the FOMENTO similar to the first one. This was made difficult by a Chilean claim against the Braden Copper Company relating to a Chilean tax law which had been in effect on capital from 1916 to 1923.[61] Department of State representatives spoke with Chilean officials on the problem and tried to emphasize that, while the United States government tried not to intervene in internal matters of other countries, public opinion in the United States would make the granting of a large Export-Import Bank credit difficult if Chile were to press on the 17-year-old issue. Guillermo del Pedregal, the Minister of Finance, took the classic rebuttal position: public opinion, alas, in Chile would resent the loan discussions being influenced by a tax matter. He assured the United States diplomats that the matter would be fairly handled by normal judicial procedures.

Despite these two problems, the Export-Import Bank officials proceeded to announce on June 13, 1940, that a $12-million credit would be given to the FOMENTO to assist in the acquisition of industrial machinery and supplies produced in the United States. Eventually, the courts did rule in favor of the Braden interests and the Chilean government also withdrew a claim for over $150 million against the American-owned telephone company soon after the Export-Import Bank loan was completed—a decision which was far beyond the hopes of the company.[62] It is difficult to conclude that Chile's actions regarding the telephone interests and the copper company were as a result of the loan. Certainly no iron *quid pro quo* was discussed. It may be, however, that to the degree that the original moves against the telephone and copper concerns were punitive, growing out of an irritation with Washington or with foreign investment in general, the loan did help soothe this feeling.

The other economic issue between the United States and Chile during

the period was the negotiation of an expanded trade agreement. A number
of factors were increasingly clouding the general trade situation. It was during these talks that Ambassador Claude Bowers's strong sympathies for Chile
first began to be evident. Bowers had been the United States Ambassador to
Spain during the most trying of times and came to Chile in September of
1939 fresh from the Spanish adventure during which he had become unacceptable to the winning forces of General Francisco Franco. He was an auth-
or and journalist of considerable reputation in the United States; he had
been the editor of the *New York Journal American* when it was one of the
great newspapers of North America. He had been a strong New Dealer, and
his faithfulness to, and admiration for President Franklin D. Roosevelt was
great. Even after his years in Spain he arrived in Chile with no knowledge
of the Spanish language and managed to leave the country fourteen years
later with that condition unimpaired. Upon his retirement he wrote an interesting account of his years in Chile in which he had almost nothing unfavorable to say about the country.[63] His Embassy colleagues were not always happy with Bowers—as is the fate of most political appointees sent
to preside over an Embassy of professional foreign service officers. He did
spend a significant amount of his time away from Santiago in some of the
pleasant resort towns which lie in central Chile.

The purpose of an ambassador is, of course, to represent the United
States in a foreign country. Frequently, however, the ambassador, if he is
sympathetic to his assigned country, also serves the function of representing
the host country's interests in Washington via his diplomatic despatches. One
reason for this sympathy may be the socialization process which the ambassador undergoes in the country. He is surrounded by, and in constant contact with, the people of the country and soon begins to acquire their outlook
and values and to identify his interests with their interests or, at least, to see
their interests as valid. Even though his language deficiencies hindered the
process, Bowers certainly did associate with Chileans.

There is another explanation (not exclusive to the first phenomenon) for
the fact that an ambassador may begin to be representative of his host country's interests in official Washington. An ambassador's job is much easier if
he can offer the host country what it wants, bring good news, and not be
forced to argue. His conversations with officials are much more pleasant if
he is not forced to say unpleasant things. Obviously, an ambassador at the
conscious level perceives of himself as the tool of his government. However,
the author would like to suggest that at an unconscious level he may be
favoring situations and actions which make his job easier. Although he may
realize that it is in the best interests of his own country to ill treat the host
country, the realization multiplies his problems enormously. So, one can
hypothesize, the ambassador in the field is obviously much more interested

in preserving good relations than is the policy planner in Washington.[64] This is partially due to the ambassador's relatively narrow perspective, but it can be due to the simple fact that it makes his job easier and, other things being equal, individuals tend to avoid conflictual situations. One might further theorize that a career diplomat, who knows he will be transferred some day and who knows his performance is being judged in Washington, would be less likely to fall into the pattern of doing "too much" to improve relations. It is a thesis of this study that one of the problems between Chile and Washington in 1942 was Bowers's desire not to bring too many unpleasant realities to the government in Santiago. The "unpleasant realities" in question will be discussed not as matters of judgment but simply to accurately present how much the United States wanted Chile to alter its existing foreign policy.

During the trade negotiations in 1939 Bowers went so far as to write Roosevelt personally in order to complain that the concessions being offered by the Department of State were "so restricted as to have little value."[65] Roosevelt's office replied strongly that the concessions were substantial and that the administration was limited by the fact that it was "facing bitter opposition to the continuance of the trade-agreements program" which was coming up for renewal at the next session of Congress.[66] Confronted by this situation and the Chilean refusal to give up her preferential arrangements with Argentina, Peru, and Bolivia, the pace of the talks tailed off in the early part of 1940. In his annual message to the Congress at the opening session on May 21, 1940, President Aguirre Cerda clearly expressed his opinion that lowering trade barriers was not in Chile's best interest.[67]

THE INTER-AMERICAN SYSTEM

The meshings of Washington's foreign policy and Santiago's policies also took place within the inter-American system. Within the system the United States was clearly the leader and dominated all the meetings. When there was serious opposition to Washington's views it was newsworthy. The important factor in the inter-American meetings up to World War II is that the leadership role of the United States usually was responsive primarily to events outside the hemisphere (and the mood in Washington), thereby making the inter-American policy of the United States simply an appendix to a European policy. The major characteristic of the meetings from 1936 to 1940 was that they represented an effort to draw together against a possible attack from the outside.

By 1936 the formal inter-American system consisted of a few agreements to keep some representative body functioning in the dignified Pan American Union building donated by Andrew Carnegie—a building which was, appropriately enough, almost in the shadow of the Department of State (and would

have been if the sun rose or set in the north). There also were a number of
uncoordinated documents prescribing methods of peaceful settlement for disputes that arose between members of the hemispheric organization. The coordinated use of force as a sanction was considered one of those topics un-
dignified for discussion among gentlemen.

However, in 1936 a special meeting at Buenos Aires had produced the
Convention for the Maintenance, Preservation, and Re-establishment of Peace,
which included among its provisions the first substantial (by Pan American
standards) move toward the formation of an alliance against outside intervention. It was a step toward the "continentalization" of the Monroe Doctrine
in which the United States lost little of its flexibility to enforce its pious
declaration of spheres of influence. Article One of the treaty said: "In the
event that the peace of the American Republics should be menanced" the
governments should "consult together for the purpose of finding and adopting methods of peaceful cooperation." The form this consultation was to
take was left open. Article Two was somewhat more specific. It stated that
"in the event of an international war outside America which might menace
the peace of the American Republics" consultation should take place so
the American republics "if they so desire, may eventually cooperate in some
action tending to preserve the peace of the American Continent."

The regularly scheduled eighth Conference of American Republics was
held in Lima during December of 1938. The international situation at the
time was not a happy one. The Axis Powers were undermining the League
of Nations, and that organization was rapidly reaching the point of collapse.
Franco was winning the Spanish Civil War with the assistance of Hitler and
Mussolini. United States relations with Mexico and Bolivia were strained by
arguments over oil companies owned by United States investors. The government of Chile was in a dilemma prior to the conference in that the Popular
Front government would not be inaugurated until December 24—at which
point the conference would be all but over. Partially because it was a transi-
tion period in Chile, and partially because of the nature of the questions and
the position of neighboring Argentina, Chile did not play an active role in
the meeting.[68] The government in Santiago did present an ambitious project providing for a permanent organ of consultation; this was blended into
an Argentine resolution which eventually became part of the Declaration of
Lima.[69] An Argentine suggestion for possible regional or leadership meetings
of American republics was objected to by Chile and dropped.[70] Such meetings would have allowed the stronger Latin American countries to face Washington without being in a position, as they were at many of the inter-American meetings, of dealing with the United States and the many votes behind
it from the Caribbean and Central American countries who were anxious to

please the Department of State. However, the meetings also would have allowed Argentina to try to dominate the southern portion of South America—
a prospect that did not appeal to Chile.

The major accomplishment of the 1938 meeting was the Declaration of
Lima. This statement, which did not take the form of a treaty, reaffirmed
continental solidarity and declared that, within "absolute sovereignty" the
nations would collaborate "against all foreign intervention or activity that
may threaten them." The device to coordinate this action was the establishment of meetings of the ministers of foreign affairs "when deemed desirable
and at the initiative of any" country. These meetings were to be held in ro-
tation in the capitals of the American republics. Thus the completely vague
nature of the agreement to consult that had been called for in previous meetings moved closer to definition. Also, the Declaration implied that the threat
prompting these meetings could come from outside the hemisphere. Thus
the Declaration constituted another step in the process whereby the inter-
American system converted from a method of settling disputes and facilitat-
ing relations among the states of the western hemisphere to an alliance in
response to coming events in Europe.

The idea of a meeting of consultation of foreign ministers produced its
first offspring nine months after the Lima conference. Hitler had finally
triggered the European phase of World War II by marching into Poland. The
United States immediately issued its statement of neutrality according to
the procedures of international law. The Latin American countries did the
same. It was also decided that since the situation did present some problems
for the hemisphere, a meeting of foreign ministers should be held. It was
convened for ten days beginning September 23, 1939, in Panama.

A commission concerned with neutrality operated on the basis of a United
States and Argentine resolution to produce a statement of rights and duties
of neutral states. The General Declaration of Neutrality made it clear that
the signatories had no desire to become involved in the European conflict.
Chile adhered strongly to this position as did the United States. Sumner
Welles, who represented Secretary of State Hull at the meeting, later wrote
that in retrospect the Declaration appeared to be "the last official expression of the belief in this modern world that the responsibility for the repression of war can be other than universal."[71] Although a case regarding the
desirability of the resolution can be made on either side of the question,
the Declaration tilted the Pan-American movement toward neutrality, which
was then difficult to reverse when the European threat became more clear.
The rhetoric of inter-Americanism at Panama became intertwined with neutrality and the blessings of observing international law. No value judgments
of the events in Europe were made. Welles also wrote later: "I am frank to

confess that at the time the Declaration seemed to me not only justified but desirable." Those at the conference had come to believe that "the war both in Europe and in Asia might in some manner be won by the forces of freedom without becoming universal." "What we did not then see sufficiently clearly was that a war in Europe in 1939 could hardly become anything other than worldwide," Welles admitted in retrospect.[72] Obviously, Roosevelt's noninvolvement position and his difficulties in rallying congressional support would have made any other position difficult for Washington to advocate.

The most unique recommendation was the Declaration of Panama. This was the proclamation of a neutrality zone extending 300 miles into the oceans around the Americas in which there were to be no belligerent activities.[73] The idea, which evidently was Roosevelt's, was supposedly justified as a measure of self-protection, springing from the concept that in the waters around the Americas the countries of the western hemisphere had an inherent right to be protected from hostile acts committed by non-American belligerents.[74] Supposedly, the measure would ensure unmolested shipping between the American republics. States were free to patrol the zone individually or collectively; however, the facts of hemispheric life meant that most of the patroling would fall to the United States. In fact, prior to signing the document Chile asked for assurance (which she received) that each country would only be expected to patrol in so far as its naval resources permitted.[75] The status of this agreement under international law was doubtful and was not accepted by the belligerents.[76] Hull evidently also had his doubts but did not feel the issue of sufficient importance to question the President's opinion.[77]

The final inter-American meeting to be considered at this point is the second Meeting of Consultation of the Foreign Ministers which was held in Havana from July 21 to 30, 1940. It had been decided at the Panama meeting to have another meeting the following year. It had also been indicated that the transfer of sovereignty of colonial possessions in the Americas would necessitate a consultation. Then in April and May of 1939 the word "blitzkreig" was added to the world's vocabulary as Belgium, the Netherlands, and Luxembourg, fell quickly, and France itself was threatened. The fact that the three small countries had been neutral was not lost on Latin American policymakers. The idea that neutrality could serve as protection for a country was dismissed after the spring of 1939, leaving defense resting on geography and military strength.

Once again Chile played a passive role in the meeting. Aguirre Cerda's administration was interested in staying out of the war and in concentrating on domestic development. The Communists, this being the period of the Hitler-Stalin rapprochement, were quarreling bitterly within the Popular

Front and charging the Socialists with being lackies of North American imperialism.[78] These problems helped force the Chilean government into a cautious position.

MILITARY QUESTIONS

As the international turmoil increased in Europe and in the Far East, the military aspect of the relationship between Santiago and Washington became more important. The question must be approached from two directions: First, the role of the Chilean military in domestic politics and its openness to influence by the United States. Second, the question of providing defense for Chile.

The Chilean military's record in the twentieth century had been relatively good in terms of staying out of domestic political processes.[79] Most authors rate it as one of the two or three least politically involved militaries in Latin America. This fact was considerably less clear at the time of World War II. Many worried about a possible military coup and there were frequent rumors of intended coups. In the early 1930s the military had been deeply involved in the turbulent events that disrupted the constitutional governing of the country. There were various plots and attempted coups throughout the period, but none of them succeeded.[80]

There was a tradition in Latin America of European military advisers and, since Germany was enjoying the reputation of having an outstanding military tradition and force, its advisers were often sought. The German techniques and ideas were usually far ahead of those of the Latin American military officers they were called upon to advise, and certainly their equipment (which they were willing to sell if there seemed to be a political advantage) was far above the general level of armament in Latin America. This was particularly true in Chile, where the quality of armaments had slipped considerably during the Depression following the nitrate boom. The actual purpose of the advisers, from the donor's point of view, was to influence the officers in the host country. Since in Latin America the military officers frequently played a key role in the political balance of the country, influence over them was particularly desirable: It was wise from a foreign policy standpoint to have influence with the influential. One writer has noted that "the distribution of German military instructors in Latin America in the postwar period [the 1920s and 1930s] was roughly corresponding with the attitude adopted by the Central and South American states toward Germany during" World War I.[81] It may also be that the relationship went the other way: The attitude adopted corresponded to the number of advisers *before* the war. Germany and Italy were well aware of the possible significance of this type of contact.

The United States had not made a serious effort in the military adviser field. At the beginning of 1938 the United States Army had only six military attachés assigned among the twenty states of Latin America.[82] According to the comprehensive official Army history of its western hemisphere operations during World War II, this minute representation was a combination of two policies.[83] The first was a political policy designed to avoid "anything that might be construed as an intrusion in Latin American military affairs," which even extended to discouraging private munitions sales by American manufacturers. The second was a military policy of limiting the United States defense effort to protection of the continental United States and its outlying territories.

The Department of State began to become disturbed as the war approached by the amount of fascist activity in Latin America and by the close relationships being formed between Italian and German military advisers and high-ranking Latin American officers. Therefore, in January of 1938 it initiated discussions with the War Department to discuss methods of increasing military assistance to the area.[84] In the late summer of 1939 the War Department received a tentative inquiry through its military attaché in Santiago regarding a possible Army Air Corps mission to Chile.[85] Part of the reason for this was a result of discontent within the Chilean Air Force over the performance of Italian planes purchased by Gustavo Ross during the Alessandri administration. A number of them had crashed, thereby attracting the attention of the press. [86] Chile was urged to formalize its request for a U.S. Army Air Corps mission and in November the Foreign Minister did this. He stated to Ambassador Bowers at the time that the Chilean government was particularly interested in the matter since it was felt that this contact would help lead to generally closer relations with Washington.[87] The Department of State strongly urged the War Department to approve the mission.[88] Eventually it was sent; although a long delay between the agreement and the actual arrival of the mission caused consternation in the United States Embassy and may have considerably lessened the mission's desired political impact.[89]

Insofar as Washington's prewar military planning had been done by the War and Navy Departments, it was concerned primarily with the Panama Canal and the passages to it and with the bulge of Brazil which lay about 1,600 miles from Africa.[90] The planners believed that German and Italian efforts would initially take the form of attempts in the direction of economic penetration. It then seemed logical to assume that the Axis would move into a pattern of meddling in domestic political processes in hopes of drawing the Latin American countries into the Axis sphere of influence, or perhaps into a colonial status. The possible establishment of military bases also seemed a danger. Bases in the virtually undefended eastern bulge of Brazil could allow direct attacks on the Panama Canal.[91] In the rather realistic planning that was done, officials in Washington found that the military capabilities of the United States did not match the rhetoric of the Monroe Doctrine. Thus one of the major war plans, RAINBOW I, called for the protection of all United States territory (but no re-enforcement of the Philippines) and areas north of latitude 10° south. This is the line that cuts South America just below the Peruvian and Brazilian "bulges," about 100 miles south of Recife and 150 miles north of Lima.[92]

Whether or not an attack on South America with the purpose of establishing bases was a realistic possibility is questionable. According to the official U.S. Army history:

> No evidence has yet been uncovered of an actual German plan in 1939 for military expansion toward the Americas, though some Nazi leaders talked vaguely about the ultimate clash that might follow a German triumph in Europe. Pending that triumph, German interest coincided [in the late 1930s] with American opinion in seeking to keep the United States officially neutral toward the European war.[93]

Army planners in late 1939 seemed to recognize this fact and to find little actual danger of an attack as long as the war continued in Europe—although pointing out that this situation could change.[94] It may seem obvious in retrospect that an attack on the western hemisphere was unlikely and the idea of the Germans or Italians making a landing in Brazil and fighting to the Panama Canal is laughable.

The unlikelihood of such an invasion was not so obvious at the time. The fact that no attack took place has solidified the idea that no attack could have taken place. Had the British been defeated, their fleet might have been neutralized in the Atlantic, thereby endangering Latin America. Also, German capabilities seemed much greater in 1939 and 1940 than they eventually proved to be. In the Latin American capitals there were fears that for one reason or another—varying, of course, from capital to capital—their particular country would be the obvious one for attack. Washington was of the opinion that if such an attack did come it would be against Brazil. Therefore, in re-estimating the Army's air requirements in December of 1939, the War Plans Division based its estimates on the amount of air strength needed to drive the Germans out of an established base near the bulge of Brazil.[95]

Another serious question confronting military planners and diplomats in the United States in the years preceding active participation in World War II was whether to attempt to raise the military efficiency of the Latin American forces to a point where they would be of substantial aid in carrying out the military duties of hemispheric defense. The major argument against this course of action was that it would be too costly and might upset the balance of power in Latin America. There was also the possibility that one of these strengthened military establishments might fall under Axis influence. The costs proved to be the deciding factor. In July of 1940 the Chief of Staff and the Secretary of War approved a policy paper stating that the objective of the Army was

> better mutual understanding; impressing Latin American officers with our military preparedness and our determination to uphold the Monroe Doctrine; affording selected officers of our Army opportunity of studying Latin America. In attaining our objective, we should concentrate on those countries of most immediate military importance to us. Our objective does *not* compromise expectations on our part of being able to use Latin American forces as effective allies in war.[96]

A facet of this question which was particularly troublesome was whether or not to provide arms to the Latin American militaries, most of which had antiquated weaponry. In mid-1938 the Army had suggested that the United States change its policy to one of encouraging sales by private companies.[97] The Department of State preferred to continue its policy of discouraging such sales, and this remained the policy until the September 1939 outbreak of war in Europe.

From 1936 to 1939 the United States sold an average of $10 million worth of armaments a year, most of which was in the form of aircraft and aircraft maintenance materials. Price was not a small obstacle in the supplying of arms. European stockpiles were more plentiful and generally cheaper. The aspect of this problem which was particularly distressing to some Washington military men was the fact that Germany and Italy were the European countries supplying the materials. German trade agreements which had built up stocks of blocked marks opened up hitherto untouched markets. Italy was, if anything, even more successful since its sales were underwritten by the government in terms of prices and terms of payment.[98] Coupled with the military advisers already in the countries, United States interests seemed directly threatened. Therefore, in November of 1938 Roosevelt told Undersecretary Welles that he wanted legislation to permit the War and Navy Departments to sell at cost some of their surplus military materials to the Latin American countries. The Army was ready to make such sales but felt that legal barriers existed. The reinterpretation of some old legislation and the proposal by the administration of some new bills opened the way for the flow of arms.[99] Unfortunately for the expectations of some of the Latin American countries, the surplus was not large and after May of 1940 the weapons went where the fighting was—to Europe and Africa. In February of 1940 General George C. Marshall said that the War Department doubted "whether, in the event of passage of the legislation now pending before

Congress . . . any orders [for new equipment] for the other American republics can be filled in less than two years."[100]

At the urging of the United States, Chile presented a request for arms in the fall of 1939. Chile first expressed interest in a large quantity of war materiel, particularly anti-aircraft guns, howitzers, and infantry mortars, which it hoped to obtain from private firms. The amount of money involved, however, proved to be more than Chile wanted to pay. Then Chile informed the Department of State that its Navy was anxious to purchase cruisers and the Army wanted anti-aircraft and other artillery pieces. The Department of State backed the request, citing the low level of equipment held by Chile. The request for large naval vessels could not be filled, but a list of available weapons was submitted to Chile in December of 1939. Included were 100,000 Enfield rifles, 100 old 75-mm. guns, and some obsolete mortars and mountain guns. Chile refused these, partially because of the price but also because it wanted more modern weapons. The United States added some 8-inch howitzers to the original list, but Chile felt the price was still too high in view of the age of the equipment.

Although there is little doubt that early in 1940 the United States was more eager to sell weapons to Chile than Chile was to buy (since she was not happy with the quality of the available supply),[101] by late summer Chile had been moved far down the priority list to a position behind Brazil, Mexico, Ecuador, Colombia, Venezuela, and the Central American countries. Chile was placed in a group with Argentina, Paraguay, Uruguay, Bolivia, and Peru, whose requirements were "to be determined after requirements for the other republics have been computed and plans to supply them have been approved."[102] This lowering of classification was in line with the War Department's realization that geographical considerations made it difficult to protect the southern portion of South America.

Also in mid-1940 as part of a general effort being made toward Latin America, the United States initiated confidential conversations between military and naval officers of the United States and Chile designed to coordinate measures of continental defense.[103] In the case of Chile, the government insisted that the trip by the representatives of the United States military be kept secret.[104] Therefore, the two officials arrived in business suits via commercial planes and left after a few days of intensive talks.[105] Following the talks Aguirre Cerda gave Ambassador Bowers an agreement based on four contingencies:[106] (1) If Chile should be attacked she would defend herself to the utmost. (2) If the United States were attacked, Chile would aid her. (3) If a third country which the United States wished to defend such as another South American country were attacked, Chile would aid that country. (4) If Chile undertook an aggressive war she would not expect aid from the United States and vice versa. Of course, since no country ever feels that it is undertaking

an aggressive war, contingency (4) was primarily designed to give Chile a way
to retreat if the United States were to involve itself in World War II on
grounds which were unacceptable to Chile. The guarantee of aiding the United
States if it were attacked did not spell out the degree of aid beyond the term
"utmost." It is difficult to find much of substance in the agreement, but it
did represent a statement of the Popular Front, with the approval of the military, that it was basically pro-Allied.

NEUTRALITY AND WAR

By early 1940 Chile was concerned with the question of defense and was
interested in cooperating with the United States, according to private diplomatic conversations. However, its public position was strongly neutral. A good
example of this is Chile's unwillingness to join in a formal condemnation of
Russia's invasion of Finland late in 1939. Santiago did favor the inter-American protest of the *Graf von Spee* incident at about the same time. In this case
the actions of the German warship were clearly in violation of the security
zone approved at Panama. Chile also expressed the opinion that the Latin
American countries should cooperate in the patroling of the security zone, if
for no other reason than to strengthen the unity of the hemisphere.[107] The
government in Santiago did manage to be offended during the *Graf von Spee*
controversy when Argentina and Brazil cooperated with the United States in
pressing Germany on the matter.[108] This seemed to relegate Chile to the role
of a second-rate South American power. Although this was an accurate evaluation of the relative military strengths of the nations involved (of course the
incident had also more directly involved the Argentine and Brazilian coasts),
it was not a reality Chile cared to have flaunted.

Events in Europe continued to raise important questions for Latin Ameri-
can diplomats during the spring of 1940. The "phony war" broke out in
April when neutral Denmark submitted to German "protection" and was
occupied over its objections. Neutral Norway did not submit, and it took the
Nazis about a month to crush the country militarily. On May 10 the Nazi
war machine crashed into neutral Belgium, Holland, and Luxembourg. The
Dutch resisted for four days and the Belgians for 17. On May 13 the British
Expeditionary Force found itself cut off, and on May 29 the heroic, but
humiliating, evacuation of Dunkirk began. On June 14 the stunned western
world saw the fall of Paris.[109] France, beseiged in the south by Italy, sued
for peace, and on June 22 the German victory over France was formalized.

The occupation of Denmark and Norway caused much pain among Chileans
and did cause a realization that what was happening in Europe was not going
to culminate in a minor shift in the European balance of power. Many Chilean
officials began to feel that more hemispheric cooperation was desirable.[110]

Among the non-Communist left there was a move away from neutrality in the direction of a policy more favorable to the Allies.[111] The Socialist Party in June issued a statement to the press calling for Latin American cooperation with North America "free from any imperialistic pretension."[112] Marmaduke Grove, the Socialist leader who had stepped aside for the nomination of Aguirre Cerda at the deadlocked Popular Front convention, told Ambassador Bowers privately that his party had decided to go along with the United States.[113] There also emerged in Santiago increased worry about a possible coup from the Chilean German element and its sympathizers. The important German colony in south-central Chile was two generations removed from the homeland, but many members clung to the old ways and tended at times to look down upon Chileans. This group was subjected to Nazi propaganda and Hitler's successes had attracted some followers.[114] Many of the movie theaters in Santiago were in the hands of Germans, Italians, or Communists (who were still not anti-fascist) and were showing German newsreels.[115] The radio stations tended to be more pro-Allied; although at least one station operated by two Italians was fined in mid-1940 under a law prohibiting the broadcasting of any kind of commentaries on war news and the limiting of news items to those furnished by news agencies approved by the government.[116]

Although the Department of State only half-heartedly considered the idea, there was some discussion of whether or not to furnish financial support for pro-Allied newspapers in Santiago. The city was full of rumors, many of which were evidently true, of large expenditures by the German Embassy for publicity. The Department feared being too obvious, and the United States generally had voluntary support from much of the press. This support was, however, usually firmly based on strong neutrality.[117]

One of the major considerations of this study is the influence of domestic politics on the formulation of foreign policy and hence on international relations. Events outside Chile obviously influenced what went on inside Chile and thereby shaped or influenced its foreign policy. And, of course, in many of the international situations confronting Chile the possible range of responses was sharply limited—perhaps at times to the point of having no flexibility at all. Nonetheless, it does seem that in her choice of responses, within the realm of the realistic, Chile was influenced significantly by domestic politics. Thus it becomes important to follow the progress of the Popular Front and its attempts to retain power.

Since the government of Chile is a presidential system, it was, of course, up to President Aguirre Cerda whether or not to keep a multi-party cabinet. The price for not doing so might have been extreme legislative obstruction. Like the United States Congress, the Chilean Congress's powers of initiation and direction were not great, but its power to obstruct was significant. So the President attempted to keep his coalition of parties together. However,

there were deep doctrinal differences between the parties, and, when the specter of Gustavo Ross as President faded, the desire to cooperate diminished considerably. The Radicals were, despite their name, committed to a much more
evolutionary approach to reform than were the Socialists and Communists, a
dichotomy somewhat alleviated by the fact that Aguirre Cerda was a reasonably
progressive Radical—although he had initially opposed joining the Popular Front.
Moreover tremendous problems existed between the two groups whose rhetoric
seemed closest together—the Communists and the Socialists.

Much of the Communist-Socialist tension grew from two sources: The first
was the aforementioned competition for the same group of voters. The second
stemmed from disagreement over international policy. From September of
1939 until the German invasion of Russia on June 22, 1941, the Communist
and Nazi parties were supposedly cooperating. The Chilean Communists' distaste for the leader of the Chilean Nazis, González von Marées, was deep and
long-standing, however; and therefore, although they supported the Communist–Nazi cooperation in Europe, they were not ready to be friendly with the
Nazis in Chile.[118] They did go so far as to follow the Moscow position of switching from public condemnation of fascism to criticism of imperialism—which
meant, in the case of Chile, to criticism of Yankee imperialism. On the other
hand, the Socialists strongly supported hemispheric solidarity and dropped
their anti-imperialist themes.[119] In the autumn of 1940 the Socialist Minister
of Development, Oscar Schnake (a former Secretary-General of the Socialist
Party), had gone to Washington to try to get more assistance from the United
States. According to one source, a "vitriolic press and propaganda attack on
North American imperialism and on the Minister of Development" was unleashed, complete with the accusation that Schnake "was becoming a slave of
Wall Street."[120] Upon his return the Minister led an attack on the Communists.
This marked the beginning of the dissolution of the Popular Front. The competition for support in the laboring class was evident in the Chilean Confederation of Labor, which though cooperating with the Popular Front had long
been an arena of struggle between the two parties. Early in January of 1941
the demand of the Socialists that the Communists be expelled from the Popular Front was refused. Whereupon the Socialists withdrew, and called for the
formation of a national non-Communist leftist bloc,[121] thereby putting great
pressures on the Confederation of Labor. On January 14 the National Direc-
torate of the union announced that it would retire from the Popular Front
and would attempt in the future to stay out of political party combinations.[122]

The final disintegration of the Front came on January 16, 1941, as a result
of a long-standing quarrel within the Radical Party. There had always been a
strong group within the party, led by Senators Juan Antonio Ríos and Florencio Duran, who had opposed cooperation with the Communists.[123] This conservative group was opposed by the left wing which favored continuing the

Popular Front without the Socialists. The leftists based their position on the successes which the party had enjoyed within the Front. They had a Radical President and about half of the cabinet posts were held by Radicals. In November a Radical had defeated the rightist candidate for the Senate in the Valparaíso-Aconcagua district which had long been a conservative stronghold.[124] However, on January 16 the Radicals voted to reassume their freedom of action, thereby breaking up the remaining portion of the Popular Front. As a coalition, the Front had lasted a little more than two years.

There were other reasons for the collapse. The Radicals and Socialists had developed hard feelings over the division of government posts both within the cabinet and outside. One North American author has written of the Radical-Socialist alliance:

> The Radicals were very strong and an immensely power-and-patronage-hungry party; it was most unlikely that after victory they would afford the Socialists a fair share of the spoils . . . the anti-fascist bond uniting the Popular Front was a mere myth. . . . Furthermore, the Radicals had little desire to implement a program of sweeping social reforms.
>
> In terms of Chilean politics the alliance with the Radicals did not really make sense for the Socialists. They allowed themselves to be dragged into it under the hypnotic effect of European political slogans that had no relevance to the Chilean political situation and thus from the beginning they felt cheated and dissatisfied. . . .
>
> The events after Aguirre Cerda's victory fully justified the Socialists' qualms. They had to be satisfied with three minor cabinet posts and with the same privilege that the Radicals had enjoyed under the preceding Alessandri administration, namely, to quote Eudocio Ravines' picturesque phrase, that of "wiping their mouths while their Radical ally ate and drank."[125]

In his book on the Popular Front, John Reese Stevenson concludes that, despite advances in social reform, the foremost success of the Popular Front was probably as an electoral instrument to beat the Conservatives and Liberals.[126]

Although the formal structure of the Front had disintegrated, there were still some lingering effects. The March congressional elections represented an overall shift to the left, benefiting the principal parties of the dissolved Popular Front. The Senate saw the Communists gaining the most (3 seats) and the Liberals sustaining the greatest loss.[127] In the Chamber of Deputies the Conservatives held their position while the Liberals lost 12 of their 34 seats. The Socialists went from 10 to 15 seats. The Communists doubled their representation in moving from 7 to 14. The largest number of seats gained was by the President's Radical Party as it climbed from 31 to 44 seats.

Although this display of confidence in the Radicals might be assumed to have strengthened the President's position, it had the opposite effect. The long-standing division within the party between those favoring the Popular Front idea in the first place and those of a more conservative bent was heightened. A change in foreign ministers in March evidently was in answer to demands that another Radical be added to the Cabinet.[128] In April of 1941 another party squabble emerged. The Central Junta of the Radical Party ordered the Radical cabinet ministers to resign. They refused and the junta expelled them from the party.[129] In June the party problems between the Central Junta and the ministers culminated in the resignation of the ministers.[130] This proved to be of some significance in United States–Chilean relations because it brought Juan B. Rossetti to the post of Foreign Minister. A newspaperman and the most prominent member of the small Radical-Socialist Party, Rossetti had a reputation somewhat of a demagogue.

ECONOMICS AND WEAPONS IN 1941

The major economic problems between the United States and Chile during 1941 stemmed from Chile's efforts to get a higher price—and particularly more foreign exchange—from its copper production. Of a number of interrelated questions involved, one was the imposition by the United States of a 4-cents-a-pound excise tax on imported copper in 1932. Moreover, the fact that the United States was currently purchasing copper at 10 cents a pound from Chile while paying domestic producers 12 cents a pound caused increased irritation.

Chile could have taken several approaches to try to make more money from its copper exports to the United States. For one, there was significant congressional support for an export tax which might have cut deeply into the profits of the copper companies (which were owned largely by United States interests).[131] A higher tax on profits was another possibility. Also, Chile could take over the buying and distribution of all copper produced in Chile (as Brazil had done with its coffee) and thereby influence the price.

Serious negotiations on the question began in mid-1941. Chile's Foreign Minister emphasized his country's need for money; but he also held over the negotiations the threat that unless the United States was willing to make significant concessions, the Chilean Congress would probably take even more drastic steps. [132] Once again we have the use of the threat in friendly negotiations. There is nothing to suggest that the Chilean executive branch would not have supported the measures under discussion in the Congress if its negotiations with the United States had not succeeded. The U.S. Department of State felt itself to be caught in a dilemma. It wished to protect the copper companies from the Chilean legislature, but the price of copper was determined by the Federal Loan Agency through the Metal Reserves Company—all under the direction of William Clayton. And Clayton, while willing to raise the price to 11¼ cents, demanded certain conditions regarding the distribution of the increased profits. When Chile greeted the proposals with disapproval, the Department of State tried to act as middleman, urging compromise between the two forces.[133] Although the Chilean Foreign Ministry may have been the middleman between Chile's legislature and the North American buyer and the Department of State the middleman between Clayton and the Chilean government, both diplomatic agencies must have realized that this was a good bargaining technique. The United States side of the negotiations was further complicated by the fact that the copper companies were vocal in their demands for a share of the increased copper revenues;[134] though any increase would have been due almost solely to efforts on the part of the Chilean government.

The bombs that fell on Pearl Harbor broke the log jam on the Chilean copper question. On December 8, 1941, the day after the attack, the Adviser on Political Relations for the Undersecretary of State, Laurence Duggan, wrote a memo saying "it seems to me that this argument with Chile about copper has gone on long enough," and that relations with Chile should not "be jeopardized because of a shortsighted attitude on the part of the Defense Supplies Corporation." The memo concluded that the Department of State "should step in and cut the Gordian knot."[135] Within the month an agreement was reached under which any increase in the price of copper over 10 cents a pound would be divided equally between Chile and the producers, provided that Chile received a minimum of 1¼ cents of the price increase. What this signified was that, at the new offering price of 11¾ cents, the companies would get an additional one-half cent of the increase.[136] Other concessions were made regarding waiving the excise tax on government purchases, and Chile arranged the exchange rate to its benefit.[137]

The agreement, which appeared in Washington to be a victory for Chile, became controversial as the war continued. One economist later wrote of it:

> Many complaints were raised in Chile over the price ceiling on copper, which made the industry, in effect, an extension of the United States wartime economy. The agreement was maintained until 1946 when, with the removal of controls, the price of copper obtained by the companies shot up from 11 cents per pound (F.O.B.) to 25 cents per pound, leveling off at 17 cents in 1949. The estimated loss of "returned value" to Chile from nonrealized price increases, owing to the agreement, has been placed as high as $500 million dollars.[138]

Although the figure of $500 million may well be an exaggeration,[139] it does point up the fact that Chile did not receive the price for its copper under the wartime agreement that it might have in a free market situation. Of course, the significant fact to remember is that almost nothing in the international economy was operating under a free market situation at the time. There were serious shipping restrictions, stockpiling of strategic materials, blacklisting, and so forth. Nonetheless, there can be little doubt that the price Chile received for her copper was not as high as it might have been under free market conditions. And immediately after the war the price rose significantly. Perhaps the situation can be marked off as Chile's not inconsiderable contribution to the war effort; however, it was later to cause ill feelings because the dollar profits Chile made during the war, when it was difficult to spend money due to shortages of goods, proved to be somewhat illusionary as they were reduced by postwar inflation of the dollar.

Even before the entrance of the United States into the war, Chile began to express fears about the possible production of U.S. synthetic nitrogen plants after the war was over.[140] The Defense Supplies Corporation agreed to purchase an extra 300,000 tons above normal purchases as a result of an understanding reached in January of 1941. This pact grew out of the visit to Washington of the Chilean Minister of the Development Corporation and was primarily an attempt to assist Chile's economic situation, since it was cheaper to produce nitrogen synthetically than it was to make explosives from Chilean nitrates.[141]

Supplying weapons to Chile occupied considerable attention during late 1940 and all of 1941. Most of the efforts centered on the negotiation of a lend-lease agreement. In mid-1940 Chile told the United States that Germany had offered to sell to Chile arms captured in Belgium, Holland, Czechoslovakia, and France at a price significantly lower than U.S. prices.[142] Although Chile said it was not interested, this thinly veiled threat did help stimulate talks. Guillermo del Pedregal of the Development Corporation visited the United States early in 1941 and discussed the question in some detail.[143] He was asking for purchases of about $40 million over several years. The talks were hampered, however, by uncertainty over the financing. Pedregal suggested that the money could come from the Export-Import Bank and be repaid by the money which had been diverted from the purchase of foreign bonds at depressed prices on the open market. This suggestion, in view of Chile's bond difficulties, was not welcomed even though the buying of the bonds on the open market was not considered a proper procedure. Chile was vocal in her complaints that the flow of arms already agreed upon was quite slow.[144] Chile also continued to be sensitive on the question of possible United States bases on Chilean soil, as shown by the fact that a United States request, arising in the Department of the Navy, for a naval observer's office at Punta Arenas (in extreme southern Chile) was rejected by Chile in March of 1941.[145]

In the spring of 1941 Washington and Santiago began negotiating a lend-lease agreement. An allocation of $50 million in equipment under the program was recommended for the fiscal period 1941 to 1944 by a committee of Army and Navy officers called the Joint Advisory Board on the American Republics. The bill authorizing this expenditure was not passed until October of 1941. This was $10 million more than the original request. Forty million would go to the Army and $10 million to the Chilean Navy. Most of the weapons were intended to provide anti-aircraft and general coastal defense equipment.[146]

When Chile was presented with the basic lend-lease agreement (predicated on congressional appropriations) in July of 1941, the pact called for deliveries of $15 million to the Army and $1 million to the Navy during the fiscal year ending June 30, 1942. Chile was expected to repay $2.5 million each fiscal year until 1947 on its total allotment of $50 million. This would mean a total of about $15 million to be repaid. The $50 million figure is significant in comparison with totals provided for other Latin American countries.[147] Mexico was operating under a different system, but of the original lend-lease offers to Latin America, Chile's $50 million was second only to the $100 million offered Brazil and ranked well ahead of the third highest offer, Peru's $29 million. Argentina was to be offered $21 million, which would be confined to use by the Navy. The comparatively high total for Chile stemmed from the facts that Chile's long coastline was poorly defended and much in need of strengthening and that the entire Chilean military establishment was in a state of decay.

These weapons discussions (and rumors of them) caused some concern in Chile. The newspaper *La Opinion* claimed on June 1, 1941, that Chile was being asked to cede bases to the United States.[148] The nationalists continually used the idea of foreign bases as a rallying issue. U.S. Ambassador Bowers denied the statements and the newspaper accepted the denial[149] —although the rumors continued. There was also considerable governmental anxiety over the slowness of the arms deliveries,[150] along with a desire to have the lend-lease arrangement not appear to be a gift. At least officially Chile wanted to pay its own way.[151] These negotiations were still not completed at the time of the attack against Pearl Harbor.

The United States was concerned about the large German population living in the south. Not unsurprisingly, Ambassador Bowers funneled a significant amount of time and effort into reporting on the question of possible German subversion. The ease with which Hitler's armies swept into France bolstered those in Chile who believed the Nazi war machine to be invincible, among whom were reported to be many lower ranking military officers.[152] There was also significant pro-Axis propaganda in Chile.[153] This tended to emphasize labor problems in the United States, criticisms of the proclaimed list (a list of companies believed to have commercial ties with the Axis nations), fears of United States territorial aggrandizement in Chile under the guise of defense, and statements of United States officials and isolationists opposed to President Roosevelt. The idea that the lend-lease agreement would saddle Chile with expensive armaments which it would have to pay for at a later date was emphasized. Old problems between the United States and Chile, such as the 1891 *Baltimore* affair, were publicized.[154] Pro-Axis spokesmen claimed that Germany would prove to be a better market for Chilean goods after the war when the United States returned to policies designed to lessen its dependence on foreign trade.

In September of 1941 President Aguirre Cerda asked the Chilean Congress for legislation prohibiting associations, parties and clubs formed by foreigners or other organizations at variance with representative democracy.[155] Since the President did not seem concerned with the internal threat by German organizations, there was some question as to whether the proposal was aimed at Communists or Fascists. Bowers wrote later that "though a democrat and an ardent admirer of Roosevelt, he [Aguirre] could not bring himself to believe that the Chileans he knew and respected could possibly engage in a conspiracy against a democratic regime."[156] Bowers felt that Aguirre believed that as long as Chile was friendly to Germany, Hitler would not cause trouble for his country.

The President, however, was experiencing declining health during 1941— which also led to rumors of a coup.[157] On November 10, 1941, he stepped down for what he hoped would be a temporary period of recovery. Gerónimo Méndez moved into the presidency in the interim. Two weeks later— about two weeks prior to Pearl Harbor—President Aguirre Cerda died. One furor that emerged from the President's illness was a comment in the November 17, 1941 issue of *Time* magazine inferring that the President had a drinking problem. All of the Santiago newspapers carried the comment and some editorialized on the insulting nature of the statement. Bowers was furious with *Time*.[158] When the Chilean President died soon thereafter, the *Time* remark took on a particularly bad flavor. This was only one of a number of incidents when remarks in the United States press were reprinted in Santiago and caused hostility. Needless to say, the Chilean government worried about the reporting of Chile in the United States, not only because of governmental sensitivity but also because it feared that the more sensational aspects of the small Nazi movement would be overemphasized abroad, thereby distorting what it perceived to be the true situation in Chile.

With the President's declining health the responsibilities and power of the Foreign Minister increased. The man who had assumed that position in June of 1941 was Juan B. Rossetti. His public image was that he was the most vocal pro-Allied figure in the Chilean government. He stayed in the position until April of 1942 when a new president was inaugurated. Although it is tempting to fall into policy explanations based on the idiosyncrasies of decision makers while ignoring the pressures of role, environment, etc., there can be little doubt that the behavior of Rossetti was not simply a reflection of the pressures which any foreign minister would have felt. A recent study of Chilean foreign policy concludes that

> the nature of the Chilean social hierarchy plus the legacy of authoritarianism prevent the construction of a smooth transmission belt to convey demands and supports back and forth from populace to party to legislature to executive. This is especially true in foreign policy formulation where the President is considered and considers himself constitutionally sovereign.[159]

With the President ill and then between presidents, the role of Rossetti in foreign policy grew in importance; although, as will be seen below, it was never absolute.

A little over 50 when he assumed the post of Foreign Minister, Rossetti had been connected with the revolutionary government of 1932, a short-lived socialist experiment. He was elected to the Chamber of Deputies in 1937 and ran the moribund Radical-Socialist Party virtually as a personal instrument. He was co-owner of the sometimes sensationally minded newspaper *La Opinion*.[160] However, Rossetti was not the average Chilean politician because he had grown up outside the traditional Chilean elite. The son of an Italian grocer, he had made his way up in politics on the basis of his brilliant debating skills, which bordered on the demagogic, and on his intelligence and fierce ambition. He was not trusted by the inner circle of Chilean politicians, who were accustomed to formulating Chilean foreign policy, and who frequently made disparaging remarks about him.

When he assumed office, Rossetti was felt to be intensely nationalistic (which was not a position of much comfort to the United States Embassy in view of the possible threat to foreign investors) and ambitious. Bowers was initially unsure of Rossetti's appointment but felt that the Foreign Minister's ambition would put him into the pro-Allied camp. Bowers also privately compared him to his predecessors by saying that Rossetti was "beyond odds the one brilliant and dynamic man among them."[161] The Foreign Minister quickly set out to prove his friendship to the United States by forcing the German Consul in Valparaíso to leave the country. The Consul had been formally ordered out of the country previously for engaging in illegal activities, but had claimed that it had received permission from Rossetti's predecessor (who denied it) to stay. Rossetti also made a strong pro-United States speech at the celebration of United States Independence Day in 1941—a statement he told Bowers in advance would represent a public "crossing of the Rubicon "[162]

In November Rossetti took the lead in proposing a joint declaration of the American nations against the German execution of hostages in France. The United States, previously in favor of a united American front, rejected the idea of adhering to the statement on the grounds that it might have a better chance of success if the United States did not sign it.[163] Throughout his nine months in office Rossetti was criticized by the old Chilean politicians for his methods, and even Bowers on occasion became exasperated with him. At one point the Ambassador even became worried as to whether or not Rossetti's newspaper was being subsidized by the Germans.[164]

Thus stood the Chilean foreign policy process on December 7, 1941. President Aguirre Cerda had been dead less than two weeks and the country was presided over by an interim executive while preparing for a general election scheduled for February 1, 1942. The Foreign Minister was pro-American and forceful, but his power was limited by the fact that he was not a member of the Radical Party and was not fully integrated into the elite. The communications media showed spotty pro-Axis influences, and the general feeling of the people apparently was that the war in Europe was not Chile's business. The stumbling economic situation was hopeful of a recovery as a result of increased demand for copper and nitrates during the war.

Despite this relatively insulated situation, Chile reacted quickly to the attack against Pearl Harbor. On December 7 Rodolfo Michels, Chilean Ambassador in Washington, phoned the Department of State to assure it that measures were being taken to protect the mines and industries owned by United States business in Chile and that precautions would be taken to insure the flow of strategic materials from Chile,[165] a flow on which the Chilean economy was seriously dependent. Foreign Minister Rossetti talked to Ambassador Bowers the following day and told him that Chile was in complete accord with Washington and would fulfill her defense agreements. He also discussed plans underway to protect against sabotage.[166] On December 9 Rossetti sent a telegram to the Governing Board of the Pan American Union asking for a meeting of foreign ministers as a result of the attack against the United States.[167] Chile's Ambassador in Washington was somewhat embarrassed by Rossetti's initiative without consultation with Washington, but he was relieved to find that the United States was anxious to have such a meeting called and glad to have a Latin American country take the initiative.[168]

As will be seen in chapter three, it was at this meeting which Rossetti was so anxious to have called that the Chilean Foreign Minister suddenly found that "pro-Allied" was defined considerably differently in Washington than it was in Santiago.

2: PREWAR ARGENTINA

No country in South America has caused the United States Department of State more anguish during the twentieth century than has Argentina. In a general sense this stemmed from the fact that Argentina did not adhere to the basic principle of Pan-Americanism: the idea that, although a cooperative venture, the United States was to be the leader. Of course, the stated ideology of Pan-Americanism does not contain the idea that the United States was "more equal" than its fellow American equals. Nonetheless, the practice, particularly in such forms as the Monroe Doctrine, has been to the contrary since Great Britain moved out of the hemisphere at the end of the nineteenth century.

There are numerous reasons for Argentina's refusal to docilely submit to the unwritten "sphere of influence" concept under which the United States was operating. In the first place, Argentina is quite distant from the United States; the capitals of western Europe are closer to Washington than is Buenos Aires. Second, prewar Argentina was a powerful and relatively prosperous nation. To be classified in Washington's eyes with Haiti or Honduras seemed an unspeakable obscenity to Argentina. Her land mass, the second largest in Latin America, is larger than many European countries and more than a third the size of the then-forty-eight states of the United States. Her population in 1935 was over 13 million,[1] the third largest in Latin America. More importantly, Argentina was a sophisticated country with a high literacy rate and with substantial material prosperity—the highest per capita income in Latin America—and the most industrialized nation in Latin America.

As a result of this situation prewar Argentina had hopes of moving Pan-Americanism out from under United States domination, perhaps into a Pan-Latin American situation with Argentina assuming the leadership. Argentina had long plagued the United States at the Pan American conferences by her refusal to recognize United States initiatives. However, the effort had been neutralized by the fact that its major rival for leadership in the hemisphere, Brazil, had a long tradition of close cooperation with the United States. Also, despite Argentina's claims of a spiritual closeness among the nations of Latin America, she was many miles from northern South America, Central

America and the Caribbean, and she did not have the military might nor the economic treasure to compete with the United States for domination of those countries.

The rivalry between the United States and Argentina was not always as open or as conscious as the above suggests. Although Argentine statesmen were more likely to recognize the situation than were those in Washington who were caught up in the mystique of the Monroe Doctrine and Good Neighbor, the competition was nevertheless not generally discussed openly and may not have been a conscious motivation of some of the statesmen at the time. Nevertheless, the functioning of the international system made close cooperation difficult. Argentina, in terms of power politics, sought influence and did not need the United States protection, which in any event the Argentines knew Washington could not provide over such distances. Her trade ties were much closer with England than with the United States. Thus it was a society relatively "unpenetrated" by North American influence. This, plus the fact that Brazil, Argentina's natural rival in South America, was closely allied with the United States, made United States–Argentine relations rest on an uncertain foundation almost from the minute British paramountcy began to be withdrawn from the hemisphere at the turn of the century.[2]

Although these deep contradictions existed, there were other, more obvious sources of irritation which had developed between Washington and Buenos Aires. The first of these was a trade rivalry that was more illusionary than real. Argentina primarily exported meat and wheat. Since her climate resembled the United States, there was some trade competition between the countries but essentially it was limited. A second problem was a strong sense of Argentine nationalism. In the western sense of nationalism there was no country in Latin America which had a stronger sense of nationalism in the 1930s and early '40s. This nationalism took a number of sometimes contradictory forms, so different groups could claim a nationalist position while holding conflicting ideas. Argentine nationalism, as will be seen in chapter six, not only caused the United States problems but also had political repercussions in the Argentine domestic political situation.

As was true in most of Latin America at the time, Argentina greeted the twentieth century with the oligarchy firmly in control although it was observing many of the amenities of democracy. Opposing this oligarchy was a rising middle-class movement, the Unión Cívica Radical (UCR) which called for moderate reforms. The UCR received its opportunity when Roque Sáenz Peña, an idealistic President drawn from the oligarchy, pushed through Congress in 1912 a law for electoral reform which gave the secret ballot to male Argentines over eighteen years of age. Although President Sáenz Peña died in office, his Vice President presided over a free election which virtually constituted a middle-class revolution in its results as the parties of the oligarchy were swept out. The relatively untested UCR leader Hipólito Irigoyen assumed the presidency in 1916. However, many of the political ills which his movement had hoped to cure worsened. He passed the presidency in the 1922 election to another Radical—though one considerably more acceptable to the upper classes. This eventually led to a split in the party, but in 1928 Irigoyen, at the age of 78, was re-elected. By this time he was "quite senile, and more irresponsible than before."[3]

Irigoyen's second term in office proved more disastrous than his first. His immediate followers, whose mentality toward politics had been shaped by their twenty-six years as an opposition force, did little to develop a consensus within the country. Also, to the new generation of Radical Party politicians, "political power represented a channel to upward social mobility and they were unwilling to share such a precious commodity with other groups."[4] The President began to meddle in military affairs through the selective use of patronage and promotion.[5] And the Conservatives, who failed to develop any capacity to "cope with the realities of electoral competition," decided that the Radicals were abusing the election laws.[6]

With the first faint tremors of the impending world depression reaching the conservative exporting elite, and with the traditional elite and military upset with the Radicals, the days of the Irigoyen regime were numbered.[7] The leader of the coup against the government, General José F. Uriburu, retained power until 1932. He had hopes of developing an authoritarian state patterned after the fascist ideas then in vogue in Europe; but his hopes were crushed when the conservatives and factions in the military pressured him into holding an election. The divided UCR, correctly assuming that the elections would be manipulated by the government in power, did not participate, and the Conservatives (running against the Socialists and Progressive Democrats) managed, to the surprise of no one, to elect their presidential candidate, General Augustín P. Justo.

During the next eleven years the conservative oligarchy, with its mistrust of democracy, dominated the government. A leading historian describes the period as one during which

> a bloc of generals and *estancieros*, supported by bankers, merchants and high clergy, ruled the country in their own behalf, crushing dissidents, staging fraudulent elections, and intervening arbitrarily in the affairs of the provinces. They viewed their war against the Radicals as a crusade for the fatherland—but these new knights proved singularly devoid of knightliness, furnishing neither new men nor new ideas. Their arrogance and their neglect of the just demands of the lower middle class and the underpaid masses paved the way for another overturn in 1943.[8]

During these years the Radicals largely managed to reunite their party, which the personality and tactics of Irigoyen had split. A few of the more right-wing, anti-reform Radicals refused to rejoin the party and continued as the Unión Cívica Radical Antipersonalista and cooperated with the conservative elements dominating the government. However, uniting the Radicals was a hollow victory because the party lacked the leadership to effectively mobilize itself against the Justo government. The fact that during its fourteen years in power the party had not been able to work the miralcles the masses hoped of it also served to discredit the UCR. There was, however, a growing reverence for Irigoyen (who died in 1933) which expressed itself in the form of increasing popularity for the Radical Party and unpopularity for the ruling Conservatives as the 1940s approached. The shortcomings of Irigoyen began to be forgotten by the masses, and the 1916–1930 period was looked back upon as one of hope.[9]

Augustín Justo served out his six-year term of office. He was a dictator, "but a gentlemanly one" as Hubert Herring has written.[10] With a background both in the military and in engineering, he was drawn from the Argentine aristocracy and was tolerant of political foes as long as they kept their dissent within bounds. The opposition was represented in Congress and its members were allowed to speak their minds. The point at which his open-mindedness stopped was at the ballot box, where the elections became shams perpetuating the Conservatives' grip on the governmental machinery. His policies did bring efficiency to Argentina and did allow the country to withstand the Depression better than her neighbors—although much of this must be credited to the abundance of the Argentine economy rather than to any conscious policy of Justo.

THE ECONOMY

At this point the discussion must digress to the important subject of the Argentine economy. Its most obvious differences from the economic systems of the other Latin American countries were its abundance and its connections to England. The economy was also unique in that it exported a large number of different products rather than being tied to one or two, such as Brazil was with coffee, Chile with her nitrates and copper, Colombia with coffee, Cuba with sugar, and the Central American countries with bananas. The enormous diversity of agricultural products for export included linseed, meat, wheat, flax, and others. The British domination of the economy had eroded during the stresses of World War I. One historian commented that "from independence until World War I, Argentina, could, with considerable justice, be considered a Spanish-speaking appendage of the British Empire."

This linkage included ownership of major portions of the Argentine transportation system and other key investments. If U.S. economic imperialism was resented in the other countries of Latin America prior to World War I, it was British economic imperialism that was the target of economic nationalism in Argentina during the period. However, such British innovations as the railroad and refrigerator ship, which made the Argentine economy overwhelmingly complementary to the British economy, also had the effect of bringing "unheard-of prosperity to Argentine landowners, in whose hands wealth remained highly concentrated."[12] It was this group which had dominated the government until 1916 and which reasserted its control in 1930. The middle class passively accepted the situation. As one author has pointed out on the basis of an extensive study of politics and beef interests in Argentina:

> The behavior of the middle classes—especially the upper-middle groups—indicates that they were by no means inclined to challenge the rural aristocracy. Their economic interests frequently coincided with those of the ranchers, a fact which nurtured social aspirations as well. Though it is hardly exhaustive, the evidence . . . strongly suggests that Argentina's upper-middle sectors sought to join the aristocracy rather than destroy it.[13]

If World War I served to loosen the British grip on the economy, the economic nationalism of the Radicals hurried the process. This brought about a gradual change in the pattern of trade during the 1920s, with British markets being replaced by trade with the United States. United States investments in Argentina grew very rapidly from 1920 to 1927 and by 1929 Argentina ranked ahead of any other South American country in terms of dollar investments (in the process surpassing English investments).[14] The trade pattern moved somewhat more slowly. Although Argentine exports to the United States in 1929 were double those of 1921, they were still far behind England's purchases and even less than Argentine exports to Belgium and Germany. But in the area of imports, by 1929 the United States was providing a third of Argentina's imports—twice as much as the previously dominant English. In 1929, U.S. exports to Argentina exceeded $200 million.[15] Argentina depended on exports to England to balance its serious trade deficit with the United States.

Argentina's prospects for riding out the Depression with relative ease experienced another severe shock in 1932 when England pledged at the Ottawa Conference to give trade preference to the Dominions producing wheat and meat over non-Dominion producers. This action, which was primarily an effort to benefit Australia and Canada, struck terror to the hearts of the rich Conservatives running the Argentine government. An Argentine trade delegation was sent to London to try to protect the Argentine position and managed to negotiate a new treaty in May of 1933 which helped to stem the declining levels of trade. The pact, known as the Roca-Runciman Treaty, was controversial in some respects,[16] but it was welcomed by the Con-

servatives who feared the loss of their precious market for exports in
England.

The impact of the Depression and Argentine trade restrictions particularly
affected trade with the United States. Its average for the years 1931–1940
was less than half that of the period 1920–1929.[17] A system of tariffs and
quotas was begun in Buenos Aires, marking a dramatic reversal of the laissez-
faire principles which the oligarchical parties had championed in the nineteenth century. A system of exchange restrictions was also initiated during
the period. The peso was devalued, some commodities were put under
government export control, and deficit financing began. One result of
these measures was to stimulate the expansion of secondary industries.[18]
This came about particularly in Argentina because the economic infrastruc-
ture in such fields as transportation already existed, along with relatively
high rates of domestic saving. The economic measures caused manufacturing
output to surpass the net value of agricultural and livestock production by
1944.[19]

This opening of the Argentine economy was the other side of the policy
to preserve the Argentine sales of beef to England,[20] and it marked a change
in the policy of economic nationalism espoused by the Radicals. There were
numerous stories, many of them substantially true, of extraordinarily lucra-
tive concessions being negotiated by foreign investors (primarily English)
during the 1930s.[21]

Given the truly catastrophic impact of the Great Depression in many
countries, it is difficult not to agree with the conclusion of one economist
who wrote that "judged without bias, the conduct of economic affairs by
the Conservative administrations through the 1930s must . . . be considered to have been passably good."[22] In their effort to preserve the meat trade,
the Conservatives had stumbled onto a policy that also encouraged industrialization.[23] The system of exchange controls, devised to favor the British,
stimulated the flow of direct industrial investment from non-British sources.[24]
Coupled with the factors that increased industrialization in most of the Latin
American countries during the Depression—that is, the inability to import
due to a lack of foreign exchange—Argentina managed to avoid much of
the force of the Depression.

Although it was not a problem of immediate major economic consequence,
to the Argentina public the most important issue complicating relations with
the United States was the embargo imposed against Argentine meat. This resulted from claims of the prevalence of hoof-and-mouth disease in Argentina.
With the Conservative interests in power after the 1930 coup, the embargo
constituted a potential threat to the rich land owners who were the support
for the government. It was not a matter of indispensable markets, but the
controversy was fanned by the fact that Argentina's beef was virtually a

national symbol to those Argentine nationalists who glorified the past and
centered their nostalgia on the great ranches of the pampas and the epic
struggles involved in settling them. Ysabel F. Rennie's *The Argentine Republic,* published in 1945, asks:

> In what country but Argentina would cabinet ministers be proud of
> being photographed with a Durham bull? In what country but Argentina
> could one imagine the President of the Republic and [the] Grenadier
> Guards parading around a show ring dedicated to the exposition of Hol-
> stein cows, Aberdeen Angus and Shorthorn bulls, Percheron horses, and
> Lincoln sheep?[25]

Without making too much of a single characteristic, it is logical to assume
that politicians will gravitate to the symbols of national unity. Thus the
banning of Argentine meat struck at more than just a product—it struck
at a national symbol.

The view was considerably different in the United States. Hoof-and-mouth
disease had long struck terror to the North American cattleman's heart. And,
of course, the possibility of massive imports of meat from Argentina had
economic repercussions for this group. In 1935 the Secretary of State signed
a Sanitary Convention which would have allowed the division of Argentina
into territories or zones in determining what cattle had been exposed to the
disease. It was felt that since the Patagonian region of Argentina had not
had a hoof-and-mouth problem, imports from there would not be dangerous.
Secretary of State Hull declared "off the record" that subjecting all of Argentina to an embargo was an "absurdity" and added that lobbies opposing
the Convention had sent "outrageously false data" to the Senate.[26] Later, a
governmental official was to state privately that the stock raisers were up
in arms about the Convention as a result of efforts of the paid secretaries
of the stock raisers organizations "who must always have a bogey to dangle
before the cattlemen so that they will continue to pay their dues and assess-
ments to the association treasuries, out of which these officers' salaries
come."[27]

Eventually, the debate came to center on an essentially technical question: Would the chances of hoof-and-mouth disease being transmitted to the
United States increase if the pact went into effect? It was not an easy question to answer scientifically because it involved two other factual questions.
The first was whether or not sufficient precautions were being taken in the
Patagonian area to prevent the area from being exposed to the disease. The
second was whether or not freezing the meat or chilling it would completely
kill the disease. Although Argentina assumed that the chilling process neces-
sary for shipping would kill the disease,[28] the United States experts in the
Department of Agriculture were unwilling to take a position. Generally, the
Agriculture Department privately accepted the pact but publicly refused to

take a position on it.[29] In an effort to avoid the wrath of the domestic
cattle interests, Secretary of Agriculture Henry Wallace even went so far at
one point as to deny any Department of Agriculture involvement in the negotiation of the agreement when testifying before a congressional committee,
although this was flatly in contradiction with the facts.[30] Agriculture had
been frequently consulted and had offered significant advice in the negotiations.

In May of 1939 President Roosevelt, in an effort to better relations with
Argentina, tried to purchase canned Argentine beef for use by the Navy.[31]
However, this ran into opposition in the Congress, and by the summer of
1939 even the Convention of 1935 was recognized as dead without hearings
ever being held in the Senate Foreign Relations Committee. The bulk of
that committee represented agricultural states which of itself made the
chances of the agreement doubtful, but outbreaks of the disease in areas
close to Patagonia raised other problems.[32] Evidently Roosevelt, in a private
talk with the Argentine Ambassador, was critical of the unrepresentative nature of the United States Senate.[33] As a result of the protest which went up
in the United States when the Ambassador later repeated his version of
Roosevelt's remarks to the American Chamber of Commerce in Buenos Aires,
both sides later denied that the conversation took place.

Professor Bryce Wood sees the moral of the dispute as being that the
United States could pursue the Good Neighbor Policy in the sense of *not*
taking actions such as landing the Marines. However, powerful interest
groups could prevent the President from taking positive steps when their interests were threatened.[34] He stated:

> The case for the Convention was logical and enlightened; it was rea-
> sonably certain that the adoption of the Convention would neither result
> in lowering the price of mutton, or in raising the incidence of hoof-and-
> mouth disease. However, no guarantee could be given, and the Department
> was never able to convince the cattlemen that no beef whatever would be
> imported if the Convention were approved. Regardless of the excellence
> of the case for the Convention on these grounds, the political argument
> for it was a weak one, because the objectives made no burning appeal to
> the powerful interests who were satisfied with the existing situation, nor,
> indeed, to anyone else.[35]

Thus the question of a very small amount of Argentine meat imports served
to cloud relations between the United States and Argentina. The entire operation seemed a guise to the Argentines, while the question managed to become a confusing scientific-political question north of the Rio Grande.

After the furor over the Sanitary Convention and the failure of the Senate to act on it, Argentina agreed to open the long-delayed trade negotiations,
evidently more or less satisfied that the meat restrictions were truly out of

the hands of the President. During 1938 and 1939 there were moments
when it seemed possible that Argentina might find a way to enter into a
reciprocal trade agreement with the United States but the talks collapsed
early in 1940. Although one can fault Secretary of State Hull's final offer,
take-it-or-leave-it negotiation style, the main problem from Argentina's point
of view was that granting the United States most-favored-nation status would
strain relations with the British by limiting the amount of official exchange
for remittance on British investments. On the United States side, vocal protests of the linseed interests set limits on the Department of State's maneuv-
erability since the agreement would have to go to the Congress. Ultimately,
the negotiations failed, not on principle, but simply because each side
wanted the other to make more concessions than it wanted to make.[36]

THE ROLE OF GERMANY

Washington was becoming increasingly concerned with the role of Germany in Argentina during the late 1930s. Argentina's relations with the Third
Reich were generally amicable until 1938. Although the large German population in Argentina operated over 200 schools, more than four times the number of English schools, these did not initially present any problems.[37] The
local Nazi Party was relatively quiet, and there were deep divisions within
the German community over the rise of Hitler.[38] It is estimated that about
40,000 native-born Germans and another 180,000 descendants who retained
German as a language composed the German colony in Argentina—about 1.6
percent of the population.[39]

Argentina's trade with Germany increased during the 1930s as part of
Hitler's aggressive foreign trade campaign. The failure of the international
payments system strengthened the demand for barter trade, which Germany
capitalized on through the Aski mark system. By 1938 Argentine exports to
Germany had doubled the 1936 figure to the 11.7 percent mark. Argentine
imports from Germany had also increased slightly, to 10.1 percent.[40] Part
of the latter increase was at the expense of the United States even though
the United States total was significantly greater. The German trade was helping to provide the growing Third Reich industrial complex with the materials
it needed. It was also producing the inevitable vested interests around the
German trade. These groups would dissent from any policy cutting Latin
America off from Germany.

In terms of the major political groups, the one in which German influence was strongest was the Army, which had long been exposed to German
training and had attracted Argentines of German descent. The army officer
who was Argentine Minister of War in 1935 had served with a German

regiment during World War I and had also been Military Attaché in Berlin for several years.[41] Numerous other high ranking officers had had some of their training in Berlin. By 1936 at least half a dozen German Army officers were functioning as instructors in the important Army War College.[42] The Army purchased many of its arms and supplies in Germany, a pattern which was strengthened after 1933.[43] Although Buenos Aires did not have a military attaché stationed in Washington to correspond to the Argentine representative in Berlin, the United States did send some military flying instructors to Argentina to help in training its pilots, thereby provoking a protest from Brazil,[44] which hoped to keep Washington solidly behind Rio de Janiero in traditional rivalry with Argentina. Cordell Hull, showing an ignorance of the history of inter–Latin American relations, said he was "unable to comprehend what objections there can be" to the sending of the instructors.[45] Within the Argentine Navy there was evidently some admiration for the United States.[46] Several naval officers from Argentina had gone to the United States during World War I, some of them bringing back U.S. wives.[47]

Robert Potash's excellent study *The Army & Politics in Argentina 1928–1945: Yrigoyen to Perón* states that very few military officers during the immediate prewar period were alarmed by Nazi ideology or German expansionism. He points to widespread pro-German feelings but says that it does not follow that military officers were anxious to see a totalitarian state established in Argentina. He concludes that

> The rank and file of officers were not political militants, nor did they want the military to govern the country. Their outlook as of 1940 was instead a confused amalgam of admiration on professional grounds for German military prowess, belief that the humbling of Great Britain would redound to Argentina's economic benefit, and determination to preserve the country's neutrality come what may.[48]

The propaganda struggle which Germany was to wage during the war was only beginning during the mid-1930s. Although the United States did not make a serious coordinated effort in this area, Germany and Italy soon began to provide subsidies and free press service to some Argentine newspapers.[49] At a meeting of some German chiefs of mission in Latin America held in July of 1938, it was decided that their propaganda efforts were ineffective and that more funds should be spent in this field.[50]

Argentine domestic politics influenced the relationship with Germany. In preparation for the 1937 presidential election, President Justo followed the traditional oligarchical practice of quietly rigging the choice in favor of his candidate while publicly attempting to give the appearance that the process was democratic. The man chosen was Roberto M. Ortiz, a former Radical who had been in Justo's Cabinet. He had been a corporation lawyer representing various North American enterprises. His choice was welcomed by most North Americans. U.S. Ambassador Alexander Weddell wrote that the new President's "direct approach to problems suggests mental process not unlike men of our own race." [51] As events were to show, the most important fact about Ortiz was that he was overweight and evidently suffering from diabetes when he assumed office. The political power of Robustiano Patrón Costas and other important Conservatives forced Justo to name Dr. Ramón S. Castillo, Dean of the Buenos Aires Law School, as the Vice President. The U.S. Ambassador stated at the time of Castillo's nomination that he was "charming but not very forceful" and "very conservative." [52] According to another author, "everyone knew his reputation as the most reactionary man in the Buenos Aires Law School." [53]

The rigged election went fairly quietly. It has been speculated that this was because there was a secret understanding between Ortiz and the Radicals that if he were elected he would allow the Radicals to regain power through honest elections. [54] This seems doubtful in the literal sense, but it may well be that the Radicals respected Ortiz's honesty and, remembering Sáenz Peña's voting law which allowed them to take power in 1916, [55] refused to cooperate in a united front against the Conservatives hoping that he would honor his pledge of free and open elections—a pledge which was dismissed as campaign rhetoric in some circles.

Somewhat due to Nazi initiatives, but perhaps partially due to a pro-Allied bias of the President, several problems began to sour Argentine-German relations in 1938. German diplomats, buoyed by Hitler's advances in Europe, were adopting "an increasingly aggressive and frequently insulting manner." [56] There also were increasing complaints regarding the cultural egocentricity of the numerous German schools. It was felt that these establishments were not developing a sense of Argentine national pride but, rather, were acting to inculcate the students with Nazi ideas. Ortiz, evidently angered by the massive plans the German community was making to celebrate May 1, the German national holiday which marked the Austrian Anschluss of April, issued a decree forbidding the display of foreign flags on May 1. [57]

The increasingly obvious Nazi activities in Argentina and the reaction against them caused Argentina to have its Ambassador in Berlin ask the Nazi government to restrain its agents. [58] A vote which had been open to Germans in Argentina concerning the Anschluss also prompted criticism. The German Ambassador, in his despatches to Berlin, accounted for this change in attitude by the government as being due to the anti-German, liberal democratic ideas of President Ortiz and his Foreign Minister José María Cantilo. [59] He also called for a series of changes in the pro-German organizations which the German Embassy was assisting in order to coordinate their activities and perhaps to tone them down. An executive decree in mid-May set regulations for foreign associations in Argentina. The thrust of the law was clearly nationalistic and emphasized the Argentine distrust of foreign things. It did lead to the dissolution of the Nazi Party; but it was replaced by the Federation of German Welfare and Cultural Societies, which was registered within the guidelines of the decree. The degree to which the German position was hurt in Argentina is shown by the fact that German Ambassador Edmund von Thermann at a June meeting in Berlin argued for a lessening of activities aimed at the organization of the German community in Argentina and for more effort toward winning over Argentines to the German cause—a plea that was only partially successful.[60] Von Thermann's stay in Buenos Aires was characterized by his continuing problems with Argentines who were vocally pro-Nazi and by zealous Nazis in Berlin who wanted Nazi control of the Argentine Pan-German organizations.[61]

HEMISPHERIC UNITY

The Eighth International Conference of American States which was held in 1938 in its regular cycle deserves some analysis in terms of the interplay of United States–German relations in Argentine foreign policy at the time. The standard interpretation generally is that Argentina was obstructionist and opposed the United States. The Argentine Foreign Minister slipped away to vacation in the lake country of Chile, thereby making compromises impossible. The United States then contacted President Ortiz directly and Argentina ended up adhering to a reasonably strong statement of hemispheric unity which contained no formal commitment binding Argentina to take action.

This interpretation is accurate in many senses and the results of the meeting were inconclusive at best. Secretary of State Hull described the ten days he spent at the meeting "as among the most difficult of my career."[62] Certainly Foreign Minister Cantilo's decision to take a vacation after the meeting opened while leaving the delegation in the hands of an individual who had almost no authorization to make concessions made things difficult for Washington. However, Cantilo's later pro-Allied stance would seem to make it clear that this was less a pro-German position than a pro-English move[63] and also may have been an attempt, which overshot the mark, to stiffen Argentina's bargaining position.

The idea that Argentina came to the meeting determined to oppose the United States or fundamentally at odds with Washington is not accurate. Although Argentina did initially oppose calling the conference, after accepting the idea the Argentine government actually presented Washington with an advance outline of its position.[64] In that document Buenos Aires advocated the strengthening of the system of consultation referred to in resolutions at the 1936 inter-American meeting. This marked a significant advance from some past Argentine efforts which had been totally disruptive of the development of the inter-American system—although even in this case Buenos Aires was careful to oppose the granting of any political power to the Washington-dominated Pan American Union. Essentially, Argentina's objection at the meeting was the emphasis on the idea of an outside threat to the hemisphere and the closing off of the hemisphere from events in Europe.[65]

After Cantilo left for his stay in Chile, the chairmanship of the delegation fell to Isidoro Ruíz Moreno whose instructions were evidently quite restrictive. Thus, after the North American delegation reached a total impasse with him and had already made several concessions from the original concept of a strong alliance, an appeal that eventually served to break the deadlock was made to President Ortiz himself. The United States always felt it had the votes to pass almost any resolution if it was willing to tolerate three or four dissenters. However, Hull did not want to have a public split in the hemispheric community, so he pressed for the unanimity which he eventually received for the "Declaration of Lima" calling for consultation of foreign ministers. It also should be noted that Argentina was not acting completely on its own in opposing the United States. Probably much of the myth of a great divergence between Argentina and the United States arose from the traditional difficulties between the countries and from the unusual situation of Cantilo's disappearance into seclusion in Chile.[66]

In line with this conclusion is the fact that the United States Embassy in Buenos Aires also felt what it believed to be a softening in the traditional Argentine reluctance to cooperate. A memo sent in late April of 1939 from the Chargé d'Affairs in Buenos Aires said that events seemed to be leading Argentina, since the Lima Conference, to "find it to her advantage to adopt a less individualistic attitude in her future relationships with her Southern neighbors" and that "there may also follow a sounder comprehension in Argentina of the advantages to be derived from a less selfish attitude and from a better spirit of Pan American cooperation." It continued:

> Despite this evidently growing belief in the significance of Pan Americanism, it would be rash to conclude that Argentina, in the event of a world conflagration, would necessarily side with the democracies against the Axis Powers, unless of course this country became the victim of a direct act of aggression by the latter. Such neutrality does not justify the belief that Argentina is in sympathy with totalitarian conceptions, but indicates rather that her present economic difficulties would force her, in the event of war, to adopt an extremely cautious attitude. Although it has been said, with a certain degree of justice, that in Presi-

dent Ortiz' endorsement of the Roosevelt messages to Hitler and Mussolini there is to be found a clarification of the Argentine attitude at Lima,
it cannot be overlooked that the reply from the Argentine Chief of State
contains an unexpressed reservation which leaves the door open for interpretation, particularly insofar as this country's future relationships
with Europe are concerned.

The memo also complained that Ortiz, having never been out of Argentina, knew little about foreign affairs and that the Foreign Minister, Cantilo,
"carries far too great a mental prejudice in favor of Europe to be able to
approach present day issues with any degree of objectivity."[67]

Hitler's invasion of Poland in September of 1939 finally toppled Europe
into war. Argentine's immediate reaction, as was true with the other Latin
American countries and the United States, was a declaration of neutrality.
There is little doubt that the bulk of public opinion favored the cause of
Britain and France, particularly the major newspapers. Even the German
Embassy's report to Berlin on Argentine reaction to the war reached this
conclusion, although within a Nazi framework. The September 28, 1939,
despatch stated:

> One frequently encounters here the foolish but accepted notion that
> expansionist ambition would make Germany a territorial and general
> threat to South America after the victorious conclusion of the war. There
> is general failure to understand Germany's policy, which usually is repre-
> sented as disruptive of peace except among a few intellectuals in the
> Army and in business who are reasonably familiar with European issues.[68]

There were others in Argentina who remembered the prosperity which
had come to the country in her neutral role during World War I and who
looked forward to a reoccurence of that situation. On the other hand, there
were at least three groups, with widely differing motives, who did not share
this sympathy for the French and English. The first consisted of those who
had long resented English economic domination of Argentina and, while not
particularly fond of the Germans, welcomed defeats and trials for the English. Second, there was a large body of public opinion favoring whichever
side was winning, and for the first two years of the struggle that side was
the Axis. Third, there was a group attracted to the ideologies represented
by the Fascist countries. Certainly the more conservative elements in Argentina had never been fond of democracy and had justified to themselves the
fraudulent elections since 1930 in terms of anti-democratic arguments. The
Italian and German communities in Argentina gained some personal satisfaction from seeing the military superiority of their ancestors. There was some
support from reactionary intellectuals and important elements within the
clergy, who saw Hitler as embodying some elements of Hispanidad ideology.

Many politically well-placed military men, trained in Germany or by German officers, were pro-Axis and also were beginning to nurture the idea that they could operate the country better than civilians. The nationalist ideas of these groups will be discussed later at a point when they have become better defined by events.

Thus, while the neutrality position was the obvious one to take in terms of the international situation, and the one which even the United States was assuming at this point, in the case of Argentina the position was also a compromise between conflicting interest groups. It should be mentioned that Hitler's cooperation pact with Communist Russia undermined some of the support for the German cause that might have been forthcoming from Argentine reactionary elements. Later, after Hitler attacked Russia and thereby freed his backers of the stigma of cooperating with the Communists, the issues became more clear-cut to many conservative and reactionary Argentines. They had long feared communism and distrusted democracy. It was much easier to support Hitler after he had proven himself to be a staunch anti-communist.

Despite an increasing propaganda campaign by the Germans after the invasion of Poland, the Argentine government generally attempted to avoid having officials identify with one side or the other.[69] But there was a pro-Allied flavor in the policy because Buenos Aires did recognize the Polish government in Paris after Hitler conquered Poland[70] and privately warned the German-subsidized press to tone itself down.[71]

The high point of Argentine backing for the Allied cause was reached in April and May of 1940 when Argentine Foreign Minister Cantilo approached Ambassador Armour with a proposal that, in terms of being pro-Allied, went beyond Washington's position at the time. The proposal was so incongruous to the commonly accepted image of a strictly neutral or lethargically pro-Axis Argentina that it has attracted analysis by at least two prominent historians, both of whom view the episode as a turning point in hemispheric relations.[72]

Cantilo began his discussion with Armour by pointing out that, in light of the fall of the neutral European countries to the German war machine, and the fact that the Panama security zone was not being observed, his government felt that the duties of a neutral, which included few rights, had become legal fiction.[73] He correctly pointed out that the United States apparently was aiding the Allies despite its official neutrality and that this aid would probably increase. Therefore, the Foreign Minister suggested, the American republics should agree to declare themselves "non-belligerents" as Italy had done. This status, as he described it, consisted of not entering into the war and permitting each nation to do what it felt to be in its best interests. It would free them from the rules of neutrality, which was only logical in

view of the collapse of international order in Europe; and, although this action would undoubtedly favor the Allies, Germany would be in no position
to protest since it had accepted the position from Italy. According to Cantilo, President Ortiz supported the idea "heartily." He felt that agreement
on the idea should first be reached between the United States and Argentina
and then Brazil should be consulted prior to the calling of any kind of an
inter-American meeting for approval.

The reaction to this idea, which was also relayed to Washington by Ambassador Felipe Espil, was a cool rejection. The Secretary of State answered
by pointing out that under the terms of existing statutory legislation in the
United States, the government was obligated to maintain neutrality. He also
condescendingly lectured Argentina on international law by stating that attempts to circumvent those ideas would lessen the validity of the international law which the American republics had always defended: "The mere
fact that nations are today openly flouting the accepted principles of international law does not . . . constitute an argument in favor of the further
derogation of those standards of international conduct." In fact, according
to Hull, such flouting made it more important to uphold the rules of international law. The Secretary also suggested that under the Argentine suggestion the various countries might end up following differing policies and
thereby hurt Pan-American cooperation.[74]

Undeterred, Argentina approached Brazil on the same proposal and met
with a similar rebuff. The Brazilian Ambassador to Argentina was suspicious
of the suggestion, feeling that it might have been a reaction by President
Ortiz to his fear of the Axis propaganda drive.[75] We now know that Brazil
was secretly stringing along the Germans at this time,[76] so it would have
been impossible for Brazil's President Getúlio Vargas to continue that strategy if the Cantilo-Ortiz proposal had been accepted.

It is interesting to speculate whether the chain of events which followed
between the United States and Argentina might have been different. However, the suggestion does emphasize one of the major problems existing
within the hemisphere, particularly at this time. The United States felt itself to be operating on a different level of international responsibility than
the Latin American states. It had the power to do something about what was
happening in Europe and had particularly close ties to England. Washington
was being torn apart by indecision regarding what should be done. Obviously
neutrality was an illusion,[77] and historians have long debated whether
Roosevelt should have moved faster to come to the assistance of England
and used his powers of persuasion to move public opinion into an interven-
tionist position. The merits of this debate need not concern this narrative
except to point out that these were the questions paramount in United
States foreign policy debate at the time. A suggestion from a country such

as Argentina, even though it shared domination of South America with Brazil, was essentially extraneous. From Washington's point of view, hemispheric relations were supposed to respond to United States foreign policy, not vice versa. The idea of Washington basing a fundamental change in its policy on a suggestion from a single Latin American country seemed hardly worth the consideration of the State Department. So the argument can be made that it would have been impossible for the United States to have responded to the idea. However, the counterargument is that Roosevelt was looking for ways (and excuses) to help England and France at this time and the Argentine suggestion, if adopted, could have helped influence U.S. public opinion.

But what prompted Argentina's proposal in the first place? Although clearly in response to events in Europe and the fiction of neutrality, it probably was the product of a political strategy and the genuinely pro-democratic propensities of Cantilo and Ortiz.

The coalition which brought Ortiz to power was divided between elements of varying degrees of commitment to democratic processes and of differing opinions as to the desirability of a Fascist victory in Europe. Ortiz appears to have been trying to support his shaky government by appealing to the political "outs" (Radicals, National Democrats, and Socialists) with his intervention to bring honesty to the election process. Meanwhile, he hoped to keep the support of pro-democratic and pro-Allied portions of his own coalition through an international policy such as non-belligerency represented.[78]

For this strategy to have worked, Argentina would have had to have been allowed to assume hemispheric leadership on the non-belligerency concept— which both the United States and Brazil opposed. It would also have had to lead to a warm response from the U.S. government in terms of generous trade agreements and support for the economy. When neither the prestige of leadership nor the material benefits of trade and aid were forthcoming, Argentina pulled back. The Radicals, who won control of the Chamber of Deputies for the first time since 1930 in the mid-April 1940 election, were supporting Ortiz. But the Nazi propaganda barrage, criticism from anti-democratic elements in his own coalition, and the military seem to have pushed Ortiz away from any continued attempt to show a pro-Allied leadership position.

At the risk of engaging in historical scenario building, if Washington had responded positively to Ortiz and at least had provided economic advantages to his government, Ortiz and Cantilo might have pulled Argentina into a position of leadership in the Allied camp. There would have been dangers of a coup; but one can speculate that, handled correctly, the Ortiz government might have attracted a wide base of domestic political support for a more activist proposal if it had been able to produce material benefits and the aura of international authority. Such was not to be. Events unfolded in the opposite direction from this point on.

THE SLOW SHIFT

On May 18, 1940, President Ortiz stated publicly that the government had no intention of involving itself in the war. On the surface the statement reflected the current policy of all the American republics, but the fact that the statement was made at all represented the beginning of a subtle change in emphasis. The United States Embassy interpreted the statement as "necessitated by criticism emanating from politically potent domestic quarters" and mentioned the military in particular.[79] With neither the United States nor powerful internal interests supporting his anti-Axis emphasis, Ortiz had modified his position. The United States Embassy in Buenos Aires also pointed out that German military successes were not helping to fortify pro-Allied feeling.

This new cautiousness was reflected in the government's handling of the sinking of the Argentine freighter *Uruguay* off the coast of Spain on May 27, 1940, by what was immediately assumed to be a German submarine. There was a public outcry in Argentina, fanned undoubtedly by pro-Allied elements.[80] Argentina officially protested to Germany and asked for payment.[81] However, Berlin beat Argentina to the punch by having Ambassador von Thermann call on Argentine officials to protest the anti-German feelings in Argentina growing out of the sinking and to point out that there was no evidence to suggest that Germany had actually sunk the vessel. The strongly worded instructions which von Thermann received also stated that even if the sinking was attributable to Germany there was no reason for Argentina to assume that the *Uruguay* was not violating contraband and blockade procedures.[82] President Ortiz had informed the Ambassador that his government was trying to restrain anti-German agitation. The note of protest delivered in Berlin by the Argentine Ambassador on June 3 requested apologies and adequate compensation, but the Ambassador seemed anxious for any possible concession that might soothe Argentine public opinion.[83] When the Ambassador called on the German State Secretary a week later he took an even more conciliatory position.[84] He emphasized friendly relations with Germany and seemed apologetic about the reaction of the Argentine press. Mentioning recent German victories, he assured the German official that Argentina had no intention of becoming dependent on the United States and suggested the possibility of increased postwar trade between Germany and Argentina. He did ask that Berlin adopt a more conciliatory attitude in the *Uruguay* case. He pointed out that a conciliatory position in Berlin following the sinking of two Argentine ships in 1917 had greatly eased tensions. Although the State Secretary knew that a German ship had been responsible,[85] he said if Argentina's complaint was justified the German government would not hesitate to take a conciliatory position. The Ambassador persisted in attempting to get an immediate gesture of friendship but was not successful.

Less than two weeks later Ambassador von Thermann was approached with a similar request. It was claimed that a conciliatory gesture in the case would help quell anti-German agitation in Argentina and would give Buenos Aires more flexibility at the Havana conference opening that day.[86] The Ambassador agreed that some sort of a written communication stating that an investigation was underway and expressing confidence in continued friendly relations with Argentina would help placate the situation. On June 26 the Argentine Ambassador in Berlin received such a note in which Germany admitted that it had sunk the *Uruguay* but refused payment because the ship was guilty of violating contraband and blockade rules.[87]

June of 1940, however, was particularly noteworthy because, as President Ortiz was beginning to make efforts to strike back at the pro-totalitarian elements in the government,[88] his rapidly declining health limited his activities. Between the death of his wife in April and his own physical condition, he was having an increasingly difficult time in carrying out his presidential responsibilities. He did not turn the management of the executive branch over to Vice President Castillo until he had no alternative. The two had clashed almost from the first when Ortiz had insisted on having honest elections.[89]

It is not difficult to argue that a dramatic change in the official attitude of the Argentine government toward hemispheric cooperation is marked by the change in presidents, but it should be noted that events were also in the process of pushing Ortiz in the direction that Castillo went willingly. Perhaps the question is only whether they assumed the position reluctantly or gladly.[90] Of course, control of the government may have slipped from Ortiz's hands by the end of May, in which case the argument for a strong difference in policy between the two men growing from personal beliefs is strengthened.

As for the case of the *Uruguay*, Argentina sent Germany a note on August 2 which stated that the sinking had not been legal but that Argentina did not wish to prolong the argument. The note also indicated that it had received the German refusal of payment in a friendly spirit and only hoped that the question would be reconsidered after the war. The pro-Allied groups attempted to keep the incident alive, and more than a year later, on September 26, 1941, the Senate passed a resolution calling on the President to press Berlin for a favorable settlement. The Foreign Office declined and reiterated that it hoped for a more favorable consideration after the war.[91]

One researcher on the question has speculated that "it is possible that the sinking of the *Uruguay* was an intentional act by the German government" to counter the anti-German attitude of the Ortiz government and Foreign Minister Cantilo.[92] Although this may seem doubtful, Argentina was clearly forced to back down in the dispute. The sinking, rather than worsening relations as might have been expected, served, along with the increasing number of Axis victories in Europe, to change the direction of the Argentine government's policy. At least, the sinking is some sort of bench mark in the shifting of policy in Buenos Aires. The fact that Germany was able to keep from sinking a United States vessel until May 21, 1941, would seem to indicate that the Third Reich was able to distinguish its targets and that the sinking of the *Uruguay* was intended as a warning.[93] It was a dangerous game for Berlin to play, because some government encouragement to protesting the sinking could have fanned anti-German sentiment in Argentina out of control. However, the leadership did not come.

Other events during June and July of 1940 help to explain Argentina's shifting attitude. Probably the most important of these is that on June 22 France capitulated to Hitler, thereby sending shock waves deep into Latin America, where French culture had long been the standard against which all other cultures were judged.[94] Also, there was the entrance of Italy into the war a few days before the French-German armistice. Since there were more Italian than German immigrants in Argentina, this was a factor of some significance; although it was offset in Argentina by the fact that the Italians did not seem to occupy the critical political posts held by some German descendants—particularly in the military. The Chamber of Deputies responded to what it sensed as a slippage toward a pro-totalitarian position by debating a measure designed to restrict the operations of foreign policy organizations in Argentina. The government introduced a similar bill; but political divisions defeated the measure, primarily because the Congress did not trust the President to carry it out in the manner intended. It feared the bill could be used as a weapon against dissent.[95] Also in June a movement called Acción Argentina was formed to serve as a counterbalance to the well-organized totalitarian activities being carried on in Argentina. Many prominent individuals affiliated with the organization and eventually it claimed a membership of about 300,000.[96] Its membership included a wide variety of opinions, but it was not sympathetic to the Communists even after the Russians entered the war on the side of the Allies. However, the organization's lack of leadership and its diverse membership caused it to bog down after an initial push, and it never realized its potential as a major pressure group.

In the meantime, the German Embassy was increasing its propaganda efforts. On June 8, following a relatively pessimistic report on the situation in Argentina, Ambassador von Thermann asked for more restraint in the Nazi-controlled organizations in Argentina so as not to stir up public opinion, for increased economic agreements in anticipation of an early end of the war, and for the transfer of increased funds to the Embassy which would be used in helping to subsidize pro-German newspapers and in immediate efforts to win over important persons (evidently through financial inducements).[97] Following the Ambassador's suggestions, Hitler disavowed any German territorial claims, placed some restrictions on local Nazis, opened negotiations for increased commodity purchases, and increased the Embassy's subsidy funds.[98] The last led to the stepping up of propaganda efforts within the country.

Another visible sign of the mid-1940 shift in policy can be seen in Argentina's performance at the Havana Conference held in late July of that year. The coming of the war to Europe had prompted the calling of a meeting of foreign ministers in Panama nine months after the Lima conference. At the Panama meeting the 300-mile security belt around the hemisphere was agreed to. Although Argentina's role at the meeting may not have been quite one of "wholehearted cooperation,"[99] it certainly was not a role in opposition to the United States. The Argentine representative felt that his instructions from Foreign Minister Cantilo were unnecessarily narrow and he wired President Ortiz requesting a loosening of his restrictions. This, according to the delegate, was granted directly from Ortiz.[100] Argentina was suspicious of the 300-mile limit but this feeling was shared by Secretary Hull, who felt the idea to be Roosevelt's seconded by Welles.[101] In retrospect, Argentina and Hull were correct in anticipating the ineffectiveness of the neutrality zone.

When the meeting was called in Havana a year later as a result of the military defeat of European countries holding possessions in the Caribbean, Argentina, now governed by Castillo, was considerably less willing to cooperate. In some respects the entire idea of a trusteeship for the colonies started poorly when the United States Senate passed a resolution prior to the meeting stating that Washington should not recognize or acquiesce in the transfer of territory in the western hemisphere from one non-American power to another. The Argentine Foreign Minister protested to the U.S. Embassy in Buenos Aires that such a declared policy seemed to preclude any discussion of the matter.[102] This was perhaps partially pique because Argentina had already adhered to a declaration barring such an action. However, at the conference, Argentina, while not openly obstructionist, was generally dubious of the entire purpose of the meeting. At one point the Argentine representative told Hull that the question of European possessions in the hemisphere was not of great interest to his country since the territories were located far from Buenos Aires.[103] Argentina also managed to irritate the Department of State by suggesting that rather than not allowing the colonies to be transferred, the colonies should be given their independence.[104] The United States leadership on the question of a statement warning against transfer of ownership of colonies in the western hemisphere (which was a portion of the original Monroe Doctrine) was successful. Another idea which had been mentioned and had temporarily found favor in Washington was the idea of an economic cartel in the hemisphere to promote cooperation and trade. This ran into significant opposition from Argentina and other states.[105] The depth of Argentine opposition to Washington did not become open until the next foreign ministers meeting held in Rio de Janeiro, but even here at Havana, and to a lesser extent at Panama, it is obvious that the two countries had fundamentally differing outlooks on the relationship of the American republics to events in Europe.

UNITED STATES EFFORTS

Although the United States clearly worried about a "too neutral" or even pro-Axis Argentina, in January of 1940 came the breakdown of the long series of trade talks with "both parties feeling a good deal of rancor."[106] In mid- and late 1940, Washington's efforts to combat the Argentine unwillingness to cooperate centered on three specific questions: a possible corn marketing agreement, talks concerning economic assistance for Argentina, and discussions of military cooperation.

An Argentine protest over the sale of 20 million bushels of U.S. corn to England in late May of 1940 first raised the question of a corn combine.[107] Argentina claimed that Washington had assisted the exporter and that this constituted an artificial barrier to trade based on the concept of free exchange of goods. In August of 1940, after some diplomatic exchanges, Washington finally proposed a relatively concrete memorandum around which talks could begin.[108] The United States suggested that an 80–20 allocation of corn exports to England (in favor of Argentina) might be a good ratio around which to begin talks, but more problems arose and it soon became obvious that Buenos Aires's interest in the talks was lagging.[109] The vision of the postwar German market closed to United States producers helped doom the discussions, but there was also the traditional unwillingness of Argentina to bind herself too closely to the United States.[110] Thus the talks were never held.

The question of economic assistance for Argentina to offset difficulties the economy was having in readjusting to the shifts in the international pattern of trade brought about by the war was raised in mid-June of 1940 by Ambassador Armour.[111] Dr. Raúl Prebisch, the general manager of the Argentine Central Bank, suggested that the United States should consider (1) financing a substantial part of Argentina's imports from the United States through the Export-Import Bank, (2) providing a loan to help Buenos Aires meet the service on the public foreign debt and other foreign payments owed by the government, and (3) purchasing large amounts of Argentina's exportable products so as to provide exchange for further imports from the United States for Argentina.[112] A telegram of June 17 from Ambassador Armour suggested that the Embassy favored the proposal in substance.[113] Eventually, discussions led to a $60-million credit which would be repaid over an eight-and-one-half-year period.[114] The U.S. Treasury Department also offered a stabilization fund operation under which it would buy up to $50 million worth of pesos during 1941 to support the value of the peso.[115]

The final question into which the United States and Argentina moved during mid-1940 was a series of talks between military officials regarding possible cooperation. This type of consultation was initiated by Washington with all the Latin American countries. On May 23, stimulated by the collapse of French resistance, the Department of State asked Ambassador Armour to approach the Minister of Foreign Affairs regarding such talks, predicated on the possibility of aggression being committed against any portion of the western hemisphere.[116] The telegram, which was more or less a form letter, cautioned that it should be made clear that the suggested discussions had no implication of a military alliance nor did they signify that the United States was about to enter the war. It only was intended to indicate that Washington felt the situation was becoming increasingly dangerous and that it would be well to plan in advance. It was suggested that appropriate military officers from the United States traveling in civilian clothes and by commercial plane could visit Argentina without publicity in order to hold private talks with officers designated by Argentina. Washington felt that the talks had already been agreed to in principle by the Declaration of Lima.

Armour's discussion of the idea with Cantilo found the Foreign Minister "in a somewhat defeatish mood," according to the Ambassador's report, as a result of the turn of events in Europe.[117] Cantilo said he would have to consult with Ortiz about the suggestion and asked what assistance Armour thought the United States could give Argentina if both the English and the French were defeated. Armour pointed out that this was to be the subject of the talks. After discussing the question with Ortiz, whose health was declining dangerously by this time, Cantilo said that the President wanted more detailed information on what could be discussed. Ortiz was, according to the Foreign Minister, inclined to doubt whether such conversations would be useful and was of the opinion that an ill-prepared defense would be worse than no defense at all since it would tend to invite attack.[118] The Foreign Minister also suggested that the best thing the United States could do for

continental defense would be to assist the Allies as much as possible. This
idea was based on the traditional British control of the seas and the concept
of the Atlantic as a barrier to the new world. Cantilo also brought up another
point which was undermining the position of those Argentines who wished to
side with the United States. Statements coming from Washington seemed to
indicate that it would probably be two years before the United States would
be in a position to assist South America materially.[119] This caused Argentina
to think in terms of its own defenses. Armour was also of the opinion that
the coolness stemmed from the internal political situation because such talks
might give pro-Nazi army officers a reason to try to overthrow the government.

On June 8, 1940, Captain William O. Spears of the U.S. Navy arrived in
Buenos Aires for talks with Argentine Navy and Foreign Ministry officials.
Spears stated that he wished to ascertain Argentina's position on several
basic points:

(1) whether the Argentine Government would be disposed to join in the
   common defense of the Western Hemisphere,
(2) whether her military and naval forces were sufficient to protect her
   own territory from attack,
(3) what assistance from the armed forces of the United States might be
   needed,
(4) what assistance Argentina would be able and willing to give other countries, and
(5) whether the American forces used in this area would be granted necessary facilities in the way of permission to fly aircraft over Argentine
   territory, make use of landing fields, have access to ports for use as
   bases of operations, etc.[120]

On the basis of the answers, Spears said, it would be comparatively easy to
work out a joint defense plan. The Argentine answer at a meeting two days
later was that they had nothing to fear from any other country at that time
and could not imagine any danger of invasion at any time in the future, thereby making the question of planning too remote for consideration.[121] When
asked if the Argentine Navy would cooperate in the defense of Uruguay or
Brazil in the case of an attack by a foreign power, the answer was that each
country should take care of its own defense. Spears attempted unsuccessfully
to point out that these questions of cooperative defense had already been
agreed upon in previous consultations and that the purpose of the conversations was to arrange this cooperation.

As a result of this deadlock, and at the suggestion of Foreign Minister Cantilo, Ambassador Armour submitted to the Argentine government a question-
naire containing a refined version of the questions raised by Spears.[122] On
June 29, 1940, a five-page memorandum was received in reply.[123] Probably

more than any other single statement or action of Argentina, this document marks the beginning of the shift in policy toward one of isolation both from the war and from inter-American cooperation. The memo basically stated that Argentina was pursuing a course of strict neutrality and did not see any danger in the near future to the American republics, although it would welcome information about such a possible menace. It also said that the government could not make foreign policy commitments without consulting Congress, and that it could not submit questions to Congress resulting from situations that had not arisen and might not arise. This was certainly an attempt to evade the issue because the President's obligation to the Congress was not so interpreted when the President wanted action or wanted to refrain from action. The note suggested that hemispheric cooperation should take the form of lowered trade barriers and declared that if a dangerous situation should arise, Argentina would participate in consultation procedures as called for in the Declaration of Lima. This answer was particularly upsetting to some military officials in Washington who felt that Germany might strike at eastern South America within 60 days after the fall of France.[124] Later in the year some informal and evasive staff conversations were held between United States and Argentine military officials in Buenos Aires, but they were equally frustrating from the U.S. point of view.[125]

With President Castillo assuming leadership from the faltering Ortiz, there appeared to be a slight slackening of overt Nazi activities in Argentina during late 1940 and into early 1941.[126] The Argentine government was doing its best not to provoke the Nazi elements and, on the other hand, the expected quick defeat of England had not materialized, thereby restraining some of the most confident German sympathizers. There were a few governmental efforts to stop some of the excesses of the Nazi-subsidized press during the period, particularly against El Pampero, the pro-Nazi newspaper with the largest circulation. Executive-sponsored legislation which would have curbed press commentary on Argentine foreign policy was defeated in the Congress due to a fear that it would be used against pro-Allied newspapers. This was part of a serious executive-legislative deadlock that was developing.[127] The beginning of an investigation of Nazi influence in the Buenos Aires police force was frustrated by the Federal government.[128] In a conference with President Castillo early in March of 1941, the German Ambassador was assured that the treatment of Germans in Argentina had improved. The President claimed to have intervened personally, as a result of the Ambassador's protest, to obtain the release of some Germans arrested in Misiones.[129] Generally, the German diplomat was cautiously optimistic about Castillo's feelings toward the Third Reich.[130]

The United States Embassy was continually concerned over the impact that German military victories were having on Argentine public opinion.[131]

German propaganda was emphasizing the glories of the Third Reich European market which would be open to its friends after the war—a most appealing thought to Argentine merchants. The United States Embassy, however, was doing very little to counter the German propaganda.[132] Partly, this was due to a fear that such a policy might "backfire," but it was also due to the embarrassing position which Washington had managed to work itself into vis-á-vis the situation in Europe. The United States was still neutral. Thus it was difficult to take a very strong position or to counter the expenditures of the German Embassy which were running 20 times as much as U.S. expenditures.[133] Britain was waging a propaganda campaign in Buenos Aires but it was aimed more at promoting British interests than at combating charges against its old economic rival in Argentina, "Yankee imperialism."[134]

The United States certainly was not without its friends in Argentina. There was criticism from some prominent Argentines regarding the foreign policy being followed by the Castillo government. Former President Marcelo Alvear (1922–1928), the titular head of the Radical Party, urged in early 1941, along with the leader of the Socialist Party, that Argentina begin to move to strengthen its ties with the hemispheric nations.[135] Part of this advocacy was undoubtedly motivated by the serious division which had developed within the Argentine political arena. After the Radicals had had their hopes raised of returning to power through free elections held under the Ortiz administration, they were dashed by Castillo's assumption of power. It was no secret that he was not about to allow this road to be opened for the Radicals or Socialists. Ambassador Armour described the new President's seemingly pro-Axis neutrality as follows:

> My own feeling is that Dr. Castillo's policy is largely dictated by internal politics. His intense hatred for the Radicals and all they stand for has clouded his vision to the extent that he sees in all their actions only attempts to attack him and his Government. He must, he feels, keep his party in power at any cost. To do this, support of the Army is necessary, and a break with the Axis would, perhaps, lose him the support particularly of the younger officers of the Army and Navy, among whose number, particularly in the former branch, are many Axis sympathizers. . . .
>
> At heart he is still the small judge from Catamarca. It is hard for him to see beyond the confines of his own province, not to speak of the country. He is a party man; the "Party" looks to him and he must not fail them by any false step which might make it possible for the opposition to gain control.[136]

Perhaps if Castillo had assumed a pro-Allied stance during 1941, the opposition parties would have taken a pro-Axis or at least a strongly neutralist position. It does appear that the Radicals and the Socialists were also responding to what they felt were the clearly aggressive policies of an oppressive German regime. Nicolás Repetto of the Socialists and Alvear both publicly spoke in terms of eventual aggression by the Third Reich against the American continent and stated that Argentina's only hope was hemispheric cooperation.[137] However, since Irigoyen had been strongly neutralist during World War I, the Radical Party did have a tradition on which it could have fallen back to justify a pro-neutrality position had Castillo begun to move toward a pro-Allied position. The point is that the political situation, as will become clearer in chapter five, cannot be separated from the foreign policy debate.

On March 13, 1941, Acting President Castillo appointed Argentina's Ambassador to the Vatican, Dr. Enrique Ruiz-Guiñazú as his Foreign Minister to replace the neutralist but essentially pro-Allied Cantilo who had enjoyed the confidence of Ortiz. He was not sworn in until mid-June following official visits to the United States, Brazil, Colombia, and Uruguay. A devout Roman Catholic, he was a diplomat of the old professional school and had been President of the Council of the League of Nations during the Ethiopian debate.[138] By reputation he was anti-totalitarian in his sympathies. He was a brother-in-law of an important Radical Party official.[139] During his visit to Washington he expressed dismay over the actions of the Axis powers against the Church in Europe.

1941: DIPLOMACY AND DOMESTIC POLITICS

During 1941 (prior to Pearl Harbor) the major contacts Washington had with Argentina revolved around three questions: the Axis-controlled airlines, discussions of a lend-lease agreement, and a possible trade agreement. A prime consideration of the Department of State was the elimination of the Axis influence in the airline companies operating in Latin America. It is impossible to consider the question in depth without becoming technical and looking at the larger effort of the United States throughout Latin America.[140] Since the United States was not at war in 1941, Washington could only pressure the airlines and was not in a position to demand confiscation or acts that were illegal under civil law. The airline question caused numerous problems because Washington's policymakers eventually became deeply involved in managing private companies. There were also questions regarding how much governmental assistance was proper to aid privately owned U.S. airlines which were in the process of being patriotic while also establishing claims to potentially valuable concessions in the form of air routes from which German and Italian interests had been displaced.

The lend-lease and military staff conversations during 1941 ran into a series of problems which illuminate the differences existing at that time between Washington and Buenos Aires. The 1940 talks in Buenos Aires had been unsuccessful because Argentina refused to acknowledge any possible threat to it from events in Europe. However, by mid-1941 Argentina was becoming interested in the weapons the United States was planning to distribute under the lend-lease program.[141] At least part of this interest stemmed from the fact that Brazil, Argentina's traditional rival for South American leadership, seemed to be in line for a large share of the program. Ambassador Armour in Buenos Aires was quick to express his opinion:

> before any material is definitely set aside for this government, we are entitled to have from the competent officials here a clear-cut statement of how those materials are to be used and what plans they have formulated under the general framework of our continental defense. Furthermore, that for this purpose officers from here should proceed to the United States to discuss these matters in order that it should be entirely clear that it is Argentina that is doing the asking, and not ourselves.[142]

The Department of State was evidently not quick to realize the problem that would stem from the situation. It telegraphed Ambassador Armour in late July that he should approach the Argentine government regarding possible negotiations for the exchange of armaments under the Lend-Lease Act. The communication stated:

> You may state that [it is] the understanding of this government that the Argentine government is disposed to renew staff conversations and that it would be happy if Argentine authorities would concur in the desirability of appointing a Military-Naval Commission clothed with sufficient authority to reach agreements subject to the subsequent approval of each government.[143]

The proposal was also given to the Argentine Ambassador in Washington, Felipe A. Espil. However, he was emphatic in stating that the memo was undesirable due to its implication that the obtaining of the equipment was contingent upon a satisfactory outcome of the staff talks.[144] The Department of State attempted to "unequivocally" assure Espil

> that the discussions . . . under the Lend-Lease Act and the staff conversations were not linked together, but parallel negotiations that might best take place simultaneously. The suggestion that the same officers who were coming to Washington to carry on the detailed discussions for the acquisition of materiel under the Lend-Lease Act also engage in staff conversations arose from the view that this was a practical procedure that would advance both questions rapidly.[145]

Although Espil preferred not to send the suggestion to Buenos Aires, Armour was advised that Argentina was willing to renew staff conversations. The

Department of State did approve the idea that if Argentina wished to renew the staff conversations in Buenos Aires rather than in Washington, this could be done.[146] Actually, Colonel Matthew Ridgway, who was involved in the talks, was of the opinion that it would be better to hold them in Buenos Aires so that United States negotiators could plead ignorance in turning away Argentine queries regarding U.S. plans for national defense.[147]

In his presentations to the Argentine Foreign Minister Armour tried to convince Argentina that the obtaining of the material was not contingent on the outcome of the staff conversations and that it was only a matter of practical advantages which had caused the two questions to be raised simultaneously.[148] The problem was considered at the highest levels of the Argentine government. Over the opposition of Foreign Minister Ruiz-Guiñazú, who feared that any agreements reached would limit Argentine flexibility,[149] it was finally decided to accept the idea of military talks with the understanding that Washington did not intend to link the subject of military cooperation with the supplying of military aid. However, the Argentine government was astute enough to recognize that its requirements for military materials were partially dependent on the decisions reached at the staff conversations.[150] The entire affair was actually an effort to give Argentine nationalism a soothing by maintaining the fiction that there was not a link between her cooperation and the providing of lend-lease materials in the sense that the materials were payment for services rendered. Obviously, the entire point of lend-lease was to help defend the hemisphere, and while the United States was not demanding detailed advance planning regarding possible foreign attacks, it was not going to provide aid to countries that were not going to use it to prepare for possible resistance of the Axis.

The United States was thinking in terms of providing about $66 million in lend-lease supplies to Argentina with a $36-million repayment.[151] The Argentine delegation left Buenos Aires on November 27, 1941, but the actual talks did not start until after the attack on Pearl Harbor. Prior to the opening of the conversations, Espil continued to argue against any possible reciprocal aspects of the lend-lease agreement. Perhaps as a result of this, the tentative agreement on which the negotiations were based contained fewer clauses calling for cooperation than the average Latin American agreements at the time.[152] Argentina, in a burst of nationalistic sentiment, also argued against any financial assistance in the form of reduced payments and said that it could pay for its military equipment and would pay cash for the weapons obtained.[153] Espil also complained that, under the tables of delivery, during the first year the Argentine Army was to receive $15 million in supplies and the Navy only $1 million, despite the fact that the over-all bulk of the aid was to go to the Navy. The Argentine Ambassador tactfully suggested that in view of the competition between the two services, this be equalized.[154] The attack on Pearl Harbor complicated the situation and, since the Argentine delegation was to have to get approval of the purchase from the Argentine Congress, the U.S. War Department recommended that any definite commitments on first year deliveries be kept provisional.[155] In fact, the attack marked such a fundamental change in the relationship between Argentina and the United States that the completion of the talks needs to be discussed in a later chapter covering the period after December 7, 1971.

The United States did have some success in negotiating a trade agreement with Argentina during 1941. Prebisch remained in Washington after the talks setting up the $100-million loan to help prepare the complicated negotiations. Washington also delayed announcing the pending talks out of fear that the idea would arouse political opposition in the Congress which could defeat Roosevelt's plans for aiding England.[156] Argentina was anxious to negotiate an agreement that would help to compensate for the loss of traditional European markets due to the war. It was argued within Washington circles that a reciprocal trade agreement with Buenos Aires would not harm United States domestic production because Argentine exports, even with lowered U.S. tariffs, would still be hampered by the increased shipping costs and other difficulties connected with the war.[157] Based on this logic, the agreement was signed in October of 1941. It was weighted in favor of Argentina in hopes of winning some support from that government for Roosevelt's policies.[158] The agreement was warmly received by Argentine newspapers that were not pro-fascist[159] but, as one study has put it, "the efforts . . . to amend the economic grievances of Argentina were too little and too late to change the course of the latter's diplomacy."[160] In response to Argentine foreign policy the Department of State slowed the ratification procedure until December of 1942, but by that time events of greater significance far overshadowed the reciprocal trade agreement.

The final aspect of the pre–Pearl Harbor period which deserves consideration is the widening split between President Castillo's administration and the Congress. The relatively free elections which President Ortiz had allowed had tilted the legislature in favor of the Radicals. In no sense was the aristocratic Castillo temperamentally prepared to work with such a body. His long reputation as a reactionary, even by his own party's standards, seemed to be reinforced by the events and conditions which confronted his administration. A retrospective dissection of the nature of the executive-legislative competition during this period is difficult, for its nature undoubtedly varied from issue to issue and from congressman to congressman. However, a few things are clear. First, part of the effort each side made to discredit the other was stimulated by the Argentine Constitution which, like the United States Constitution, provides for a continual struggle between the two branches of government through the separation of powers doctrine. Second, there was party rivalry which irritated the situation. The Radicals were fighting for their political lives against a Conservative President who did not hesitate to rig elections against them. This led the Radicals to oppose the President at every turn and by every method. Finally, the question of cooperation with the other American republics was in itself a divisive issue. There had long been a debate in Argentina on the question. President Castillo's adherence to strict neutrality during the period and his unwillingness to antagonize the Nazi elements forged an anti-totalitarian and pro-Pan-American consensus within the Radical and Socialist political groups. Otherwise, these groups might have been willing to sit back and profit from the war's effect on the Argentine economy. There is empirical evidence to support the generalization that foreign policy was becoming politicized. Peter Smith's excellent analysis of voting in the Argentine legislature, *Argentina and the Failure of Democracy: Conflict Among the Political Elites, 1904-1955*, shows that the 1942 session was the only one during the time span he covers in which foreign policy per se was an issue. And what is most interesting about his figures is that it was the major issue in that session and produced the most party cohesion of any issue between 1924 and 1955.[161] This means that it was an issue on which the interests of the various parties were most clearly at variance. Congressmen tended to see the future of their parties linked to the foreign policy issue either in terms of preservation or as a method of discrediting the other party. In the last half of 1941 we see the Radicals and the Socialists on the attack which culminated in the rigid dichotomies that dominated the 1942 legislative session.

In June of 1941 the Radicals began to press for something that had been suggested on numerous occasions: a congressional committee investigation of subversive activities in Argentina. On June 18 such a committee was constituted with broad powers to investigate the situation and with the right to raid private homes.[162] Deputy Raúl Damonte Taborda, who had taken the lead in proposing the group, was made chairman. Designated the Anti-Argentine Activities Committee (the Damonte Committee), it was charged with investigating the activities of individuals and organizations whose ideologies and methods were contrary to Argentine institutions and directed against Argentina's sovereignty. The Committee was also given the mandate to ask for the assistance of national and provincial governments in its investigations.

Obviously, this maneuver was welcomed by the pro-democratic press in editorials that had distinct anti-Administration overtones. After a slow start, the Committee, with some police cooperation, began to stage a series of raids on Nazi groups and even made some arrests, although the individuals were seldom held. Testimony was taken and large quantities of Nazi propaganda and records were seized. The Minister of the Interior, following some raids in July of 1941, began to be more antagonistic toward the Committee's activities. On the grounds that the actions of the Committee were violating constitutionally guaranteed individual liberties, he said that the police would not be allowed to participate in future raids except under court order.[163]

The raids continued, however, and produced mountains of information for the Committee's evaluation. Late in July the Committee went so far as to seize some diplomatic baggage which was coming from the German Embassy in Lima to the Embassy in Buenos Aires. The Federal Court upheld the action.[164] By late summer the approval of the Committee's activities being expressed by the major newspapers and leading Argentine political figures was forcing the executive branch of the government to take some action. For example, early in August of 1941 the German and British embassies were asked to halt propagandizing efforts within Argentina on the grounds that it was injurious to the public order. On August 11 the British and German ambassadors delivered written promises to stop the actions.

On August 29, the Committee finally released its first public report.[165] The seventy-five-page statement charged that the German residents of Argentina were organized into military-disciplined groups under the direct orders of Berlin. Funds were raised from the groups, cells formed, and oaths of allegiance demanded. An espionage system among the German community was also outlined. Evidence was offered indicating that money collected for charitable purposes was simply handed over to the German Embassy for propaganda activities. The major newspapers and many members of Congress rallied behind the report, which seemed to justify the suspicions many of them had long held. There began to be serious public talk that Ambassador von Thermann should be declared persona non grata by the government.

A week later the Committee released its second report.[166] The document revealed that the German Embassy had spent about 6 million pesos during the previous fiscal year—about seven times the expected expenditure. This report (of 95 pages) recommended that Axis-controlled investments in Argentina be frozen so as to not be put at the disposal of Germany. It went into more detail on the question of forcing Germans to contribute to the German "charity" drives. It linked the newspaper *El Pampero,* long the most circulated, most outspokenly pro-Nazi paper, to the German Embassy. And it criticized the German Embassy for abusing diplomatic privileges by using Argentine mail facilities for large amounts of propaganda. Again the newspapers urged strong action against the Embassy, with *La Prensa* writing that "it is time to put an end to vacillation" and expressing astonishment that these actions had been tolerated by the government.[167] The day after the report was made public, the Chairman of the Committee accused the German Ambassador of being the director of more than half a million Germans organized as storm troopers throughout Latin America. On September 9 von Thermann protested the report's statement that his Embassy was financing anti-Argentine activities.[168]

On September 17 the third report was issued.[169] It stated that the German government was using the Transocean news agency as an instrument of policy. It claimed that Transocean had spent over a million pesos since 1937 while collecting less than fifty thousand pesos in receipts, with Berlin making up the difference. It also mentioned that the news agency Stefani was controlled by the Italian Embassy. *El Pampero*'s records were opened to show that in its first six months it had spent over a million pesos with receipts of only slightly over six hundred thousand pesos. Understandably, the reaction of the pro-German press was becoming increasingly critical of the investigation and of the slights against von Thermann. The position of the Argentine Minister of Foreign Affairs was that the government was not responsible for statements made by the Chamber of Deputies and that the Chamber's statements did not represent official government policy.

The fourth report of the Damonte Committee ran almost 200 pages and was issued on September 30, the day the body recessed.[170] It dealt with the German schools in Argentina in which Nazi political and radical theories were being taught, supposedly on orders from Berlin. The report included examples of the Nazi teaching materials being used in some schools. It also included draft legislation providing for stricter controls over any foreign language schools in Argentina, including the replacement of teaching and administrative staffs with Argentine citizens. The fifth report was made public late in November.[171] It was concerned with labor organizing done by German elements in Argentina and throughout Latin America. Supposedly, the Nazi-dominated unions had been dissolved previously, but the Committee offered evidence that this had largely been a subterfuge.

The situation growing out of these reports caused concern in Berlin. In late August the Argentine Ambassador to the Third Reich was summoned to talk with Foreign Ministry officials and admonished for the actions of the Damonte Committee.[172] According to the German memo on the conversation, "the Ambassador disavowed this commission in no uncertain terms" but admitted that the Argentine government could not ignore the effects of the group. The memo also discussed the seizure of diplomatic packages, and actions against the German schools in Buenos Aires, and the interrogation of Consul General Barandon from Chile. It closed with the State Secretary asking von Thermann to make a personal appeal to the Argentine Foreign Minister, "a close acquaintance and friend of mine, who undoubtedly would understand perfectly well that these goings on had to be stopped."[173]

However, by September the Radical criticism of von Thermann had caused him to doubt whether "as a result of internal political weakness and

external political pressure" the government could resist the pressure to declare him persona non grata and suggested that if this appeared likely he
should be recalled immediately.[174] A conversation a few days later between
the Ambassador and Foreign Minister Ruiz-Guiñazú found the Argentine
apologetic about events, according to von Thermann, but saying that there
was nothing he could do to stem the criticism. The Foreign Minister did,
however, ask "in all friendliness" and confidentially if perhaps the German
government might not consider shifting him to another post since his term
in Buenos Aires had already been eight years.[175] Ruiz-Guiñazú promised
that the Ambassador's departure would be attended by every honor. This
same message was relayed by the Argentine Ambassador in Berlin.[176] In
mid-September the Argentine Chamber of Deputies, with only one dissenting
vote, declared that Ambassador von Thermann had exceeded his function
and called upon the President to declare him persona non grata.[177] This unleashed further press criticism in both Buenos Aires—largely against von
Thermann in the major newspapers—and in Berlin—against Argentina. In the
end, the Argentine government resisted taking the recommended action
against the Ambassador.

Retired President Ortiz, whose health was failing rapidly, was becoming
more critical of Castillo's unwillingness to cooperate with the Allies and
blamed it on the men around the President.[178] He even went so far as to
urge Armour to put more pressure on Castillo. The Embassy was convinced
that Ortiz was preferable to Castillo. The Embassy was convinced that
Ortiz was preferable to Castillo and had shown it by bringing in a special-
ist to examine Ortiz in hopes of correcting the blindness which made it impossible for him to sign the numerous documents necessary to operate the
government. The verdict of the doctor was that there was no hope. By late
October the Radical Party's central organization was demanding that President Castillo be impeached. Although the situation was aggravated by the
question of von Thermann, the specific complaint was his meddling in the
politics of the city of Buenos Aires to keep the Radicals out of power.

Acción Argentina, the large pro-Allied organization, was scheduling rallies
for November 29, 1941, which would be aimed at consolidating criticism
of the government's isolationist policy and the government's toleration of
the activities publicized by the Damonte Committee.[179] The Acting President, through the Minister of the Interior, asked the state governors not to
allow these rallies. In most provinces they were repressed; although in Entre
Ríos the Governor allowed them to go forward, thereby precipitating a
crisis in that area.[180]

At the same time Berlin was resisting the polite requests of the Argentine
government that it might be simpler to transfer von Thermann to another
embassy. Ambassador von Thermann received instructions on December 1

that he should protest the attacks on the Embassy and its staff; but he was told to state that Germany might take the option previously suggested by Argentina that he (von Thermann) might be replaced at the same time that there was a change in Argentina's ambassadorial post in Berlin.[181] The suggestion was received with some relief by Foreign Minister Ruiz-Guiñazú,[182] who pointed out that getting a new Ambassador for Berlin might be difficult in view of the fact that the Senate was adjourned until May, but that simply withdrawing the Ambassador was not a problem.

The most striking point in this analysis is the degree to which the Argentine political situation obscured the issues and forces influencing the formulation of foreign policy in Buenos Aires. The portrayal of the Radicals as true friends of the United States or as followers of Pan-Americanism is misleading. Foreign policy had become a political issue. One sees this most clearly in the criticism of Cantilo and the non-belligerency proposal by the Radicals and Socialists.[183] And the Radicals opposed the planned credit from Washington to Argentina in September of 1941. At that time the Radicals, with the assistance of five Antipersonalistas, managed to defeat the agreement by four votes after making their support of the loan conditional on government guarantees of unhampered voting in an upcoming election in Buenos Aires province.

Even the Damonte reports, which certainly turned up a great deal of useful information, were so blatantly political that they could be ignored by many. The fact that the German winter relief funds stayed in Argentina essentially proved nothing, since presumably they could have been freeing money for winter relief that otherwise would have had to be sent from Berlin to run the Embassy in Buenos Aires. The documents regarding the highly structured German community in Buenos Aires and elsewhere were misleading.[184] Plans may have been made, but there is little evidence to suggest that such proposals as forming a paramilitary operation within the German community were ever more than an idea on paper.

Moreover, attempting to preside over all this was the figure of President Castillo. The dilemma he faced at the end of 1941 is well put by historian Robert Potash:

> Dr. Castillo . . . was walking a political tightrope between those officers who favored a German victory abroad and saw no threat in Axis activities within Argentina and those officers like the War Minister who saw a danger in both. Lacking a strong political base of his own, unwilling to be merely a bridge for General Justo's [former President] ambitions, and as yet having no firm understanding with nationalist sectors the Acting President could only pursue a tortuous course.[185]

3: COMPROMISE AT RIO

After the relatively successful inter-American meetings in 1938, 1939, and 1940, internal State Department discussions began early in 1941 on the desirability of another consultation. Prompting the proposed talks was the fact that, after the declarations of neutrality and non-involvement at Lima, Panama, and Havana, and in the face of a worsening European situation, the United States was preparing to change its policy. The declarations of neutrality had amounted to verbal photographs of United States policy at each particular point. Now Washington was becoming openly pro-British through such measures as lend-lease, and despite the flexibility of international law, it did appear that United States policy was daily diverging more and more from the policies it had pressed for in the inter-American meetings. Philip Bonsal of the Department of State sent a memo to Sumner Welles in mid-February of 1941 responding to criticisms of this divergence from Pan-American commitments or obligations. He advocated calling a meeting of consultation, but not simply in the interests of legal niceties, he emphasized. He saw the meeting as a practical measure of continental defense in order to bring the positions of the other American republics into line with the United States. "The object should be agreement on the principle of aid to the democracies," Bonsal suggested.[1] He also mentioned measures to take over ships immobilized in American harbors, financial controls, and others. The first step would be to find out how far Argentina, Brazil and Mexico would be willing to go in support of United States policies.

Approximately a month later Bonsal sent Welles a similar memo[2] and Undersecretary Welles expressed some interest. The Undersecretary replied that he felt it was undesirable for the United States to take the initiative again in suggesting a meeting of consultation, but said he wanted to discuss the matter with President Roosevelt.[3] Perhaps as a result of his talk with the President, Welles began to speak in terms of an early May meeting in Rio de Janeiro—but with some other country taking the initiative in requesting the consultation.[4] The countries put forth as possibly interested in calling the meeting (with some encouragement from the United States) were Chile and Mexico. The Department of State memo on the subject confidently stated

78

that although the Latin American countries continued to be theoretically neutral, "the governments and the immense majority of the peoples of the other American republics are in agreement with us regarding the attitude which we have taken toward the war."[5] Noncompliance with the Panama safety zone was mentioned as a subject for discussion as was the question of economic dislocation caused by the war.

A memo of April 9 included a possible agenda for the meeting. It was designed to produce a strong statement against aggression and to emphasize the idea that the countries of the western hemisphere would provide assistance to those states resisting aggression. This was, of course, the position of the United States at that time. There was no mention of breaking diplomatic relations.[6] Late in May, in a conversation between Welles and the Mexican Ambassador to Washington, a meeting was discussed, at which time Welles expressed the opinion that, because of the rapidly changing situation in Europe, it might be well to postpone any final decision. The Mexican Ambassador, according to Welles's account of the conversation, agreed with the idea of delaying any move.[7] The death blow to such a meeting came in June when the United States Ambassador to Brazil, Jefferson Caffery, wired the Department of State that the rumors that Brazil's Foreign Minister, Oswaldo Aranha, and the new Foreign Minister of Argentina (Enrique Ruiz-Guiñazú) favored an inter-American meeting had been specifically denied by Aranha who said both he and his Argentine counterpart felt the time to be inopportune.[8]

The Japanese attack on Pearl Harbor and the furious response of the United States clarified the issues. Chilean Foreign Minister Juan B. Rossetti's quick reaction in asking for a foreign ministers meeting was welcomed by the United States. Brazil had been irritated that the 1940 Havana meeting had not been held in Rio de Janeiro and was cool to the idea of being the next nation for the new foreign ministers conference, although a resolution adopted in Havana called for the next conference to be held in Rio. Rossetti wanted the meeting for Viña del Mar, the luxurious Chilean ocean resort, and when Aranha did not express open opposition to the idea he interpreted this as approval and began to press for having the meeting in Chile.[9] In the end, it was made clear that Rio de Janeiro was next in line and Chile stepped aside. Evidently, Brazil's reluctance was primarily residue of its unhappiness over the 1940 decision to go to Havana and was not due to opposition to to the meeting itself.

Meanwhile, the Department of State began preparing Washington's position for the conference. Many of the subjects discussed were in the areas of either restricting Nazi activities in the American republics through such efforts as financial controls, control of communications, and export controls, or of preparing hemispheric economic systems to withstand the inevitable strains of the war effort. Ideas included such measures as mobilization of shipping, possible arrangements for increased production of basic and strategic materials, pooling of strategic materials such as copper or oil, and plans for assistance for expanded industrialization and better agricultural production.[10] The idea of an Inter-American Defense Board to help coordinate hemispheric defense was also born within the Department of State. Although the United States military departments tended to oppose the Board on the grounds that it would be too slow and unwieldly and could constitute a possible security leak for defense information,[11] the Department of State insisted on the Board, and the concept was adopted at the meeting.

The Dominican Republic, with its dictator Rafael Trujillo anxious to curry favor with Washington by assuming an anti-fascist position, suggested a possible joint declaration of war against the Axis for consideration even though preliminary inquiries by the U.S. Department of State of other American republics revealed their opposition to this proposal.[12] The major United States effort went into a draft resolution, circulated to some other foreign ministers, which provided that all the American republics would break relations with the Axis.[13] It spoke of "the treacherous attack committed by Japan," the Axis plans for world conquest, and finally declared:

Consequently, [the American republics] announce that by reason of their solidarity and for the purpose of protecting and preserving the freedom and integrity of the twenty-one Republics of the Americas, relations, whether political, commercial, or financial, can no longer be maintained by any of them with Germany, Italy, and Japan, and they likewise declare that, with full respect for their respective sovereignty, they will individually or collectively take such further steps for the defense of the New World as may in each instance seem to them desirable and practicable.

Even prior to the beginning of the meeting it was becoming obvious that Argentina was going to be a major stumbling block to unity behind any strong measure. Less than three weeks after Pearl Harbor Ambassador Norman Armour was reporting pessimistically from Buenos Aires regarding Argentina's international position.[14] It was primarily the Argentine government's attempt to halt pro-Allied propaganda that bothered the United States Embassy. The state of siege measures, according to Ambassador Armour, were operating "to prevent public expressions of support for the United States on the part of the large majority of the press and public which favor the democratic cause." In the same despatch Armour mentioned the suspension of an homage to Roosevelt at which Armour had been scheduled to read a message from the President, and he speculated on the influence of "various pro-totalitarian sympathies . . . including various National elements" in getting Castillo to stop the mass meeting. Armour closed his day-before-Christmas memo with the comment that

> I believe that the government will continue to follow a day-to-day policy of procrastination and evasion, and will be influenced in its final decision with regard to the commitments to be undertaken at Rio largely by the course of the war and the position taken by the other American Governments.

Two weeks later, immediately before the Rio meeting, Armour submitted a long memo regarding his expectations of the general attitude and position the Argentine delegation would assume at Rio. Armour felt it was "virtually certain" that Buenos Aires would not agree to declare war on the Axis and predicted that the same would probably apply to the breaking off of diplomatic relations with the Axis powers although "this is not so certain." The fact that there was a significant Italian and German element in Argentina was mentioned as a factor making a declaration of war against Japan more likely. According to the Ambassador, there was a fear that if Argentina did declare war, the Axis might well make " an example" of Argentina by sabotage or attack. Armour did feel that Argentina would be willing to cooperate in patrol activities and some other measures short of convoying. He emphasized the deep political implication of any strong anti-Axis moves in view of the fact that the out-of-power Radicals had been advocating this position and had made the question a political issue.[15]

The Argentine motives seemed particularly suspicious from Washington's point of view when Argentina made great efforts to have Latin American diplomats traveling to Rio stop in Buenos Aires for talks. Several delegates, including those from Paraguay, Uruguay, Chile, and Peru did stop in the Argentine capital.[16] The Bolivian Foreign Minister declined the invitation, but, when his Panagra air schedule was inconvenient, he informed United States Minister to Bolivia Douglas Jenkins that the decision was being reconsidered. The Minister suggested to Washington that perhaps a special flight could be arranged although he did not feel that the Bolivian group would "be unduly influenced" by Argentina.[17] The Department of State, while assuring itself that it did not wish to influence the travel plans of the Bolivian Minister of Foreign Affairs, did arrange for a special flight.[18]

A week before the official opening on January 15, Argentina communicated a protest to the United States over the fact that a pact of alliance had been signed in Washington by twenty-six countries (nine of them American) declaring war on the Axis.[19] Argentina pointed out that this action had been taken "without previous consultation" and that the action "exceeds any regional concept and approaches an almost universal position." This, according to the memo given to Welles by Argentine Ambassador Espil, raised "doubts as to the utility of any consultation in Rio."

> There is a certain contradiction in inviting us to participate in the study and adoption of measures of common defense at the same time that nine countries proceed without prior exchange of views in defining in absolute form their double position, intracontinental and extracontinental, with the consequent risks and responsibilities of a state of war.

Argentina stated that "any nation jealous of its sovereignty" would find the procedure "objectionable inasmuch as consultation is undertaken subsequent to the resolution adopted." Argentina's position was logical if one assumes the inter-American system to be of the utmost importance, as the United States had stated at times during its period of neutrality. Of course, the point was that the United States (and those Latin American nations it could convince) had diverted its attention to Europe and the Pacific and had managed to drag eight Latin American countries into the same legal position.

Meanwhile, Rossetti, who had taken the lead in calling for the meeting, was continuing in his pro-Allied position, much to the delight of Ambassador to Chile Claude Bowers. The Chilean Foreign Minister asked in advance if he could consult with Welles prior to the opening of the Rio meeting.[20] Bowers felt that Rossetti was "most eager to please us in every way at Rio."[21] Rossetti also admitted that he might not continue as Foreign Minister with the incoming President; therefore, he said, he was anxious to have a firmly committed pro-Allied policy when he left office. He also expressed displeasure with Argentina over its unwillingness to fortify the Strait of Magellan (in southernmost South America), which is shared by Argentina and Chile, as had been agreed upon. Argentina's argument, according to Rossetti, was that the fortifications would be vulnerable even when completed and therefore would encourage an attack.[22] Rossetti informed Bowers that after the Magellan decision he had been angry enough to refuse to visit Buenos Aires on the way to Rio de Janeiro, except that he did not want to make a public scandal by changing his itinerary. During his stop at Buenos Aires, Rossetti, in answer to a speech by Ruiz-Guiñazú stressing legality and similarities in tradition, culture, and language between Argentina and Chile (the implication being that the United States was excluded from this company), stated that Chile did not recognize any distinction among the American republics,[23] and he privately told Ambassador Armour that he hoped that the Dominican Republic would not press for its declaration of war resolution since Chile was in no position to defend herself.[24]

With Sumner Welles, a man of long experience in Pan-American affairs, leading the Washington delegation, the United States began to lobby immediately for the resolution calling for a break in diplomatic relations. According to a telegram sent January 7, 1942, from Welles in Washington to Armour, the Department of State felt that all the countries except Chile and Argentina had agreed to break relations.[25] Ambassador Armour had discussed the point directly with the Argentine Foreign Ministry and had been told that Buenos Aires would not sever relations. During the conversation the Argentine official confirmed that both the Army and the Navy were opposed to the idea, although Argentina would help in the prevention of Axis propaganda and subversive activities, besides furnishing strategic materials and port facilities.[26] The Foreign Minister had given an interview to *La Nacion* in which he answered a question concerning a possible break in relations with the comment that, while American solidarity was of value, it did not mean that Argentina would automatically follow any policy that might be suggested and that Pan-Americanism should not be mistaken for a military alliance.[27]

By the second day of the conference, Welles was telegraphing Secretary of State Hull that he agreed with Hull's feeling that "every effort should be made to preserve unanimity" and that, if Argentina was unwilling to sever relations, it "should be allowed to proceed alone."[28] Welles stated that in his initial talks with Ruiz-Guiñazú, he found the Argentine delegate "wavering and vacillating, and obviously very much under the impression of the strong line taken by the other delegations and by the general state of public opinion in Brazil."[29] He left Welles with the impression that he would cable the Acting President for possible new instructions which would allow some modification of the stand against breaking relations. As for Chile, Welles felt that if Argentina agreed, Chile would be forced "without question to adhere to any joint declaration."[30] However, Welles was unhappy with Rossetti's position during the early days of the meeting because he seemed to be bargaining for more military assistance and financial assistance in return for support for the resolution demanding a break in relations.[31] Later in the meeting Welles decided that Rossetti's attitude at the opening of the meeting was based on commitments he had made to the Cabinet and to congressional committees, on the "real fear" that breaking relations would prompt an attack on a defenseless Chile, as well as on the belief that an attitude of "aloofness" would result in offers to Chile of significant economic and financial cooperation.[32]

Although the Peruvian Foreign Minister was also reluctant, the other American republics (particularly the Central American and Caribbean delegations) backed the United States strongly. The Cuban Ambassador had assured the Department of State in advance that the Cuban delegation could be considered, according to the words of one State Department official, "as really an extension of the United States delegation" and it "would be very glad to introduce any resolutions which the United States delegation felt might better come from some other country."[33] This statement points out the degree to which the abrogation of the Platt Amendment was a legal rather than a substantive action. Cuba remained, in terms of politics and economics, a "client" of the United States.

In many ways the role of Brazil in this gathering deserves special analysis. Brazil was following its traditional pro–United States policy publicly. However, President Getulio Vargas actually kept lines of communication open with Germany late into 1941 through discussions with the German Ambassador, conversations of which the Brazilian Foreign Minister was not informed.[34] According to what Foreign Minister Aranha and President Vargas told Welles, they felt that if Ruiz-Guiñazú were given the credit for solving the troublesome Peruvian-Ecuadorian boundary dispute during the meeting, it might serve to mellow his (Ruiz-Guiñazú's) position.[35] This tactic had been successful with Argentine Foreign Minister Carlos Saavedra Lamas during previous meetings.[36] Although Ruiz-Guiñazú did claim credit for the settlement when he returned to Buenos Aires,[37] the solution came relatively late in the meeting and had little observable effect on the current Argentine Foreign Minister, who did not have the freedom of decision which Saaverdra Lamas had enjoyed. Prior to the meeting, Brazil's Aranha had assured the United States Ambassador in Rio that Brazil planned to support Washington's policy but that it did not want the other republics to know this. According to Aranha, this would strengthen the United States position if it was known only to the Department of State that Brazil was committed to this position.[38] There was in the Brazilian assurances the tacit implication that only Brazil could really be trusted and that the Argentine government would not be a good ally under any circumstance and probably should not receive much military or economic support. Aranha was not slow to report on Argentine perfidy,[39] or on Brazil's valiant efforts to resist possible Nazi pressure;[40] he even spread the story that Brazilian agents following Rossetti had found that on two occasions he met secretly with the Japanese Ambassador to Brazil.[41] All the time, beneath this pro-Allied attitude in Brazil's government, a struggle was going on between President Vargas and the military, with the Army fearing a strong anti-Fascist position.[42]

One minor flurry of anxiety was produced when Senator Tom Connally, Chairman of the U.S. Senate's Foreign Relations Committee, commented in a Washington press conference that the United States felt that either President Castillo would change his mind or the Argentines would change their President in the forthcoming elections, although he admitted that the government machinery might function to perpetuate itself in power. After a talk with Secretary of State Hull, Connally issued a statement that his views were his own and the Secretary of State issued a statement that Connally's views were not to be construed as being those of the White House.[43]

Faced with almost unanimous opposition to their positions, both Rossetti and Ruiz-Guiñazú began to feel the pressure. Rossetti had instructions which allowed him to support the United States in every way possible up to the breaking of diplomatic relations with the Axis.[44] Evidently on January 19 he wired a request that his instructions be modified to support breaking diplomatic relations.[45] As a result of this he was given permission to vote for the breaking of relations subject to congressional approval. The reasoning in Santiago was that, since the appropriate congressional committees which had helped to formulate his instructions were not available to approve the decision, the reservation was necessary. This was also an effort by the interim government not to make a decision which would arouse a storm of criticism in the Congress. Acting Foreign Minister Guillermo del Pedregal told Bowers that the agreement would be submitted to Congress immediately after the elections, at which time it was likely that the government would have a better majority in the Congress. Although in Santiago Rossetti's actions seemed strongly pro-Allied, he was seen in Rio as vacillating. Welles said he found Rossetti's position "anything but clear."[46] Actually, at the time the original instructions were formulated, to agree to go along with the United States on everything short of breaking relations seemed quite pro-Allied to the Chileans. This produced a Foreign Minister who talked pro-Allied but was unable to support the United States on the question which the entire conference soon began to use as a test of hemispheric cooperation. There was little enthusiasm in Santiago for breaking relations during the conference. There was frequent mention of the possibility of a Japanese attack.[47]

The Argentine delegation also felt the pressure of the other delegations, except that Buenos Aires responded with less flexibility than the government in Santiago. Ruiz-Guiñazú, according to Welles's account at the time, had expressed the opinion to the Undersecretary that the Argentine government would be willing to break relations. However, he feared that with the congressional election scheduled for March, raising the issue immediately prior to the voting would cause serious problems for the government.[48] When Chile seemed to be changing its position, the pressure on Argentina was increased. On January 19 Ruiz-Guiñazú suggested to Welles a statement that any American republics that felt it impossible to break relations could adhere to the declaration later. This would supposedly have cleared the way for Argentine action in April while preserving the essence of the Washington-originated resolution.[49] Welles replied that if Argentina was unable to sign the final declaration it would clearly demonstrate to the world that Argentina was unwilling to cooperate. At the same time, the United States was making

it clear that its resources would only permit the giving of economic assistance
to those countries that were cooperating in the effort against the Axis.

With the large pro-Allied newspapers in Buenos Aires emphasizing hemispheric unity during the meeting, on January 21 the heads of the delegations
of Chile, Argentina, Brazil, Peru, and the United States managed to work
out a compromise agreement. The operative section of the new agreement
was:

> The American Republics consequently declare that in the exercise of
> their sovereignty and in conformity with their constitutional institutions
> and powers, provided the latter are in agreement, they cannot continue
> their diplomatic relations with Japan, Germany and Italy since Japan has
> attacked and the others have declared war upon a nation of the Con-
> tinent.[50]

The Argentine and Chilean Foreign Ministers—both of whom said they
could accept the draft under their instructions[51]—insisted on the phrase "in
conformity with their constitutional institutions and powers." Rossetti, according to Welles, said that his government would break relations before the
elections (which were nine days away). The Acting Foreign Minister in Santiago, in explaining the compromise to Ambassador Bowers, said that Chile had
favored the phrase regarding constitutional institutions because, even though
severing relations was the responsibility of the executive, in this case it might
lead to war, and therefore it was felt necessary to have congressional approval.[52] Ruiz-Guiñazú said that Argentina would also inevitably break relations although probably not until after the congressional elections.[53] He mentioned the need for congressional approval because such a break would mean
almost immediate entry into the war.[54]

Evidently the Argentine government originally approved the formula on
the basis of a telegram from Ruiz-Guiñazú which indicated that the compromise left the matter of breaking relations more or less up to the individual
countries.[55] The President would therefore not be obligated to urge the Congress to act on the question. However, when the actual text arrived President
Castillo felt the wording obligated him to send a presidential message to
Congress recommending the action. In terms of the spirit of the resolution,
the President was correct in his interpretation. Perhaps the idea of not having to recommend the action might have appealed to Castillo because it
would have allowed him to remain on friendly terms with Germany. But
speculation on Castillo's motives and on the intricacies of the often-ignored
Argentine Constitution is, at this point, largely fruitless. The result of the
situation was that Ruiz-Guiñazú was forced to report to the conference that
his President had rejected the formula approved by his Foreign Minister. It
also might be noted that the compromise possibly was not acceptable to

Secretary Hull, but Argentina had disowned it before Washington could completely evaluate it.

The negotiations consequently began again. Argentina brought forth a new draft that was unacceptable to the major delegations.[56] Undersecretary Welles sent word back to the Department of State that the entire Argentine delegation was unhappy with Ruiz-Guiñazú.[57] Welles also said that "all" the other delegations had decided to sign the joint declaration for breaking relations and that "if Argentina is not prepared to go along, the others . . . will go along without her."[58] However, late in the afternoon of January 23 there was agreement on a new version of the troublesome Article Three. In its new form the article was converted to a recommendation. It read:

> The American Republics consequently, following the procedure established by their own laws within the position and circumstances of each country in the actual continental conflict, recommend the rupture of their diplomatic relations with Japan, Germany, and Italy, since the first of these states had attacked and the other two have declared war upon an American country.

Thus, after days of difficult talks and dashed hopes, the tired delegates joined to accept the idea that the breaking of diplomatic relations should only be in the form of a recommendation and not a flat statement of policy which signators presumably (but not necessarily) would be legally obligated to follow.

Although it may have been a ploy to obtain more military equipment, Chile showed its fear of attack by declaring at a plenary session on January 24 that "without the slightest shadow of a doubt, Japan immediately is going to attack Chile."[59] Early the following morning Rossetti visited Welles and asked him to sign a document including the pledge that

> the United States would take precautionary defense measures in the waters of the Pacific adjacent to South America and that should some emergency occur, Chile could count upon effective military assistance from the United States and that technical details of such assistance would be agreed upon in the immediate future.[60]

The Chilean Foreign Minister also said that he had received assurance that Chile was now prepared to break relations without delay. He stated that he had telegraphed Ríos, whose election he felt to be assured, for approval to announce the actual break in relations on the final day of the conference. Welles saw no objection to signing the agreement but asked for instructions.[61] The Department of State sent back a revision toning down the Rossetti document's preamble, which included the statement that Chile was "notoriously open to attack." The new version stated that in accord with unequivocal assurance to go to the assistance of any nation of the western hemisphere which has been the victim of an attack by a non-American aggressor, the United States in the event of an attack by a non-American country against Chile will take immediate steps to send naval, air and land forces to repulse this aggression. In the meantime precautionary defense measures have been taken to render as unlikely as possible attack upon the coastline of Chile.[62]

The telegram from Washington also said that Rossetti should be warned of the limits of the United States' capabilities to patrol and that Chile could not expect preference. Both parties signed the agreement. It may well be that Rossetti sought the document for political reasons in order to protect himself against accusations that his pro-Allied position was suicidal for Chile.

It is regrettable that public interest at the time and afterwards came to be focused on the recommendation that all countries break relations when there were so many other significant measures passed at the meeting.[63] This made it easy later to ignore less-publicized agreements in other areas. Cooperation was agreed to in such matters as financial controls and shipping limitations, but many of the measures were difficult to administer through the sometimes reluctant and sometimes inept Latin American bureaucracies. The measures themselves were often of a complex and absolute nature and unlike the compromise legislation passed in most Latin American legislatures.

It is illuminating to view the aftermath of the Rio conference in terms of three of the leading negotiators: Ruiz-Guiñazú, Rossetti, and Welles. The Argentine Foreign Minister, who had misinterpreted his government's instructions, alienated the other members of his delegation, and wavered in the face of the opposition, managed to become a hero to the Argentine isolationists. Upon returning to Buenos Aires he supposedly limited his airport remarks to a less than illuminating "long live the fatherland."[64] The pro-Nazi press hailed him as the hero of the conference despite the fact that it was Castillo who forced him into a stronger position. The Rio agreements were submitted to the Congress only for its information, and Castillo did not request any action on them.[65] The promises to break relations after the March elections were ignored.

Rossetti, who had pressured his interim government from Rio to change his instructions, seemed to return to Chile somewhat a fool in the eyes of many for his vacillations. Of course, there were those in Santiago who desired for political reasons to detract from the potentially powerful Rossetti. Rossetti's role was greatly complicated by the fact that he was first and always a politician, and his actions tended to be interpreted (correctly or incorrectly) in that light. Bowers defended Rossetti's role in a letter to Welles in which he stated that Rossetti "was miles ahead" of most of the public officials

in Chile in regard to pro-Allied sentiments and pointed out that when Rossetti
went to Rio he had ironclad instructions not to agree to a break in relations.[66]
When the Foreign Minister returned to Chile he insisted that he would present
the resolutions to Congress for speedy ratification and assured Bowers that
within a month the Axis missions would be ejected from Chile.[67] Then problems began to emerge, although Rossetti continued to be optimistic regarding
possible ratification. Bowers expressed the opinion that unless Ríos intervened
against ratification (which the Ambassador doubted), approval would soon
be forthcoming following the Rio conference.[68] However, with the exception
of the Communist paper *El Siglo,* the major newspapers were not advocating
a quick break in relations.[69] Rossetti, however, continued to assure Bowers in
early March that the Congress would be called into session.[70] Rossetti also
complained that he was greatly embarrassed during his efforts to have the Rio
agreements ratified by the fact that Welles had decided not to sign the Chilean
Lend-Lease Agreement until Chile's foreign policy had been clarified.[71] On
March 10 he assured Bowers that he now had the approval of the Acting
President to summon a special session of the Congress.[72] Despite public apathy
toward the session, Rossetti a few days later said that on March 16 the special
session would be called.[73] Chile's ambassador relayed the same word to Washington.[74]

The special session never came. Ernesto Barros Jarpa, who replaced Rossetti
when Ríos took over the presidency, later told Bowers that the regime opposed
the submission of the agreements to the Congress because it would have been
a recognition of a congressional role in foreign policy. Barros said that it was
the President's prerogative to break relations and not his duty nor his intention to consult the Congress.[75] Of course, the argument that had been given
at Rio was that such a step might lead to war and, since only Congress had
the power to declare war, it would have to approve the breaking of relations.
It might have been easy for Ríos to have tacitly allowed the Congress to have
been called into special session in order to break relations and thereby remove
any possible onus from his administration. Evidently he did not approve of
the action and a fear of strengthening Rossetti's position may have been one
reason for his position. Rossetti, out of office, returned to his newspaper *La
Opinion,* where he was critical of Ríos's refusal to break relations[76] and was
generally an implacable foe of the regime.

Welles also ran into problems with the latitude allowed him under his instructions. When Secretary of State Hull heard that Welles had accepted the
breaking of relations clause in the form of a "recommendation" rather than
a flat commitment, he was upset and ready to force Welles to repudiate the
compromise.[77] Hull arranged a three-way telephone conversation between
Welles in Rio, and Roosevelt and himself in Washington. During the argument
which ensued over Welles's action, Hull, according to the description, spoke

to the Undersecretary "more sharply" than he "had ever spoken to anyone in the Department."[78] Roosevelt broke off the discussion and stated that it should be accepted. According to Hull, Roosevelt said it was too late to repudiate the agreement.[79] Welles's account has it that the President said that he was going to take the judgment of the man on the spot and said he approved of what had been done.[80] Although the accounts are not directly contradictory (the approval of the action could have been prefaced by the statement that it was, after all, too late to repudiate), the tone in their respective memoirs is indicative of the feelings which unfortunately existed between Hull and Welles.

Welles's defense, both in the telegram of explanation which he immediately sent to Roosevelt and in later writings in which he discusses the question,[81] centers to a large extent on the figure of Brazilian President Vargas. According to the Undersecretary, he spoke privately with the chief executive of the host country after a warning from Foreign Minister Aranha that, if Argentina remained aloof from the resolution dealing with breaking relations, Brazil did not think it could support the United States as originally planned. During a conversation with the Brazilian President, Vargas mentioned to Welles that important Army and Navy officers feared a war if Argentina were neutral and said that the conference's problems were insuperable unless some formula acceptable to all sides could be found. Welles also claimed that the recommendation was really not different from the previous resolution—although there is some question whether Cordell Hull would have approved the previous one if the Undersecretary was referring to the compromise rejected by Castillo after being accepted by Ruiz-Guiñazú.[82] Welles argued that if the Argentine President did not recommend the breaking of relations, Buenos Aires was in violation of its commitments. He also mentioned Hull's distaste for Argentina, which, he said, he and Roosevelt had discussed prior to the Rio meeting and which the Undersecretary felt was a result of Hull's dealings with Argentine Foreign Minister Saavedra Lamas during the 1936 Buenos Aires Conference. Welles also later wrote that during the stormy telephone conversation with Roosevelt and Hull, Hull stated that the recommendation approved at the conference would also be evaded by Brazil, Ecuador, Peru, Bolivia, Paraguay, and Uruguay—none of which did evade the obligation.

Hull's memoirs seem to blame all future problems with Latin America on the Welles decision, and he claims that his own health was partially undermined by his disappointment over the Rio settlement.[83] Hull stated that on the opening day of the conference Adolf Berle sent Welles a communication (will Hull's approval) stating:

> In the Department from Secretary Hull down, the feeling is in accord on
> the belief that rather than a compromise formula a breach in unanimity

would be preferable. The Argentines must accept this situation or go their own way, and in the latter event reliance may be placed upon the overwhelming public feeling in Argentina to supply the corrective.[84]

Events were to prove that the "overwhelming public feeling" would not supply a corrective.

The major criticism that can be made against Welles during the conference is that he did not keep Hull well informed of what was happening. Apparently this was far from the first incident of this nature.[85] His telegram of January 7 indicated that he went to the conference believing he had the support of all the delegations except Argentina and Chile.[86] Welles's claim that Brazil's sudden decision not to cooperate unless Buenos Aires did was the key to the eventual compromise either was not emphasized by Welles in his telephone discussion with Hull and Roosevelt or did not seem relevant to the Secretary because it is not mentioned in Hull's memoirs as one of the reasons given by Welles for his actions. There can be little doubt, however, that Vargas was under significant pressure from his military to do nothing to irritate relations with Argentina or to drag Brazil into the war in Europe.[87]

There is also the fact that Welles was not respectful of Hull's knowledge of Latin American affairs; but this is not an excuse for a failure to inform his superior. Welles may have felt that in view of Hull's ignorance of the area he had been given a relatively free hand to operate as he chose at Rio. Welles does state in his book, *Seven Decisions That Shaped History*, that he had wired the Department of State the information about his conversation with President Vargas;[88] but the wire is not in the Rio conference files, which would at least indicate that it was not considered relevant to the meeting when received.

In retrospect, it is difficult to see what advantage Hull's course of action would have had except to bring the hemispheric split out into the open sooner. Chile was not going to leave itself vulnerable by approving a document rejected by Argentina. Passage of a strong resolution might have strengthened the pro-Allied elements in Argentina temporarily, but probably not enough to topple the Castillo government. The greatest significance of the meeting may have been the degree to which it deepened the split between Hull and Welles. Welles claimed that the Secretary refused to see him when he returned from Rio or to brief him on events during his absence.[89] The fact that such deep feelings could originate in a question of little historical substance probably demonstrates that the clash between the two men was a clash of politician versus diplomat, aristocrat versus rural judge, friend of the President versus outsider.[90] Eventually, Welles was pressured out of the Department of State in August of 1943 when his name was linked to a scandal.[91]

This description of the Rio meeting centers on the resolution dealing with the breaking of relations because it was on this question that the divergent foreign policy views of the United States, Argentina, and Chile most clearly show themselves. The conference did serve a valuable purpose in that it set up cooperation on a range of technical matters relating to the war effort and established understandings on how the pressure should be applied on domestic Axis interests. This proved helpful as the war progressed. Argentina and Chile were not opposed to the resolutions based on these understandings even though the measures frequently called for strong anti-Axis actions. Particularly in the case of Argentina, the resolutions were simply not carried out. Why Buenos Aires agreed in the first place is perhaps accountable to the fact that these were technical questions, and the ramifications of enforcing the blacklists and other procedures were simply not explored at Rio. Certainly later protests from Washington (both to Santiago and Buenos Aires but also to some of the other governments) were frequently greeted by surprise that the country had agreed to such-and-such at Rio.

Despite the stream of pronouncements about the glories of Pan-Americanism at the meeting, it is not difficult to interpret this gathering in terms of simple power politics. The dominant power wanted to arrange for a co-ordinated effort and was willing to pay for this in economic and military assistance. Most of the states either stood to profit in some way from the coordination or were too weak to oppose Washington's wishes (or both). But the rhetoric of Pan-Americanism served to soften the realities of the situation by giving the Latin American countries a sense of participation.

4: CHILE TEMPORIZES

The days following Pearl Harbor found Chilean–United States relations dominated by two themes: Chile's desire for weapons from the United States and the inevitable stresses caused by the Chilean presidential election campaign. The interest in weapons grew from the fear of a Japanese attack on the undeniably vulnerable Chilean coast. This in turn led to a reluctance on the part of the Congress to take a strongly pro-Allied position. In retrospect, the attack on Pearl Harbor clearly strained Japanese capabilities to the limits, and the resources of the Imperial Navy and the interests of its policymakers both operated to make a possible attack on Chile an impossibility unless the United States was soundly defeated in the Pacific. This was, however, not so clear at the time—particularly in Chile— and even the faintest possibility of an attack was sufficient to cause alarm.

Shortly after Pearl Harbor, and prior to the Rio Conference, Foreign Minister Rossetti came to U.S. Ambassador Bowers and asked if he could have a signed protocol (predated to Pearl Harbor) for secret use in influencing the Congress. The protocol would be a statement that the United States would support Chile if it were to be attacked by any nation outside the hemisphere. Bowers urged Department of State approval since this had been the understanding for some time.[1] Undersecretary of State Sumner Welles wired back that there had been "many unequivocal assurances" of the intention of the United States to come to the defense of any nation in the western hemisphere that was a "victim of foreign aggression," and therefore it did not seem desirable to add a secret protocol.[2] The Undersecretary argued that adhering to such a document was incompatible with the idea of continental solidarity and that, since other nations had "unhesitatingly declared war upon the Axis Powers," it would be inappropriate to make a special agreement with Chile. He did, however, authorize Bowers to deliver to Rossetti a signed communication reiterating specific promises of military assistance made in the past.[3] As noted in the previous chapter, Welles did consent during the course of the Rio meeting to sign what amounted to a special agreement with Chile.

But written assurances carried less weight with Chilean policymakers than weapons. Bowers, in a telegram to Washington early in January of 1942, stated:

> The belief is widespread in Chile that the United States is not in a position to extend at this moment aerial and naval protection to the vulnerable Chilean coast and that Chile had better be careful at this time not to precipitate a break with the Japanese. If this Chilean judgment is factually wrong then we should be advised and news communications originating from here and from the United States should take an appropriate line.[4]

This "widespread" belief, unfortunately for the United States, was substantially correct. The weapon supply was far from bottomless. The War Plans Division of the General Staff informed the Department of State less than three weeks after the attack on Pearl Harbor that it was "practically impossible to find anything for immediate or even reasonably prompt delivery to Latin American republics."[5] The Chief of the United States Military Air Mission in Chile urged that planes be provided for shore patrol immediately rather than waiting for the anticipated attack. He particularly feared an attack on the electrical plants powering the production of copper. He also expressed the opinion that before the Axis would launch a major attack against the continental United States, it would try to control such outposts as Chile.[6]

While Rossetti was at the Rio meeting, the Acting Minister of Foreign Affairs, Guillermo del Pedregal, said that the Japanese Minister had assured Chile that if it maintained its neutral position it would not be attacked by Tokyo. Del Pedregal told Bowers that if Chile had military equipment she would not only break relations but would go to war.[7] The Ambassador advised Washington that he felt, if the United States would immediately send sufficient reconnaissance planes and fighters to ensure protection of the vulnerable coast installations, Chile's reluctance to break relations (which was being shown at Rio) would dissolve.[8] The following day Bowers sent the revised estimate formulated by the U.S. Air Mission regarding the minimum number of planes and anti-aircraft guns needed to defend against surprise attack along the strategic areas of an 800-mile stretch of Chilean coast. It called for twelve long-range bombing reconnaissance planes, preferably thirty-six but at least twenty-four interceptor pursuit planes, forty-two 20-millimeter anti-aircraft guns, and twenty 37-millimeter anti-aircraft guns. He closed by asking the Department of State, "Could you promise immediate arrival of such equipment? "[9]

On the same day the Department of State was in the process of notifying Bowers of the materiel which would be made available to Chile when she adhered to the lend-lease agreement:

—about 15 airplanes of advanced trainer type with Army crews to train Chilean personnel

—about 25 scout cars
—134 81-mm. morters
—4,000 rounds of 155-mm. howitzer ammunition
—approximately 300 motor vehicles of various types
—3 Stearmann training planes
—2 Observation Scout OS2U-3
—cement, oil and gasoline as may be requested.[10]

Although, according to Hull, the State Department felt an attack on Chile "was perfectly possible," regardless of whether or not Chile was willing to break diplomatic relations, the United States would have many difficulties in supplying the equipment.[11] Bowers wired Washington that the list of materiel was not responsive to the requests Chile had made. Chile welcomed this materiel, but, the Ambassador stated, "it in no way meets the immediate danger of a Japanese hit-and-run air attack." Bowers declared:

> Our Air Corps Command has apparently not been able to grasp the military and political significance of South America and particularly the vulnerability of Chile. If something should happen now to Chile in her present defenseless situation it is going to throw our whole policy out of gear and our relations will be adversely effected for a very long time to come since it will be said that we urged Chile to take a step which it felt was unwise.

The Ambassador gave his opinion that "if you could give assurance of the immediate (repeat immediate) delivery of the material . . . I believe it would decisively clinch full Chilean cooperation."[12]

This at times arrogant communication from a nonprofessional diplomat angered Secretary of State Cordell Hull. In a memo to President Roosevelt on January 24 he stated:

> It does not seem to me that Mr. Bowers appreciates the exceedingly heavy demands which are now being made on our war production or that the War and Navy Departments, at your direction, made a real effort to furnish to Chile whatever they could spare.[13]

Roosevelt's telegram to Bowers was almost as blunt:

> It would be inexcusable to disregard the possibility of a Japanese hit-and-run attack on Chile. On the other hand, it would be equally inexcusable to suppose that any Japanese plan would be in any way affected by the particular state of Chile's diplomatic or other relations with Japan at the time. Therefore I hope that the "full Chilean cooperation" mentioned in your telegram . . . will be immediately forthcoming, since it will be a most valuable contribution to the placing of both our countries in the best possible position to meet all eventualities.[14]

Roosevelt was probably correct in his statement that Chile's breaking of diplomatic relations with Japan would not alter whether or not Japan chose to attack. Of course, in retrospect, we know that there was no plan to attack under any circumstances; but with Japan winning major victories in the Pacific during January and February, there was a tendency to exaggerate the Japanese military might. The possibility remains that even if the weapons had been furnished to Chile immediately (an almost impossible task) Chile still might have followed the diplomatic course she did since there were strong pro-neutrality forces. Ironically, the United States was refusing arms to Argentina with the excuse that countries breaking diplomatic relations were incu. ng additional risks.[15]

The other factor complicating United States–Chilean relations during late 1941 and early 1942 was Chile's second presidential campaign within three years. The leftist coalition which had narrowly brought President Aguirre Cerda to victory was having difficulties in regrouping itself for the February 1, 1942, election. The international situation was much more a factor in this election. During the 1938 campaign events in Europe had seemed far away and of little consequence to Chile, unless the situation should happen to open up new markets as World War I had done. Now, however, there were elements in Chile who viewed the war as a moral issue, and other elements who felt that Chile's self-interest dictated backing the Allies.

The first candidate to proclaim his candidacy was the ever-present Carlos Ibáñez. His strategy for the 1942 election was to gather a coalition of the right. The Radicals, the largest party in Chile, had a difficult time in deciding on a candidate. Eventually the choice was Juan Antonio Ríos who had managed to defeat Gabriel González Videla (representing the left wing of the party) in an extraordinarily close party primary (14,953 to 14,222).[16] Ríos attempted to build a coalition of center elements with hopes that the far left would support him as the lesser evil.

Although in retrospect some of the more moderate rightist leaders certainly could have worked with Ríos, the powerful Conservative and Liberal parties turned their support to Ibáñez. However, this decision helped to splinter the Liberal Party. Joining in the right-wing coalition was the Nazi Party, endorsing its old friend Ibáñez. This placed the left in the dilemma on which Ríos was counting. He certainly was no friend of the left and was strongly anti-Communist. The Socialists initially backed Oscar Schnake while the Communists were trying to persuade González Videla to run as an independent.[17] However, when the right began to coalesce behind Ibáñez, the leftist elements were faced with the possibility of probably contributing to the election of Ibáñez by splitting the votes if they nominated Schnake. In a choice between Ibáñez and Ríos the choice for the left was relatively clear: Ríos. So the Socialists and Communists reluctantly cast their lot with Ríos in a coalition that was based strictly on electoral necessities, and with no plans for cooperation such as had been formulated prior to the election of Aguirre Cerda.

Foreign policy was not a clearly articulated issue in the election campaign. But it was an issue in the form of vague implications and frequently at the level of rumor. Neither candidate declared that he was ready to break diplomatic relations with the Axis, nor were they vehement in arguing against such a course of action. The Radicals and the left heavily emphasized Ibáñez's past connections with the Nazis. The United States Embassy was careful not to express any public opposition to Ibáñez, although it initially seemed to assume that he was a front man for the Nazis and that his campaign was financed by Germany.[18] Ibáñez tried hard to deny these charges, and shortly after the attack on Pearl Harbor offered to appoint Carlos Dávila, a strong supporter of the United States, as Ambassador to Washington if he won the election.[19] Evidently some North American business men in Santiago (who normally associated with Conservative and Liberal circles) tried to convince Bowers that Ibáñez was not pro-German or anti-Yankee, but Bowers adhered to his opinion that in view of his past associations and his silence on continental solidarity, Ibáñez was not to be trusted.[20]

If the Embassy didn't support Ibáñez, it also did nothing to help Ríos. Although it is often assumed in Latin American capitals that the American Embassy is a prime source of campaign funds, there is no evidence to suggest that Ríos received money from the United States Embassy despite the fact that the Embassy viewed the election as a grave one. In fact, Bowers told United States companies in Chile that the Embassy "looks with disapproval" on their contributing to Chilean election funds.[21] Bowers later wrote in his memoirs of Chile:

> Before I went to Chile it was charged that some of these corporations contributed to the campaign coffers of the presidential candidate, and the reaction was bad. However, in justice to these corporations, they had been pressured by important politicians to furnish money. In the presidential election of 1942 I formally notified our people that if they intervened in domestic politics and found themselves in trouble they could not count on the protection of the Embassy.

Bowers commented that his order pleased the corporations because it gave them an excuse not to contribute.[22] The major Department of State argument against assisting a candidate was not a moral one. It simply was the fact that such operations were likely to be found out and cause a reaction against the Washington-supported candidate. The Department of State also objected to any efforts on the part of the Allies to help a candidate such as Ríos.[23]

In the closing days of the campaign ex-President Arturo Alessandri, who had been friendly to the right during his second administration, spoke out strongly in favor of Ríos. This, plus the fact that the left was reluctantly supporting Ríos and that many of Ibáñez's vocal supporters were Nazis, gave Ríos a substantial victory, with approximately 56 percent of the vote. Ibáñez received the remainder in the two-way race for the presidency.

The period from Ríos's election on February 1 until his inauguration on April 2 was an uncertain and difficult one for the United States Department of State. It was soon obvious that Rossetti would not be retained as Foreign Minister but that he would stay in the post until Ríos took office and that several matters of continuing importance would be discussed during the period. Rossetti evidently was distrustful of the degree to which Ríos would support the Rio recommendations and also piqued over what he felt to be a lack of appreciation on the part of the United States for his efforts in Chile to promote inter-American cooperation.

Rossetti's unsuccessful efforts to have the Rio agreements ratified in a special congressional session have already been discussed. However, another substantial set of negotiations which transpired during the two-month period grew out of Rossetti's attempts to procure anti-aircraft guns. Since Chile was primarily worried about a hit-and-run Pearl Harbor–type attack against its unfortified coastal installations, anti-aircraft guns and airplanes were the logical pieces of equipment to seek from the United States. In response to Chilean requests on February 4, 1942, the United States offered to ship in mid-February four batteries (16 guns) of 155-millimeter cannon with 300 rounds of ammunition per gun. These would presumably be set up in northern Chile, and the War Department suggested that approximately 300 men would accompany the batteries to handle the guns. Chileans would then be trained to operate them. Bowers's instructions were to see the President-elect personally and to state that, if the guns were desired, it would be advantageous to sign the lend-lease pact.[24]

Rossetti, however, did not want the American Ambassador negotiating with the President-elect and, with Ríos not seeking an active role, Bowers had little choice. The Chilean Foreign Minister felt that after the weapons had arrived, Ríos should simply be told "we are armed."[25] In any event, the idea of 300 North American troops accompanying the four anti-aircraft batteries was not well received. It was feared that this would appear to be the first step toward the much dreaded establishment of foreign bases on Chilean soil.[26] Therefore, after a meeting of the Chilean Council of Defense, Rossetti informed Bowers that his government accepted the various stipulations in the offer of planes and batteries with the exception of requiring a reduction of the 300 men to 100.[27] According to the Ambassador, Rossetti said that "however foolish it might be, it [is] impossible in view of Chilean psychology at this time to permit any except extremely limited numbers of foreign military advisers to enter upon Chilean soil."[28] The United States reluctantly accepted the limitation. It did manage to have the figure raised to 108, and warned Chile that this number of men would mean that in the beginning the batteries would not be manned by experienced personnel and that this would lessen the effectiveness of the guns at first. The weapons were furnished without the formal signing of a lend-lease agreement because the Department of State was beginning to have some second thoughts in view of Chile's reluctance to carry out the Rio recommendation that she break diplomatic relations with the Axis.[29] A few relatively minor problems over the degree to which Chile was to control the gun installations were resolved in favor of Chilean control.[30] It probably should also be pointed out that the weapons were obsolete from Washington's point of view and so did not mark a significant sacrifice of war materiel.[31]

The uneasiness of this interim period between presidents was increased when, in the darkness of the morning of March 13, 1942, the Chilean cargo ship *Tolten,* steaming off the coast of the United States between New York and Baltimore, was sunk. The incident, which might have helped ignite Chilean public opinion against the Axis, ended up bogged down in controversy over the circumstances surrounding the incident. The ship had left New York against instructions but had been sailing with its lights on in order to allow any submarines to identify it as a neutral, Chilean ship. It was intercepted by the United States Coast Guard and told to obey the rules of the Atlantic seaboard during the emergency and to turn off its lights and proceed to a safe port during the night. After it turned off its lights, it was sunk.[32] The Chilean government did everything possible to try to soothe public feelings over the incident, much to the dismay of Ambassador Bowers who felt that the Santiago government should use the incident to rally pro-Allied feeling. Bowers suggested to Washington that the *New York Times* or some other prominent North American newspaper publish an editorial denouncing the sinking with arguments showing it was primarily the fault of the Axis.[33] However, the feeling in the Department of State was not to spotlight the incident because publicity regarding the number of sinkings tended to indicate that the United States was on the defensive and could not police its own waters.[34]

According to Rossetti, the Japanese Minister gave him a promise that Chilean merchant ships would not be attacked, although he exempted possible attacks on the Panama Canal. The Foreign Minister, according to his own account, refused to accept the limitation regarding the Canal and the Japanese Ambassador went away angry.[35] The Axis diplomats acted together regarding the *Tolten* sinking in assuring immunity but again placing the Panama Canal out of bounds. Rossetti, according to what he told Bowers,

warned Italian Ambassador Clantz that Chile would consider an attack on
the Canal a cause for war.[36] Although the Department of State regarded the
negotiations over immunity for Chilean merchant vessels within the Canal
with some amusement,[37] Rossetti and his successor claimed to have received
assurances from Germany, Italy,[38] and Japan that Chilean commerce con-
voyed in Chilean ships would be allowed to continue unmolested.[39]

As pointed out previously, in the waning days of Rossetti's term he made
a strong effort to obtain congressional ratification of the Rio agreements.[40]
This may have been designed to force Ríos into a pro-Allied policy without
his consent, but it was probably to some extent an attempt by Rossetti to
justify his change in position at Rio, which had brought forth a great amount
of personal criticism (most of it from people who were already critical of
him). The Foreign Minister did tell Bowers that the actual breaking of relations probably should be reserved as a courtesy for Ríos even if the Rio
agreements were ratified. Rossetti also continued to insist that Japan would
attack and that the attack was "inevitable" regardless of whether Chile broke
relations.[41] However, by mid-March Rossetti had doubts about any imminent
break in relations with the Axis, unless there would be a change in the
course of the war in the Pacific (the Japanese were apparently winning) or
the United States could begin to supply large amounts of equipment.[42]

The man designated by President-elect Ríos to be the new Minister of
Foreign Affairs was Ernesto Barros Jarpa. In many ways he was by background the most pro-United States Foreign Minister of the period. Yet, by
the time he left office, he had caused Bowers many sleepless nights. He was
fluent in English, which was a major advantage for anyone hoping to deal
with Bowers. In his late forties, educated in law, he had some diplomatic
and journalistic experience. He had previously been a cabinet member and had
been made President of the Chilean Electric Company in 1936 by Finance
Minister Ross. He had written a book on peaceful settlement. He had been
a lawyer for the Braden copper interests[43] and a president of the Chilean–
North American Cultural Institute.[44] Bowers found him nationalistic but
initially "aggressively pro-United States, as a matter of principle and conviction."[45] In short, he was the stereotype of a member of the clientele elite.[46]

Despite this background, Barros Jarpa made it clear in his first conversation with Bowers after being named Foreign Minister-designate, that he opposed breaking relations. This sentiment Bowers first thought to be based on
the conviction that the war would end with a German victory or in a stalemate. In either case, Chile would be in a better position to trade if she had
been officially neutral.[47] The Department of State felt it would be a good
idea to have Barros Jarpa visit the United States prior to taking office in
order to discuss the general situation between the United States and Chile.[48]
Although Ríos approved of the visit, Barros Jarpa opposed it because he

felt that since Chile was not ready to break relations, his visit would only bring forth increased criticism in the United States press of Chile's reluctance to break diplomatic relations.[49] In all likelihood this evaluation was correct. Barros Jarpa did, however, assure Bowers that Ríos would change the policy toward American business interests for the better.[50] Thus, from the North American point of view, he became the right Foreign Minister at the wrong time.

ON BREAKING RELATIONS

From the day of Ríos's inauguration on April 2, 1942, until January of 1943, United States relations with Chile centered on the question of Chile's breaking diplomatic relations with the Axis as recommended by the Rio meeting. These were ten extraordinarily difficult months during which tempers in the United States frequently frayed in the face of Chile's seeming ability to resist pressure from Washington. It would be easy to present an account of this period interpreting Chile's reluctance in terms of cowardliness and greed. It would also be easy to present the period as one in which poor, innocent Chile was trying to resist the bullying efforts of the United States to get her to take a diplomatic act of no substantive importance and one which might well have caused her serious difficulties after the war.

Regrettably, the situation was not that simple. The motivations of various policymakers in both countries varied considerably even if the policies pursued were reasonably uniform. At the time, the situation was complicated by the tremendous pressures brought to bear by the strains of fighting in the Pacific, Europe and Africa. The United States felt itself to be launched upon a holy crusade and tended publicly to see its supporters as saints and to see those slow to participate as sinners. This reaction was inevitable but it nevertheless presented difficulties. Actually, Chile may have been able to view things with a little better perspective, and this in itself was frequently maddening to Washington. This is not intended to portray Department of State officials as zealots, but they were responsive to a population and press which was fiercely involved in the war. A total, concentrated war effort was the prime consideration, and the wishes of other countries were largely ignored.

A second general comment should be made concerning the nature of the act the United States was trying to get Chile to perform. As a legal act the breaking of relations has little, if any, significance. However, Chile and Argentina's failure to break relations, after the Rio resolutions had been adopted in a flurry of supposed inter-American cooperation, seemed to signify a major crack in the wall of unity. In some senses the desire to have

Chile break relations was almost an exercise in bookkeeping. Eighteen of the twenty countries had filled in the blank marked "relations broken." Two boxes remained unchecked: Chile and Argentina. And so the books cannot be closed until they are completed. It is difficult to believe that the morale of soldiers fighting the Axis was undermined by the knowledge that Chile had not broken diplomatic relations with Germany.

At the time, Chile's reluctance to break relations was often treated as though it constituted some sort of active, deviant policy of a particularly perverse nature. In terms of inter-American cooperation it was certainly not going along with the majority. However, in terms of Chilean politics, the forces of inertia and status quo were on the side of not breaking relations. To break relations involved an action on Chile's part. Had relations been broken when Ríos took office undoubtedly he would have sustained the status quo and not re-opened them. With a delicate balance of government, it simply stirred up fewer waves in the initial stages of 1942 not to break relations. Perhaps the United States was not happy, but it was obvious that Britain was not putting much pressure on Chile in this direction.[51] Chile could always point to a number of contributions it was making to the war effort: shipment of materials to the United States, cooperation with the proclaimed list (a dubious claim), arrest of Axis agents, giving the United States non-belligerent status, accepting the coastal batteries, etc.[52]

There is, however, another side to diplomatic relations besides the symbolic one. Carrying on relations means an embassy in the other country. This embassy can be a center of subversive organization. Certainly the Nazis were showing a propensity both for intrigue and for attempts to influence public opinion via the communications media. Therefore, it might have been well to have the Axis embassies closed. However, in retrospect the question must be asked: What did the United States want from Chile during World War II? The answer is, clearly, that the United States wanted Chile (1) to protect herself against an attack from the outside (although such an attack was highly unlikely), (2) to protect herself against internal subversion (of which there was very little) or a coup, (unlikely), and (3) to keep up the flow of needed materials to the United States. Certainly providing these raw materials was very much to Chile's benefit, so there was no question that this would continue. With British control of the Atlantic it would have been impossible to sell these materials to Germany.

Thus with the calmness of hindsight, the substantive reasons for breaking relations were not so great. Chile's slowness in cracking down on possible subversive activities was probably justified by the meager danger such efforts presented. But the United States was following a strategy of over-kill and feared the potential of the Axis diplomats to encourage secret operations. A massive sabotage of the copper industry would have been a serious blow to war production, and, because the German Embassy seemed the logical co-ordinator of any sabotage, officials in Washington wanted the Embassy closed.

A few other comments about United States policy should be made prior to attempting to analyze the reasons for Chile's refusal to break relations. From the first many persons connected with the Department of State were aware of the difficulties in pressuring Chile. A ranking officer in the Embassy in Santiago wrote the Department of State in March of 1942 that he was disturbed lest there develop a tendency to use pressure as the principal method of bringing Chile into line. He claimed that any pressure would have to be disguised because no country in Latin America was more resistant to pressure.[53] Therefore he advocated playing on Chile's feelings of hemispheric solidarity. Later, he also advocated that the United States persuade the other Latin American countries to pressure Chile,[54] a course of action which was urged on Bolivia, Colombia, Uruguay, and Peru. The general effort to persuade Chile was primarily at a gentle level in the beginning. President Roosevelt wrote Bowers in April of 1942 that no deliberately unfavorable action was contemplated toward Chile.[55] He also pointed out that naturally those countries breaking relations would be given preferential treatment. As the situation progressed it became increasingly difficult to tell when an action by the United States was simply a reward to those countries that had broken relations and when it was a punishment for Chile. Obviously Chile had a tendency, since she felt herself to be cooperating in the war effort, to interpret United States actions favoring other countries as punishment.

CHILE'S RESISTANCE

No single factor was *the* reason for Chile's resistance during the first ten months of the Ríos administration to the United States demand that she break diplomatic relations with the Axis. Many forces were coming to bear on the decision not to sever the ties. Of the reasons that will be discussed, none of them could have accounted for the decision in isolation from the other factors. Combined, they provided a hard-core resistance motivating different groups in the same direction. Perhaps in the case of one or two of the reasons offered for not breaking relations, had that hard-core resistance not existed the relations might have been severed; but this is purely guesswork, since the point is that the factors did exist and were largely interrelated.

It will be remembered that during the foreign ministers' conference in Rio,

both at the meeting and in Santiago, the United States received strong indications that large amounts of military aid would help persuade Chile to
break relations. It may well be true that significant amounts, by the standards of what was being supplied to Latin America, might have tipped the
decision toward a break. The Chilean military was a powerful interest group
and in that interim between Aguirre Cerda and Ríos, it could have brought
about a change in the policy of neutrality. However, these requests from
Chile caused three major problems for the Department of State. First, the
United States was short on such materials. Second, to have favored Chile for
doing something the other countries had already done would have caused considerable dissension within the inter-American community. Third, the offer
initially impressed the United States as an attempt on Chile's part to profit
from carrying out what seemed to the United States to be Chile's moral obligation. These problems continually plagued the negotiations. Chile hoped
to obtain something in return for her concession (a time-honored custom).
The United States was so involved in its moral crusade that anything which
hinted of setting up a quid pro quo reeked of opportunism. As the situation
progressed, the provision of armaments came to be less important; the problem developed an impetus and rigidity of its own and other interests rallied
behind the idea that relations should not be broken. It was probably easier
to break relations before opinions solidified, but the shortage of arms was
an important factor in preventing this action at the time.

The actual form this demand for arms took was a series of separate attempts to obtain the weapons. After sending the four batteries and fifteen
airplanes (plus some supplementary material) the United States decided that
since Chile was refusing to sever diplomatic relations it was not advisable
to sign the lend-lease agreement which had been negotiated with Chile.[56]
In May Laurence Duggan, the Department of State's Adviser on Political
Relations, suggested that the Chilean military not be informed of what weapons were available until "we see what Chile's international policy becomes."[57]
Discussions regarding the sending of twenty-five PT-19 aircraft were stopped
in late June.[58] In mid-July of 1942 Douglas Heath of the Embassy in Santiago wrote Duggan that he felt the holding off of military supplies was having a slow and favorable reaction.[59]

Most of the discussions over possible supplies of arms took place in
Washington, where lend-lease operations were centered. Late in July, when
Chilean Ambassador Michels discussed his country's situation with Welles
after returning to Washington from a trip to Santiago, he seemed more optimistic that a break in relations would come soon. He stated that the President did not want to give the impression of negotiating favors in return for
breaking relations; but, unless Chile could obtain military and naval materials putting it at a minimum level of self-defense capability, public opinion

(fed by pro-Axis propaganda) would not support his (Ríos's) breaking of relations.[60] Welles replied that the first thing would be to determine what the defense requirements would be. Then, if the United States could meet them,
a tentative agreement could be worked out regarding the amounts and times
of delivery of the equipment that would be furnished under a lend-lease agreement. Welles states in his memo of the conversation:

> I said that once such an agreement had tentatively been agreed upon,
> we should then be in a position to assure Chile that if Chile severed re-
> lations with the Axis Powers this government would then be prepared to
> sign a lend-lease agreement with Chile and deliver material to Chile under
> the schedules carried in such agreement. The Ambassador stated that
> this would be most satisfactory to his government.[61]

The War Department, however, cast some doubt on this arrangement.
A spokesman stated that it would be "exceedingly difficult, if not impossible, to supply Chile anything like what we consider Chile's minimum requirements to be." Army officers said that the demand for anti-aircraft
guns, combat planes and other supplies was "far greater than the supply
or prospective production." This led the Department of State to adopt a
"go slow" attitude for fear that the situation would lead to a great deal
of haggling with Chile.[62] On August 5 Ambassador Michels had a long
talk with President Roosevelt, during which Roosevelt told Michels that
he could foresee little danger to Chile except from an isolated bombard-
ment of the Chilean coast by a Japanese submarine, and, with the batteries
furnished by the United States the more vulnerable positions were protected.
The President explained that the United States was doing most of its patrolling of the Atlantic coast with small planes with a flying range of no
more than two or three hundred miles. He assured the Ambassador that
if Chile were to break relations Washington, under the schedules being
prepared for a lend-lease agreement, could furnish "at least fifty to one
hundred planes" of the type the United States had been effectively using.[63]
On August 7 Welles gave the Ambassador the list of materials available
under lend-lease.[64] It included 97 airplanes, and an additional 50 to 100
that were not included because no decision had been reached on the type
and specifications.[65]

The U.S. War and Navy Departments, confronted by the size of Chile's
requests, began to question whether the United States was not paying too
high a price for a diplomatic act, and one which it viewed as unimportant.
This precipitated a minor and short-lived debate in the Liaison Committee
in which Welles's position, backed by Roosevelt, prevailed.[66] On October 3,
Duggan was informed by Ambassador Michels that Chile would be very
glad to accept the armaments listed in the event that she broke relations

with the Axis[67]—hardly a very satisfactory response from the Department of State's point of view.

In any event, at this time the real issue was beginning to center on the proposed visit of President Ríos to the United States and its eventual cancellation. (This is discussed in detail below.)

Ríos's visit was cancelled on November 13. The Chilean Ambassador called on Sumner Welles again on the same day and once again raised the question of military and naval assistance in the event Chile severed relations with the Axis. Welles reiterated his previous position: when Chile aligned herself with the Allies the United States would follow the same procedure with Chile as it had with the other American republics in attempting to furnish all practicable assistance for the defense of its territory.[68] On November 2, the Chilean Foreign Office, which by this time had pledged itself to break relations, had asked if as much as possible of the promised lend-lease equipment could be delivered *prior* to the breaking of relations. This, the Office argued, would relieve fears within the military and would be an expression of confidence in Chile's pledge to break relations. Of course, it would also counter the charge that Chile was simply breaking relations in order to get arms. Bowers "urgently supported the request."[69]

The Department of State, this time maddened by Chile's cautiousness in taking what seemed to the Department to be a harmless step, wired back a strong "No,"[70] and offered several reasons for its position. First, Chile, for several months after the outbreak of the war, had been treated the same as American republics who had either declared war or broken relations; moreover, the amounts of arms and munitions already sent compared favorably with other countries and this flow had been based on "many authoritative and official expressions reported by [Bowers] that Chile intended to comply with her obligation." Second, other nations of the hemisphere would be upset if Chile continued to receive favored treatment. And third, the Department insisted,

> so long as Chile maintains relations with the Axis, all details regarding arms and munitions which might be sent to Chile, as well as the disposition, location and use of such arms and munitions would be immediately made known to the Axis, thus reducing materially the potential value of such arms and munitions in the defense of Chile and of the continent.[71]

In a separate transaction, the Department of State decided early in December of 1942 to thwart the sale of four Lockheed Lodestar airplanes to Chile even though, in theory, the planes were commercial. When Chile's position on breaking relations was clarified, the question would be reviewed.[72]

On December 17 a special envoy from Chile, Raúl Morales Beltrami (accompanied by Ambassador Michels), had a conversation with Roosevelt and

Welles.[73] Morales presented a message from President Ríos stating that Chile had decided to immediately break relations with the Axis. He expressed some fears regarding the vulnerability of the Chilean coast, and Roosevelt suggested that this question be discussed privately with Welles. When Morales and Michels caucused with Welles, the Undersecretary agreed to accept a revised list of Chile's requirements for military supplies based on the list presented in August. The new request would be prepared by military and naval personnel attached to the Chilean Embassy in Washington.[74] However, the demands of the list presented went far beyond the expectations of the Department of State. Duggan called it "fantastic,"[75] and it evidently angered several Department of State officials whose tempers had been frayed by the negotiations with Chile. The list included the addition of forty-eight 40-mm. anti-aircraft guns instead of the twenty 27-mm. guns originally specified, fifty more 20-mm. anti-aircraft machine guns, eighteen P–43 pursuit planes, eighteen dive bombers, twelve 75-mm. howitzers, twelve motor torpedo boats, and other supplies.[76]

On December 22, 1942, Welles again discussed the situation with Morales and Michels. Rather than a flat refusal, he took a more subtle diplomatic position. He restated the United States position that it would aid Chile in all ways possible if a break took place. In regard to the additional arms request, he said it raised a question that would cause difficulties between the United States and Chile. According to Welles, such an arrangement would foster the "unfounded" interpretation that Chile "was now prepared to break relations with the Axis Powers because of a new bargain struck between the United States and Chile, a bargain furnishing Chile additional quantities of defense material not already contemplated by the government of the United States."[77] The Undersecretary said he felt it would be better for both countries to avoid actions that would give rise to such an interpretation. Of course, this "unfounded interpretation" was precisely the one some Department of State people were already putting on the request. Welles suggested that after the break in relations problems of additional materials could be worked out by military and naval experts of both countries. Ambassador Michels, who frequently had assured Welles of his disagreement with the Chilean Foreign Office's policy of not breaking relations immediately, reminded Morales that the United States had already been continuing to make defense materiel available to Chile without an agreement, so Chile could certainly trust the United States to carry out its word. Minister Morales expressed satisfaction, and Michels mentioned January 15 (the anniversary of the Rio Conference) as an appropriate date to break relations. Welles was not pleased by the delay and suggested it be done within the next two or three weeks. Actually, the time involved was not much since January 15 was only 24 days away. The Minister said that he would report to

Santiago that Washington had been understanding of Chile's desire to join the Allies and that he would emphasize that no pressure was applied.

Immediately prior to the break Chile continued to make requests for the furnishing of some military aid in advance of the severing of relations.[78] One factor which cast some doubt upon the validity of the need for the equipment was the extremely slow utilization of the anti-aircraft batteries which had been sent several months previously.[79] Also, it was felt that the Chilean Navy was not making maximum use of its equipment, part of which had been furnished by the United States.[80]

The slowness in using available materiel raises another question: Was fear of an attack by Japan actually a reason for Chile's reluctance to break relations? As has been expressed above, there is serious doubt that the Axis would have even considered an attack and also doubt as to whether Chile's diplomatic stance would have made any difference one way or the other *if* an attack had been possible and desirable for Japan. If the other countries of Latin America had refrained from breaking relations, then an attack on Chile might have served as an example of what happens to countries that break relations with the Axis. Under the circumstances, however, if an attack was going to come in order to demonstrate to Chile the disadvantages of breaking relations, it should have been on a country such as Peru which had been strongly anti-Axis.

Regardless of this, there apparently was a significant fear on the part of many Chileans that an attack might come. It is easy for a citizen to see his country somehow as the key to everything else. Certainly the Chilean coast lacked effective defenses. The fact that the *Tolten* could be sunk near New York City made Chile's 3,000-mile coastline appear impossible to defend.[81] Part of this fear may have grown out of the fact that the government used its vulnerability as one of several reasons for not breaking relations, and in the process of justifying the policy, Ríos may have managed to oversell the danger. Thus Santiago could, during the latter stages of the negotiations over the break, claim that Chilean public opinion would not accept the break easily due to the fear of an attack. While this *might* have been an accurate representation of Chilean public opinion, the responsibility for the fear rested partly with the government.

But what did the government believe? There are indications that it did actually fear such an attack. For example, late in July of 1942, when Ríos was apparently seriously considering the break, he asked the United States for promises of economic assistance in case of military attack. He feared that assaults on the Chilean mining industry could throw 100,000 workers off the job and he wanted financial help to see Chile through the difficulties created by this unemployment.[82] Of course this, and other such incidents, could have been simply ploys to emphasize to Washington how much Chile needed weapons. President Roosevelt and the Department of State on several occasions attempted to soothe Chile with promises of protection,[83] but their guarantees never seemed to have a major impact on Chilean policy. Possibly this was because Chile doubted whether the United States actually had the power to extend protection so far into the southern hemisphere— a doubt that was shared by some military experts in Washington.

Another reason sometimes given for Chile's cautiousness on the question of breaking diplomatic relations with the Axis Powers was that it expected, or feared, an Axis victory in the war. A memo prepared by a member of the Santiago Embassy staff in April of 1942 argued that the strongest motive behind Chile's reluctance was the "fact that Chile has not yet decided who will win the war."[84] Key to this argument is the idea that the United States, *assuming the war ended in a stalemate*, would be more understanding of Chile if she did not break relations. Of course, if Germany won the war and dominated continental Europe, Chile would certainly be in a good position to trade with her. Chile had had a large amount of trade with Germany prior to the war, and policymakers in Santiago, remembering the tremendous depression which struck the country after World War I, were very conscious during World War II that Chile needed to take steps to protect herself after the peace was made.

Did Chilean opinionmakers actually believe the Axis might win? The evidence would suggest that there was a belief in the eventual victory, or at least a stalemate, among important Chilean circles. There are numerous statements suggesting that Foreign Minister Barros Jarpa particularly was not convinced that the Allies would eventually win.[85] Supposedly, the Chilean Ambassador to Berlin was confident of a German victory on the Russian front, as were many people in Germany at the time. This information may have helped to shape the Foreign Minister's thinking.[86] When Ambassador Michels returned to Washington after visiting Santiago in mid-1942 he reported that President Ríos was misinformed about a number of questions, including the world situation. According to Michels, he spent some time trying to convince Ríos that the Allies would win.[87] It was pointed out in the Department of State, perhaps unfairly, that Ríos's interest in visiting Washington coincided with United States naval victories in the Pacific.[88] It does not seem illogical, when one reviews the first year of United States involvement in the war, that an observer might have been unsure of the ultimate Allied victory. It was not until November of 1942 that the Allies landed in their sweep against North African ports. November was also the time of the deepest German penetrations into Russia. Certainly the military effort against Japan was proceeding with "agonizing slowness" in 1942–1943.[89] Ríos viewed his responsibilities as being to protect the interests of Chile, and aligning the nation with the losing oido in a world war certainly would not have been a wise course of action.

The unwillingness of the United States to make economic concessions to Chile in connection with the severing of relations, plus the form the negotiations took, was another reason for delay in breaking diplomatic ties with the Axis. During the Rio meeting there had been some efforts by Chile to gain economic advantages in return for cooperating with the other American republics. There can be no doubt that Chile and the United States looked upon this situation from completely different points of view, thereby leading to confusion. The Chileans felt that such concessions, besides being Chile's just and long-overdue compensation, would be necessary to convince public opinion that Chile's action (which might precipitate an attack by Japan) was worth the risk.[90] However, from the point of view of the United States, including those diplomats who were willing to make the concession, the Chilean position seemed to be one of trying to make a profit from an international catastrophe. In April the Second Secretary of the United States Embassy in Santiago clearly stated the case for economic concessions:

> The present government is headed by an individual who prides himself on his business acumen. A good business deal would appeal to him. If we could present concrete proposals, such as assurances for some years to come against the loss of European markets which Chile has suffered through the war; if we could convince him that Chile would remain as prosperous as is conceivably possible in a chaotic world, then, I feel convinced, Señor Juan Antonio Ríos would willingly furnish the leadership required to conduct Chile toward complete cooperation with the United States.[91]

Ambassador Bowers also seemed willing to make significant economic concessions but only "as part of an over-all settlement of outstanding problems, notably the taking by Chile of a clear-cut position on the war issue in support of the United Nations."[92] In other words, he opposed aid designed simply to shape public opinion or to influence Chile's President unless there was a specific quid pro quo.

The clearest Chilean approach on the question of economic concessions came early in June in a conversation between the Chilean Ministers of Finance and Commerce and a member of the United States Embassy staff. Stating that they were also speaking on behalf of the Minister of Development, the Chilean ministers said that they favored breaking relations and were willing to use the sinking of a Chilean ship as an excuse; however, they wanted some economic concessions in principle in order to help influence public opinion. They specifically mentioned, according to the account of the Embassy,

(1) . . . an increase in the copper price, a reasonable increase, and a reasonable guarantee from Santiago for a minimum fixed tonnage and minimum fixed price for a reasonable period after the war;

(2) a reasonable increase in the price of Metals Reserve (a U.S. government agency) purchases . . . and a reasonable assurance of the continuance of this Metals Reserve market for a reasonable period after the war;

(3) a reasonable increase in the price of nitrate and iodine and guarantees regarding the market and price for a reasonable period after the war emergency;

(4) reasonable guarantees to the effect that synthetic ammonia plants now being erected under the defense program will not be used after the war to cut the throat of the nitrate industry of Chile;

(5) a loan of X millions of dollars, but something that might approximate $100,000,000 to do the following things:

(a) Approximately $48,000,000 so that the Chilean government can carry out the scheme by the Minister of Interior to liquidate the arrangement made with the electric company to take over all its holdings to solve problems of locomotion in Santiago and vicinity;

(b) $21,000,000 to carry out electrification of state railroads and thus solve combustion problems of coal and oil;

(c) the remaining X millions to be spent by the government partly on its armed forces, and partly for the material to be bought in the United States so as to keep small industry alive in Chile.[93]

The ministers stated that they realized this proposition might seem like bargaining, but since they assumed that some agreements would be forthcoming from any break, they wanted only the agreement in principle before acting. They also indicated that Foreign Minister Barros Jarpa did not know of the proposal, though they felt President Ríos was ready to go along with the break if Chilean military forces were not asked to leave the country. Given the climate generated by the war, plus an increasing U.S. dissatisfaction with Chile's policy, this proposal was not accepted calmly by Washington. The answering telegram to Bowers stated strongly that the severance of diplomatic relations was "not a subject for bargaining."[94] Hull stated that he felt the severance was at least as much to Chile's advantage as to the United States. He also pointed out that it would be unfair to those who had already broken relations.[95] The Secretary of State assured the Ambassador in Santiago that all possible assistance within the limits of circumstances would be given to Chile should it sever relations; however, he added, "we cannot discuss this assistance until after we know what Chile's policy is to be."[96] Thus the United States was willing to discuss the question of assistance only after the break while Chile wanted to discuss it "in principle" prior to the break. At least some of the United States reluctance may have grown from knowledge that it could not meet Chile's demands, and part of

Chile's position may have stemmed from a realization that this was probably the case and that its bargaining position—if the United States would bargain— was better prior to the break in relations while it still had something to offer.

On June 11 Ambassador Bowers met with President Ríos and Foreign Minister Barros Jarpa. The conference took place because it was felt that the answer to the proposals by the ministers should be handled through regular diplomatic channels.[97] The President began by making the proposition official. The Ambassador then gave the Department of State's reply, which included the accusation that Chile was trying to bargain on the question of breaking relations. The accusation considerably distressed the President, who denied it. He said that perhaps the Finance Minister, in pursuit of his own special problems, had inadvertently tied together the questions of economic aid and breaking relations. He indicated that Chile was taking strong action against the local Nazis as proof of where Chile's heart lay. Bowers took a very tolerant position toward the government of Chile regarding the incident. He suggested in his report on the conference that perhaps the Minister of Finance had told the President of the economic propositions without indicating that the breaking of relations was to be a consideration. Bowers also, after reading Hull's telegram to Ríos and Barros Jarpa (including the statement that the question was "not subject to bargaining") softened the blow considerably by stating that perhaps the language was a little strong since it was not intended to be delivered verbatim and had only been sent for the Ambassador's guidance.[98]

It is interesting to note that in November Welles was willing to go so far as to use a threat in linking the question of economic assistance with Chile's breaking of relations. Discussing Chile's postwar economic situation, he said that "the republics which were now joined together in the war effort had established that kind of indispensable basis for further cooperation in the postwar period which would prove invaluable to all of them."[99] He then went on to say that he regretted that Chile was not taking part in this cooperation "since her participation would be greatly valued and would certainly be, from every standpoint, to the interests of the people of Chile."

Some discussion of economic considerations continued between Chile and the United States during discussions concerning the severing of diplomatic relations. The United States more or less adhered to its position that no specific negotiations should take place until the break actually came about.[100] In retrospect, it seems difficult to fault Chile for trying to protect herself against the loss of European markets if Germany won, or to protect herself from the type of depression that followed World War I.

A few Chileans suggested that by remaining neutral Chile was able to ship its supplies unmolested to the United States and thereby to bolster the Allied effort more than if it broke relations or declared war.[101] The flaw in this argument is that only a very small percent (4 to 8) of Chile's exports to the United States was carried by Chilean merchant vessels.[102]

Although it has been touched upon previously, the question of Chilean public opinion as an influence on Chile's foreign policy demands some dissection. Public opinion is a complex and shifting concept because it is amenable to leadership and influenced by events, or at least influenced by the way events are presented to the public. In Chile in 1942 there were few ways to measure public sentiment. Newspaper editorials are a poor gauge. Public opinion polls were not in use in Chile at the time. Thus, in view of its uncertain and transient nature, perhaps public opinion is not a concept worth considering. However, Ríos several times told friends that the people of Chile would not stand for a break in relations in mid-1942.[103]

Ambassador Bowers, in his later book on Chile, is particularly vehement in stating that the main reason for Chile's slow movement toward the severing of relations was the restraining force of public opinion. At one point he seems to explain the entire question with the comment that the break did not come immediately "because public opinion, which determines the actions of a democracy, was not yet prepared for such a step."[104] Displaying his sympathy for Chile, in which it became almost a virtue not to break relations, he says:

> When, after Pearl Harbor, some American republics, under dictators, broke relations because neither Congress nor public opinion had to be consulted, a portion of the North American press, ignorant of the institutional system of Chile, pointed an accusing finger at her, while praising the dictatorships. These accusations ignored the very essential fact that Chile is a democracy, a government of law, not men, with a Constitution that is respected, and that no one man, by a scratch of the pen, could commit the nation on an international issue. It was clear to me that there would have to be a definite crystallization of public opinion.[105]

There are two basic flaws in Bowers's argument. First, had Ríos decided to break relations there was significant party strength behind him; he would not have been alone. Second, Ríos did almost nothing to crystallize opinion until the last moment—at which point the break was taken relatively calmly.

The United States Embassy in Santiago did attempt to do what it could to shape public opinion toward the war but its means were rather limited. For example, in mid-July of 1942 *La Critica,* one of the few newspapers pleading for a break in relations, was about to fold.[106] Bowers suggested that the paper could perhaps be paid a high fee ($7,200 was the figure mentioned) by some North American newspapers interested in helping the

Department of State in return for some articles on Chile. A difficulty presented itself in that *La Critica* was tied to the Socialist Party; therefore,
financial support would almost be in the form of subsidizing the Socialists.[107] The United States business community in Santiago would have preferred, were a party to be subsidized, that it not be the Socialist Party, regardless of its foreign policy. Despite some backing for the idea of helping
La Critica, it was finally decided to adhere to the standard policy of opposing
ing "direct subsidization or . . . requesting United States companies to contribute directly."[108]

Foreign Minister Barros Jarpa should also be specifically mentioned in
terms of the delay in breaking relations. In examining a topic such as Chile's
resistance, it would be easy to overemphasize the role of the individual and
to neglect the more difficult-to-define pressures coming to bear on his role.
However, besides the pressures which have been mentioned above, there is
evidence to suggest that the Foreign Minister's personal propensities had
some impact on the policy. There are numerous despatches indicating that
Barros Jarpa was more against the break than was the President. Had he
remained as Foreign Minister, which he could not have for political reasons,
the break would certainly have come sooner. Barros Jarpa's supposed belief that Germany might win has already been mentioned. However, even
after Barros Jarpa left office, and at the time Ríos was about to make the
break, he continued to oppose the action, which would seem to suggest
that his position on the issue was not totally the result of the pressures of
his office, although one could explain this in terms of an attempt to justify
his record in office.[109] Barros Jarpa must have felt some bitterness because
he had come to the office as a friend of the United States. Perhaps his reputation put him somewhat on guard against seeming too friendly. In November of 1942, after leaving office, he wrote a letter to the press stating that
history would show that his period in office was the apex of bad United
States diplomacy.[110] Given the competition for this honor, Barros Jarpa's
claim is certainly an exaggeration. Had Ríos been a more vigorous President,
the role of the Foreign Minister would not have been so important, but all
accounts indicate an initial reluctance to become involved in diplomatic de-
cisionmaking. Of course, it is a standard ploy for a President to allow a
Minister to act as a lightning rod for criticism so as to protect himself, and
such may well have been the cautious Ríos's strategy.

Although the substance of the issue involved and the reaction of the
individuals concerned should not be forgotten, the flow of information
between the United States and Chile must also be questioned. Much of what
has been written assumes an understanding of the other country's position,
if not its motives. However, there were a number of times during the
period of stress over the breaking of relations in which the upper circles of

the Chilean government seemed to be indicating that they did not understand how badly the United States wanted Chile to break relations. Assuming this was not a guise, part of the blame for this falls on the shoulders of Ambassador Bowers. After the break actually took place, a high-ranking Department of State official, who had been instrumental in the negotiations over the break, made the following supplemental comment regarding a letter which had been drafted for President Roosevelt praising Bowers for his role in bringing about the break:

> This reply is couched in terms which are perhaps more enthusiastic than are in reality warranted. Unfortunately, the thrust of the matter is that, owing to Claude Bowers' unwillingness after a period of ten years to learn even a few words of Spanish, he has been prevented from talking informally or freely with members of the Chilean government or of the Chilean Congress, and during the very difficult months which have elapsed since the Rio de Janeiro Conference he has consequently been very greatly handicapped in putting over the point of view of this government with regard to Chile's attitude. No one admires his great ability more than I do, but I think it is only just to say that from the complaints made to me by several Chilean senators and congressmen who have visited Washington during the past four or five months, there is a very definite belief on their part that had Bowers taken the trouble to talk frankly to them and to tell them clearly what the views of yourself [Roosevelt] and the Department actually were, a modification of Chile's foreign policy would have taken place many months ago.[111]

It is difficult to judge such a charge because it involves numerous "what ifs." Part of the criticism may stem from the previously mentioned traditional State Department bias against political-appointee ambassadors, a category into which Bowers clearly fell. Reading his memoirs of his years in Chile (he stayed until 1953), one does not get the impression that he found the post particularly demanding, and some Department of State officers undoubtedly resented his privilege of slipping off to relax in the pleasant little communities near the ocean. Certainly Bowers's memoirs tend to de-emphasize the need for Chile to break relations in 1942 and to apologize for Chile's slowness. He may have been correct in casting some doubt regarding how necessary it was to break relations; but the point is that his unwillingness to really press the issue was at variance with the Department of State position.

Of course, Bowers's despatches at the time indicate that he was in support of United States policy. He wrote Roosevelt in April of 1942 that he felt "the time has come to talk rather bluntly to our friends."[112] He wrote a few weeks later, at which point he seemed to believe that Chile was about to break relations, that he felt his "blunt talk" was "having effect."[113] However, as mentioned previously, a month later he attempted to soften Roosevelt's statement that Chile's breaking of relations was not subject to bargaining (after seeing the effect the statement had on Ríos) by remarking that the language was perhaps a little strong since it was more of a guide than a message to be delivered to Chile.[114]

There are also numerous statements that Ríos felt he was doing what the United States wanted during 1942 and that the breaking of relations was not really that important to Washington. In April of 1942 some Department of State officials responded to these rumors by sending a memo to Welles suggesting that Chile did not understand the United States position toward it and that Bowers's instructions should be clarified. Welles rejected the idea with the comment that Santiago did understand, but the following month he was willing to admit that perhaps the government of Chile was confused on the matter.[115] Ríos, according to secondhand accounts, several times later in the year assured people that the United States was satisfied with Chile's position.[116] It may have been that President Ríos did not want to understand the policy, or it may have been, as Bowers suggested, that Barros Jarpa was not furnishing correct information to the President.[117] At other times Carlos Dávila, who had briefly been President during the troubled days of 1932 and had later been Ambassador to the United States, was misrepresenting the viewpoint of Washington.[118] Ríos even supposedly claimed in a conversation with another Chilean, that Ambassador Michels felt the United States approved of Chile's position.[119] This seems particularly difficult to believe because in his relations in Washington Michels gave the impression of strongly urging the break. On September 1 Michels went so far as to tell Welles that if the break did not come he would immediately resign.[120] This statement came more than four months before the break, but from that point on it was reasonably assured that the severing of relations would take place and the Department of State concentrated on hurrying the process as much as possible.

In a discussion of the efficiency of the lines of communication between Chile and the United States, it is well to mention that the extreme friendliness which Ambassador Michels showed the Department of State may also have been misleading or dysfunctional. It is difficult to believe that if Michels had been accurately reporting the degree of comfort he was giving the U.S. Department of State, he would have been retained as Ambassador. If the policy was *not* to break relations, either he was not informed of it or he did not choose to relay the message very forcefully to Washington. Of course, by being agreeable, he made his job easier. On the other end of the line, Bowers's attempts to be reasonably pleasant in delivering an unwelcome demand, besides his lack of language competency, served to soften the United States position. President Ríos may have expected that if the Colossus of the North actually wanted a break in relations it would speak in a harsh and commanding voice. When the message did not come in that style, it took a while for Ríos to realize the situation. Thus one finds explanations for the comments about Santiago not understanding the position of the United States, and for the comments of Ríos that Chile was willing to do whatever the United States wanted it to do. For example, late in July of 1942 Ríos stated through Ambassador Michels that Chile would cooperate fully with the United States and would take such action as the United States felt necessary for hemispheric defense.[121]

The point is not that Bowers was incompetent. He may simply have been the right man in the right place at the wrong time. Then in his early sixties, Bowers had led a long and active life. He had hoped "for a period of rest and relaxation . . . in an atmosphere of serenity amidst the beauty of Chile" when he was appointed.[122] Instead, he was thrust into an extremely delicate diplomatic situation. It should be noted that Bowers's (or his staff's) analysis of the Chilean political situation was evenhanded, and he certainly did receive some unjust criticism. For example, at one point he was criticized within the Department of State for not making the necessary contacts with the Chilean right,[123] while later he was criticized because the Socialists and Radicals felt they didn't have any contact with the American Embassy.[124] From reading his memoirs one gets the impression that he did have a personal friendship with Alessandri and Barros Jarpa, but in both cases after they had left office.

So part of the analysis suggests that Bowers had become overly sympathetic toward the Chilean case. This is not an uncommon situation among diplomats;[125] it does allow them to soften conflicting situations if they can always bring the host government good tidings. But in the case of Bowers, he may have been "too friendly" and not sufficiently ready to push Washington's case and thereby have impeded one channel of communication between the two countries.

The figure of Juan Antonio Ríos, President of Chile from April of 1942 until his death in office in 1946, also must be discussed. An austere, personally conservative man, his own reticence seemed to carry over into his politics. His upper-class background was hardly conducive to any position other than the preservation of the status quo. Although within the Radical Party, he was in no way radical. Certainly the party as a whole was not extremist and Ríos stood clearly in the conservative wing of the party. To the outside observer, his political approach was largely indistinguishable from the Conservatives and Liberals. His Cabinet did contain some Socialists and representatives of other parties, but there was never any doubt that he had the last voice in any important matter.

The President was inexperienced in foreign relations. He had risen to power through his astute playing of the game of Chilean politics, and it may well be that the quid pro quo nature of bargaining in the domestic

political arena led Ríos into some of the international diplomatic misunderstandings that plagued his administration. One of these misunderstandings
was the invitation to visit Washington which came from Roosevelt during a
talk with Ambassador Michels and which may have been somewhat less than
concrete when originally mentioned.[126] Welles did not learn of it until after
it was made, but Ríos was quick to accept. In view of Chile's unwillingness
to break relations, the proposed visit presented a particularly difficult series
of problems in Washington regarding how warmly Ríos should be received.
From Chile's point of view it may have been that Ríos felt this was an opportunity to directly plead his case with Roosevelt.[127] The Department of
State, however, apparently assumed that Chile would break relations with
the Axis before President Ríos arrived in Washington.[128] Ríos, on the other
hand, wanted to go without advance commitments.[129]

With the trip set for late October, 1942, the Department of State continued to try to convince Chile that the break should be made before Ríos
left. Its argument was that if the President of Chile broke relations after
the visit, the Axis propagandists and the opponents of the President would
say that the step had been taken due to pressure from the United States
government.[130] It also pointed out that since this would be the first time
that a Chilean President had visited the United States it was important that
he receive a friendly reception, but, if Chile still had not broken relations
when he arrived, the general public's reception was likely to be hostile.[131]
The argument made by Barros Jarpa opposing the break in advance of the
trip was that the President would be able to state upon his return that, after
visiting the United States and the other Latin American countries in which
he was planning on stopping, he found a consensus in favor of the break
and therefore was taking the step in the name of inter-American cooperation.[132] Ríos was also planning to bring a number of economic advisers
with him, thereby giving credibility to the story that Chile would make a
strong effort to obtain economic concessions during the visit.[133] Welles was
emphatic in informing Bowers that the only change in policy toward Chile
that would be forthcoming as a result of a break in relations with the Axis
would be in the area of providing more armaments and possibly some economic assistance in the "unlikely event" that an Axis attack on the Chilean
mines would cause substantial unemployment.[134]

Evidently, partially in response to the ongoing process of events in Argentina, but also as a result of a fear that Ríos's visit would be interpreted
as support for Chile's foreign policy, Undersecretary of State Welles attempted
to make it clear prior to the visit that the United States disapproved of Argentina's and Chile's refusal to break relations with the Axis. His vehicle was
a speech to the Twenty-ninth National Foreign Trade Convention in Boston
on October 8, 1942. Although such papers as the *New York Times* did not

emphasize the Undersecretary's criticism, his words aroused strong feelings in Buenos Aires and Santiago and apparently at home with Cordell Hull.[135] The specific portion in question was:

It is true that the remaining two [American] republics of the 21 have still refrained from carrying out the unanimous recommendations of the Inter-American Conference of Rio de Janeiro . . . that all of the Americas sever all relations with the Axis, and are still permitting their territory to be utilized by the officials and the subversive agents of the Axis as a base for hostile activities against their neighbors. As a result of the reports on Allied ship movements sent by these agents, Brazilian, Cuban, Mexican, Colombian, Dominican, Uruguayan, Argentine, Chilean, Panamanian, and United States ships have been sunk without warning while plying between the American republics, and as a result many nationals of these countries have lost their lives within the waters of the western hemisphere. But I cannot believe that these two republics will continue long to permit their brothers and neighbors of the Americas, engaged as they are in a life-and-death struggle to preserve the liberties and the integrity of the New World, to be stabbed in the back by the Axis and emissaries operating in the territory and under the free institutions of these two republics of the western hemisphere.[136]

To United States diplomats in Santiago the remarks came at an inopportune time because the Embassy had just been cheered by the fact that the Chilean government had arrested three German spies reputed to be of some importance and had also denied use of codes to Axis missions in their communications. There also had been several assurances supposedly given by Ríos that he would break relations immediately upon returning from Washington.[137] Although Bowers had great respect for Welles, some irritation over the Undersecretary's speech shows through in the Ambassador's memoirs of Chile.[138]

The day after the speech the Chilean government issued an official statement, signed by Barros Jarpa, which declared that the Welles speech departed from all diplomatic practices. It stated:

A few days ago we received from other American authorities words of understanding and respect for the collaboration which Chile is rendering to the United States' war effort by sending large quantities of essential strategic materials. The very invitation of President Roosevelt to His Excellency President Ríos to visit that country was formulated as evidence of confidence in the friendly disposition of the government of Chile and accepted in demonstration of the sincerity of our intentions.[139]

The statement went on to deny Chilean responsibility for any sinking of Allied ships and concluded that the speech "offends the dignity" of Chile.

On October 10, amid rumors that Ríos would cancel the visit, Ambassador Michels went with Undersecretary Welles to visit President Roosevelt. The Ambassador read a brief message protesting the Boston address and asking for a "clarification" of the remarks. He concluded by asking if Ríos's visit would not be regarded as "inopportune" at the present time.[140] Roosevelt stressed four points in his reply: The address contained no accusation that Chile was assisting or sponsoring the activities of Axis agents; the facts set forth were unfortunate but true; he believed the visit of Ríos to be of the highest importance; and he hoped that Ríos would come as planned.[141]

Nonetheless, on October 11 President Ríos notified Roosevelt that he had decided to cancel the visit. He stated that he found it a "regrettable necessity" that he could not visit because of "the last official information released in the United States concerning the international position of my country which has created an unfavorable atmosphere."[142] He assured Roosevelt that Chile would "continue cooperating . . . in the defense of the continent." Roosevelt's official reply stated that he was "sorry" to learn of the decision and expressed a "deep personal regret in not having the opportunity of meeting and knowing you personally." He also stated that he hoped the Chilean President would "come to Washington a little later and that I can consider your visit" as merely postponed.[143]

Although the entire misunderstanding (or dispute) originated in the deadlock over Chile's refusal to break diplomatic relations with the Axis Powers, the issue of the controversy soon came to center on whether or not Chile was taking sufficient anti-Axis actions, not on whether relations would be broken. This grew from Chile's claim that the United States had never told it of any information that activities taking place in Chile were resulting in the sinking of ships. In terms of the realities of the situation as pointed out earlier, the interests of the United States lay more in the area of cracking down on Axis activities than on whether Chile-Axis relations were continued.

As early as April the United States was taking substantial steps to help Chile take action against suspected Axis maneuvers. In that month the United States sent radio monitoring equipment to Chile to help track down some clandestine broadcasting which was reported.[144] Barros Jarpa told Bowers in mid-May that he hoped to take drastic action to wipe out all Nazi agents and propagandists in Chile and that the government was investigating them at the time.[145] On June 30 Bowers presented Barros Jarpa a long memo prepared in Washington concerning espionage activities in Chile.[146] The report listed eighteen individuals accused of being Nazi espionage agents and said that they were transmitting to Germany such information as:

(1) boat arrivals and departures from ports on the West Coast of South America;

(2) information on the activities of the United States government in connection with military and other aid furnished to the countries on the West Coast of South America;

(3) information relating to the exports of the United States;

(4) information on defense measures taken by Latin American countries;

(5) general information from the United States; and

(6) political information, chiefly pertaining to Chile.[147]

The information was received, according to the report, from other Axis agents operating in Argentina, Colombia, Ecuador, Guatemala, Mexico, Nicaragua, Peru, Venezuela, and the United States. Why an agent in Argentina would transmit information to Chile must cause some suspicion. The report also contained information on the formation in Chile of a unit responsible for sabotage which received its direction from the High Command of the German Army. The report implicated some German commercial firms and members of the German Embassy.

Since early in 1942 the Department of State had been making efforts to close down channels of communication (particularly in code) between Germany and South America.[148] There were numerous legal problems connected with the efforts since there was substantial European ownership, including some German and Italian, in the companies handling the communications. Most of the measures the United States pressed for had been approved in resolutions at the Rio conference but both Chile and Argentina refrained from complete cooperation. However, Chile did show a slow, but perceptible, movement toward cooperation. On June 22, 1942, Foreign Minister Barros Jarpa called on Ambassador Bowers and said that he planned to inform the missions of Germany, Italy and Japan that they could no longer communicate with their governments in code. He indicated that this action would lead to a controversy resulting in the break in relations desired by the United States.[149] The Foreign Minister expressed the hope that the United States would accept this action as proof of Chile's intention of breaking relations. Bowers was cheered by the conversation and offered the opinion that the breaking of relations could probably be expected "very soon."[150]

A few days later Bowers presented the above-mentioned memo on subversive activities. During July the Ambassador, under Department of State orders, continued to encourage Chile to cut off all communications from Chile to Axis territories.[151] This position was backed by the presentation of translations of telegrams intercepted from the German Embassy transmitted over regular telecommunications circuits. These contained what the United States felt to be proof of subversive activities by the German Ambassador and his staff. In mid-August of 1942 Chile cracked down on some types of messages in code but the step was a small and disappointing one from the point of view of the State Department.[152] Early in September, in a personal interview with Ríos, Ambassador Bowers reiterated the unhappiness of Washington with Chile's reluctance to cut communication channels with the Axis. The Ambassador pointed out that, according to United States figures, the German Embassy's wires had increased 216 percent since 1941 and that this seemed particularly significant in view of the fact that commerce had been cut.[153] Bowers again presented copies of intercepted telegrams. The President asked the Ambassador if he had shown these to Barros Jarpa and, according to Bowers, expressed "astonishment" when told that he had.[154] The interview may suggest that either Ríos did not want to know what the situation was vis-à-vis telecommunications or that Barros Jarpa had not been informing him of the situation. However, there is a third alternative: perhaps Ríos was simply stalling. In the same despatch reporting this conversation Bowers also relayed the fact that the Chilean Minister of Commerce and Supplies had told Bowers that Barros Jarpa claimed he had proposed cutting off use of codes by Axis embassies and that Bowers had opposed it[155]—a statement which, if Barros Jarpa actually made it, was a complete distortion of the situation, but it also could have been an effort to discredit the Chilean Foreign Minister by a fellow member of the government.

After much effort, Transradio Chilena, which was primarily a British company, decided on October 8, 1942, to refuse to transmit any messages in code to or from any non-American country.[156] This was the situation at the time Welles gave his speech in Boston. Ríos later explained to Bowers, evidently to Bowers's satisfaction, that the reason for the slow action on the espionage memo of June 30 was that when Ríos came to the presidency he found the investigatory agencies of the government in disorder.[157] Therefore, he claimed, it took time to check out the accusations made by the United States and that arrests were about to take place—and did take place within three days—when Welles made his speech.

The question of the degree to which administrative difficulties were responsible for Chile's failure to enforce various measures against possible enemy influences, as opposed to an unwillingness to take the measures, continued throughout the period under question. It may be true that Chile was not prepared to investigate the situation, but it also may be that the warm friendship which Bowers later developed for Barros Jarpa clouds his memoirs. At the time, Bowers did all he could to encourage the removal of the Foreign Minister, however, his power to do this was strictly circumscribed, and it often seemed as though he spent more effort trying to keep it from appearing that the United States was pressuring Chile in this direction than he spent actually pressuring.

With Washington clearly unhappy with Barros Jarpa and the Socialist Party having passed a resolution specifically calling for his dismissal, the entire Chilean Cabinet resigned in order to give Ríos a chance to start with clean hands in the area of foreign policy and elsewhere. Ríos decided at this point that it might be well to find a foreign minister without party connections and he picked Joaquín Fernández y Fernández, then Ambassador to Uruguay. Fernández was not identified with any party and had been Chile's representative on the Political Defense Committee in Montevideo, a role in which he had not distinguished himself by his support of U.S. proposals although he doubtless was simply following the directives of his Foreign Office. Ríos's new Cabinet had five Radicals, three Socialists, one Liberal, one Democrat, and three non-partisan representatives. Generally, it seemed to be more pro-Allied in its composition; although the old Cabinet, if left to an uninfluenced vote, probably would have voted to break relations. After this point Ríos seemed to take much more control in the area of international relations. Fernández stayed in the background. Soon after returning to Santiago he took a much more militantly pro-Allied position, which helped to soothe Department of State worries that had arisen over his actions as a member of the Committee on Political Defense. After the intense political involvement and brilliance of Rossetti and the charming stubbornness of Barros Jarpa, Fernández, who was almost a technician, was a great change.

During 1942 when most of the public attention was devoted to the question of whether (and when) Chile would break its diplomatic relations with the Axis, there were at least two other major complications in relations between the United States and Chile: the proclaimed list, and the shortage of imports, particularly gasoline. From the first month of 1942 onward, the United States warned Chile that gasoline restrictions would be necessary. The problem did not stem so much from a shortage of oil in the United States, although this was a problem, as it did from a shortage of tankers to bring the oil to the countries of South America. However, the beginning of restrictions caused ill feeling in Chile when rumors began to spread that similar restrictions were not being applied in the United States.[158]

In mid-May of 1942 Ambassador Bowers issued a declaration intended to correct the idea that Chile was being asked to suffer gasoline shortages while none existed in the United States. This did not improve the situation noticeably, and in mid-June Bowers informed the Department of State that

> from the outset the Chilean government has shown unwillingness to face the facts regarding the petroleum situation. Instead of accepting the evident necessity for a sharp reduction in normal consumption and making an honest effort to meet our ideas, it has tried, through bargaining tactics, to get just as much as possible. . . . Furthermore, the government has done nothing to correct the false impression in the midst of the

public resulting from misleading and inaccurate press stories that there is not a shortage even of tankers sufficient to justify the present curtailment of supplies and consequently that the United States is merely exerting pressure on Chile.[159]

An announcement of a further reduction less than three weeks later fell "like a bombshell" in Chile and brought about a special Cabinet meeting.[160] Bowers appealed for more publicity on the merits of the United States position but stated that it was well known in Chile that Peru, Argentina, Colombia, and Venezuela were not being forced to ration.[161] Although Bowers sided with Chile in the sense of believing that the restrictions were too severe, he was also distressed about the continued unwillingness of Chile to make any significant cutbacks. In mid-August of 1942 he expressed the opinion that the latest Chilean request for gasoline included a total figure that was "entirely arbitrary and is evidently put forward as a trading proposition." He also reported that there was little evidence of gasoline rationing in Chile.[162]

In pleading the case for a higher Chilean quota, Bowers made two major points. The first, which was put forth while Ríos was still planning to visit Washington, was that a drastic cut "at this stage of our political negotiations" could be harmful.[163] The second point was that, according to the estimates of the Embassy, in 1941 (the control year) non-war-essential consumption of petroleum was only 23.7 percent of Chile's total consumption, while the Department of State was asking for a figure equal to 40 percent of Chile's total consumption in 1941.[164] In his reply, Hull pointed out that the Department's planning was based on fulfilling war-essential requirements plus 40 percent of the 1941 consumption.[165] Bowers again pleaded that supplying at a level less than 60 percent of the 1941 figure, besides the war-essential figure, would be "disastrous" to the Chilean economy.[166] Bowers also pointed out, in mid-September, that

> just at this critical juncture, with lines closely drawn here, we are already creating the impression of bringing pressure in the case of nitrate and copper, and it certainly seems unwise to me knowingly to strike a disastrous blow at Chile's economy that may easily turn public opinion bitterly against us in the midst of difficult negotiations that are making progress. I am so positive that I am correct that I cannot assume the responsibility without again making clear to the Department the dangerous political reactions that would follow the disruption of the Chilean economy.[167]

In early October of 1942 the Department did delay the date of the quota reductions so as to avoid the crisis that would have resulted from Chile's unwillingness to begin a new level of restrictions until the last moment.[168] The entire situation was quite complex, and it is doubtful—in view of some of the suggestions put forth by Chile—that U.S. policy was actually understood by Chilean high officials for the first several months. The United States hoped to supply all "war-essential" needs, a figure Washington felt to be unusually high in the case of Chile.[169] Thus, with the increased production due to the wartime demands for copper and nitrates, Chile was, according to the Department of State, receiving *total* deliveries that were actually at a rate above the 1941 figure.[170] This total figure was, however, "a somewhat irrelevant figure" in the words of Emilio G. Collado, the Special Assistant to the Undersecretary of State specializing in economic problems. Another difficulty was the fact that there were differences in the figures concerning the oil stocks on hand.[171] The United States was trying to keep the gasoline situation, which it said was strictly dependent on the amount of shipping available, outside the realm of diplomatic or political bargaining, but both Ríos[172] and Barros Jarpa[173] brought pressure to bear on Bowers. In retrospect, it seems difficult to believe that the Department of State felt it could prevent this matter from becoming a political question.

Chile also made some efforts to obtain additional shipping on her own in order to increase her gasoline supplies. The problem with this approach was that the Latin American states were pooling their shipping resources, plus what the United States could spare, and then each country was to have a percentage of that pool. Any additional shipping was supposed to become part of the pool, an arrangement which did not encourage countries to seek extra shipping since the amount of benefit they would derive was small. If Chile had left the pool, the shortage of available shipping tankers probably would have cut the supply even further because of the small size of the Chilean fleet and the lack of private shipping outside the pool. Meanwhile, Bowers was again pointing out on October 30 (three weeks after Welles's speech and during the period of Cabinet reorganization in Chile) that "extremely serious political and social disturbances may develop" unless the petroleum situation was improved. The Ambassador reported that enemies of the United States "are effectively exploiting the general discontent and have been successful in creating the belief . . . that the United States is trying to force Chile's hand by withholding petroleum supplies."[174] The situation was not "solved" during 1942, but a special State Department representative who was an expert on oil distribution did fly to Chile and did manage to find a working arrangement in late November of 1942.[175]

As it did for all the United States embassies in Latin America, the proclaimed list caused Bowers and his staff endless problems. Under the system arranged in Washington the United States refused to deal with private companies which it felt to have ties with Germany, Italy, or Japan. The Latin American countries had agreed to participate in the system at the Rio conference, although it is doubtful that they realized the problems that would issue from the measure. In some ways Chile was the most reticent of Latin American countries in carrying out these measures (although Argentina was more blatant in its refusal). A Department of State despatch of August 1942 commented that

> alone among the American republics Chile has made no move to curb within her borders trading and financial transactions harmful to hemispheric interests or to prevent commercial intercourse with the Axis Powers, and at times has taken steps affirmatively beneficial to the enemies of the other American republics.[176]

In theory, the government of Chile had instructed its agents to avoid transactions with firms on the blacklist, but there was little evidence that this was being observed[177] and the United States was not anxious to have Chile involved in the determination of who would and would not be on the proclaimed list.

THE ACTUAL BREAK

As for the actual break in relations, as the discussion above indicates, there were several false starts. Ambassador Michels evidently returned from his July 1942 visit to Santiago and talks with Ríos assured that the break would come soon. According to Michels, his final conversation with Ríos included a statement that the United States government should be told that Chile would be prepared to break diplomatic relations with the Axis if the United States felt this was desirable.[178] Ríos, however, linked the offer to the arrival of more military materiel and economic support in case of a disruption of industry by an armed attack. From this point until the scheduled October trip of Ríos there was optimism that the trip would bring forth the desired severing of relations. This did not come about, although the events did manage to bring an end to Barros Jarpa's term as Foreign Minister.

The Department of State, stung by the claim Chile made after Welles's speech that it had not been given any notice that dangerous subversive activities were going on in Chile, began to consider late in October the idea of publishing the memo on Axis subversives in Chile that it had given the Chilean Foreign Minister on June 30.[179] This could have been handled by leaking it to the press in Washington without mentioning the source. The argument in favor of this course of action was that it would prove that the United States had warned Chile previously and would also help alert Chilean public opinion to the dangers of not cracking down on possible subversives. The release could be timed for a special session of the Chilean Congress which was scheduled for November 15. Bowers was uneasy about the idea.[180] He warned that "the apparent spirit" in which the memo was released was important. If it seemed primarily to be an indictment of the Chilean government for its failures, Bowers argued, the effect could be very bad, particularly since the Ambassador felt the government was finally beginning to take some actions against Axis espionage.

Washington was not convinced that the actions being taken in Chile were going to be effective but it did realize that the release of the document was fraught with dangers of unleashing anti-Yankee sentiment.[181] Thus the decision was made to have the Montevideo-based Emergency Advisory Committee for Political Defense release the contents of the memorandum and thereby relieve the United States of some of the responsibility.[182] Although the Chilean and Argentine representatives on the Committee opposed the plan, the Chairman of the Committee managed to get a resolution passed favoring publication of the document.[183] When the Chilean press published the communication, with much publicity a number of papers were critical, particularly those that opposed a Chile-Axis break and that interpreted the action as indiscreet.[184]

The Minister of the Interior issued a long statement following publication of the U.S. note.[185] The statement outlined the extent to which the government of Chile had arrested, or was arresting, individuals whose names were in the memo. That statement also indicated that the U.S. memo had forced the government to rush its actions before the Chilean investigators had really terminated their investigations.[186]

As a result of what some saw as Chilean public opinion moving slowly toward favoring a break in relations,[187] Ríos re-opened the proposal of his making a trip to Washington. Bowers felt that the Chilean President's pledge to break relations solved any problem.[188] Welles, however, insisted that the break should take place prior to the trip. The Undersecretary wrote Bowers that, although the invitation to Ríos still stood, the President of Chile would have to be prepared to accept the fact that popular and press reception would be questionable if Ríos "were to take advantage of President Roosevelt's invitation before carrying out the official and authoritative commitment as a result of which that invitation was extended."[189]

Under the circumstances, Ríos's interest in making the trip waned, but in December he did send his young Minister of Interior, Raúl Morales Beltrami, to help explain Chile's position and to make some final arrangements relating to the forthcoming break. In his meeting with President Roosevelt on December 17 Morales renewed the Chilean demands for more protection. There is a revealing statement in a memo he presented the President. The document closed by pointing out that Chile had to reach the decision to break relations "in the absence of the dramatic atmosphere of the conflict, stimulating it within abstract principles, without acts of war to precipitate it."[190] In conversations with Welles he stated that Chile would like a specific pretext for the break. A possibility was the presentation of specific evidence that Axis espionage in Chile had led to the sinking of vessels.[191] It was also in these talks that Morales presented the above-mentioned list of weaponry, a list that one State Department official termed "fantastic and totally out of the question."[192] Morales was provided with a specific statement showing that, at least in the eyes of the United States, American ships sailing from Chile had been sunk in the Caribbean due to clandestine radio messages sent by Axis agents in Chile.[193] The desire for a specific action that would justify a break in relations emphasizes the extent to which Chilean politics had allowed the question of breaking relations to reach dead center. It was also during this visit that Welles countered Morales's request for arms with the opposite argument: such a large flow would give rise to the interpretation, "quite unfounded," of a bargain with the United States.[194]

On January 20, 1943, after some compromises by the United States in terms of guarantees of protection and vague promises of the settlement of some other questions *after* the break, President Ríos honored his word and broke relations with the Axis. The Chilean government kept Bowers closely informed of the situation. A week and a half prior to the break former President Alessandri publicly urged that Chile not sever its ties, a position also evidently backed by Ibáñez and Barros Jarpa,[195] although all protested their friendship for the United States. Gustavo Ross spoke out in favor of the break shortly before the action was taken.[196] Foreign Minister Fernández presented the policy to the Senate—although the decision was constitutionally the President's—where it passed by 30 votes to 10, with two abstentions. There was some debate regarding the possibility of "suspending" relations rather than breaking them but this was not accepted.[197] Limited opposition came from the parties of the right, the Liberals and the Conservatives.

On the evening of January 20, President Ríos broadcast the news to his nation that diplomatic relations had been broken with the Axis Powers. He declared that the action was a moral obligation and he defended the legality of not breaking relations previously.[198] In an obvious attempt to placate the many Germans and Italians and their descendants who lived in Chile, he emphasized that the action was not aimed at the peoples of the Axis countries but at their governments.

So the gesture the United States wanted Chile to make was made. There was only limited criticism in Chile of the action, and it did not bring the feared Axis attack upon the country's often deserted shoreline. However, as will be seen neither did it bring the results the Department of State had hoped for, because the United States had begun to view the break of relations as a panacea for all the problems that existed surrounding Chile's cooperation in the war effort.

Although this narrative has perhaps been excessively detailed in describing the problems connected with the break, there is one final point that deserves some comment. It was difficult to discuss it earlier because it was not evident until the 30-to-10 vote just how ready the Senate was to break relations. With this support, why didn't Ríos do it sooner? Innumerable reasons have been suggested above, but one other factor should be mentioned. It deals with the source of the opposition—the right.

Frequently today one assumes that the United States can get along with dictatorships of the right but not with democracies of the left. However, during the 1930s and 1940s this was not so true, and certainly it was not true in Chile where the situation was, in fact, reversed. Of course the conservative elements were friendly to the United States when profit was involved; but, as Frederick Pike has pointed out in his volume *Chile and the United States, 1880 to 1962*,[199] the rightists in Chile of this period resented the social mobility and equalitarian ideas of the United States. The political ideology of the rightists in Chile was extraordinarily conservative by later standards. While the parties of the left disliked the United States for its "exploitation" of the workers, they did find much admirable in the system of the United States. The criticism of the Communists was muzzled during the war, and the Socialists in Chile were a tame or "responsible" group at the time. Ríos was from the centrist party of the time, the Radicals. In theory, this might seem to put him outside the streams of anti-U.S. or pro-U.S. thinking, but it did not. Ríos was a wealthy businessman and definitely of the Conservative wing of the Radical Party, and in a party as nebulous in ideology as the Radicals, Ríos was able to be quite conservative. His party had a middle but he clearly was not part of it. He did not attempt to "undo" the reforms of Aquirre Cerda but he did nothing to advance them. Those who voted against the break in the Senate were conservative—certainly the group from which Ríos was drawn even though the patronage-hungry Radical Party was his political home. The nationalist spirit of the Conservatives, plus their fear of communism and social change in general, made Chile's participation in the war on any basis other than a moneymaking one distasteful. This is not to say that Ríos shared their distaste for the United States—his almost childlike desire to visit the United States disproves this.[200] But he did identify with the Conservatives and was strongly influenced by their thinking.

THE MOVE AGAINST THE AXIS

As has been pointed out, breaking relations with the Axis was primarily a symbolic act. Unfortunately, it is not always clear that the United States knew this fact in advance. Many in Chile felt the actions already being taken against pro-German elements in the field of preventing espionage and in financial controls were sufficient and that the breaking of relations was merely the final act on a spectrum of action. The Department of State viewed the action as quite the opposite—the *first* act on a spectrum of restrictions against Axis interests. On the day of the break, the Department wired Bowers that when Chile severed relations the Embassy should "follow closely the action of the Chilean Government . . . offering such informal suggestions and assistance as, in your judgment, may be appropriate."[201] It then went on to suggest a number of areas of action: The first was the thorough implementation of the Rio Resolutions, especially in the area of telecommunications, and the Washington Resolutions on economic and financial controls. The communication discussed the problems of repatriation of diplomats, but also mentioned that under "Chile's new relationship" the production of strategic materials "will be of primary importance" and that an anti-sabotage control program should be instigated.

Less than a week later President Ríos advised the Ambassador Bowers that an order had been signed to pick up 200 "enemy agents et cetera." Foreign Minister Fernández at the same time said that Ríos was displeased that the Minister of Interior had not taken action to suppress certain papers. Bowers, a long-time newspaperman, urged that this be done and also urged that Chile freeze Axis credits to be used as compensation against any damage done by enemy nations.[202] The detention of the suspected agents was part of an initial flurry of actions taken in connection with the break in relations.[203] Checking at international points was tightened and there was a suspension of communication facilities with Axis and Axis-controlled territories. Axis news agencies were limited and travel restrictions placed on some Axis nationals. The right to carry firearms was denied Axis nationals and the German Club in Santiago was closed down, as was at least one pro-Axis newspaper. The Japanese Minister and his staff were held incommunicado for a time in their Legation.

After the smoke from this initial series of acts accompanying the break had cleared, however, the United States Embassy became increasingly dissatisfied with the restrictions against Axis nationals. In mid-June Ambassador Bowers reported to the Department of State that "there are no indications that Nazi organizations in Chile have been materially undermined or that the state of morale among German elements has sunk" due to the government's actions or the fact that the war was going against the Axis.[204] German sports groups, for example, continued to function.[205] Typically, Bowers urged that too much pressure not be brought to bear on the Chilean government to increase its restrictions.[206]

Part of the reluctance on the part of the Chilean government to take vigorous actions was of the government's own making. It did not publicize the trials of some of the Nazi Party members who were accused of spying and therefore generated little public pressure to take further steps. Not surprisingly, it soon became evident that the basic policy of the government was to avoid offending any more Chileans than necessary. Washington wanted much tighter controls on the German community in Chile. President Ríos preferred, for reasons of political stability and because he felt the Embassy exaggerated the danger these people presented, to do very little. There was no evidence of extensive involvement of the German community in subversive activities, so from the point of view of Chilean stability it may have been wiser not to provoke the group. Washington went through one period of particular worry early in 1944 over the possibility that "an Axis-inspired revolution" might take place in Chile.[207] This worry was heightened by the coup in Bolivia, and, on the suggestion of Bowers, a United States cruiser was sent to Valparaíso under the guise of a demonstration of North American friendship toward the Chilean government.[208]

Also early in 1944 there was the uncovering of an Axis spy ring in Santiago, complete with contacts outside the country, documents buried on San Cristobal (a hill rising in Santiago which is a major tourist attraction), large sums of money, and forged passports.[209] The Chilean judicial system, despite the urgings of the United States Embassy, and evidently encouraged by Ríos, moved slowly in the case. However, after urging action, the Department of State was then reluctant to provide copies of intercepted messages broadcast from Chile for use in the prosecution of the captured enemy agents.[210] State feared exposing the extent of United States intelligence activities in the country and possibly revealing sources of information. Bowers pointed out that the Santiago newspapers had previously reported the assistance of U.S. intelligence in the discovery of the spy ring and that "it would be hard to find a literate person in Chile so unimaginative as not to believe that we have an intelligence service here in wartime."[211] The Department of State reversed its decision and made some documents available.[212]

The other area of United States demands relating to the Axis involved questions of financial restrictions on the movement of funds held by those sympathetic to the Axis and the general administration of the proclaimed list. In this field the pressure of the United States was considerably less effective than even its feeble successes in the area of espionage, although the reasons for its failures were the same as those for the slowness of the Chilean government in moving against what the United States felt to be Axis espionage threats. Thus in 1943 and 1944 the United States Embassy spent a great deal of effort attempting to get the Chilean government to do things the government was not fully convinced were necessary and which were certain to cause domestic political problems. In fact, the speech in which Ríos announced the interruption of diplomatic relations emphasized the purely diplomatic nature of the action and promised that Germans, Japanese, and Italians would continue to enjoy the legal protections of the Chilean judicial system as long as tranquillity was maintained.

Washington, with some British cooperation, pushed for stricter controls on, or the taking over of, some of the German banking institutions. The Embassy's Counselor for Economic Affairs early in July of 1943 suggested that, as a result of the slowness of the Ríos government, the United States withhold "favors from the present cabinet-administration" so that Washington would "have something substantial in the basket to pass out to a pro–United Nations cabinet" in order to show the appreciation of the United States and also to allow the Cabinet to gain some popularity.[213] Ambassador Bowers opposed the idea because he felt it would take "a fanatically leftist administration" to nationalize the many Axis firms then listed as dangerous or nonessential and that this was not probable.[214] There was registration of almost $25 million of alien property under decrees in mid-July of 1943.[215]

The Department of State was also urging Ambassador Michels to encourage more decisive action from Ríos and promised to assist Chile in case the financial measures harmed her economy.[216] The Department admitted that the actual impact of the measures might not be so great, but emphasized the "psychological" aspects that this would have in Washington among those agencies dealing with Chilean affairs. This constituted a blatant attempt to imply that the rewards for such actions would be worthwhile while avoiding any definite commitment which could be branded as a bribe. The Department was not advocating that all firms on the proclaimed list should be liquidated or subjected to nationalization.[217] The term "inherently bad" was applied to those firms actually owned or controlled by interests in Germany and which Washington hoped to see disbanded. Other firms which had cloaked for Axis firms or those that traded with blacklisted outlets were supposedly placed in other categories.

Besides the destablizing pressures which would have been unleashed against the Ríos government had these measures been vigorously enforced, another important factor is Chile's seeming reluctance to move. The measures had a complexity and severity which the Chilean bureaucracy was simply not capable of handling without considerable effort and pressuring from the President. This difficulty was found in many of the Latin American countries whose support of the Allied cause was much more consistent and outspoken than Chile's. A Department of State survey, made at the end of 1943, of compliance of the Latin American countries with the Rio Resolutions found that there were widespread difficulties and a consistent slowness in the administration of the legislation dealing with the severance of commercial and financial relations with Axis-tainted groups.[218] Brazil, Mexico, Panama, and Peru were said to have adequate legislation and effective administration, although Peru was singled out for its "temporizing and irregularities." Honduras and Uruguay were said to have the necessary legislation but lax administration and inadequate controls. Bolivia and Paraguay were lumped with Chile as having done little to implement the Rio resolution dealing with commerce and finance. Colombia and Venezuela were also having problems, and Argentine performance had been totally inadequate up to that time.

In January of 1944, with the course of the war well turned in favor of the Allies, the President and his Cabinet finally propagated four strong control decrees.[219] The first called for the offices of two German banks (Banco Alemán Transatlántico and Banco Germánico) to be liquidated under the supervision of the Chilean government. The second demanded registration by all persons in Chile who had money, bonds or other assets for, or in the name of, persons in Axis countries or Axis-occupied territories. This decree also prevented the transfer of, or negotiations concerning, these holdings. The other two decrees helped tighten the blacklist considerably. However, these strong measures still were hindered by questions of enforcement and existing loopholes in the laws. The steps taken against the German insurance companies in Chile presented other complications[220] as the "spearhead" Axis firms were moved against.

The problems caused by these maneuvers in terms of work they forced on the United States Embassy were staggering since it was difficult to apply the general rules issuing from Washington to specific proclaimed list cases. The government of Chile was more interested in pleasing the United States without bothering Chileans than in worrying about possible subversion. By August of 1944, at which point the Santiago government was finally beginning to put many of the decrees into effect, Washington was already preparing to dismantle the blacklist operations on the correct premise that the war was almost over in Europe. In September of 1944 the liquidation of the German banks was still not complete.[221]

Thus the United States policy in the months following the January 1943 break in relations was to press for Chilean actions against possible spies and German business interests. On the other side, the Chilean policy was to press for military goods and economic aid or guarantees of protection for the Chilean economy.

Although the United States policy on supplying weapons to foreign countries during World War II centered on resistance to Axis encroachments (external and internal), there can be little doubt that Chile's interest in weapons eventually centered on her relations with her neighbors and the general

balance of power in southern South America. One of the reasons given by
the Ríos government in its congressional presentations supporting its foreign
policy was the increasing military power of Peru.[222] There were numerous
rumors circulating in Chile regarding the vast amounts of armaments supposedly
received by Peru. It was widely believed in Chile that Bolivia and Peru were
not eager for Chile to break relations because in the meantime the two traditional enemies of Chile were able to benefit disproportionately from lend-
lease supplies.[223] Again late in 1943, in a conversation with Bowers, President
Ríos raised the specter of Chile as being threatened by her neighbors. He
specifically mentioned Bolivia, Argentina, Paraguay, Uruguay, and Peru, an
unlikely combination for any unified action. Bowers himself feared that the
Nazis were attempting to open a second front in South America which evidently was to be spearheaded by pro-Nazi governments in Bolivia and Argentina.[224]

On March 2, 1943, following the break with the Axis, the long-delayed
lend-lease agreement with Chile was signed. Under the agreement Chile was
to receive about $50 million worth of arms and munitions and was to repay
approximately 30 percent of this. With some exceptions,[225] the limited pro-
Axis sympathies in the Chilean military tapered off considerably after this
agreement and as the war progressed. Since the country was relatively late
in entering into a lend-lease agreement, it was particularly threatened when
the United States, in the autumn of 1943, began to discuss scaling down the
original amounts of lend-lease aid.[226] Although United States war production
had finally reached a level in the spring of 1943 to permit regular arms deliveries, "by that time the fundamental change in the strategic outlook raised
the question of whether or not it was desirable to continue to supply" the
amounts originally contracted under the lend-lease agreements.[227] In June of
1943 the War and State Departments had agreed that arms to Latin America
strictly for defensive purposes were no longer needed. This brought about a
shift in emphasis to materiel for anti-submarine efforts, the preservation of
internal security, training those units from Brazil and Mexico that were
actually going abroad, and the maintenance of existing equipment.[228]

With the Department of State moving in this direction, Chile became increasingly impatient during 1943 over the amounts of lend-lease it was receiving. By the end of the year Ambassador Michels was protesting to Duggan
that, between the slowness of arrival of Chile's supplies and the large amounts
received by Peru, the traditional balance of power on the west coast was
being disturbed.[229] In a second conversation with Duggan and Cecil Lyon
of the Division of the American Republics held on December 30, the
Chilean Ambassador was accompanied by the Chief of the Chilean Military
Mission and the Chief of the Chilean Air Force Commission in Washington.[230]
The Army representative complained that Chile had received only 15 percent

of the agreed-upon material. He said that he hoped the Chilean Army would replace its German equipment with United States equipment, something which the United States also hoped for. The General, in his effort to bolster Chile's case, raised the idea of a possible attack on Chile by Japan, a rather unlikely prospect at that late date.

When the Department of State consulted with military officials in an attempt to speed up the flow of equipment, the opinion expressed in the War Department was that the material being requested had no bearing on the war except to the extent that providing it prevented Chile from being intimidated into aligning with Argentina.[231] Evidently, the Chilean Air Force was particularly unhappy over its inability to get airplanes while the naval authorities in Chile were somewhat more content. Chile continued to play on the suspicions of the United States regarding Argentina. In early February of 1944 General Oscar Escudero, the Minister of Defense and General in Command of the Army, spoke to a United States diplomat and pointed out that Argentina's equipment was much better than Chile's and that his country felt it must prepare to repel outside attack. The General was in a particularly strong position to make these approaches because he had long held an openly pro-Allied position.

In 1944 Chile did begin to receive more lend-lease materials. It reached, in the eyes of the Department of State, a level comparable to the amounts furnished the other American republics that had broken relations but had not declared war.[232] By mid-1944 the lend-lease program had furnished Chile such items as:

    12 attack planes
    123 training planes
    30 liaison planes
    30 light tanks
    50 scout cars
    10 half-tracks
    385 trucks
    36 105-mm. howitzers
    32 anti-aircraft guns
    78 machine guns[233]

Although the Army adhered to the policy during 1944 of cutting lend-lease back as much as possible unless it was contributing directly to the war effort,[234] steady pressure from Santiago caused the flow of materials to Chile to pick up considerably during the second three-month period of 1944.[235] In September 1944 a memo from the Office of American Republics stated the policy that some flow of armament should be continued but "just enough to keep [Chile] quiet until the [military] staff conferences are held."[236] Chile was also pressing for considerable assistance in the improvement of its airfields. This did not particularly appeal to the United States since by mid-1944 it was not felt to be of any particular military advantage and might have been of great benefit to Chilean commercial operators in competition with United States–owned Panagra.[237] However, a request for a naval mission, which was made late in 1944, was honored. This was part of a continuing effort to extend United States influence into Latin American military establishments thus replacing the previous German and Italian interests.

Besides this desire for weapons, Chilean policy toward the United States focused on the South American country's worries about her postwar economic situation. The war had managed to pull her out of the Depression and she worried continually during the conflict about the effect the end of the war might have on her economy. There was ample justification for this concern in view of the disastrous depression Chile experienced following World War I. The economic negotiations moved in two directions: talks regarding continued nitrate purchases, and talks regarding postwar economic assistance from the United States.

The nitrate question was fraught with problems. Factories constructed in the United States during the war were pouring out tons of artificial nitrates at a relatively low cost. Thus the production of natural nitrates did not appear to be a healthy basis on which to rest a considerable portion of a country's economy as the war neared its end. The explosives market was sure to collapse, thereby freeing the production of artificial nitrates for use in the few areas where Chilean nitrates were still being used. Although Chile realized the dangers of not moving away from dependence on nitrate exports, it had few alternatives to their continued production. The United States was aware of what a drastic cut in nitrate purchases could do to the Chilean economy. Discussions in March of 1943 for the fiscal year July 1, 1943, to June 30, 1944, concerning the nitrate trade were held between Department of State officials and members of agencies concerned with nitrate production in the United States.[238] The economic agencies said that under the most favorable (for Chile) of conditions, the United States could import only about 600,000 short tons of nitrates and that the figure might drop to 300,000 tons. The imports during the previous year had been about one million tons and the Department of State wanted to retain this level. In response to this situation, in April the Department of State began to advocate the stockpiling of nitrates if it was felt necessary in order to keep the Chilean economy stable. Part of the justification for this measure was that disruption of the Chilean economy might hinder the flow of copper, and copper was a vital material from Washington's point of view. Also, a store of nitrates might prove valuable if the tide of war should shift against the Allies.[239] However, at this same time elsewhere in the Washington bureaucracy talk was already beginning in terms of converting the defense plants to the production of nitrates for agriculture, an idea that caused considerable consternation within the Department of State.[240]

The Chilean Embassy began its formal pressure for a high level of guaranteed nitrate purchases with a lengthy memo presented on July 10, 1943. It stated that unless the United States purchased 1,000,000 tons during the 1943-44 fiscal year, a serious unemployment problem would result and forecast that unless the same purchase was made during 1944-45, a similar situation would arise. The note reminded the United States that Chile had asked Washington not to construct artificial nitrate plants and had promised to meet the needs of the United States:

> Because of considerations of defense, the construction of plants was begun on a moderate scale, and Chile remained calm because it was declared that such construction would not endanger the natural nitrate sales for agricultural purposes, nor consequently the economy of Chile.[241]

The note reviewed the greatly increased Chilean production for wartime consumption and pointed out that in the past it had provided fertilizers to the United States on a regular basis. The aide-memoire concluded by asking that the United States not assist in the construction of new synthetic nitrogen plants internationally and that it wait until after the war to decide in consultation with Chile the fate of the wartime plants.

In effect, Chile was asking the United States to take a measure that had no economic justification. Nitrates of equal quality could be produced more cheaply in the United States—why should they be purchased in Chile? The dilemma was a classic one: on the one hand, the uncertainties of the international market, and on the other the desire to prop up the Chilean economy. In a sense, the United States owed Chile no debt—it had paid for its nitrates and to continue purchasing them represented a direct subsidy to an inefficient producer. It seems doubtful that the mood of the U.S. Congress was such as to allow the United States to provide direct assistance to the Chilean government; therefore, what would now be called foreign aid could only be supplied by purchasing goods at artificially high prices in order to assist a foreign country. Such purchases made no sense to those agencies which viewed purchases from a strictly economic point of view and thus a dichotomy emerged between these groups and the Department of State, which felt some necessity to keep the Chilean economy healthy. The irony of the situation is that the United States was probably seriously underpricing such goods as copper, but the pressures of the war had so completely jumbled the international trade system that it seemed to operate more on the basis of memories of past prices than on existing patterns of supply and demand—an outgrowth of the necessities of winning the war. Thus an incongruous situation

arose: a foreign country requesting a voice in how the United States managed
a string of domestic nitrate factories.

Less than a week after the delivery of the Chilean note, officials of the
Chilean Nitrate Sales Corporation met with representatives of the Department of State and the Chairman of the War Production Board. The position
of the board was that the figure of 700,000 tons under consideration was
the amount necessary to the United States (actually it was somewhat in-
flated due to the efforts of the Department of State) and that the Board
would not oppose a figure above that. There were, however, serious shipping
problems involved in the question. The Chileans stated that lowering the
figure to 700,000 tons would mean 12,000 to 15,000 people would be out
of work.[242] The following day the Corporation officials met with Secretary
of Commerce Jesse Jones and Assistant Secretary Will Clayton. The Chileans
again emphasized the economic dislocation connected with the 700,000
figure and also stated that if the government turned the nitrogen factories
over to private enterprise after the war it could ruin Chile. Jones and Clayton indicated that perhaps the 1-million-ton figure was possible but that
shipping that quantity would cause great difficulties. As for the postwar situation, the Department of Commerce officials stated that this was totally up
to the United States Congress.[243] On the same day the Food Administrator
heard the Chileans and indicated that he would recommend 1 million tons
and perhaps more.[244] Officials of the Department of Agriculture and the
War Department were approached the following day.[245]

On August 26 Ambassador Michels discussed the question with Secretary
of State Hull in a last effort to prevent the 700,000-ton figure from being
accepted. Despite the relative sympathy which had been shown to the
Chilean Nitrate Sales Corporation officials during their visits, the economic
arguments against the 1-million-ton figure had been accepted. Michels said
that Chile was going to ask for an increase of $2.50 per ton to cover the
increased production costs which he claimed amounted to over $3.00 a ton.
He argued that $1 of the increase represented the higher price Chile was pay-
ing for United States petroleum. Another $0.50 of it came from higher prices
Chile was paying for materials imported from the United States and the
higher Chilean freight rates traceable to the increased oil price. The other
half of the claimed increase originated in salaries necessary to maintain the
standard of living in the face of rising costs.[246] The question was also difficult because the United States was simply never sure of Chilean costs so it
had to guess as to the accuracy of Santiago's claims of increases.[247]

On August 30 and 31 State Department representatives again discussed
the situation with Michels. The Chilean Ambassador re-emphasized the adverse impact the 700,000-ton figure would have on his country and warned
that funds to compensate for the dislocation would probably have to be
obtained through new taxes on the copper industry. This semi-veiled threat

was coupled with the idea that the people of Chile, who had cooperated during the war, would be shocked by a cutback to 700,000 tons. Duggan correctly claimed that the Department of State had argued for a higher figure but that other agencies also had important interests to protect and that the shipping limitations had been real. Duggan suggested that Chile take advantage of the 700,000 figure and then attempt to get an additional 300,000 tons later.[248]

This was the course Chile took but the additional 300,000-ton allotment was not forthcoming. The United States did, however, grant half of the requested price hike—thereby moving the price from $21.00 to $22.25 per ton, or its equivalent in freight rate reductions on petroleum products and other imports. The local cost in Chile was a question not considered in the actual negotiations.[249] The United States Embassy in Santiago estimated that the 700,000-ton figure would probably directly influence about 2,800 workers.[250] Although the United States did not so argue publicly, such a decrease probably served as an inevitable reminder to Chile that the nitrate purchases simply could not continue at the wartime level and that some adjustment had to be made.

The question of copper supplies during the latter stages of the war was considerably easier to solve since this was not a question of overproduction, and the material was badly needed for the Allied war effort. Chile cooperated in a plan of distribution in which the United States did most of the planning.

The flow of some copper to Argentina caused minor problems during the period when the United States was attempting to take the edge off the Argentine economic boom (see chapter six). Copper production in the large mines boomed although some smaller producers were driven out of business by the low prices.[251] After the wartime price freeze was lifted, copper prices did increase substantially and there was a clear deterioration of the terms of trade to the disadvantage of copper producers.[252] This is further evidence that the United States-controlled price for copper was artificially low. But, to return to a previous point, the war had wrecked any concept of supply and demand in international trade.

If Chile's supply of copper to the United States was relatively problem-free, the ability of the United States to supply gasoline and paper to Chile was quite the opposite. Although there was gasoline rationing in the United States and some problems with obtaining newsprint, the basic impediment to the supplying of Chile was a shortage of shipping space. Chile was reluctant to adopt gasoline rationing and continually procrastinated over initiating cutbacks. The Chilean government apparently felt that the United States quotas were expandable and Ríos did not want to irritate the motorcar owners.[253] In the case of paper, there were frequent complaints that countries such as Mexico were experiencing no shortage although they also were supposedly limited in their supplies due to shipping shortages.

One North American attempt to better relations with Chile soon after the break in relations took the form of a visit by Vice-President Henry Wallace in March of 1943. Bowers called the visit "one of the best things in Chilean-American relations that has happened since the 'good neighbor' policy was enunciated."[254] Although the impact of such visits is impossible to evaluate, it does appear that this was a particularly opportune time to have a high-ranking Washington official visit Chile because the country was still a little uneasy over the recent breaking of relations with the Axis. Bowers, perhaps with some exaggeration, said that "never in Chilean history has any foreigner been received with such extravagant and evidently sincere enthusiasm."[255] From the point of view of the United States, the advantage of this type of diplomacy was that it was inexpensive.

Although Vice-President Wallace's visit was welcomed, Chile was much more interested by this point in the question of postwar economic assistance, and felt the United States should assist Chile in adjusting to the economic dislocation of returning to a peacetime economy. The U.S. Department of State included many officials who hoped that the United States could provide some financial assistance after the war; but it was impossible for the Executive Branch to make any firm commitments in this regard because of the necessity of getting the approval of the Congress. One study done for the Department of State by an economist suggested several promising areas of Chilean–United States cooperation.[256] In view of Chile's continuing exchange problems, one obvious possibility was the inclusion of Chile in any postwar arrangement to stabilize international currencies. On the copper problem, the survey suggested that the United States do away with or reduce its excise tax on copper, that it guarantee a minimum market of 100,000 tons annually for ten years, and that it help establish an international copper cartel. Another cartel was suggested for nitrates, along with a market guarantee of 500,000 tons which would be reduced 50,000 tons a year for ten years. Marketing agreements for agricultural production were also mentioned. Finally, the study included a tentative suggestion that capital for industrial development be provided in exchange for concessions such as the abolishment of exchange controls and quotas, limitation on new duties, and general trade liberalization.

The idea that Chile should open herself to more imports from the United States clearly was not in her interest. Postwar trade statistics show that in the period 1954–1959, the United States purchased over a quarter less from Chile than during the period 1940–1945.[257] Meanwhile, imports from the United States for the postwar period actually rose slightly, thereby worsening the balance of payments difficulties. The same statistics show that the per unit value of Chilean exports after the war lagged behind the per value unit of her imports.[258]

During 1943 and 1944, despite the requests of Santiago, the Department of State continually ignored questions of postwar economic relations with Chile and concentrated on the development of multilateral international economic cooperation.[259] The thinking in this area did not progress far, except in the case of Europe. Questions of bilateral cooperation were largely lost within the Department. Chile's policymakers clearly felt that the country deserved more in return for its wartime cooperation and Bowers agreed, sometimes to the irritation of the Department of State.[260] The worries of the Latin American countries that postwar relief would not be forthcoming proved to be justified. When the war was over, the pro-United Nations and pro-Europe internationalists in the Department of State came into dominance and Latin America was left to protect itself from the strains of adjusting to peacetime.

DECLARING WAR

A final test of Chile's cooperation in the closing days of the war provides an interesting insight into the nature of the relationship which had developed between the United States and Chile. The decision had been reached, at the insistence of the Soviet Union, that invitations to attend the San Francisco Conference for the writing of the United Nations Charter go only to those countries who had actually declared war on the Axis. Roosevelt was not pleased with the decision for he realized that many of the countries in Latin America had not been encouraged to declare war. Washington had been satisfied in most cases to have them break diplomatic relations and to receive their economic assistance during the conflict.

Thus the Department of State found itself in the awkward position of having to approach the government of Chile in December of 1944 to inform it that membership in the international organization was dependent on a declaration of war. On December 5 Bowers, who found his mission unpleasant, spoke to Foreign Minister Fernández who was "startled," (to use Bowers's term) by the news regarding the prerequisites to the organization. Fernández asked the Ambassador what reason the Chilean President could give the public for such an action. He complained that a dictatorship such as Bolivia could be included under the requirements while democratic Chile might be excluded. He also stated that a declaration of war would require congressional approval and that he feared great embarrassment when it became obvious that the requested declaration of war was more or less an order from the United States.[261] Questions of internal politics undoubtedly complicated the situation because the Conservatives and Liberals had made gains in the April 2, 1944, municipal elections; the two parties of the right polled more votes than the Radicals and Socialists.

Secretary of State Edward R. Stettinius, Jr., sent a rather disconcerted telegram to Bowers on December 7, 1944, saying that the United States would continue to take the position that Chile was entitled to a seat in any postwar conference and that the question was one for Chile to decide but that it should be informed of possible requirements for participation. A show was made of Chile's sovereignty throughout the discussions. Of course, Chile could have declined to declare war, but participation in the postwar organization was virtually a symbol of sovereignty and it would have been quite difficult for Chile to have stayed outside the United Nations. It was the almost-necessary nature of participation in the United Nations Organization that made the question so delicate. Chile had little choice.

James Wright, Assistant to the Director of the Office of American Republics, came to Chile to help in the discussions of the matter. He tried to emphasize that Washington, in delivering the news, was simply acting "as old and good friends of Chile informing them of a situation which exists and there was not the slightest pressure."[262] On December 11 Wright and Bowers met with the President and Fernández in Viña del Mar. The Chileans stated that they definitely wanted to declare war and were "seriously searching their minds for ways and means to do it," according to Wright. Chile raised the possibility of military assistance in connection with the declaration. This assistance, apparently, would be for protection against Argentina rather than the Axis.

But Bowers and Wright urged caution against applying any pressure on Chile in the matter. It was felt that Ríos needed time to sound out prominent senators on the question and that the situation was complicated by the election scheduled for March. However, on December 26 the Department of State pressed Bowers for information on whether Chile would attempt to lead the nonwarring nations of Latin America into a declaration of war. Otherwise, the United States ambassadors in those countries would be informed of the need for a declaration of war. The hope of Washington was that Chile's declaration would trigger similar statements from the other countries of Latin America who had not yet declared war. Chile was being given a chance to appear to be the leader. It was also hoped in the Department of State that the chance to appear as the leader would be sufficient compensation to Santiago to persuade the Ríos government to take the initiative. This ploy did not work.

The legal justifications Washington suggested Santiago might use were (1) under the Lima and Panama declarations, aggression against one American republic was aggression against all, and (2) when President Ríos had broken diplomatic relations it was an action tantamount to war, and (3) the acts taken by Chile against the Axis did constitute acts of war; therefore, the situation could be put before the Chilean Congress in terms of formally aligning with the United States by recognizing a pre-existing state of belligerency. The fact that this was also a prerequisite for membership in the coming international organization could be soft-pedaled.[263]

On January 3, 1945, Secretary Stettinius, after making warm statements of appreciation for Chile's role in World War II, threatened to approach the Latin American countries individually if Santiago did not act quickly. When the Ríos government failed to respond, on January 12 the State Department notified Bowers that it was proceeding with individual approaches to the Latin American countries that had not declared war.[264] Bowers was informed that President Roosevelt was going to send personal letters to the presidents of Chile, Ecuador, Peru, Venezuela, Uruguay, and Paraguay stating that in view of the fact it was being increasingly urged that invitations to the coming United Nations Conference on a world security organization should be limited to those nations which were signatories of the United Nations Declaration, the President ventured "to suggest that your government may wish to consider the desirability of formalizing its present position by taking the necessary steps to becoming a signatory of that Declaration."[265] The necessary step was not mentioned specifically but it was, of course, the declaration of war against the Axis. Washington rejected Chile's idea that the matter be discussed at the Mexico City conference.[266] Then the problem was further complicated in Santiago because the *New York Herald Tribune* leaked the story of the letters to the Latin American presidents in a way that cast the note in terms of pressure. This caused angry editorials in the newspapers in Santiago.[267] Foreign Minister Fernández told Bowers that the letters showed an ignorance of the Latin American psychology because they implied a threat. He said that with the congressional campaign in full swing it would weaken the position of the friends of the United States for Ríos to ask for a declaration of war, thereby unleashing an unpleasant debate.[268]

At this point Chile came up with what it obviously felt was a means of avoiding a direct confrontation with the issue. Ríos decided that Chile would simply adhere to the United Nations Declaration since the country was already connected with the war effort. Acting Secretary of State Joseph Grew wired back that Washington had tried to make it as clear as possible in private conversations that according to the wording of the United Nations Declaration only nations "at war" were eligible to adhere.[269] Ríos then decided that if he signed the Declaration—and the Congress approved—it would constitute a declaration of war. However, since the action would have to be completed prior to the United Nations meeting in San Francisco, Fernández wanted the meeting delayed so that the debate in the Chilean Congress could take place after the March 4 election and after Fernández had returned from the Mexico City conference.[270] Bowers approved of the idea but Washington was not about to consider delaying the entire meeting in order to ease domestic political difficulties in Chile.

It was finally agreed early in February in Washington that Chile could sign the Declaration if it adhered to a formula suitable to the Department of State. This took the form of a letter from President Ríos to President Roosevent which included the following statement:

> The exceptional circumstances of the present hour have induced me, with the unanimous approval of my Council of Ministers, to declare the state of belligerency existing between Chile and Japan and to obtain for such Declaration the sanction of the National Congress as required by our Political Constitution.[271]

Although the Congress did not approve the Declaration until April, this compromise was sufficient to allow Chile to avoid embarrassment.[272] The degree to which Santiago compromised on the question emphasizes the fact that once Chile had cast its lot with the Allies, as opposed to following a policy of semi-neutrality, it had very little choice except to do as Washington wanted it to do. On the other hand, as long as Chile was willing to follow Washington, the United States was willing to make its requests in the correct form, pay elaborate respect to Chile's sovereignty, provide it with what Washington felt were benevolent prices for its goods, and so forth. It was a relationship that did not need the rhetoric of Pan-Americanism, and little of it was used in the case of declaring war; but the feeling of cooperation with other Latin American nations in declaring war made it easier to take the step. Chile had hopes of using the idea of Pan-Americanism to help pressure Washington for special treatment after the war, but this rhetoric proved to be a feeble weapon when the United States saw Western Europe threatened by a Communist takeover.

5: THE LAST DAYS OF
CIVILIAN GOVERNMENT IN ARGENTINA

The Japanese attack on Pearl Harbor had repercussions on the deepening splits in the Argentine political arena because it altered the international legal and military situations. But the biggest change it brought about was that it shifted Washington's attitude regarding neutrality. At times prior to the attack President Roosevelt seemed to be asking Latin American countries to take steps which he himself hesitated to take in the face of congressional pressures. Washington's policy had been aimless until December 7, 1941, when an act of outright aggression against American territory stimulated action. United States policy was shoved off dead center and Washington entered the war with the sense of self-righteousness necessary for victory. This brought about a complete change in the pattern of hemispheric relations and forced the Argentine government to make a series of difficult decisions it would have preferred to avoid.

Although many of the other Latin American countries reacted to the attack on Pearl Harbor with declarations of war or the severing of diplomatic relations while Argentina hung back from these actions, there were only a few hints in the initial Argentine reaction to suggest the problems that would follow. Foreign Minister Ruiz-Guiñazú called U.S. Ambassador Armour the day after the attack to inform him that Argentina would declare neutrality between Japan and Great Britain but, with reference to the Declaration of Lima and Havana, would take the position that the United States was not a belligerent.[1] Under the terms of international law, such a posture was clearly favorable to the United States.

On December 9, Acting President Castillo wired a statement to President Roosevelt which invoked Declaration XV of the Havana meeting in referring to "extracontinental aggression against the sovereignty of the American States and the violation of its territory."[2] It stated Argentina's position that the United States was not a belligerent and also that Argentina would "in due course" negotiate "the necessary complementary agreements" as mentioned in the Havana document. In response to Armour's suggestion, motivated by Washington, that Buenos Aires take measures to prevent the use by the Axis

Powers of any domestic communications facilities in a manner inconsistent with hemispheric security,[3] Castillo assured the United States that his country would take the necessary internal measures to deny the use of the facilities in a manner endangering the security of the continent by Japan "or its allies."[4]

Another contact immediately following Pearl Harbor between Washington and Buenos Aires policymakers was a December 10 conversation of Welles and Alonso Irigoyen, the Financial Counselor of the Argentine Embassy. Supposedly a friend of Castillo's, Irigoyen gave United States Undersecretary of State Sumner Welles the personal assurances of Castillo that he was ardently pro-United States, despite his reputation of being pro-German. According to the conversation, Castillo believed Germany would be defeated and hoped that England and the United States would win; also the Argentine government was willing to follow the letter and spirit of existing inter-American agreements. Irigoyen said Castillo wanted Welles to know that the Argentine naval and military mission on its way to Washington was going to propose that Argentina take over the job of patrolling the coasts of Argentina and Uruguay. The Financial Counselor also said that the Cabinet had given its approval to a demand that the German government recall its Ambassador in Buenos Aires; but it had been modified into an agreement that the Ambassador would leave in January of his own volition, and it had been secretly agreed that he would not return.[5]

Regarding the general public in Argentina, Ambassador Armour judged that the Japanese attack had done much to arouse strongly pro-United States reactions "in all levels of Argentine society."[6] A number of newspaper owners called on the U.S. Embassy or expressed sympathy, as did a number of Argentine legislators, including the conservative President of the Senate, Dr. Robustiano Patrón Costas, who the Embassy felt had the reputation of being unfriendly toward Washington.[7] A number of military officers also seemed to find new sympathy for the United States, as did some Cabinet officers.

On December 16 President Castillo declared a state of seige. Under the Argentine Constitution such an order could be issued to keep the public order by waiving certain civil liberties "in the case of domestic disorder or foreign attack."[8] According to the Constitution this could only be done by the President when the Congress was not in session and for a limited period. The preamble of the decree stated:

> Whereas the gravity of the international situation imposes upon the Executive Power the obligation to take all measures tending to strengthen the moral unity of the nation in order to be able to maintain fully and effectively the position adopted with regard to the war, it is necessary to this end to suppress all activity tending to increase the passions aroused

by the war which in disturbing public order may endanger public tranquillity by subversive appeals or undesirable means of expression.[9]

The decree went on to refer to "international undertakings" which Argentina had accepted in the latest Pan American conferences for neutrality and continental defense and which could not be carried out within the normal constitutional guarantees.

The declaration of a state of seige has a long history in Latin America, and, even though there had been no obvious "internal disorder or external attack," it did not initially seem an unusual action. The language seemed innocuous, but the declaration quickly took on a sinister light to the United States Embassy when Castillo used it to prohibit rallies of Acción Argentina, the pro-Allied group. The government did ask the bitter, pro-Axis newspaper *El Pampero* to stop publishing objectionable cartoons ridiculing Roosevelt, but it certainly took little immediate action along the lines suggested by the Anti-Argentine Activities Committee.[10] Even a meeting scheduled to honor President Roosevelt was canceled. The Embassy felt this was an obvious effort to dampen public sympathy for the United States, despite the Minister of the Interior's assurances to the Ambassador that similar restrictions would be applied against totalitarian demonstrations.[11] It also soon became evident that the decree had strong political overtones because it was a convenient presidential weapon for stopping the rising tide of press, radio, and Radical and Socialist criticism of the regime. Given the political atmosphere in Buenos Aires at the time, a rally honoring Roosevelt might well have been seen by Castillo as an attempt by the opposition to criticize the administration for its failure to back Washington more strongly. Newspapers were warned to abstain "from all tendencious discussion of the international situation and publicity of anything that might disturb internal political tranquillity."[12]

Other distressing signs were noted by the United States Embassy. The negotiations for the ousting of Axis-dominated airlines did not seem to be going well. The Argentine government gave extensive publicity to its decision to reserve all tungsten exports for the United States when the decision was economically rational and inescapable in terms of the availability of shipping space. Moreover, according to Armour, Castillo had at one time assured him that if the United States declared war on any non-American power, Argentina would immediately join in a similar declaration of war[13] —a promise that was obviously not being kept. The United States was also disappointed that Germany's Ambassador von Thermann was not being ousted, although the Embassy had been informed of the supposed agreement to have him recalled.[14]

In a series of arrests rumored to coincide with the opening of the Rio meeting of foreign ministers, twenty officials of the Nazi benevolent and cultural societies were jailed for fraud based on an investigation showing that the funds they had collected for German charity had actually been used by the Embassy to support the Nazi propaganda effort in the Buenos Aires area.[15] These cases were not pressed, however. A Ministry of Interior sub-division for Vigilance and Repression of Anti-Argentine Activities had been created, but it had been placed under the direction of a person the Embassy felt to be sympathetic with the Nazis.[16]

Had Washington been aware of the private assurances Castillo and Ruiz-Guiñazú were giving the German Ambassador in Buenos Aires, undoubtedly the Department of State would have been even more disturbed. When von Thermann called on the Foreign Minister on December 11, the German Ambassador was "given to understand that Argentina would try to continue its policy of neutrality as far as possible within the framework of Pan American agreements."[17] On the same day von Thermann telephoned Berlin asking for his own recall in order to strengthen the hand of Ruiz-Guiñazú; this request was initially refused. In a conversation with President Castillo on December 15 the German Ambassador was assured that Buenos Aires intended to remain neutral and that the Rio Conference would not obligate countries to break diplomatic relations with the Axis or to declare war.[18] This blatant attempt of Castillo's to placate both sides gives credence to the observation of Argentine historian Sergio Bagú that the Argentine President was primarily interested in deciding who was going to win the war.[19]

Nonetheless, Argentine foreign policy was being pushed into a crisis by the Rio meeting. Without this conference it would have been relatively easy for the foreign office to muddle along and to attempt to remain friendly to the Germans while mouthing the rhetoric of the neutralist Lima–Panama–Havana Pan-Americanism. But at Rio, Ruiz-Guiñazú had been faced with the problem of voting on substantive resolutions regarding an either/or action—the breaking of diplomatic relations with the Axis. One either broke relations in accordance with the resolutions, or one did not and thereby violated the agreements. There was no middle ground in Washington's initial draft resolutions. As discussed in chapter three, Argentina managed to find an alternative, at least to her way of thinking, by forcing the final resolution to be considered a recommendation, which she then ignored. The other resolutions, some of which were quite harsh against the Axis, were complicated and did not receive the publicity the question of breaking relations received. Thus Argentina, evidently without much enthusiasm, adhered to various resolutions promising to cooperate with the hemispheric nations in systematically discriminating against Axis economic interests in the Americas.

When Chile and Argentina refused to follow the recommendations of the Rio meeting promptly, the Department of State felt obligated to re-evaluate its position toward those two countries. In the Chilean case, as chapter four shows, the situation was never one in which the government clearly failed to break relations. First there was the question of the Chilean presidential election; then there were the continual misunderstandings and delays in taking the action. Santiago's breaking of relations frequently seemed just around the corner. Argentina, however, made her refusal to break relations much more clear-cut, although she had pleaded at the Rio meeting for a delay due to the upcoming congressional elections. This fraud-marred voting saw many National Democrats and Antipersonalists (the conservative parties) elected in support of the government's neutrality policy. The largest drop was in the Radical camp, with the Socialists picking up a good deal of support compared to their dismal showing in the previous election. The Chamber of Deputies distribution was as follows:[20]

Party	Elected in March	In Mid-term	Total
National Democrats	37	17	54
Antipersonalists	10	7	17
U.C.R. (Radicals)	23	42	65
Socialists	12	5	17
Others	3	2	5

However, even after this election of questionable fairness, the Radicals and Socialists could muster eighty-two votes and therefore a majority. The coalition moved quickly upon convening in May to take advantage of this majority to vote that the state of seige be lifted. The President's support in the Senate allowed Castillo to ignore the action.

Argentina's behavior at Rio, and her seeming unwillingness to move quickly to implement the Rio resolutions at a time when many of the Latin American countries were going beyond what had been agreed to, forced Washington to begin treating the government in Buenos Aires differently from the rest of the hemisphere (except for Chile). This took the form of not favoring Argentina in the same sense that the United States was attempting to favor those who were appearing to be acting on the Rio accords. From the Department of State's point of view, it was not a policy of reprisal and was never referred to as such within the Department. Undersecretary of State Welles, who had been instrumental in the formulation of the policy, explained the U.S. position on February 9, 1942, to Argentine Ambassador Espil. He said that demands were being made for urgently needed military aid and economic assistance from all parts of the world. Since those nations that had openly sided with Washington "had consequently incurred the dangers inherent in the position they had assumed," the United States felt it imperative to give "immediate and prompt consideration to their defense requirements."[21] Argentina had not adopted such an attitude, Welles told Espil; therefore it was obvious that the requirements of the other nations were more urgent and thus deserved preferential attention. The irony of this position, as mentioned in chapter four, is that simultaneously, and later, the United States was telling Chile that it was not incurring extra dangers by cooperating—an attempt to allay fears in Santiago of a possible attack against the country's exposed coastline if it were to break relations.[22]

Whatever the logic of the United States position, Argentina perceived Washington's policy as an attempt at coercion. There were, indeed, voices in the U.S. government which seemed to agree that the policy was coercion, or at least counterproductive. On the question of allocations and priorities, the Acting Chief of the Division of the American Republics, Philip Bonsal, argued that Argentina should be treated on the same basis as the other American republics. In a memo to Welles he argued that "to proceed otherwise would be to fail to take a realistic view of Argentina's importance to us and to the British at this time."[23] Bonsal also argued in March of 1942 that the policy being followed really amounted to economic warfare and yet was not of sufficient magnitude to do anything more than merely cause irritation without changing Argentina's policy.[24] He did approve of the denial of military material since it placed Argentina at a disadvantage in relation to Brazil and was a point of pressure on important political groups in Argentina, including the military.[25] The U.S. Board of Economic Warfare and its Director Milo Perkins also argued against the policy on the grounds that without British cooperation it would not be effective and England was not in a position to apply the pressure. This meant that the economic pressure resulting from the policy was virtually unilateral and could not be made "completely effective." He also warned, in a memo to Secretary of State Hull, that the policy "may lead to serious misunderstanding with resulting harm to the best interests of the United States."[26]

MILITARY AID AS AN ISSUE

The other prong of this policy was the attempt of the United States to use lend-lease supplies to tempt Argentina into changing its position. Once again the policy was never referred to in terms of coercion—it was always spoken of in terms of the idea that these supplies were desperately needed by many countries and those states showing the strongest pro-Allied tendencies were bound to rate the highest priorities.

There did seem to be some recognition in Washington that the United States was using weapons sales to "buy" favors. The Argentine military delegation sent to Washington to discuss an arms deal began its talks a few days after the attack on Pearl Harbor (and prior to the Rio meeting). It was the understanding of the U.S. negotiators that the purposes of the meeting were to discuss hemispheric defense plans suggested by the two countries, to prepare a a program of acquisition of armaments based on the plans for defense agreed upon in the staff conversations, and then to negotiate a lend-lease agreement to help furnish these arms. It was hoped within the United States military establishment that only *after* this supposedly purely military agreement had been negotiated would it be presented to the Argentine Foreign Office and the U.S. Department of State.[27] This would seem to show a staggering ignorance of the connection between military affairs and diplomacy at a particularly delicate moment. However, it may be that Washington hoped to give Buenos Aires a way of changing its political position by first shifting its military policy. It also could be that Washington hoped to create a pro-Allied interest group in the Argentine military via these negotiations.

The Argentine Embassy insisted on participating in the discussions at which the position of Washington was clear: "American countries which have already declared war against or broken relations with the Axis Powers will be first to receive available war material."[28] Ambassador Armour strongly advocated this policy when he communicated with Welles. In the meantime, Armour was having a continuingly difficult time with the Foreign Ministry in Buenos Aires. In a talk on January 30 with the Acting Minister of Foreign Affairs, Dr. Guillermo Rothe, he was told that Buenos Aires's not having broken relations placed her in a better position to assist the United States because Argentine shipments of materials would not be molested by German submarines.[29] Armour pointed out that this technicality had not prevented German submarines from sinking United States vessels prior to its abandonment of neutrality. He was assured by Rothe that if an Argentine ship were sunk it would lead to a quick break in relations or the declaration of war by Argentina. Rothe also expressed another Argentine position which had been heard previously: the country was not in a position to defend itself and a poor defense would be an invitation to an attack, and he added confidentially that the internal situation made it impossible for Argentina to break relations at the time.

Meanwhile, the military delegation had arrived in Washington to find itself under difficult cross-pressures. On the one side there was the reluctance of such officials as Ruiz-Guiñazú to any agreement that might lead Argentina into the orbit of the United States.[30] On the other side there was significant worry among Argentine military officials that the supplying of lend-lease, particularly to Brazil, would seriously tip the balance of power in South America unless a similar source of supply was found for Argentina. Buenos Aires had considered itself to be significantly stronger militarily within the area than its traditional rival. However, the enormous flow of military aid to Brazil from the United States had greatly impressed General Juan Tonazzi, Argentina's

Minister of War, after he attended a September 7, 1941, military parade in Brazil.[31] Thus the Argentine delegation went to Washington in a position of wanting the weapons but unable to make any concessions that might conceivably be interpreted as infringing upon its position of neutrality.

From the United States point of view, there were two surprises when the negotiations or discussions commenced. First, although the United States had spoken in terms of $66 million in allocations over a six-year period, Argentina was asking for $450 million in materiel.[32] In view of the difficulties the United States was having meeting other demands for materiel, the request seemed out of question and Argentina soon modified its request. The second surprise came on the question of cooperation. According to Adviser on Political Relations Laurence Duggan, the naval plan presented by Argentina "goes far beyond any indication heretofore received from the Argentine government of its willingness to cooperate." However, the plan was premised on Argentine entry into the war on the side of the United Nations and would not go into effect *until* the necessary materiel had been furnished.[33] Why Argentina at this point showed such a willingness is difficult to explain without getting into the murky waters of speculation regarding which political clique had helped draw up the instructions and which group of officers had represented the military interests. It appears that the "bait" of weapons and the fear of Brazil were both strong. Also, the pro-Axis nationalist groups had not yet rallied their forces within the government.

Part of the good feelings which originally characterized these talks also grew from the military-man-to-military-man nature of the discussions. The U.S. naval officers were even reluctant to give Department of State officials information on the plan being formulated.[34] Officials of the Navy and War Departments wanted to finish the agreement, sign it, and then allow the onus of not approving it to rest on the Department of State or the President.[35] This would allow the friendly relations between the navies to continue. The President could claim that, since the recommendation from the military talks was premised on the assumption that Argentina was going to enter the war as an ally of the United States, and since this assumption seemed unwarranted, it would be impossible to supply the materials needed. It illuminates the nature of bureaucratic competition to note that the Department of State showed some interest in having the recommendations submitted to the Navy and War Departments in order to have those two bodies declare the recommendations not acceptable. This would have avoided any implication that the State Department was attempting reprisals against Argentina for her foreign policy.[36] The situation was further complicated at the time by the fact that both Argentina and Brazil were claiming that the other had concentrated troops on their common border as a prelude to a possible attack.[37]

In response to Undersecretary Welles's query as to how Armour felt about approval of the agreement, even though it would not be implemented, the Ambassador in Buenos Aires advised against it.[38] Otherwise, he reasoned, the Argentine government would act as if the United States was going to provide military equipment regardless of Argentina's international stance. He said that if the agreement were signed it certainly would include "a carefully worded statement" that no lend-lease agreement had yet been negotiated.[39] Such a communication was prepared, including the statement that "no negotiations are under way with respect to a lend-lease agreement and none are contemplated at the present time."[40]

The Argentine government's representatives in Washington were encouraging the Department of State to allow the plan to be signed. The Chief of the Division of the American Republics in the Department of State was warned that a continuation of United States reluctance would weaken the political position of the pro-Allied elements in Argentina and strengthen the neutralist, pro-fascist elements.[41] Welles finally decided upon a method of avoiding a hard "yes" or "no" on the question: he simply raised the requirements for Washington's approval. He feared that signing the agreement would allow Argentina to claim that the United States had undertaken a moral commitment to provide arms "so that Argentina could be in a position to fulfill its obligations in the event that it were to enter the war." Moreover, he feared that, as Armour had suggested, the agreement would be used by the Castillo government to fortify its claim that it was following a policy in harmony with Pan-Americanism.[42]

The specific proposal the United States set forth was that Argentina cooperate with the United States in convoy activities in areas near the Argentine coast.[43] The answer from the military representatives was that the question was "a political matter, therefore it is outside the orbit and attributes of this Delegation for consideration." Espil, after the delegation had turned down the question on the grounds of jurisdiction, told Welles that such a proposal would involve Argentina in the war and therefore was unacceptable.[44] On March 20 the Argentine and Washington delegations had their final meetings and United States Admiral James O. Richardson made the following statement:

> The United States delegation has welcomed the discussions with the Argentine Delegation regarding certain military questions and has appreciated the spirit of understanding and comradeship of the Argentine Delegation which is traditional between the navies of the two countries. It is understood that the arrangements discussed between the two delegations are to be held in abeyance pending their further consideration by our respective governments.[45]

Although the military experts had completed their discussions, the diplomats continued to consider the question. There is no doubt that

Argentina wanted the lend lease assistance quite badly. On March 24, 1942, Ambassador Espil delivered a note to Secretary of State Hull outlining Argentina's position.[46] It stated that during the talks Argentina had "offered a plan of defense which, in revealing its war preparations, signifies a great demonstration of friendship towards the United States." It also claimed that the Argentine government had already decided to accept the proposed basic agreement with only a few modifications in the area of amounts and times of delivery. The major Argentine complaint with the lend-lease agreement, prior to the addition of the convoy requirement, was that the materiel scheduled to be furnished "would be insufficient to assure the adequate organization" of a defense of the zones within its responsibility under the U.S.–Argentine "war plan which has just been discussed in Washington." The note went on to point out certain preparatory measures it had already taken for defense. These included an increase in the Army, the provision for a possible calling up of the reserves, strengthening of certain points on the South Atlantic, and the installation of air bases in Patagonia. However, Argentina lacked some of the military equipment needed to carry out these plans and much of this equipment was "practically impossible to manufacture in the country within a short period." Thus, the note concluded,

> it is obvious that the effectiveness of our cooperation in continental defense is closely bound to the equipment and materials which the Argentine Republic has a probability of receiving in due time to complete the operative value of its Army and Navy.

A formal note from Undersecretary Welles to the Argentine Ambassador in Washington on April 3 repeated the United States offer to "immediately enter into negotiations with the Argentine government for the purpose of signing a lend-lease agreement" if Argentina was willing to accept Washington's proposal on the control and protection of shipping.[47] On April 23 Ambassador Armour had a conversation with Ruiz-Guiñazú which was followed by a note the next day from the Argentine Foreign Ministry. The note stated, first, that Argentina had "understood that the loan to be obtained under the Lend-Lease Act did not necessarily depend on the conversations . . . for the study of a common defense plan." Second, without lend-lease aid, Argentina could not possibly carry out her share of the defense plan which had been negotiated in Washington. However, the note said, the Argentine government had authorized its delegation to sign the plan of cooperation "insofar as it implies the recognition of a policy of collaboration adopted in accordance with the obligations assumed by the country, which it is disposed to fulfill in the measures that its resources may permit." Only the last-minute inclusion of the convoy idea by the Department of State had prevented a successful conclusion of the talks.

Third, Argentina argued that the convoy requirement had not been made in regard to other Latin American governments who were obtaining lend-lease assistance. This, according to the note (and probably accurately), discriminated against Argentina, and also created "a situation of belligerency which the country does not desire and for which it is not prepared."[48]

In his conversation with Ruiz-Guiñazú the day before the delivery of the note, Ambassador Armour had said that the United States was not discriminating against Argentina in the convoy proposal; rather it was making an exception in Argentina's case by agreeing to sign a lend-lease agreement when Buenos Aires had neither declared war nor broken relations. The Foreign Minister said that the Rio Resolution was not binding on Argentina because it was qualified by references to the geographic position of certain countries, and Argentina's geographic position had not changed. Armour then stated that German submarine warfare constituted a blockade against Argentina which was an aggressive act. The Ambassador also took the opportunity to state that the United States was concerned over the increasingly hostile tone of the United States press toward Argentina and that Washington wished it had some information to help change United States opinion toward Argentina. This not-so-subtle suggestion that public pressure was building up in favor of Department of State actions against Buenos Aires was a clear attempt to apply some extra pressure. Overlooking the question of the fraud involved, Ruiz-Guiñazú answered that the recent Argentine elections, which had gone in favor of Castillo's government, represented a desire of the Argentine people to stay out of the war. It will be remembered that at the Rio Conference the Foreign Minister had indicated that his government would have to wait until after the elections in order to take some of the strong steps agreed to. Now that the election was held and the government victorious, the new explanation of the process was that it represented a victory for a neutral foreign policy. Undersecretary of Foreign Affairs Roberto Gache, in a conversation with Armour a week after the delivery of the Argentine note, stated that his government felt the convoy proposal was more likely to involve Argentina in the war than the breaking of diplomatic relations.[49]

On May 13 Ambassador Armour received a note from the Department of State for delivery to Ruiz-Guiñazú in answer to the Foreign Minister's note of April 24. The Washington reply said that, despite statements which had been made that the supplying of lend-lease materials did not depend on a defense plan, this position had been drastically changed by the attack on Pearl Harbor. (In fairness to Argentina, it should be noted that Argentina had not been informed of this prior to the talks.) The communication repeated that Argentina was not being discriminated against; because there was not sufficient materiel to supply all the countries requesting assistance,

United States policy was simply to supply the most help to the countries that had "placed themselves in the forefront of hemispheric defense." The convoy idea, Washington's note argued, would have allowed Argentina to be part of this program despite the fact that it had neither declared war nor broken diplomatic relations with the Axis. It also disputed the contention that participation in the convoy would have created a state of belligerency on Argentina's part. Although not precluding a change in attitude if Argentina were to reverse its decision, the note stated flatly that there was no chance under present circumstances for the United States to provide lend-lease materials to Argentina.[50]

Without actually delivering the message, Armour spoke with President Castillo a few days later and brought up the question of a possible plan to protect ships off the Argentine coast. According to the Ambassador, Castillo "appeared interested in [the] proposal and promised to study the matter further with the Minister of Foreign Affairs." Armour said he later learned that Castillo had mentioned the matter to the Minister of the Interior which led the Ambassador to express the opinion that the President "is giving serious consideration to it."[51] With this in mind, Armour suggested delaying delivery of the note until the situation had clarified itself. Five days later, on June 1, 1942, word came from Washington that Armour should deliver the note.[52]

In their book *Argentina's Foreign Policy, 1930–1962*, Argentine writers Alberto A. Conil Paz and Gustavo E. Ferrari characterize the note from Hull as "cutting" and seem to indicate that its delivery marked the end of any chance for an accommodation on this question.[53] Undoubtedly the note was strong. For example, in stating that it could not give aid to Argentina, it said that the policy was to refuse those countries "which have made no effective contribution to the cause of hemispheric defense."[54] But in view of other events at the time, of the Rio meeting, and of the problems which were to follow between the two countries, it seems difficult to conclude that this note closed the door to an agreement. It was part of a much larger problem.

Doubtless the military establishment in Argentina was upset by the failure of the lend-lease negotiations on the one hand and on the other by the fact that Brazil was receiving a tremendous flow of material. The Argentine reaction took two forms. The first was to begin to deprecate the quantity and quality of the United States military goods furnished Brazil and to begin to exaggerate the number of concessions Brazil was forced to make in order to receive this equipment.[55] The second form, although this was not known to Washington at the time, was to open secret negotiations with Germany for military equipment. Private intermediaries made some unofficial approaches to the German Embassy in February or March on the matter.[56]

In July the tempo of the discussions increased,[57] and when Brazil declared war with Germany on August 22 an official approach was made to Berlin via the German naval attaché in Buenos Aires for submarines, airplanes, munitions, and anti-aircraft weapons. German shortages (and transportation problems) caused the talks to slow down in October of 1942.[58]

On April 17, 1942, the Argentine tanker *Victoria* was hit by two torpedos from a German submarine. The captain and crew left the ship but were later returned to it by the United States Navy which had managed to make sufficient repairs on the ship to allow it to limp into New York on April 22. There was a disposition in official Argentine circles when the news first came to doubt that the ship actually had been torpedoed.[59] At least part of this resulted from government attempts to keep Argentine public opinion from being stirred up on the issue of the war, although some of the newspapers were making hostile comments about Germany.

Under the rules of the sea, the United States was legally justified in claiming ownership of the vessel which had been abandoned. After a discussion between the Navy Department and the Department of State, it was decided not to make the claim.[60] Hull stated at a press conference:

> This government is patrolling the seas in that area with a view to doing all in its power to protect the shipping and interests of the American nations. It has no interest in taking up or raising a question of salvage [in the case of the *Victoria*].[61]

The Navy made it clear privately that its waiving of rights applied only to the case of the *Victoria* and that it did not intend to make this a standard policy.[62] The owners of the *Victoria*, as a gesture of thanks for saving the ship and rescuing the officers and crew, donated $20,000 to the Navy Relief Society.[63]

Late in May the captain of the *Victoria* returned to Buenos Aires, thereby prompting another flurry of publicity on the question.[64] He defended leaving his ship by saying that most ships, hit in the manner his had been hit, did sink. He stated categorically that the ship had been torpedoed, an admission the government had not been willing to make up to that point. Exactly two months after the attack the Argentine government announced that a note had been received by the Argentine Embassy in Germany in which Berlin acknowledged its responsibility for the attack and expressed its regret over the error. It claimed that the light was obscure at the time and the ship's markings faded. It also, unlike the case of the *Uruguay*, offered compensation for damages. The Argentine government accepted the note,[65] doubtlessly glad to have this potentially volatile situation defused.

Less than a week after Argentina received the note concerning the *Victoria*, a second Argentine ship, the freighter *Rio Tercero*, was torpedoed and sunk off the U.S. coast. Argentina protested this sinking and Germany again replied by expressing regret and offering to compensate, although the note commented that Germany felt the ship was not observing the rules regarding markings of neutral ships.[66] The Argentine Foreign Minister stated flatly at a news conference after the receipt of the note that the ship had been suitably marked. He also remarked that he considered the incident closed, since it would not serve any useful purpose to press the point, and that the Argentine government believed that the German submarine had not intentionally targeted an Argentine ship.[67]

The significance of these two submarine attacks was viewed considerably differently in the three capitals involved: Washington, Buenos Aires, and Berlin. Washington obviously hoped that the Castillo government would use these attacks to justify a more pro-Allied policy. Buenos Aires, however, did everything possible to keep the incidents from arousing public opinion which might thereby bring into question the desirability of neutrality. Late in June when the German government announced a submarine blockade of the eastern United States, the Argentine government ordered Argentine merchant vessels to avoid East Coast ports.[68] The submarine attacks also outline a change in the position of Berlin since the time of the sinking of the *Uruguay* prior to Pearl Harbor. There is some possibility that the first sinking may have been a premeditated attempt to impress Argentina. If it was an accident, the Third Reich diplomats used it to intimidate Buenos Aires. Now, however, Germany wished to keep Argentine following the policy of neutrality, so it did everything possible to soothe ruffled Argentine feelings and to give the Castillo government an excuse for not pressing for satisfaction.

The Department of State was making one serious effort toward bettering relations with Buenos Aires during the early days after Pearl Harbor: continuing pressure on the Department of Agriculture for the removal of the ban against Argentine beef and mutton. Welles sent a note to the Secretary of Agriculture shortly after Pearl Harbor stating that Argentina had gained a new confidence in the United States as a result of the Good Neighbor Policy. The memo then argued, rather naively, that this feeling accounted for Argentina's declaration of non-belligerency status for the United States "thereby making available Argentine ports and airfields to our Navy and Army." This new confidence could only be sustained, according to the Undersecretary, if the United States showed a willingness to lift the trade barrier against meat from zones untouched by hoof-and-mouth disease.[69]

A trip to Argentina by an investigator from the Department of Agriculture led to a report that said there was no hoof-and-mouth disease in Tierra del Fuego, but the report was unwilling to admit that there was no possibility that it would be introduced into the area.[70] Irritated with Argentina as a result of its foreign policy, President Roosevelt began to slacken his opposition to the ban and the Department of Agriculture remained committed to the existing policy of exclusion.[71] Agriculture also avoided dealing with the reality that the Department of State was more interested in doing away with the embargo for propaganda purposes than to facilitate trade. Agriculture suggested, for example, that the United States might purchase 2,000 tons of mutton from Tierra del Fuego and arrange to have it sent to England.[72] Armour hoped for a lifting of the ban as it would "be of far-reaching help to us now as well as in the future." He also cautioned that "an adverse announcement is unthinkable without the fullest scientific justification." If the decision were to be unfavorable, he suggested it might be well to announce it at a later date.[73]

Armour's telegram was probably designed to bolster the Department of State's case in an April 16 discussion between Secretary Claude Wickard of Agriculture and Sumner Welles. Wickard stated that at the time the importation of meat from Argentina would seem to involve a foreseeable risk of hoof-and-mouth disease. According to the Department of State memo of the talk, the Agriculture Department's representative who had toured Argentina had knowledge of an outbreak of the disease in Patagonia but it came from a source so confidential that he did not want reference made to the outbreak. Wickard also feared that cattle which had been exposed might be smuggled into the area.[74] Welles declared that he did not want the meat admitted if there was any reasonable risk involved but wondered whether there were any possible actions Argentina and Chile might take to lessen possible danger. The Secretary of Agriculture finally agreed that if steps were taken which removed the danger of possible shipment of cattle or sheep into the uninfected areas, his Department would agree. However, he doubted whether this was possible and showed no enthusiasm for the idea.

Argentine Ambassador Espil called on Duggan of the State Department the following day and asked about the outcome of the State-Agriculture talk. Duggan conveyed the impression that the way was open for the importation of Argentine meat if additional safeguards were instigated. The Ambassador expressed Argentina's willingness to do this and asked what safeguards the Department had in mind. Duggan admitted that these had not yet been worked out. The Ambassador asked what he should tell his own Secretary of Agriculture when he made an expected inquiry about possibly sending 2,000 tons of meat from Tierra del Fuego to the United States. Duggan said that his latest information indicated that the British had offered to buy all the meat produced in the area and therefore the problem was not an immediate one.[75]

On May 11 Ambassador Espil wrote the Secretary of State asking that the matter be clarified.[76] Welles's answer was that it was still under study by the Agriculture Department and that since England was buying the entire production, Washington hoped that some satisfactory solution could be reached prior to the next year's slaughter.[77] The State Department viewed this as the only possible course of action and hoped that Roosevelt might be convinced to pressure the Secretary of Agriculture about the matter. Since by this time diplomatic relations between Buenos Aires and Washington were in a state of decay, the Department felt that Argentina would become even more intransigent if it believed the United States had gone back on its position regarding Tierra del Fuego as an acceptable point of origin for meat imports.[78] The worsening political situation and a serious outbreak of hoof-and-mouth disease in Argentina late in 1942 led the Department of State to stop pressing for a concession on the question after mid-1942.

WASHINGTON'S STRUGGLE AGAINST AXIS INFLUENCE IN ARGENTINA

Although the failure of Argentina to take the step of breaking diplomatic relations with the Axis and its inability to reach a settlement on the question of supplying arms loomed large during the early portion of 1942, an even larger preoccupation in Washington began to center on the degree to which Argentina was allowing itself to be used as an "open city" for espionage and Axis influence. Immediately after Pearl Harbor some crackdowns evidently were made by pro-Allied officials who had not yet gotten the word from the Castillo government that nothing should be done to anger Germany. On the other hand, numerous actions which seemed to protect Axis activities occurred. There were some arrests, for example, of pro-Allied elements on the grounds that they were engaged in Communist activities.[79] The censorship program operated rather clearly to muffle pro-Allied opinion, while publications such as *El Pampero* and *Crisol*, which were virtually Axis propaganda organs, were able to operate in relative freedom. Part of this may have arisen from the fact that the Axis propagandists appealed to Argentine nationalism and also took the position that the neutralist policy was good. The pro-Allied press was operating under the disadvantage of being critical of the government policy and thus if it went too far in its advocacy was likely to offend. The State Department also felt it had information that Axis agents were circulating freely in Argentina and that visas were knowingly issued to spies.[80] Many Argentine military men were expressing pro-Axis opinions although no leader had emerged for this group.[81] The propaganda campaigns of the Axis embassies were extensive. Propaganda material was being mailed from Buenos Aires to other Latin American countries.

In June of 1942 the Argentine government issued decrees providing for supervisors for local enterprises which were managed or controlled by belligerent countries outside the western hemisphere. This was in line with Resolution V of the Rio meeting of foreign ministers. Actually, only thirteen of the more than one hundred sizable firms were given inspectors.[82] The Argentine government evidently also attempted to assure the German government that these actions were not designed to be effective but were merely paper efforts to appease the Pan-Americanists. By September of 1942 the actions of the inspectors had declined even further.[83]

The failure of Argentina to break relations with the Axis Powers and the lackadaisical attitude it was showing toward Axis activity was bringing a wave of press criticism in the United States. For example, the April 18, 1942, issue of *Colliers* magazine had an article titled "Argentina: Axis Gateway." This article and much of the other public criticism was repressed before it reached Buenos Aires and therefore not available to the Argentine public. Late in May of 1942 Ambassador Armour told President Castillo that he hoped Argentina would take actions to discourage this type of comment in the U.S. press. The President said he would stress solidarity with the United States in his May 28 speech to the Congress.[84] Castillo also contended that Argentina was already taking action to implement the Rio resolutions. The President, according to the account of the Ambassador, seemed concerned about public opinion in the United States and "appreciated our Government's concern over the effect this might have on future relations."[85]

When Castillo finally made his speech it proved to be a disappointment to the United States Embassy. He repudiated any automatic commitment to collective action under Pan-Americanism. He repeated the argument that the maintenance of neutrality of greater usefulness to Washington than a break with the Axis. He interpreted the rigged March elections as indicating approval of his policies. He defended the state of seige under which Argentina was operating as necessary to preserve the internal tranquillity in the face of "professional agitators" who, he felt, were "attempting to spread ideas and principles contrary to the institutions of Argentina."[86]

This speech, and the general situation in the country, prompted an informal memorandum from the United States State Department to the Foreign Ministry of Argentina on July 6, 1942. The note particularly protested what it felt to be the continued operation of Axis agents in Argentina. It pointed out that the Embassy had supplied the Argentine government with information on the subject but that the cases had not been prosecuted. It protested the fact that "certain newspaper offices, radio broadcasting stations and publishing houses" were "centers for the dissemination of totalitarian propaganda" and were operating openly. It also raised the question of continued telecommunications with Axis countries. The note closed:

> During the past five months the government of the United States has
> awaited with serenity and confidence the positive action which it has
> felt sure would be taken by the government of Argentina to implement
> the resolutions subscribed at Rio de Janeiro. The government of the
> United States does not doubt that this confidence is justified.[87]

On July 8 Armour also renewed his own vigorous protests to President
Castillo over Argentina's disappointing attitude toward the Rio resolutions.
Castillo denied any position other than being pro-Allied but said that the
one thing his Government would never do was to break relations with the
Axis countries. Short of this, he claimed, Argentina would lend the fullest
cooperation.[88] The President told Armour at the time that his government
was asking its ships to stay out of the belligerent zone established by Germany along the Atlantic coast but that it was also protesting Germany's
right to establish such a zone. Armour suggested that if Buenos Aires hoped
to avoid the appearance of giving in to Germany, it might be well to publish its protest prior to issuing the decree.

The Argentine Foreign Minister appeared in July before the Chamber of
Deputies in secret (at his insistence) session and evidently used portions of
communications from Washington to the Argentine government to try to
convince the body that the United States was attempting to coerce Argentina into changing its policy of neutrality.[89] It was also here that he made
disparaging remarks concerning the quantity of war material the United
States was furnishing the other American republics.[90]

A few days prior to his presentation to the Congress, Ruiz-Guiñazú had
replied to Armour's note of July 6. The Argentine communication stated
that "the Ministry believes that only through erroneous information" can
one claim that Argentina was permitting continued Axis activities in the
country.[91] It did not specifically deny some of the charges in the Washington note relating to failure to implement certain Rio resolutions. It did
point to legislation aimed at stopping foreign organizations from operating
in Argentina. These were precisely the laws which the pro-Allied factions
felt to be potentially directed against them. The reply also mentioned the
office of "Vigilance and Repression of Anti-Argentine Activities" which had
been added to the Ministry of the Interior to combat "any activity contrary to the democratic systems and institutions" of Argentina.[92] However,
the head of this group had several times told United States Embassy officials that he had been unable to function due to a lack of funds.[93] Also the
Embassy felt that the energies of the police had tended to be aimed at
suppressing pro-democratic feelings. The note praised the Argentine activities—which actually had been quite slow—to control communications with
Axis countries. It claimed that efforts were being made to control

internal and external movement of funds which might be of danger to continental security. The Foreign Minister ended his note:

> This summary of background information, the clear significance of which admits of no doubt, permits the assertion that the Argentine government has instituted, in defence of the security of the continent, a plan of control in keeping with the resolutions of the Meeting of Rio de Janeiro, which will be gradually completed in the methodical and progressive manner which the organization and the administrative requirements of the country may permit.[94]

The Embassy in Buenos Aires disagreed with this conclusion. It felt that the action that had been taken toward fulfilling the Rio resolutions was "negligible and the true intentions of the Argentine government are best revealed" by its docile acceptance of the sinking of the *Rio Tercero* and "the attitude of intransigent isolation" which Castillo had displayed in his July 6 speech.[95]

On October 8 Undersecretary Welles–who had the prime Department of State responsibility in the area of Latin America–made his controversial talk before the National Foreign Trade Council in Boston in which he was critical of Argentina and Chile. The Argentine Embassy in Washington quickly stated the "extreme displeasure" with which the Argentine government received the speech. It claimed that the statements were "in open contradiction to reality in the present state of our relations with the United States and other American countries," and protested the "unprecise and general terms" used in the speech which did not specify cases and therefore supposedly made it difficult for Argentina to reply. It stated that it was hard to understand why the ship sinkings were attributed to reports sent from Argentina. It also claimed that Argentina was "gradually broadening the measures called for by the Rio de Janeiro recommendations insofar as Argentina's position and needs permit."[96]

As had Chile's reaction to Welles's speech, Argentina's objections put pressure on the Department of State to provide evidence to support Welles's statements. The Embassy in Buenos Aires was ready to provide that evidence. It pointed out that "there is reasonable certainty that the Germans are aware that we are acquainted with some aspects of their local military espionage set-up."[97] The Embassy felt that specific information fortifying Welles would be of significant benefit to Washington's position in Buenos Aires.[98] Although the Embassy mentioned the slowness of response to information provided in past cases, it felt that a note might help Argentina realize the dimensions of the infiltration. On October 22 the Embassy sent the draft of a long note it proposed to give to the Argentine government.[99] The memo, which was approved with a minor change, claimed there were at

least four groups of espionage agents working in Argentina. It stated that
Brazil had been the center of Axis espionage activity but restrictions in
that country had successfully closed down the organization. The Embassy
explained that the Germans had used "couriers on Spanish and other neutral ships, the diplomatic pouches, and the facilities of ordinary mail for
transmittal of their information between the United States and South America." From South America the information was transmitted, according to
the information of the United States, by clandestine radio to the German
High Command.

The memo referred vaguely to "citizens of South American countries"
who cooperated in the transmittals and to "bribery of police and other
government officials." It also mentioned that "a number of the main espionage agents have diplomatic status" or were attachés to German embassies.
The information sent via these channels included ship arrivals and departures,
political information, weather reports, movement of military equipment
within the hemisphere, details regarding hemispheric defense, the Panama
Canal, etc. After listing thirty-three members of the four espionage groups,
the document enclosed copies of some of the messages these groups sent
to Germany over clandestine radio transmitters. Although the Embassy felt
that the Germans were probably aware that the United States had most of
the information in the memo, the Embassy's note states:

> Inasmuch as the Germans probably are not aware that copies of these
> messages are in the possession of the government of the United States,
> it is requested that they be regarded as strictly confidential and be
> treated with the greatest of care.

Meanwhile, the Castillo government was coming under increasing criticism from the Chamber of Deputies. In late September the lower house
had called for the approval of the Rio resolutions and had passed a specific
resolution favoring an immediate severance of relations with the Axis
Powers; however, the bills went to the Senate too late for consideration
before adjournment. The Radicals had taken a pro-break position as early
as April.[100] The Socialists had been much slower in formally advocating
the severance, but, in arguing for the resolution Socialist Mario Bravo, one
of the leaders of the pro-Allied faction in the Chamber of Deputies debate,
picturesquely stated:

> What they [Castillo and Ruiz-Guiñazú] lack is human feeling. These
> people do not feel the war, do not see it, they ignore it. It is present
> in the five continents, in every corner of the world; the catastrophe
> approaches with apocalyptic force and no one can stop it, but against
> this catastrophe of events that is falling upon the people of the world

it only occurs to the President of the Republic to say to those who advise him to adopt a strong position: Very well; if there are any bellicose persons let them go to Europe to fight. This is the truth, and it is a bloody sarcasm, when there are millions and millions of men who are dying on the fields of battle; when all the nations of the world are mobilized to defend the ideas of democracy; and these nations are struggling with the immense problems which the war has brought with it, that a President of the Republic, a republic bound to the world situation together with that of America itself, should make remarks of this kind—is it not the truth that this should revolt the patience of the Argentines.

On the question of neutrality, Bravo said:

People believe that we are living in a neutral state. The people must know that we are living hypocritically in a neutral state; that the official mask is the mask of neutrality; that we are living in a state of war, not in a noisy war of bombardments and battles of bloody fields, but the other war, the undercover, the economic, the political, the war of peaceful penetration, of the fifth column. . . .[101]

In any event, the Executive Branch, which at Rio had insisted on clauses making the agreements subject to Argentina's constitutional processes, informed the Chamber that the management of foreign relations was the prerogative of the President,[102] a position which was probably correct under the Argentine Constitution.[103]

Moreover, September also saw the acquittal in the Court of Criminal Appeals in Buenos Aires of the twenty-one persons charged with fraud and unlawful association in connection with the raising of funds for German charities.[104] The grounds for the ruling were that the organization doing the collection was essentially a continuance of the Nazi Party—despite the fact that the Party had been ordered to dissolve these groups.[105]

Against this background the Department of State now had to make a decision which it realized had the potential of influencing the course of Argentine politics: How much publicity should the United States give to the memo it presented on November 3 to the Castillo government in which it "exposed" the German espionage activities in Argentina? Certainly the Embassy wanted to rally Argentine public opinion against the Axis countries but there were several problems. The first was whether this could be done without the appearance of intervention in the domestic affairs of Argentina, since making the contents public would be designed to strengthen the hands of the anti-Castillo elements. Second, the Embassy wondered whether publicity regarding the delivery of the note might give notice to Axis agents to

take cover. It was also suggested that making such information public might
give the Argentine government the excuse that its efforts to apprehend the
agents had been frustrated by premature publicity. The Embassy felt the Argentine government should be given an opportunity to act prior to any
publicity being given the note.[106] The Department of State replied that in
view of the public protests from Argentina that Welles's statements were
vague, the Department reserved the right to give publicity to its memo but
would, for the time being, not move in that direction.[107] The Department
was strengthened in this position by the fact that Argentine Ambassador
Espil in late October had recommended that the United States, upon presenting the note, state that it intended to make the information public in
the relatively near future. This, the Ambassador believed, would stimulate
action in Buenos Aires.[108]

Ambassador Espil, however, changed his position on the question after
the memo was presented. His initial reaction upon reading it was that the
November 3 message was desirable and he was sorry the step had not been
taken sooner. Welles pointed out that Argentina had not heeded earlier information given to it, and the Undersecretary was particularly vehement
on the subject of telecommunications between Axis agents and Europe.
Ambassador Espil laid much of the blame for the situation on the domestic
political situation. Espil admitted that his own position in the government
had deteriorated but said he hoped the memo would not be made public
"if the Argentine government took effective and prompt steps to correct
the situation" (according to Welles's account of the conversation). The Ambassador said that such a disclosure would only increase the bad feelings
between the countries, but Welles left the question of publicity open.[109]

On November 5 Ambassador Armour wired the Secretary of State that
he felt the Argentine officials were beginning to take some actions as a
result of the memo and that he strongly urged that no publicity be given
the note for the time being. Later that same day the Embassy wired that
the police had made some arrests of specific agents mentioned in the November 3 memo. Armour also stated that the publication by the Political Defense Committee in Montevideo of the memo presented to Santiago relating
to espionage activities in Chile, and the rumors that a similar report was
forthcoming on Argentina, might have given Axis agents a warning of the
impending raids.[110] The following day the Ambassador warned that "the
sincerity, extent and effectiveness" of the actions remained to be seen. In
the same note Armour advised that he felt the reaction of the Argentine
public to publication of the memo would be favorable only if a sufficient
amount of time had elapsed so that it would not appear that the purpose
of the note was simply to embarrass the Argentine government.[111]

On November 7 Ambassador Espil called on Undersecretary Welles with a memorandum making a plea that the U.S. memorandum relating to espionage should not be given publicity immediately.[112] When Welles said he could not give assurances that the memorandum would not be made public, the Ambassador asked to see Secretary Hull, in hopes of getting a firm commitment from him. The impact which the publication of the Chilean memo was having was readily observable and the Argentine government hoped to avoid the pressure. Actually the memo was already in the hands of Washington representatives on the Committee for Political Defense. Other pleadings not to release the memo were made on the grounds that it would play into the hands of extreme nationalist elements which would claim that the arrests in Argentina were ordered from Washington.[113] Hull's memoirs indicate that in his meeting with Espil he agreed not to publicize the memo at that time, although there was a brief statement in the papers that the United States had presented memos on subversive activities in Argentina at the request of the Argentine Embassy following Welles's speech.[114]

Officials in the United States Embassy in Buenos Aires soon began to complain that only fourteen of the forty-four names on the original memorandum had been arrested or detained.[115] Armour, in a conversation with the Minister of the Interior, threatened that Washington would be forced to publish the memo unless concrete, positive actions were taken. He noted the fact that the police supposedly had not been shown the complete memo; and he said he was unimpressed by the efforts being made regarding the memo by the local police, which he characterized as "superficial and extremely 'hit or miss.' " Actually, in some cases confessions were obtained; but in others, including some in which the United States felt there was a great deal of incriminating evidence, accused agents were given favorable reports by the police. The Ambassador also theorized that, until one key agent unexpectedly confessed, the intention had been to discredit the United States memo.[116] The Embassy began to prepare for a counterattack from Axis sympathizers who were expected to try to expose actions of American agents operating in Argentina.

The Department of State was divided on the question of the wisdom of releasing the memorandum. The question was never one of whether it was proper to attempt to influence Argentine public policy, but only one of whether policy could be influenced in the proper direction. One suggestion was that a definite deadline be set for effective action by the Argentine government against the spy organizations mentioned in the November 3 communication.[117] There was also some feeling that the threat of publishing such a memo might be sufficient to obtain results. As in the case of Chile, it was decided that if the memo were published it should go through the Committee for Political Defense in Montevideo so as to avoid making it appear to be too much a unilateral attempt by Washington to pressure Buenos Aires.

Two factors finally prompted the Department of State to have its representative on the Emergency Advisory Committee for Political Defense in Montevideo urge the publication of the information. The first was that by mid-December of 1942 it was becoming increasingly obvious to the Embassy that the Argentine government was not going to vigorously pursue the individuals and groups named in the memo. Early in December the Embassy had been of the opinion that "we are at last beginning to obtain to a certain degree the kind of cooperation we have wanted" and have advocated giving the Castillo government more time.[118] Disappointment soon set in and the Department reached the conclusion that it was "becoming increasingly clear that Argentina is not following through vigorously with respect to the memo on Axis activities" and that it was doing nothing on its own to pursue the question.[119] The other factor prompting publication of the note was Chile's decision on January 20, 1943, to break diplomatic relations with the Axis. From Washington's point of view, Chile's decision served to further isolate Argentina and to emphasize the fact that Argentina was alone in its dogged efforts to avoid commitment. The U.S. hope was that between Chile's break in relations and the publication of the memo by a relatively sterile source, the Argentine government's policy would be shaken.

The memorandum submitted by the United States was prepared for final release in Montevideo and attempted to limit its discussion to the existence of German agents in Argentina. Care was taken to avoid including anything that had not already been presented to the Argentine government, though no specific mention was made of this fact.[120] On January 22 the Emergency Advisory Committee for Political Defense met to consider the memo. A resolution by Brazil calling for immediate publication was approved by five of the seven members. Chile, which had previously taken a position that there should not be any publication under such circumstances, abstained. Argentina centered its opposition around three arguments. The first was that the document was closely linked to diplomatic exchanges between the United States and Argentina and hence could not be published without the approval of both countries. Second, Argentina defended its efforts to prosecute the agents mentioned in the memo. Finally, it was argued that publication of the note would prejudice justice in the Argentine courts. The majority of the Committee argued that the memo presented to the Committee was not a diplomatic note between Argentina and the United States and that prejudicing judicial proceedings was a technical question. The Committee could only be guided by whether publication would promote the defense interests of all the American republics. The Argentine efforts to curb Axis agents were also criticized in the debate.[121]

The Argentine government made no effort to ban national publication of the memo, and it received wide reprinting in major newspapers, most of which were opposing the Castillo government. On the day of its release the Foreign Office issued a decree stating that there was nothing new in the memo, that the courts were prosecuting the cases mentioned, and that the publicity would undoubtedly hinder further investigation and prejudice judicial decisions.[122] It also quoted Ambassador Armour saying that the "government of the United States appreciates the effective action taken by the Argentine government with regard to the apprehension of certain subversive agents of the Axis." Actually, the quotation was drawn from a note which was quite critical of Argentine efforts.[123] The decree indicated that the executive would adjust its position to the judicial findings—a hint that, if the charges were substantiated, the government might change its position. Although allowed to publish the memo, the newspapers were evidently barred from making favorable editorial comment on it while those who objected were free to criticize.[124]

TELECOMMUNICATIONS

Another consequential issue between the United States and Argentina was the question of closing telecommunications linking Argentina (and Chile) with the Axis countries as agreed to at the Rio meeting. The technical question of how difficult it would be to circumvent such a stoppage made the issue incredibly complex. Soon the United States government also realized that the varying nationalities represented in the financial interests which controlled telecommunications made it possible for limited opposition to veto effective action. Finally, it was clear that Argentina and Chile would have to cooperate in the closing, and those two countries hoped to avoid any unnecessarily hostile act.

By April of 1942 the United States was seriously concerned, and studying the telecommunications situation because messages from Buenos Aires and Santiago were continuing to flow to the Axis capitals. It had been hoped that, concurrent with Resolution 40 of the Rio meeting, these channels would be closed. In both Latin American capitals the major station under consideration was operated by a local company which was a subsidiary of the Consortium Trust Affiliates, a combine of United States, English, French, and German interests.[125] The composition of the local committees managing the companies was a subject of consideration because initially in Argentina there was a fear of offending important local financial groups. In contrast to Argentina, where local financial opposition was being spurred in its opposition to halting the flow of telecommunications by German business interests, the problem in Chile was fear of offending Japan.[126]

Originally, it was hoped that the governments of Argentina and Chile would take it upon themselves to stop the messages. When it became obvious that the Argentine government was not going to take action, Allied diplomatic interest shifted to getting the companies to take the step on their own. However, the companies feared that if they took such an action, the government of Argentina might use this as an excuse to take over the companies. Then, too, there began to be hints that the companies, even the branches in England, did not want to lose the revenues from the messages.[127] The U.S. Department of State became increasingly displeased by mid-1942 with the actions of Sir Edward Wilshaw, Chairman of the Board of Cables and Wireless, Ltd., and Sir Campbell Stuart, Chairman of the Commonwealth Communications Council, for what it felt to be excessive hesitancy.

Information gathered by the United States Embassy showed that during May of 1942 the number of messages sent had remained relatively stable as compared to the prewar month of November 1941;[128] but there had been a substantial decline in messages to and from the United States and some decline in messages to and from other South American countries. There had been a substantial increase in messages sent to Europe, particularly to Spain, Germany, Italy, Switzerland, and Sweden. There had also been a more than 20-percent increase in messages to Japan. The United States felt it had other evidence that these circuits were being used for the transmission of information regarding ship movements, cargoes, and other intelligence messages. On the other hand, it was feared that if communication channels to Germany and Italy were cut off, messages might be relayed through such neutrals as Spain, Switzerland and Sweden.[129]

There was a burst of hope in July of 1942 that Argentina would take action as the Minister of the Interior issued instructions for the complete implementation of the Rio resolution dealing with telecommunications.[130] However, the Director of Posts and Telegraphs refused to implement the instructions on the grounds that such instructions would have to come from the Foreign Office.[131] This was not the first time that the Foreign Ministry counteracted pro-Allied decisions made by other agencies,[132] and it should not necessarily lead to a conclusion that the Foreign Ministry was exceeding its administrative boundaries because the decisions it had interfered with were decisions with strong diplomatic implications. Of course it does highlight the differences of opinion within the Argentine government.

Although England frequently appeared to be dragging its feet in these efforts,[133] Washington suggested that the two countries cooperate to utilize their voting majorities on the boards of directors of the Argentine subsidiaries. Washington had finally decided that it was unlikely that the Argentine government would undertake to operate the circuits to the Axis capitals if the companies ceased to accept messages. Such an action by Buenos Aires would clearly have been an act hostile to inter-American cooperation, while most of Argentina's previous resistance had been simply non-cooperation rather than active opposition. This opinion, however, was not unanimous in the Department of State. The Chief of the Division of American Republics, Philip Bonsal, argued that the companies had no right under Argentine law to break off communications. That step, he said, would certainly give impetus to possible nationalization, but he noted that nationalization might be desirable under some circumstances.[134]

The Argentine government, then under pressure from the November 4 memo from the United States, began to talk about a possible action to prohibit the use of coded radio messages outside the continent. This would allow only cable communication, and the cable channel passed through London, thereby making it vulnerable.[135] On November 24, 1942, in Ambassador Armour's first informal meeting with Acting President Castillo, Castillo complimented him on the recent United States military victories and assured the Ambassador that Argentina was investigating the espionage charges of the United States. He also agreed with Armour's suggestions that Buenos Aires should promptly issue a decree prohibiting the use of cipher messages by radio outside the continent.[136]

The word soon reached the Embassy in Buenos Aires that the decree would not deny such use by embassies, a change Armour felt was due to pressure from Axis diplomatic missions. On November 26 Armour was told that the Argentine government would restrict messages in code to a limited number of words. Undersecretary for Foreign Affairs Roberto Gache said that completely to forbid the use of code by the embassies would run counter to his government's neutralist policy. Armour argued that Germany was already violating Argentina's neutrality through its spy network which was being slowly exposed. Gache argued that in view of Washington's protests about the increasing number of code messages from the three Axis embassies, the limitation would sorely effect their operation. Armour asked to see Ruiz-Guiñazú before the degree was approved.[137]

After some reluctance, the interview was arranged for November 2, 1942, and Armour reported the results as being "most discouraging." Ruiz-Guiñazú used many of the same arguments and mentioned a maximum of no more than 100 code words per day. Armour said that the planned decree was "entirely unsatisfactory" and argued against the allowance of 100 words in code. The Minister of the Interior had privately suggested that the best hope was for the private companies to simply close the circuits to Europe.[138] On December 1 Secretary Hull wired Armour suggesting that he point out to the Argentine government that during World War I the United States, while still neutral, had refused to send any messages in code for the diplomatic missions of the Central Powers unless the Navy had been furnished the code.[139] Armour decided, however, not to bring up this alternative at the time because the British Embassy was pressing for a prohibition against all radio communications in code outside the continent. Although Armour believed the decree would be issued over his protests, he felt at the time the idea of forcing the messages to be in a code known by Argentina could be suggested. The Ambassador also warned that even if all code messages to the Axis capitals were cut off, there was still the ever-present possibility that the Germans would be able to transmit messages through European neutrals.[140]

Armour's uneasiness proved well founded. On December 3 the Argentine government issued a decree suspending international exchange of radiograms in code excepting 100 code words a day which could be sent by embassies or consulates. Attempting to convince the United States Embassy that the decree was of some significance, an Argentine Foreign Ministry official pointed out that some of the local Axis missions had been sending as many as 2,000 code words a day and therefore the reduction was more than a gesture. He also pointed out that communications by private citizens were being cut off. According to Armour, it was hinted that if the United States could show concrete evidence of subversive information being transmitted by Axis embassies, a further crackdown might follow.[141]

The coming of the 100-word allowance decree ends one stage of the debate over telecommunications. The Department of State interpreted it as a defeat of serious proportions for Washington. One State Department official suggested that the time had come to seriously consider the beginning of agitation via the public media in Argentina, the United States, and the other American republics in order to arouse public sentiment against the existing Argentina government. The memo, written by Louis Halle, pointed to the impact of the Welles speech in Boston as having "shown that the Argentine government is not altogether insensible to the atmosphere of public opinion."[142] The Embassy in Argentina went through the formality of protesting the allowance of 100 words with the statement that it was ineffective as a device to limit communications with the Axis.[143] Armour also reiterated his previous suggestion in a December 18 telegram to Washington stating that "we would be in a much stronger position to press for total elimination of coded messages by radio if we could show [the] Argentine government copies of any subversive messages sent by local Axis missions."[144]

The effort now shifted back to trying to get the United States and the British business interests to simply refuse messages in code between Buenos Aires and non-American countries. In line with this policy, on January 15, 1943, Ambassador Armour presented a memo to the Argentine Minister of Foreign Affairs.[145] It stated that the United States could not allow United States companies to provide services to the Axis Powers which enabled the

Axis "to destroy personnel and shipping" of the Allies. Henceforth, the Argentine government was notified, the government in Washington was prepared to instruct United States interests in Transradio International to work in conjunction with British interests toward the goal of "terminating the transmissions of all messages to or from non-American countries in secret language." The note referred to the Rio resolutions as justification and asked for "the sympathetic understanding of the Argentine government" for this step.

Undersecretary of Foreign Affairs Gache, who received the note, attempted to dissuade Armour from formally presenting it—although he did not argue against taking the action without notification. He said that speaking as "a man in the street" it might have been more effective not to notify the Foreign Office of the action in advance.[146] Armour stated that he wished to be on record as having informed the Argentine government of the action Washington was about to take. He also said that he hoped Buenos Aires would support the move, at least to the extent of not making it impossible for Transradio to comply with the instruction. Dr. Gache admitted that it did seem illogical for a United States firm to take an action detrimental to the defense of the United States such as sending out information containing espionage information. What Gache did not say, but clearly implied, was that by presenting the note Washington was forcing Argentina to either protest the action or tacitly admit that espionage activities were taking place in Argentina without obstruction by the Argentine government.

Upon returning to his office after the conversation, Armour received a call from Gache asking again if Washington would not reconsider the idea of presenting the note and, rather, simply instruct the company. Armour said that he doubted whether the company would agree to taking the action unless it had some intimation of what Argentina's governmental attitude would be. Armour asked if he could inform the companies that the Argentine government had no objection and would confirm this decision if approached by the representatives of the firms. The Undersecretary, "emphatically," according to Armour's account, said he did not believe the Foreign Minister would agree to such a procedure. Then Gache asked if perhaps the aide memoire could be kept on his desk without becoming a matter of official record until Ruiz-Guiñazú returned. Armour, who knew that a similar request had been honored by the British Ambassador, said he would not object.[147] An official of Transradio was called to the office of the Chief of Radio Communications that afternoon and cautioned against any halting of the code traffic without prior governmental approval—an action the local Transradio board was evidently not going to take without official approval anyway.[148]

On January 19 the Ministry of Foreign Affairs officially replied to the

Washington memo and arranged for Armour to see the Foreign Minister the following day. The Argentine reply threateningly commented that the United States memo of January 14 "again raises the problem of foreign interests in corporations which function in" Argentina.[149] It stated that the government had long made it clear that its position was that "companies which function in the Republic may not accept orders emanating from foreign governments." It said that particularly in the case of Transradio, which was a public service company, there was no question but that it was "subject exclusively to the provisions of its respective concession and to the control of the Posts and Telegraphs authorities." The memo outlined the actions already taken to halt the flow of subversive information and concluded:

> The memorandum under reply adduces no proof whatever substantiating the aforementioned abuse which might warrant the suppression of telegraphic service in secret language, within the existing regulations.[150]

In his conversation with Ruiz-Guiñazú, Ambassador Armour shifted the emphasis of the United States note by indicating that Washington was not asking to direct the company to stop the flow of code words unless the Argentine government agreed—a nuance which the Foreign Minister said had escaped him. It probably escaped others because it is difficult to read this into the statement. It may be that the memo was purposefully worded so as to give Armour the "out" of arguing this position if the government of Argentina should choose to become offended. Judging from his own accounts of his previous conversations with Gache, Armour certainly had not been emphasizing this as the reason for wishing Ruiz-Guiñazú to see the memo prior to the Embassy's issuing it and giving instructions to Transradio. Armour also took exception to the implications of the previous day's memo that there had been other recent instances of Washington giving orders to investors in Argentina. The Minister said the note had merely intended to emphasize the policy.

Armour then went back to the argument he had made to Gache, that since the messages being sent in code undoubtedly contained information leading to the sinking of Allied ships, it was improper for Transradio to be forced to continue sending them. The Ambassador asked whether recent espionage exposés did not convince the Foreign Minister that the embassies were abusing their code privileges. Ruiz-Guiñazú said that the complicity of embassy members in espionage did not necessarily prove that the sending of messages in code had any connection with the sinking of United Nations shipping. He reiterated that if the United States had such evidence, he would be anxious to see it. The Foreign Minister said that if deciphered copies of messages sent since the 100-word maximum was put into effect showed them concerned with reporting ship movements, the Argentine government would be in a position to act. To do this would, of course, have put the United States in the position of revealing if it had broken the code, and despite repeated requests from Armour to the State Department for information of the type requested by the Argentine Foreign Minister, it was not furnished.[151] An April 1 message from Adolph Berle informed Armour that "the Department regrets to inform you that this inquiry has not now established that evidence of this nature can now be produced." He did state that there seemed sufficient circumstantial evidence on which to base the assumption but that the "categorical evidence" simply was "not available."[152]

The January 20 conversation became even more of a vacuous debaters' tournament as it progressed. Ruiz-Guiñazú assured Ambassador Armour that the Argentine government would issue strict instructions to its interventors in the radio offices that they should satisfy themselves that the code messages from the Axis embassies were innocuous. Armour asked how this could be done and received an answer which he termed "incredible": the officers could insist that the embassies tell the interventors what was in the messages or give them a reading.[153] When pressed on the fact that Argentina did not seem to be living up to the Rio resolution on communications (the text of which Armour read to the Foreign Minister), Ruiz-Guiñazú stated that it had only been a recommendation. He also said that there had been so many resolutions at the Rio meeting that there had been little time to closely study them. Therefore, he maintained, it was not reasonable to take the resolutions too seriously or to interpret them too strictly. Armour commented in his despatch:

> This astounding statement, surpassing even anything I had already come to expect from Dr. Ruiz-Guiñazú, was too much. I told him that it was evident that no useful purpose could be accomplished by continuing the conversation, and departed.[154]

Thus by the end of January 1943 the United States and Argentina had reached a stalemate on the question of stopping telecommunications with the Axis capitals. The situation remained unchanged until the fall of the Castillo government.

Although there is always a tendency to explain events in terms of the individuals involved since it is much simpler than dealing with the complex processes involved, the figure of Ruiz-Guiñazú deserves some special mention in this narrative. He appeared to dominate Argentine foreign policy from late 1941 to mid-1943. Whether he was in fact in control is questionable because the policy frequently seems comprehensible only in terms of domestic political considerations. A Foreign Minister who seems to be controlling the President's policy can serve as a useful tool for the President, as Barros Jarpa may have in Chile. The Foreign Minister can act as a lightning rod for criticism while the President remains unscathed. It cannot be overlooked that the Foreign Minister must please the President, so the degree to which his control of the policy is absolute is sharply limited.

Ruiz-Guiñazú was described in his 1967 obituary in the *New York Times* as "an urbane lawyer whose aristocratic appearance was enhanced by a pince-nez and well-tailored Savile Row clothes" and "the embodiment of the old-school diplomacy pursued by . . . President Ramon S. Castillo."[155] His memoirs published in 1944 argue that World War II was not a matter of direct interest to the Latin American countries.[156] During his visit to Washington in May of 1941 when he was returning from his post as Argentine envoy to the Vatican he had impressed Sumner Welles with his favorable attitude toward the United States.[157] At the time he had been quite upset by German policy toward the Catholic Church and by the fall of France. He did, however, seem "somewhat antagonistic," according to Welles, toward the British and out of touch with inter-American affairs. The Undersecretary was later to write that Ruiz-Guiñazú was "one of the stupidest men to hold office" in Argentine history.[158] Certainly he did at times seem unable to comprehend Washington's view of the situation, but this could have been simply a good diplomatic tactic: what I don't know, I can't be held accountable for.

Welles quotes Ruiz-Guiñazú as saying that General Franco was his idol. The Undersecretary claimed that the Foreign Minister took "no trouble to conceal the extent of his admiration for Mussolini's brand of fascism."[159] Welles in 1944 also described Ruiz-Guiñazú as having

> a strong prejudice against the United States and a barely concealed belief that the civilization of this country was so decadent and inefficient, because of its democratic institutions, that it would not conceivably be able to stand up against the power and might of the Axis nations.[160]

There seems little doubt that he did feel Mussolini had done for Italy what needed to be done in Argentina. He fell into the "Hispanidad" stream of Argentine (and Latin American) nationalism, which considers "Madrid the center of the civilized world"[161] and the crass materialism of the United States to be decadent. His speeches in Argentina appealed to Argentina's "unblemished tradition of international honor" in which neutrality served "the real interests of the international community."[162] In his efforts to rally support for his position, he emphasized the pressure the United States was applying to Argentina.[163] There is also evidence that he hoped to mediate an end to the war in mid-1941.[164]

Another factor sometimes mentioned in regard to the Foreign Minister is his son, a writer of nationalist and corporate state tracts.[165] In calling for revolution, young Ruiz-Guiñazú wrote that "the historical destiny of a people depends above all on the character of its race." Although feeling that the biology of the race was important, the highest level, he argued, was spiritual. His position against immigrants seems particularly inappropriate in view of the nature of Argentina's development. He called for a return to the land and larger families with work a "right and duty." He asked for an end to electoral democracy. "To replace universal suffrage there is no other road than that of popular representation through syndicalist and corporative organization." Much of his most bitter criticism was directed at the legislative branch of government in Argentina. But whether his writings affected his father, cannot be known; nor can it be known how much effect the elder Ruiz-Guiñazú's ideas had on his son's thought and work.

In the light of the Foreign Minister's antidemocratic beliefs, it is interesting to contrast his attitude with that of Argentina's Ambassador in Washington, Felipe Espil. Again, as with Chile, this channel of communication between the two countries had its political aspects. The Ambassador in Washington was in the difficult position of being asked to present to the Department of State a policy with which he often disagreed. This, of course, made his task frequently unpleasant since the Department of State did not welcome the policy either. Welles was of the opinion that Espil's fear of being caught in the middle of a serious diplomatic struggle may have worked in both directions—Espil was also "not disposed to communicate unpleasant truths to his government."[166] When Espil was about to return to Buenos Aires for a visit in August of 1942 he assured Welles that he would do everything within his power to influence a change in his government's policy.[167] At the time he said he felt the leadership of the Foreign Office was intransigent and that his best chance for a change was in a personal talk with the President. He also expressed the opinion, which proved to be inaccurate, that if Chile broke relations with the Axis it would cause an uneasiness in the Argentine Army and Navy which would lead the government to modify its policy.

After his return from Buenos Aires he even encouraged Welles to threaten the Argentine government with disclosure of the information regarding espionage agents in Argentina as a method of stimulating a change in policy.[168] This could not have helped but encourage the presentation of the November 4 memo only a week after the remark of Espil. In terms of a model of diplomatic bargaining, Espil was dysfunctional. Rather than presenting the response of Washington back to his government, he was at times almost an adviser on Argentine affairs to the Department of State. And he was not a particularly good adviser in that he was not in sympathy with the general policy and not close to the group controlling the Foreign Ministry. The fact that Espil was "too" pro-United States hindered his effectiveness as a channel of communication between Buenos Aires and Washington. Perhaps he was clearly stating the North American position to his own government (although this seems doubtful), but he was sometimes softening the Argentine position in his presentations to the Department of State.[169] Thus the role of Ambassador Armour became important. He was convinced of his government's policy, and he was a professional. There is no evidence to suggest that Armour was anything other than a diplomat of the old school, in the best sense of the term. He seldom exercised sovereignty in questions of basic policy once Washington had chosen its course of action. He did, however, voice his opinions within the framework of the decision-making process.

With the nationalists of the right using United States pressure as an excuse for not taking certain actions, the Embassy's problem of staying out of domestic Argentine politics was made more acute. This did not stem from any neutrality regarding Argentine political issues, of course, but rather from the dangers of getting caught trying to influence the policies. Undersecretary Welles warned Armour shortly after the Rio meeting to make sure that American business interests in Argentina did not allow themselves to be maneuvered into a position that would leave them vulnerable to charges of intervention.[170] The "outs" in the Argentine political process evidently entertained some mild hopes of involving the United States in plans to topple the government. Soon after the Rio meeting a prominent Radical politician had been soliciting United States firms in Argentina for financial support to assist Radical activities against the government—thereby prompting the Welles warning. In passing along information about this situation, Armour said that Castillo was "reliably reported" to know about the case and that it was said to have caused bitterness on his part and a further drawing together of the anti-Allied elements of the government.[171] A month later Armour was approached directly by another prominent Radical in the Chamber of Deputies with a request that a small number of arms be provided to Radicals in the provinces so they could resist possible government intervention in the provinces of Córdoba and Entre Ríos.[172]

Another problem faced by the United States Embassy in Buenos Aires and the Department of State was that of coordinating its Argentine policy with that of England. More specifically, from Washington's point of view, the question was of getting England to coordinate its policy with that of the United States. The difficulties in coordination stemmed from the completely different relationships between England and Argentina and the United States and Argentina. Argentina was a major source of English meat and a primary area of English investment. There were long, close ties between the countries. To simplify, Argentina was economically more important to England than it was to the United States. This situation served to circumscribe British ability and willingness to pressure Argentina. The loss of trade with Argentina or a crackdown in Buenos Aires against British investment would have been a serious blow to England.

Certainly in the case of telecommunications and other incidents there was a distinct reserve in British policy as to its willingness to go along with Pan-Americanism. The Pan-American idea held no appeal in England, where it was interpreted as a sphere of influence concept lacking the mystical qualities attributed to it in the United States. On August 1, 1942, Duggan was sufficiently concerned about the lack of cooperation on the part of the British to write a memo on the subject. He felt that part of the British reticence stemmed from some Englishmen who were thinking primarily in terms of postwar trade. While he did not feel these individuals were being encouraged by the British missions in Argentina and Chile, he did not feel that the postwar projections were being discouraged either.[173] Finally, in October of 1942 the British Foreign Office sent a circular instruction to its missions in Latin America denying that Britain opposed Argentina's possible breaking of relations with the Axis.[174] At least part of the kind of rumor that would necessitate such an instruction must have originated with individuals in Argentina who were pro-Axis in sympathies, but the reserve of the British on questions of Pan-Americanism reinforced the idea.

Ambassador Armour had hoped in early 1943 that the British government might be persuaded to use its meat purchase negotiations (which were being held in London) as a lever to influence Argentina in the direction of a more pro-Allied diplomatic stance.[175] His reasoning was that these talks were really much more important than other economic questions because the negotiations directly affected the owners of the large cattle-growing estates in Argentina, a group of considerable political power and the primary backing for President Castillo. He felt that if "concern" could be created among this group that Britain might attempt to secure its meat elsewhere, it could quickly lead to a halt in telecommunications. This in turn could have forced Ruiz-Guiñazú, the symbol of strong neutrality, to resign— thereby opening the way for more cooperation. The United States Ambassador admitted that such a threat on the part of the British would be a "bluff" and that it had the disadvantage of possibly endangering the flow of important products to embattled England. Still, Armour stated, "so long as the Argentine government knows that all the meat the country produces will be taken by Great Britain," the other restrictions on Argentina designed to soften its attitude would be weakened.[176]

WASHINGTON RECONSIDERS ITS POLICY

There were so many aspects to Argentina's reluctance to cooperate against the Axis that it is simplistic to emphasize any particular one. However, the aspect which came to be most symbolic of her resistance was the question of breaking relations with the Axis Powers. As in the case of Chile, this was an action easily comprehended by the public and one which either had been done or had not been done—there was no question of degree such as made evaluation of actions against Axis espionage difficult. During the months after the meeting in Rio there was hope in the Department of State that relations would be broken although public statements from Argentine public officials could hardly have been less encouraging. For example, in late May of 1942 during the lend-lease controversy, President Castillo had told Armour that Argentina would cooperate with the United States on all matters up to the breaking of diplomatic relations but that this final action simply would not be taken.[177] The President's public repudiation of the "automatism" of collective international agreements in his speech to the Argentine Congress a few days later reaffirmed this position. By early February of 1943 Duggan was stating within the Department of State that "there is little ground for hope that Argentina will break diplomatic relations with the Axis . . . during the remaining months of the presidency of Castillo."[178]

Besides the refusal to break relations, there were many Argentine actions in relation to the proclaimed list, financial transactions, provision of raw materials, and protection against espionage which were not easy to evaluate.[179] Even the Department of State was sometimes baffled regarding whether or not Argentina was following the Rio commitments she supposedly had assumed in these areas. The questions were frequently so complex that it would be months after a law was passed or a decree issued before it would become known whether or not it was being enforced or whether it was simply an effort to appease Washington or pro-Allied elements in the government. There was, of course, also the fact that unenforced decrees could sometimes result simply from governmental ineptness rather than from any unwillingness on the part of Buenos Aires.

As these reports regarding Argentine slowness to take actions against German and Italian interests in almost all fields accumulated, the Department of State began in the autumn of 1942 to re-evaluate its economic policy toward Argentina. In September Emilio Collado, Executive Secretary of the Department's Board of Economic Operations, sent a memo titled "Economic Policy Towards Argentina" to Acheson, Welles and Hull.[180] Essentially, it was an answer to those who wanted to "crack down" on Argentina. The basic argument it made was:

> The economic balance with Argentina is of such a character that strong economic pressure can be brought against Argentina only by a combination of the most vigorous economic policies applied by a coalition of the United Nations.

Based on this general line of reasoning, Ambassador Armour and the officers of the Department of State felt that the gains from such policies would be more than offset by sacrifices forced upon the populations of the United States and England without bringing about the desired changes in policy. Collado pointed out the English dependency on Argentine beef and the problems in regard to meat shortages and general shipping shortages which would occur if the United States tried to meet the need. The memo also pointed out that Argentina was supplying the United States with some important materials. Since the costs of "cracking down" were so high and the gains doubtful, Collado rejected this course of action. He also argued that it was even more evident that a policy of partial pressure would not bring about a change in Argentine policies.

The recommendations made in the memorandum, which represented the consensus of the Buenos Aires Embassy and Department of State feeling on the subject (with some exceptions), fell into several categories. As far as purchases from Argentina, Collado's memorandum suggested that England continue her meat purchases and the United States continue to purchase such Argentine strategic commodities as could be shipped in Argentine vessels. It suggested allocating no United Nations–controlled ships to the United States–Argentina route, and it presented a tentative monthly schedule designed to limit the goods going south to Argentina to supplies not needed in the United States or materials essential for Argentina to keep up the production the United Nations needed.[181] Until Argentina agreed to participate in the tanker pool, she should be denied equipment she wanted for her own petroleum industry. The memo suggested some other measures in the area of finance and the proclaimed list: Proposed Export-Import Bank special credits should be halted and no further credits should be extended to the government in Buenos Aires. The effectiveness of the proclaimed list should be increased (actually a reorganization of the Embassy staff to better handle the list was already underway). Intelligence work connected with the proclaimed list should be expanded and improved. In collaboration with the Treasury Department, the Department of State should work to halt transactions involving assets within the United States or transactions by U.S. concerns when such transactions might indirectly or directly help the Axis countries.

As part of this re-evaluation both Armour and Duggan prepared statements of suggested policy early in February of 1943, each reflecting a somewhat different emphasis. In his memo Armour advanced the idea of a bluff on the part of Great Britain that she might not buy Argentine beef, which might well serve as the catalyst for a change in policy.[182] He felt at the time that the Casablanca meeting, Roosevelt's interview with Brazilian President Vargas, and the announcement of a $20-million loan to Uruguay, all served to introduce uncertainties into the Argentine calculations which might result in a change in Argentina's policies. Armour admitted he could understand the difficulties of London's assuming this position, but said he felt that so long as Argentina was confident of this market, other economic restrictions were going to be less effective.

Armour did have a suggestion for a policy which he felt might be effective. In view of the uneasiness in the Argentine public and government of the foreign policy being followed by Buenos Aires, Armour felt that it would be wise to try to provide an excuse for a change in policy since he felt that already the government was debating whether or not to change the policy. Armour's idea was, not to stage an incident of any kind, but rather to simply begin ignoring Argentina while doing everything possible to "build up" the image of Brazil, Uruguay, Paraguay, Chile, and the other countries cooperating in the war. This would involve press, newsreels, and radio releases emphasizing the military equipment going to the latter countries. Also laudatory articles stressing the industrial and economic development of these countries in cooperation with the United States would be emphasized. A boycott of indifference should be shown within the hemisphere toward Argentina. He also suggested that the President and Secretary of State should in press conferences make it clear that the United States was no longer interested in what Argentina was doing and that the policy of Buenos Aires was strictly its own business. This might, Armour felt, hit Argentina in what he felt to be its weak spot—its pride. It also had the advantage of not having the element of coercion which other policies had, an element bound to rally Argentine pride (or nationalism) against the policies of the United Nations and perhaps make Argentina even more belligerent in its resistance to requests for cooperation.

Duggan's approach was more dependent on economic pressure.[183] He felt it unlikely that there would be any change in policy so long as the Argentine economy continued to prosper from the policy of non-involvement. "When things are going well, people just do not make drastic decisions," he reasoned, and continued:

> This is not to say that it is necessary for grass to grow on Calle Florida [a main street in Buenos Aires], or that Argentine industry slow to a standstill, or that hundreds of thousands of workers in Buenos Aires roam the streets unemployed. But it does mean that the boom in the Argentine economy be brought to a halt. It means that an element of uncertainty, of question, of doubt, be injected into a situation that looks mighty good to everyone, from the *estancia* owner down to the dock worker.

Duggan felt sure that the overwhelming bulk of the Argentine population favored a United Nations victory but had decided that it was easier, and more profitable, to let the United States and England carry the burden.

Duggan emphasized that the policy would have to be carried out in conjunction with other countries—otherwise the United States would be vulnerable to Argentine claims of coercion. His memo, by his own admission, did not discuss ways of executing the policy but he expressed optimism that there were no insuperable difficulties.

Evidently Armour's opinions on the matter of cracking down on the Argentine economy reflected the opinions of other members of his staff. Voicing many of the same arguments as the Ambassador, the Commercial Attaché in Buenos Aires also urged ignoring Argentina and dropping harsh efforts toward pressuring her for a break in relations. He argued that the alternatives were between a friendly neutral and an unfriendly neutral.[184] He did argue that the other Latin American countries should be favored over Argentina in such things as trade and military goods but not to the point of obvious discrimination. The United States policy should not be to shut down Argentine factories, he said; just to slow them down a little.

On March 4, 1943, a new State Department policy memorandum was drawn up by the Board of Economic Operations and the Division of American Republics which seemed to follow these recommendations. Its thrust was mainly in the direction of dampening the Argentine war boom without cutting off the flow of critical materials and supplies from Argentina to the United States. It called for favoritism towards those countries assisting in the war effort but it recognized that goods and services would have to be made available to Argentina in order to keep up her production of critical materials. In essence, the memorandum advocated putting trade with Argentina on a very businesslike basis: Argentina should get only what was necessary to continue her production of goods needed for the war effort.[185] This flowed from the reasoning of an earlier Armour memorandum arguing that "the present Argentine government has no ideals. Appeals and protests based on anything but self-interest are therefore largely futile."[186]

Even this relatively mild economic pressure was a compromise policy. Milo Perkins of the Board of Economic Warfare felt by May of 1943 that the restrictions called for in the March 4 statement were too severe and would interfere with production in Argentina. This disagreement represented the differing roles of the Board of Economic Warfare (BEW) and the Division of American Republics. The Board approached the problem at this time within the terms of its own sphere of interest—the economic viewpoint. Its responsibility was to feed raw materials into the war-time industrial complex in order to sustain production. Argentina was an important source of supply of some of these materials. The problem was also a jurisdictional dispute between the two groups, and some petty remarks were made within the Division of American Republics regarding BEW's role in foreign policy formulation.[187]

At this time, in the spring of 1943, there was much more pressure from those advocating a punitive policy toward Argentina. Particularly as events progressed, those who favored harsher action became more vocal. Thus in August of 1943, when the Argentine Embassy wrote a memo defending the March 4 policy statement, it was primarily a defense of the policy against those who advocated "stronger" actions. At the time, five months after the policy was adopted, Armour argued that the "weak" policy had not really been implemented and that it remained his recommendation.[188] Once again he emphasized that Argentina was a sovereign nation and that there were definite limits to the United States capability to influence its policy. The memo returned to the theme that Argentina should be ignored as much as possible.

Since the Chilean and Argentine ambassadors to Washington have been criticized previously for being too pro-Washington and Bowers for being too pro-Chile, mention should be made at this point that Armour was favoring a "softer" policy toward Buenos Aires than many officials in Washington. Armour may have been judging the situation on its merits—certainly the ability of Washington to pressure Argentina, a country with more wealth and three-and-a-half times the population of Chile, was limited. But Armour was, it is only fair to note, favoring policies which made his job less complicated. It is surprising that all four ambassadors discussed seem to have been somewhat more sympathetic to the government to which they were posted than their home government was. However, there is a major difference between Bowers in Chile and Armour in Argentina in that there is little evidence to suggest that the Ambassador in Buenos Aires was less than vigorous in carrying out Washington's policy or that he did not believe that Argentina's policy was essentially against the interests of the United States. He was never an apologist for Argentina's policies, and Armour's recommendations showed a realistic perspective of the limits of United States power in Argentina and its possible dysfunctional effects on the Argentine domestic political scene. As will be seen, this "weak" policy (to the degree it was followed) did not prove especially successful, but there is nothing to suggest a harsh policy would have fared better.[189] As an example of the relative leniency of the policy, it was decided to allow materials to be sent to Argentina to help in the maintenance and upkeep of existing units and equipment for the Argentine armed forces.[190] This was in hope, not only of keeping the military in Argentina from becoming upset with the United States, but also of preserving its ability to function if drawn into the war on the Allied side.

One of the most ticklish aspects of supplying Buenos Aires was the newsprint question. The Embassy in Buenos Aires hoped that through the use of the restricted list, the flow of newsprint to pro-Axis publications could be halted. Initially, the policy seemed to be successful.[191] Locally manufactured newsprint, which was not of good quality, was also difficult for pro-Axis publications to obtain since the producers did not want to be included on the proclaimed list as a result of their sales to proclaimed list firms.[192] However, according to Embassy reports, the Ministry of Agriculture began buying local newsprint and distributing it to pro-Axis newspapers such as *Cabildo*.[193] It does seem to be a clear infringement upon the flow of information within Argentina to have an outside force such as the United States attempting to declare which newspapers could publish and which ones could not. In the face of the purchase and distribution of local newsprint by the Argentine Ministry of Agriculture, the suggestion was made that perhaps all the materials needed for the manufacturing of newsprint in Argentina should be denied until the government changed its position on the supplying of newsprint. The difficulty with this policy was that no single imported material seemed essential to the manufacturing of the paper; although it was felt that a type of bronze wire screen produced in Sweden and used in the papermaking process might be the most vulnerable part of the process. Therefore, in February of 1943 the decision was reached that the screens would be denied export licenses from the United States to Argentina.[194] This attempt to cut off the flow of screens proved unsuccessful, however, evidently because of administrative difficulties but more probably because of the reluctance of the British to support the idea.[195]

The second side of the newsprint problem was to make sure that the pro-Allied papers continued to get the newsprint they needed from the United States and Canada.[196] There was some fear that in the efforts to keep the major pro-Allied mass circulation newspapers in Buenos Aires in business, the innumerable small publications might be forced out of business. These small publications were the ones which were most likely to utilize the material distributed by the Coordinator of Inter-American Affairs.[197] Eventually, the large newspapers did cut down on their size and in some cases increased their prices. Besides attempting to pressure the United States Embassy for larger newsprint allocations, the papers also attempted to influence the Argentine government. When the government in Buenos Aires did make concessions, the United States Embassy saw them as attempts to win favor with the large newspapers.[198]

The newsprint difficulties raised another, and more serious, problem for United States policymakers. This was the attempt of the United States Embassy in Buenos Aires to administer the proclaimed list. The entire operation was enormously complicated, and at one point reached such a degree of complexity that it was decided not to protest Argentina's failure to carry out restrictions against German economic interests because to explain the situation would call for a memo so long that "the indictment would lose its effectiveness."[199] Undoubtedly the Embassy received virtually no cooperation from the Argentine government.[200]

The major questions were (1) halting any possible help from United States sources (and, if possible, Argentine sources) to companies connected with German interests, and (2) preventing the transfer of funds to help the Axis finance its war effort. The Argentine Central Bank, then directed by Rául Prebisch, was the Embassy's target for early efforts to block fund transfers. Although Prebisch seemed sympathetic to United States efforts, and perhaps did all he could, the Central Bank was not an autonomous agency, and had to answer to the country's President. In March of 1942, for example, the head of the foreign exchange section of the bank told a member of the Embassy staff that some of the Washington requests were going to have to be denied on instructions from the Ministry of Foreign Affairs.[201] Also, it was frequently quite difficult to judge the degree to which a private business was complying with the efforts of the United States to stop transactions with proclaimed list firms, though everyone seemed to be ready to assure Embassy officials that they would comply.[202]

In May of 1942 the U.S. Treasury Department proposed that Argentine funds in the United States be frozen.[203] The Department's argument was that financial institutions with headquarters in Buenos Aires were holding large dollar resources in the United States in evasion of controls that applied to Germany and Italy. This allowed them to operate as fences for looted currency and securities, and consequently, according to the Treasury, allowed Germans to obtain dollars from the sale of stolen assets. It was suggested that all Argentine financial transactions in the United States be subject to license, with the Treasury permitting only those transfers of dollars that it felt were wholly divorced from Axis interests. This policy had the additional benefit, according to the foreign policy analysis of the Treasury Department, of demonstrating to Latin America that the United States was determined to win the war.[204] The proposal was the first shot in a bureaucratic duel, which went on for months, between the Secretary of State Cordell Hull and Secretary of the Treasury Henry Morgenthau, Jr., and between their respective departments.[205]

The Department of State opposed the idea of a freeze, perhaps partially because it clearly represented an intrusion of the Treasury into the diplomatic realm. At the time, State was willing to argue that Buenos Aires actually was cooperating in some ways. It specifically mentioned Argentina's willingness to allow armed U.S. vessels to use her ports, her refusal to allow aviation gasoline to be sold to Axis airlines, and her sales of strategic materials to the United States.[206]

Export-Import Bank officials predicted that a freeze would force Argentina into a formal alliance with Germany and could lead to an attack on Brazil. Secretary of War Henry Stimson entered the lists by stating that the real problem presented by Argentina was that spies were providing Germany with information on American ship movements, and he could not see how a freeze would halt this.[207] President Roosevelt eventually decided against the Treasury proposal as being "not in accord with the Good Neighbor Policy."[208]

As called for in Resolution VI of the Rio meeting, an Inter-American Conference on Systems of Economic and Financial Control was held in Washington from June 30 to July 10, 1942. All the American republics attended the meeting and there was a general show of harmony. The talks covered topics, and reached policy decisions, in such areas as financial and commercial transactions with aggressor nations and nations under their domination, general problems of financial and commercial transactions with countries outside the western hemisphere, transactions among the American republics, control of the movement and transfer of securities, standards for the application of financial and economic controls within the hemisphere, standards of effective blocking, control of business enterprises whose operations were considered counter to the war effort, and schemes of reciprocal cooperation among the American republics.[209] Despite the fact that Argentina raised no particular problems at the Washington meeting, the Embassy in Buenos Aires continued to be plagued by countless major and minor problems in the prevention of the transfer of funds to, or trade with, Axis countries or agents. In September of 1942 Washington decided to halt the allocation of Export-Import credits to Argentina.[210] Initially, the feeling had been that perhaps the fund transfer problems were matters of procedural rather than substantive disagreements between the countries. By January of 1943 however, Ambassador Armour had clearly decided that in the area of financial controls the poor Argentine performance in meeting the Rio and Washington resolutions was not an administrative problem. He suggested that pressure for Argentine action "be shifted from the Central Bank to the Argentine government itself."[211]

As this detailed account illustrates, it was becoming increasingly obvious that Buenos Aires was not simply inept but was purposefully not enforcing the financial resolution. Thus the American Embassy began early in 1943 to draft a memo stating the case for enforcement of the proclaimed list. It was probably designed as much for public record and for consumption by other American republics as for convincing the Argentine government.[212] The formal reason for making the document public was that it was an answer to a June 8, 1942, memorandum from Argentina. The long note,[213] which was delivered on April 3, 1943, began by emphasizing the reasons for the proclaimed list and the degree to which the American republics had cooperated in its formation. The Argentine note had pointed out that Washington had protested the British blacklist in 1916 on the grounds that it violated the United States rights as a neutral. Washington answered this seeming contradition with the arguments that (1) the United States had changed its posi-

tion when it entered World War I (which was not a good point to make since
Argentina had not entered World War II), and (2) that the activities of the
Imperial German Government "were as nothing, in character or scope, as
compared with the subversive, 'fifth-column' activities of the Nazi regime."
Emphasizing the threat, the note stated: "Today the heart of the matter is
to prevent the fires of Hitlerism in this hemisphere from being fed with our
own resources." The note assured the Argentine government that the purpose
of the proclaimed list was strictly of a temporary, emergency nature and not
for the purpose of permanently influencing trade patterns. It also stated that
it was not difficult for innocent victims of incorrect listing to have their
names removed.

The suggestion in the Argentine note that perhaps the government in
Buenos Aires should participate more completely in determining who was
placed on the list was rejected. The note stated that "it is common knowledge" that when the Argentine protest was made in June of 1942, "Axis
and pro-Axis commercial, financial, and other enterprises were operating ex-
tensively and freely in Argentina." The United States felt that the situation
had not been "materially altered" in the meantime. The "venomous pro-
Axis propaganda enterprises" in Buenos Aires were pointed to as examples
of pro-Axis activity. The magazine *Clarinada* was specifically mentioned,
with the claim that it was making "scurrilous and revolting pro-Axis attacks
upon the President of the United States of America." *Clarinada* was worthy
of mention, according to the note, because it "regularly carries full-page
advertisements of Argentine governmental and semi-governmental agencies
and institutions." Although the ads might not have been authorized by
responsible officers of the agencies (which Argentina claimed), "it nevertheless did give the publication a respectable status" according to the Embassy.
The note did not close the door to the Argentine suggestion for more cooperation. In fact, despite the coolness of the note regarding the possibilities
of more consultation on proclaimed list questions, it did formally advocate
the idea.

The situation, from the perspective of the United States Embassy, continued to worsen. The ever-present harrassments from the Argentine government on financial controls caused the Embassy, in late May of 1943, to
charge in a memorandum to Washington that Argentina was not only refusing to comply with the Rio and Washington conference agreements, but
that "Argentina has allowed her financial facilities to be used for the aid and
comfort of the aggressor nations and the nations dominated by them."[214]
The memo pointed out that the Central Bank had taken some steps and
had enforced them but many loopholes continued to exist. The question of
remittances of free funds from Argentina to Axis, or Axis-dominated, nations
was particularly emphasized. It was also claimed that *El Pampero,* the most

important of the pro-Axis newspapers, was in effect being subsidized by the government because it was being sold newsprint at a price below the market rate.

This, then, was the state of United States–Argentine relations in mid-1943. The Castillo government's unwillingness to take actions against Berlin-controlled interests was causing the Department of State to seriously consider much stronger sanctions against Argentina. In the midst of this dilemma a domestic political crisis of grave international consequences occurred in Buenos Aires and changed the entire political environment in which the United States had been operating.

6: SANCTIONS AGAINST ARGENTINA

The military coup which toppled the Castillo regime on June 4, 1943, is one of the turning points in Argentine history. The relatively peaceful event is important because it opened the door for the rise of Juan Perón, the man who, thirty years later, still loomed like a dark cloud over the Argentine political system.

At the time, however, the important issue from the U.S. Department of State's point of view was the possible impact the change in government would have on Argentina's cooperation with the United States.

It is necessary to discuss the internal nature of the forces which produced the coup because, in this instance, even more than in most such cases, international events became intermeshed with domestic political considerations until the two were no longer separable. This is not to imply that the events of June 4 were caused by pressures outside Argentina. They were shaped by international forces but certainly were not caused by them.

The underlying fact necessary to understand the coup is that the Castillo government simply was not popular. This lack of support did not grow from a burning desire in broad sectors of Argentine public opinion to participate in World War II.[1] Quite simply, there had not been a government in Argentina since 1930 that had enjoyed substantial public support, and Castillo was probably only less popular than were his predecessors. His attempt to reverse the Ortiz effort to build a coalition of democratically minded conservatives with the Radicals and the other political "outs" met with little success. In a sense, his administration was the culmination of the now-aging oligarchy that had taken power from the military men who had executed the 1930 coup.[2]

Besides this lack of public support, several sources of political tension emerged during the early months of 1943. The first of these was the election scheduled for later in the year. It has been demonstrated that the months immediately prior to an election or immediately after the balloting are the least stable for Latin American governments,[3] and pre-election pressures clearly developed during mid-1943 as election speculation began to fill the air. By law and by the understanding of the ruling group, Castillo could

not succeed himself. Customarily, however, he could name his successor.
The man favored by Castillo was sixty-five-year-old Robustiano Patrón
Costas, who had been instrumental in 1938 in obtaining the vice-presidential
nomination for Castillo. Enormously wealthy and a kind of political boss
over the province of Salta,[4] Patrón Costas had been a lawyer in Buenos
Aires and had come to be the provisional President of the Senate. Although
from the landholding class, his close economic ties with the industrialists
caused uneasiness among older aristocrats, who mistrusted industrialization.
Likewise, his orientation toward opening the country for foreign capital
conflicted with those who distrusted the foreign economic penetration of
Argentina.[5]

The fact that the nominee was pro-Allied shows the degree to which
domestic political questions took precedence over foreign policy issues. Tensions at the time were heightened by rumors of a deal between the Radical
Party and the Minister of War, General Pedro Pablo Ramírez, which would
have made the powerful military man the party's candidate. A Radical
Party–military coalition of sorts would have been a powerful one and probably pro-Allied. Eventually, it was actions by Castillo to prevent the Ramírez
candidacy which triggered the coup.[6]

The international situation was not contributing to political stability.
The degree to which Castillo's regime seemed to be favoring the Nazis, or
at least allowing Nazi sympathizers to be favored by members of the government, provoked uneasiness among some. Economic conditions in the country
were combining with the political situation to accentuate the class divisions
within the nation. The economy was prospering but the developmental
process had been dysfunctional in terms of stability.[7] There had been a
growing disparity between the wealthy elite and the masses. The lower class
workers had not developed any effective political defense for their interests.
The idea that the Radicals were interested in protecting the working class
had proven illusionary.[8] The foreign financial penetration had helped general development but had left key economic sectors in the hands of foreigners. Also, the heavy tide of immigration from 1856 to 1930 had brought
new groups into the country, which added to the social and cultural diversity
of Argentina.

These problems were deepened by the Depression. That things were worse
in other Latin American countries was of no solace to the Argentines. They
saw their harvests worth little on the international market, they saw slums
springing up and disfiguring the outskirts of Buenos Aires, and they saw
their democracy being replaced by repression. The Argentine dream had
collapsed. Optimism about the future, about a Europeanized Argentina,
waned. Argentines began to ask what had happened to their country. "This
question ran like a unifying thread through practically all of the essays, much

of the historiography, and many of the novels produced during the 1930–
1943 period," according to Mark Falcoff.[9]

It is in the search for an answer that nationalism becomes important.
Nationalism explains a country to itself. In their treatment of contemporary
Latin American nationalism, Arthur Whitaker and David Jordan, both stu-
dents of Argentine politics, wrote:

> Argentina has led all Latin America in the development of nationalism.
> She has been first in point of time, first, probably, also in intensity, and
> first, certainly since 1910, in the variety of nationalisms supported by
> rival groups.[10]

As a political force, nationalism is extraordinarily complex to analyze and
evaluate. It is often difficult to connect the feeling of nationalism, which is
of a psychological nature, and actual political behavior of historical significance. It is easy to take the writings of a widely read author as the catalyst
for events actually growing from long-standing political conflicts over the
base questions of who gets what. One also finds many types of nationalism—
so many that it might behoove writers on the subject to declare a moratorium
on typologies of nationalism and to begin to work in a comparative vein.

In the beginning of their book on nationalism Whitaker and Jordan attempt to develop the idea that there are five primary types of nationalism
in Latin America. The first, "traditional rural," was discussed in the second
chapter of this study. It is the feeling of the land owners that "their" Argentina was "the" Argentina and that what was good for the great estates
benefited Argentina as a whole. A second type suggested is the "old bour-
geois" nationalism, which favored development through foreign investment
and the adoption of foreign ways. This outlook among some Argentines
allowed the government to make the economic concessions it did to English
interests. A third type suggested by Whitaker and Jordan is the "new bour-
geois." Its followers reacted to the nation's domination by foreign interests
by calling for discrimination against outside capital or at least limitations
upon its use. These three types were definitely in operation in Argentina
during the period in question.[11]

There are obvious disagreements among the three concepts, and these
conflicts of ideas, heightened by the questioning brought about by the Depression, helped to produce tension prior to the 1943 coup. The new bour-
geois nationalism had gained momentum under the impact of Irigoyen's cam-
paigning, although not under his policies. His preachments against imperialistic enterprises accounted for much of the popularity of the theme of economic nationalism[12] which Perón was later to ride to power. However, Irigoyen
also believed in democracy, and this belief split the followers of new bour-
geois nationalism into two camps: those who favored democratic approaches,

and those who would find solutions more along the lines of the corporate organization of the state. Also a split between liberal economics and state intervention complicated the issues.[13]

One stream of nationalism produced by this mix is what can be called "nationalists of the right,"[14] or "Fascist nationalism."[15] This can be characterized as in opposition to the inevitability of the class struggle and as in support of government rule by an elite. It favored governmental actions that "sought to enhance rather than to overcome the cultural, religious and moral traditions deemed essential in [the] country."[16] Followers opposed the idea of political parties and shared the Radical demand that British penetration of the Argentine economy be reduced. Although they had strongly supported the 1930 coup against Irigoyen, they were attracted to General José Félix Uriburu who lost out in the power struggle to Justo.[17] Justo's economic liberalism had more appeal for the oligarchy.

Castillo's presidency presented the nationalists of the right with a dilemma. Because of his extreme conservatism, many of his ideas were well received by them, but he did not share their view that Argentina's society and politics needed a radical restructuring along corporate lines such as one could see in Spain, Italy and Germany.[18] Throughout his term in office "the Nationalists of the Right were in the awkward position of having to attack the oligarchy because it was liberal." On the other hand, according to a long study of Argentine corporate nationalism by Marysa Gerassi, they had to defend the Castillo government "because they considered the alternative—radicalism—mob rule."[19]

This nationalism of the right was primarily an indigenous movement but it had gained impetus from the rise of ultra-nationalism in Germany, Spain and Italy. Anti-Semitism was the major intellectual current added to the native nationalism of the right by the rise of the Nazis.[20] Rightist nationalism had sympathy for the totalitarian states but recognized that Argentina's economic ties and her geographical position made support for the Axis impossible. Also, the neutralist tradition was, in the eyes of these nationalists, "one of the few traditions not imposed" on Argentina by foreign pressure.[21]

The candidacy of Patrón Costas, with his pro-British reputation, caused the nationalists of the right great uneasiness. The irony of the situation was that Castillo had been turning more and more toward the right for support during the latter stages of his administration in his effort to build a coalition among those who opposed a return to free elections.[22]

What groups were followers of this brand of nationalism? Gerhart Mauser writes in his study of nationalism in Latin America that Italian fascism had a significant appeal to the sons of the *estancieros* who had been hurt by the Depression. It also attracted some intellectuals who wanted to return to the old, simple life untouched by liberalism and communism.[23] The Roman

Catholic Church in Argentina was widely considered to be a prime backer of the movement. John J. Kennedy's excellent study suggests that the idea that the Church's emphasis on authority was a contributing factor to this stream of thought may be overemphasized. The German Embassy reported to Berlin in 1938 that the Catholic Church had been hostile to its attempts to organize Germans in Buenos Aires.[25] However, there is little doubt that some elements of the Argentine clergy were quite sympathetic at least to Franco's brand of totalitarianism and probably also to Mussolini's.[26] Besides the fact that some priests did sympathize with the nationalists of the right, what can be misleading is the fact that the nationalists always made a great show of their religiosity. One study of Argentine nationalism recounts the following incident:

> Shortly after coming to power, General Ramírez, amid much ceremony and attended by many military and Church leaders, made the Virgin of Merced a general in the army, decorating the statue with epaulets, sash and sword. . . .
> [Perón] commissioned the Virgin of Carmen de cuyo a general in the army. This involved a special trip to Mendoza by many dignitaries. Nuns, a company of cavalry dressed in white uniforms, many generals, and clerics were present. Assisted by the nuns, Perón solemnly placed upon the statue the insignia of rank, a sash, and a sword. A twenty-one gun salute was fired and a flock of doves was released.[27]

The emphasis on the purity of the Spanish way of life compared with the immorality of North American civilization may have drawn additional support from clerics, but one cannot know whether the public attachment to religion of many of the nationalists of the right grew from a clerical influence that touched on other matters of policy or whether the claims of faith by the nationalists drew the clergy along.

THE POLITICS OF THE COUP

The labor unions were not important in the change of government. The movement generally lacked leadership and accepted the new military government calmly, if not hopefully.[28] The Socialist Party, one of the least elitist of parties in terms of leadership, was the logical group by which the labor movement could have galvanized. Although the Socialist Party had a reputation for honesty, the unions had fallen on bad times after 1930. The industrialization process in Argentina had been hard on the laboring man; and, although a consciousness was beginning to develop that the unions needed to band together in order to make their voices heard, no political movement seemed to do this. Also, as long as the conservatives were thwarting free elections, the laboring classes were not of great value to any political party. These factors, plus rent controls and other sops to the masses during the early days of the military junta, kept the unions out of the political arena during the June 4 coup. It remained for Perón to integrate the unions into a political movement.

The Radical Party had an ineffectual role in the events surrounding the coup. The party was torn by internal feuding and political opportunism. Its two former Presidents of Argentina, Irigoyen and Alvear, were both dead, leaving the party without strong leaders. Still, the party could probably have won any free election, a fact which the conservatives could only interpret as proof of their distrust of the masses. Certainly there was much in the Radical Party to justify the criticism. However, from the point of view of the United States, the fact that the party was both pro-Allied and relatively popular made it attractive. The military had not cared much for the Radicals because Irigoyen had refused to increase military expenditures. Also, the smell of corruption that haunted the party and its internal squabbling offended the discipline-minded military.

Clearly the most important factor in the 1943 coup was the position of the military establishment. Like the other forces involved, it too was split into factions. There were pro-Allied elements in the Army, and this thinking seemed at times to dominate the Navy. German influence was to be found throughout the organization.[29] On the right wing of the spectrum of military thinking was the GOU lodge of officers which "produced one of the few Argentine examples of a distinctly military nationalism."[30] The group came to view itself as the potential savior of the country. The GOU capitalized on two images among professional soldiers. The first was the fear that the military balance between Brazil and Argentina might be fundamentally altered by the quantities of lend-lease aid going to Brazil.[31] The second, and more important, factor was a disillusionment with civilian politicians, particularly as represented by the Radicals and the National Democrats (conservatives). Certainly the civilian politicians had not distinguished themselves, but from the outside the task of running the country undoubtedly looked easier than it proved to be after power was seized.

So the coup came. Few mourned the passing of the Castillo government since it had managed to offend virtually every major sector of political support in some way. The nationalists of the right were quick to vociferously support the coup.

The events of June 4 brought a little-known General named Arturo Rawson to the presidency. This caused bewilderment among the foreign diplomats in Buenos Aires who were primarily interested in speculation as to whether or not this was a pro-Allied change of government. There were numerous statements by participants in the change of government which seemed to indicate that the new regime was going to honor the Rio obligations but the vagueness of these commitments was not immediately satisfying. Later the truth began to emerge: foreign policy was not the issue that bound the conspirators together. While each individual had foreign policy ideas (and often initially believed they were widely shared among the participants in the coup), as a group there was no single foreign policy which was definitely pro-Allied or pro-Axis in the initial turbulence. The pro-Axis newspapers, which had been widely praising the foreign policy of Castillo, immediately began to laud the new government in the most patriotic of terms.

The initial Rawson statements seemed to be pro-Allied, but the Cabinet included at least two individuals who were clearly friendly to the Axis; one of them was José Maria Rosa who owned the blacklisted publishing house which was responsible for *El Pampero*. A sensationalized account by an American journalist in Buenos Aires, Ray Josephs's *Argentina Diary*, which later sold well in the United States, effectively captures the bewildering deluge of rumors surrounding the events of the moment.[32] The accounts being sent back by Ambassador Armour's staff also reflect the massive confusion.[33]

The bitter discussions among the military leaders in the days following the coup apparently revolved around both the question of who was to wield the power and the question of what policies were to be advanced.[34] Outside the broadest generalizations, such as a call for a national purification of the Argentine spirit, the holders of power began to discover that they had moved against Castillo for a wide variety of sometimes contradictory reasons. This chaotic situation toppled Rawson on June 7 after three hectic days as President. The new leader was General Pedro Ramírez, the Minister of War under Castillo, who had been mentioned as the Radical candidate for the 1943 presidential election. Ramírez's new Cabinet included only one civilian, Minister of Finance Jorge Santamarina. The new President's speech, upon being sworn in, called for cooperation under the existing hemispheric treaties but in such generalities as to be meaningless. However, in a private conversation with the Paraguayan Ambassador to Buenos Aires, Ramírez said he intended to better relations with Washington and also to work toward a break in relations with the Axis. This statement was immediately relayed via the Paraguayan Ambassador to the United States Embassy.[35]

The possibility that it might not be recognized by the other hemispheric states worried the new government. Washington favored collective nonrecognition until there was a more substantial indication of the future direction of Argentine foreign policy. The United States was ready to use pressure but realized the dangers of rallying Argentine public opinion against Washington. On June 9 a meeting of diplomats to Buenos Aires from the American republics was held to discuss the situation. Brazil took the lead of those insisting on immediate recognition while the United States argued against the idea. Despite efforts in Rio de Janeiro by United States Ambassador Jefferson Caffery, Brazil decided to go ahead and recognize the Ramírez government. The Brazilian government offered privately a number of arguments in favor of immediate recognition;[36] however, the basic reasons stemmed more from long-standing geopolitical considerations rather than any belief in the effect this action would or would not have on the new government. Brazil did not want to offend Ramírez, and Brazilian President Vargas was uneasy about a possible military coup within his own country by those elements sympathetic to events in Buenos Aires. Ambassador Armour speculated that by acting unilaterally Vargas hoped to demonstrate to his military that the Brazilian government, despite its close cooperation with Washington, was capable of acting on its own.[37]

On June 10 the new government replaced the 100-word-a-day limit on diplomatic code messages by wireless with a complete ban on this type of communication. With this as a sop, and with Brazil having broken any possible united front of American states, the Department of State (much to the relief of the Ramírez clique), recognized the new government on June 11. It seems difficult to believe that continued withholding of recognition after the change in the code situation could have accomplished anything other than bolstering the nationalists of the right in their claims of United States pressure. This is not to argue that the Ramírez government at this point had shown any particular pro-Allied position or "deserved" recognition in terms of fulfilling past inter-American recommendations, but simply to argue in terms of possible impact on domestic politics.

There was some limited optimism in Buenos Aires among Allied diplomats that the Ramírez administration might prove to be pro-Allied. This optimism, however, was not shared by the Department of State, which went so far as to send Armour a communication stating that if the Argentine government should break relations with the Axis, Armour should receive the action coolly unless it was accompanied by serious efforts to fulfill the entire range of anti-Axis resolutions adopted at Rio and Washington.[38] The Department of State, far from the rumors and intrigues of the Casa Rosada, was judging the new government strictly on the basis of its acts, not on its words or the rumors floating around Buenos Aires. In retrospect, it appears that the view from the Embassy was more realistic than that from Washington. The new government undoubtedly did contain strong pro-Allied elements but they were limited by the general political situation. It was also true that the new government did initially gain a significant amount of popularity based on its overthrow of an essentially unpopular regime and on such actions as decreeing rent reductions throughout the capital.

A diplomatic problem which quickly assumed importance between Washington and the new government in Buenos Aires concerned negotiations, begun in 1942, under which the United States would supply a quantity of material needed by the Argentine oil industry for the exploration and refinement of oil. In return Argentina would supply specified oil exports to the American republics. Besides relieving the strain on oil production to a limited extent, the bargain could have relieved an even greater strain on the supply of available tankers.

Less than a week before the coup, the U.S. Embassy in Buenos Aires successfully completed its long negotiations with the Argentine government.[39] After the coup the Department of State notified the Embassy that it should attempt to evaluate the proposed agreement in terms of Argentine political considerations while Washington was also examining the question.[40] However, the Department informed the Embassy that, after consultation with other interested executive agencies, and "considered completely on its merits," the agreement was unsatisfactory.[41] The reason given was simply that the bargain cost the United States too much. The Embassy protested that this decision would create a bad impression with the Ramírez people and that it would undermine future negotiating by the Embassy if the Buenos Aires leaders felt that the Embassy did not represent the Department of State.[42] Washington stood firm in its refusal to honor the understanding, even though the Embassy continued to strongly argue its position.[43]

Perhaps this is a case in which the problems confronting the Embassy were so near and so real that it was difficult to see the merits of the decision taken in Washington. The Embassy was involved in the ticklish business of trying to establish friendly relations with a new, inexperienced government. Now the Department of State had made a decision that could easily be interpreted as an attempt to punish the rudderless Ramírez regime. And it may well be that Washington was insensitive to the changing situation in Buenos Aires. Judged as a political decision, the Department's position does not seem wise; if it were an economic question, then it becomes difficult to judge without a lengthy evaluation of shipping needs and supplies. It is clear that there had been a failure of communication within the United States government. Washington had been kept generally informed of the goals of the negotiations by the U.S. Buenos Aires Embassy. The Department of State had certainly adopted a most peculiar procedure in waiting until the agreement had been signed before beginning its deliberations on the matter. Thus it becomes difficult to accept the rationalization that the

decision was an economic one. During the course of the talks there had
been little to indicate that the Embassy was not acting as an agent of the
United States government but, rather, was acting as an adviser to the Argentine government in helping it to draw up a proposal to be submitted for
the approval of Washington. In essence, this was the position taken by the
Department in disavowing the agreement.

As in the case of Chile, although the breaking of relations was to an extent only a gesture unless accompanied by a series of other actions, it was
the question of Argentina's diplomatic relations with the Axis that continued
to dominate Department of State thinking toward Argentina. At Duggan's
suggestion,[44] on June 28 Welles sent a long letter to Armour discussing the
Department's point of view. Referring to Armour's opinion that one of the
major reasons for the June 4 coup was the desire of the Argentine Army and
Navy to procure armaments, Welles pointed out that the new government
seemed if anything less inclined than the Castillo government to return to
the constitution. Since the people were apathetic toward the new government, he recommended that the United States also remain distant. Of course
the implication that the nonconstitutionality of the government made it difficult for the United States to cooperate with it was ludicrous in view of
Washington's close cooperation with governments headed by such men as
General Jorge Ubico in Guatemala.

The Undersecretary called the new regime's foreign policy "somewhat
two-faced" but did admit that it seemed to be pointed toward greater collaboration with the war effort. He particularly mentioned the prohibition of
coded radio transmissions. Welles warned that no matter how friendly the
Buenos Aires government now became, it could not be rewarded more than
those countries which had been pro-Allied during the darker periods of 1942.
He also cautioned that only actions, and not promises of actions, should be
the basis of any modification of United States policy. "Nor is there any use
in Argentina's attempting to bargain to find out what rupture is worth to
us," Welles continued. However, the government should be "understanding
and accommodating" of efforts in that direction. Welles suggested that these
views be quietly presented to the new government, although with an emphasis that the United States was not attempting to dictate Argentina's foreign
policy. Welles closed by warning that since Argentine Ambassador Espil was
not willing to take much part in the negotiations or discussions, most of the
burden would have to fall on Armour.

Late in June the Embassy began to receive some encouragement for the
idea that Argentina was at last ready to break relations with the Axis. A
member of the Embassy staff in Buenos Aires was told by a Cabinet minister
that there would be a break soon.[45] Then at the Fourth of July dinner held
by the North American community, Foreign Minister Secundo Storni spoke

strongly in favor of hemispheric cooperation. Later, speaking privately with Ambassador Armour, Storni told him that the speech had been made with the approval of the President and was designed to bring forward those elements in the armed forces who opposed breaking relations. Storni said only one Cabinet minister opposed the break and that if the action did not come within the month, he intended to resign his position as Foreign Minister.[46] He also, according to Armour's account of the conversation, suggested that if the break came, Argentina should use its destroyers for convoy activities and, if they were attacked, the country would immediately declare war. He continued with the statement that, although he understood that Argentina could not be favored in the supplying of materials, perhaps some of the oil machinery could be furnished and some reconditioning of naval vessels could be done. Storni cautioned that public opinion would have to be prepared and that Ramírez's position was not strong enough to allow him to act precipitously.[47]

On July 6, 1943, Ambassador Armour was able to have a long unofficial talk with the President.[48] Ramírez repeated much of what Storni had said. He told Armour that he hoped the United States would understand why it was impossible to break relations with the Axis immediately. He did feel that the climate for the break was improving and that 80 percent of the people favored it. He also felt that the armed services in Argentina were beginning to appreciate the military might of the Allies. He promised that the break would be made not later than August 15, 1943. Evidently in response to the rumor that Argentina would break relations in order to get its share of lend-lease materials, he stated that Argentina would not ask for materials when it did break relations. He did, however, express some uncertainty regarding Brazil's motives. For his part, Armour promised to look into the question.

Although Washington was getting these private assurances, the new Argentine government's actions were frequently disquieting. In a mixture of State Departmentese and bewilderment, Ambassador Armour's long survey of the situation, sent July 13, began: "I have the honor to report that the policy of the Ramírez government during its first month in office has been confused and at times inconsistent."[49] In mid-July five pro-democratic groups (and two Nazi groups) were ordered dissolved.[50] It was also becoming more and more obvious that conservative elements in the Catholic Church either had influence on some members of the new government or were being used to justify actions by these officials.

Apparently, these contradictory assurances and actions were surface manifestations of a turbulent period of negotiations taking place within the new government as each group attempted either to gain power or to control policy. The significant nucleus of the issues dividing the military was not foreign policy per se. The issues all had international aspects and each faction used patriotism as an argument, but it was essentially a domestic question of who would have the power and the future role of constitutional democratic government in Argentina that divided them. With the coup growing from a distrust of civilian politicians, the military leaders had not faced the long-term question of what policies to follow once they were in power.

The United States, of course, wanted Argentina to crack down on the Axis and increase the Argentine role in hemispheric defense. Ambassador Armour originally felt that minor appeasements should be offered the new government, such as the petroleum agreement, a few spare parts, etc., in order "to show that we have faith in the good intentions of the new government."[51] However, influence in the movement began to fall into the hands of those who opposed cooperation with the Allies, and by July 15 the Foreign Minister was privately expressing discouragement to Armour. With the situation in such a state of confusion, and the question of possible assistance to the Argentine government so delicate, Secretary Hull and the Department of State, which was less impressed with the good intentions of the new government than Armour,[52] asked the Ambassador if he could possibly return to Washington for consultations sometime in early or mid-August.[53] The communiqué also mentioned that it might be easier for the Argentine government to break relations with Armour out of the country.

THE STORNI NOTE

An interview Ambassador Armour had with Foreign Minister Storni on July 29 produced a dramatic reversal.[54] The Foreign Minister said that Ramírez had decided that sentiment among Army officers made it impossible to break diplomatic relations. Storni said the internal support of his backers had weakened. The nationalists of the right in the government seemed to be gathering strength on one side and he perceived rising Communist threat on the left. Storni was critical of the treatment being given Argentina in the United States press. Confronted with this change in policy, Armour asked if he could have a clear written statement of the Argentine foreign policy position to take to Washington when he left Buenos Aires in two weeks for consultations with the Department of State. The Foreign Minister said that such a statement was already in the process of being drafted but warned that it would not be able to mention the weaknesses in the government itself. Storni also backed away from his earlier promise to resign unless diplomatic relations with the Axis Powers were broken. He said he felt he could accomplish more by staying within the government and working for a return to constitutional government. One unique argument for not breaking relations that was advanced, and would be repeated in the note, was that with Italy having collapsed, to enter into the war now would make it appear that Argentina was simply getting in on the side of the winners. This position overlooks the fact that some officers had argued against siding with the Allies earlier in the war because the Axis Powers were winning. Of Storni personally, Armour commented that he "had lost much of his earlier fire and enthusiasm. It is apparent that he has been subjected to considerable pressure and is no longer so sure of himself."

The following day Storni passed along to Armour another of the many inexplicable factors involved in not breaking relations. He said that a newly arrived Chilean naval attaché had supposedly said, in an effort to convince Argentine officers to break relations, that Chile had been very worried in the past year, prior to its break in relations with the Axis, that Peru and Bolivia might attempt to occupy the northern provinces of Chile. Because Chile did not have the arms to protect herself, it was decided to break relations in order to get the necessary arms for her defense. Then, supposedly, the attaché drew the parallel between that situation and Argentina's position vis-à-vis Brazil and Paraguay. The idea was that, if Argentina broke relations, she would then be in a position to secure the arms she needed. According to Storni, this argument enraged the nationalistic Argentine officers to the point where they supposedly said they would fight with gaucho knives if they had no other weapons but would never break relations. Storni also claimed that this situation had been partially responsible for Argentina's decision not to break relations.[55] As seen in chapter four, Chile's decision to break relations was a good deal more complicated than this. It is true that Chile was uneasy over Peru's and Bolivia's level of armament. But it is difficult to believe that the Chilean Ambassador flatly affirmed the story, if for no other reason than that it reflects so poorly on Chile's national pride. Of course it may be that the naval attaché actually believed this to be a true account. What the anecdote probably shows more than anything is the state of the rumor market in Argentina at this time and the fact that people were willing to believe unquestioningly almost anything that agreed with their perception of the situation—a fault not confined to Argentine Army officers.

Shortly before he left for Washington in early August, Ambassador Armour received the promised note from Storni.[56] In this exceptionally candid communication addressed to Secretary Hull, Storni denied that the neutrality of Argentina and the sympathies of Ramírez were pro-Axis. The note pointed out the degree to which Argentina's non-belligerent status was favorable to the Allies. The note candidly admitted that it would be difficult to change the policy because Argentina was enjoying "an atmosphere of peace, work and comparative abundance." He also mentioned kinship ties with foreign countries and the existing fear of communism. Changes in foreign policy could only be made "as rapidly as the internal situation may permit," according to the memorandum. The memo also cautioned that unless the United States halted its delaying of materials, Argentina would find it difficult to meet its continental defense obligations. He seemed to be pleading for a dramatic event to use as an excuse for declaring war.

With Armour visiting in Washington, August became a month in which a serious re-evaluation of Argentine policy occupied much attention within the Department's American republics echelons. Communications from London on the matter seemed initially ready to attribute many of the problems within the new government more to ineptness than to design.[57] Elements within the United States Embassy, however, were beginning to be increasingly critical.[58] A memo from the Financial Controls Section of the Embassy relayed the suggestion early in August that Argentina be designated a blocked country—the same category as Switzerland, Portugal, Spain, and Sweden.[59] This would mean that the Argentine Central Bank would have been asked to certify that no enemy interest was involved in connections with each financial transaction. The argument made was that Argentina was profiting from her neutrality while it acted as a center for Nazi espionage and subversion. The Financial Controls Section also claimed that Buenos Aires was a prime market for Berlin's disposal of looted securities. The blacklisting program had accomplished little. The memo did admit, however, that there was no conclusive evidence that Argentina was a center for the financing of espionage and subversion and that the dangers from this type of action were declining rapidly with the Allied successes in Europe. The Department of State rejected the suggestion because it felt that the proposed action would not be powerful enough to cause a change in policy but would certainly cause irritation that might be used by the nationalist elements.

It was finally decided in the Department of State to send a reply to Storni's note. Bonsal evidently wrote the original draft of the reply, with Duggan, Collado, and Berle collaborating. Considering the circumstances, the final document sent to Storni, signed by Cordell Hull and dated August 30, 1943, was one of the strongest diplomatic documents ever to leave Washington, in terms of its criticism of another government.[60]

The note began amicably enough, but by the third paragraph it was informing the Argentine government that the "undoubted sentiments of the Argentine people" were not being represented by the foreign policy of Buenos Aires. The Department of State document reprinted most of the Rio agreement concerning the recommended break in relations. It also quoted the Argentine delegate at the meeting as favoring economic and financial control measures over alien businesses threatening the hemisphere. The Department then proceeded through other responsibilities the United

States felt that Argentina had accepted at Rio de Janeiro. In reply to Storni's contention that the Argentine people would accuse the government of caving in to foreign pressure if it began to use sanctions against the Axis, the communication pointed out that Argentina had freely adhered to the Rio agreements. As for the great benefits Argentina claimed its supplies were having in support of the Allied war effort, the note observed that "equitable prices" had been paid and that Argentina was enjoying great prosperity.

In reply to Storni's request for airplanes and other armaments so that Argentina could restore the equilibrium in Latin America, the Hull message claimed that this type of balance was "surely inconsistent" with the inter-American ideas of peaceful settlement of disputes. The note also pointed out that United States arms going to Latin America were solely designed to help the hemisphere protect itself against aggression. "Since Argentina, both by its words and its actions, had indicated clearly that the Argentine armed forces will not under present conditions be used" in this manner, the note said it would be impossible to include Argentina under the lend-lease agreements.

When the communication was given to Ambassador Espil on September 7, 1943, he replied heatedly that the position Washington was taking was highly legalistic and that it would have a bad effect on United States–Argentine relations.[61] He also claimed that the answer was taking advantage of a friendly attempt by Storni to clarify Argentina's position. Armour, who was still in Washington, stated that Storni had said he intended to publish his letter in order to inform Argentine public opinion of the situation. The claim of Espil that the reply was legalistic was largely correct, but legalisms had come to be the diplomatic language within the hemisphere. Perhaps part of the friction with Argentina came from a confusion on the part of both parties between the political realities and the legalistic language which was used in communication.

Delivery of the note prompted an emergency Cabinet meeting in Buenos Aires to consider various responses. It was decided to go ahead as planned and to publish Storni's note to Hull along with Hull's reply. Elements of the military government evidently reasoned that Argentines would rally behind the government in the face of this blast from the United States. Newspapers were given freedom to editorialize on the exchange.[62] However, the understanding apparently was that the editorial reaction would be critical of the U.S. response, and some papers managed to get themselves into trouble by supporting Hull's comments.[63]

The furor over the communications forced the resignation of Foreign Minister Storni. On the one hand, he had said in his note that Argentine public opinion favored the breaking of relations, a position many of the

military leaders denied.[64] On the other hand, his effort to be mildly con-
ciliatory and to operate openly had been harshly rejected by Washington.
The British Ambassador to Buenos Aires, Sir David Kelly, later described
Storni as

> perhaps the most friendly, honest and straight forward of all the mem-
> bers of the various Argentine governments during my residence there; a
> man quite devoid of the tendency to self-seeking intrigue and party cal-
> culation so common in all political life; and he had the rare distinction
> of qualifying in every way to be called a gentleman.[65]

Kelly felt strongly that Washington's reply to Storni was a mistake. He
called the original Storni note "a genuine appeal for American goodwill and
trust." In retrospect, it is difficult to interpret the communication of the
Argentine Foreign Minister as anything but an exceptionally candid public
document designed to clarify the issues between Buenos Aires and Washington. Historian Robert Potash has suggested that GOU leaders had written
parts of the letter with the hope "of provoking a harsh reply and thus precipitating a crisis from which they could benefit."[66] This would be credit-
ing the GOU leaders with a tremendous ability to forecast the repercussions
of the exchange of letters. It was the reply of the Department of State that
caused the difficulties, since it spotlighted and ridiculed the more candid
portions of Storni's note. However, one can argue in support of Potash by
pointing out that the military leaders had the means of controlling the flow
of information within Argentina and therefore could determine what the
public's reaction would be.

Obviously, as a tactic designed to accomplish a change in the attitude of
Buenos Aires, the message from Hull was a failure. One Argentine book
later referred to the note as a "model of crudeness."[67] Another Argentine
wrote that Hull "had not been educated in the diplomatic school of Talley-
rand but in that of King Kong."[68] There is no doubt that the published
communications did serve to inflame some sections of public opinion against
Washington.[69] The rightist newspapers that had been supporting the new
government managed to direct their ire at both Hull and Storni and helped
lead to the change of foreign ministers. Alberto Gilbert, a military man who
had been identified in his term as Minister of the Interior with the nationalist elements, replaced the Admiral. Ambassador Espil was recalled from
Washington and replaced by Adrian Cesar Escobar, a former Ambassador to
Madrid, who was less friendly to the United States.

The resignation of Storni is a clear turning point in relations with Argentina, although the turn may have been inevitable in view of the forces
at work.[70] By mid-October events were proceeding so rapidly that the Department of State felt that the question of Argentina's possible breaking of

diplomatic relations with the Axis had become unimportant. "The real question," according to a memo from Adolf Berle to the new Undersecretary of State Edward R. Stettinius, Jr., "is whether Argentina is going Fascist or not."[71] Further signifying the turn of events was the resignation of the few remaining pro-Allied top officials in the government over a declaration signed by 150 Argentine leaders in which a return to democracy and a recognition of international obligations was demanded. Ambassador Armour saw President Ramírez on October 20 and found him particularly irritated by the manifesto.[72] The President denied any unfulfilled international obligations and pointed out that the Rio statement on the breaking of relations had left the decision to individual countries. However, he did say that he hoped to be able to take the action eventually. Ramírez then began to criticize the United States for a number of recent statements concerning Argentina—several of which were protests over the closing of the Jewish newspapers in Buenos Aires.[73] Armour closed his report with the remark that "the interview lacked entirely the cordial tone which marked my talk with [Ramírez] last July."

The continued movement of the Argentine government away from democratic practices provoked continued unrest as the year 1943 waned. Protests in the universities and the refusal of recognized educators to assume control of the universities plagued the administration, and the government's crackdowns on various Jewish groups caused increased problems. However, Buenos Aires was moderately successful in an attempt to strengthen political and economic relations with its neighbors. Chile agreed to a new commercial treaty and a joint Chilean-Argentine commission was announced to study the off-again, on-again customs union idea. Paraguay signed another commercial agreement, and when the Bolivian revolution came about in late 1943 it was widely held that it had been planned in Buenos Aires.

One of the major issues within the United States government was a continuing debate over the question of whether or not to freeze Argentine assets in the United States. The idea had been advocated for some time by the Department of the Treasury, and by October the Embassy in Buenos Aires was also advocating the action.[74] The resignation of Raul Prebisch as head of the Central Bank was accepted in mid-October and this marked the end of his attempts to mediate between the Argentine government and the United States Embassy. This action also apparently tipped the Embassy in the direction of increased pressure against Buenos Aires. The Embassy argument was that the government was becoming increasingly unpopular. The people's appreciation of the original rent and utility rate lowerings had worn thin. An action such as the freezing of assets would constitute a clear statement of United States dismay over events in Argentina and this might lead to the fall of the Ramírez administration or at least change the composition of the leadership. The Embassy felt that the Ramírez government represented what the Allies were fighting against in other parts of the world.

The hard-core Department of State officials with direct responsibility for Latin America such as Duggan, Bonsal and Collado (Welles was gone by this time) argued that any action aimed at overthrowing the Buenos Aires government constituted clear intervention. They also argued that it was likely that the Argentine people would react defensively against such an action by Washington and thereby bolster the leverage of the nationalists of the right. This State Department clique did feel, however, that multilateral hemispheric action would be acceptable and less subject to charges of intervention.[75] The problem was one of finding any action that would be agreed to by a large number of Latin American countries. The Department also believed that sanctions against Argentina would probably not be supported by Great Britain and that attempts at punishment could cause Buenos Aires to cut back on its limited support of the war effort.[76] The Department of State recommendation in October of 1943 was "that Argentina be left to stew in its own juice for the time being. The political pot is seething and may boil over of its own account."[77]

The Treasury Department had been vehemently advocating the idea of freezing Argentine assets for some time. This particularly irritated Hull, who felt that the Treasury Department was attempting to meddle in the conduct of foreign policy.[78] After the President again ruled against the suggestion in October, the story that the action was contemplated was leaked to the press—thereby putting the Executive Branch in the position of not being able to simply review the action weekly as originally contemplated but rather in the position of having to do it immediately or not be able to have as many Argentine assets to freeze in United States banks as a result of hurried movements of funds. The Department of State claimed privately that the leak was an intentional effort by the Treasury to force action on the matter.[79] Some money was transferred because of the rumor, but it was decided again early in November of 1943 not to apply a general freeze to Argentine assets and transactions. Treasury, however, was given the task of closely monitoring Argentina's international transactions and of subjecting to special blocking those transactions that would be of benefit to the Axis. Since England was unwilling to freeze Argentine sterling balances, the impact of the United States decision was dubious from the first.[80] The Treasury continued to press for action, and some capital movements were halted, but not enough from the Treasury's perspective.

In January of 1944, against the backdrop of Allied military victories in Europe, the government of Argentina continued to move its domestic policies more and more in the direction of a kind of corporate control over all sectors of Argentine life. The major thrusts were toward the schools and the news media. Compulsory religious training was instituted in the schools with the support of important elements of the Catholic Church hierarchy in Buenos Aires. Newspapers began to be subjected to new decrees further limiting their ability to criticize the government, although some of the decrees were also aimed at prompting a so-called higher level of morality in the nation. The government also attempted to prevent any selective placement of advertisements into papers on the basis of political viewpoints, a practice of United States advertisers who tried to use only pro-democratic papers.[81] The first notable victim of the law was *La Vanguardia,* the Socialist daily, which closed down claiming it could no longer fulfill its duty of pursuing the truth under the new censorship requirements.[82] The comment of the Embassy upon the closing was that "there remains no newspaper in Buenos Aires prepared to defend principles of democracy and oppose the actions of the present Argentina regime in open and forthright language," although the Embassy did point out that *La Prensa* and *La Nacion* were willing to speak up at times.[83]

A SUDDEN BREAK

Early in 1944 events in Bolivia began to intrude into U.S.–Argentine relations. A military coup had taken place in Bolivia during December of 1943 and it was widely believed that Argentina had been involved in some way. Victor Paz Estenssoro, the intellectual leader of the Movimiento Nacionalista Revolucionario (MNR, one component of the revolutionary forces), had visited Argentina a few months previously. Coupled with the rumored Argentine influence was the belief that a number of Axis sympathizers were present in the new government. Argentina's President Ramírez supposedly admitted to a foreign diplomat that certain nationalist elements had been implicated in the coup and that dissident elements in other neighboring countries had visited Buenos Aires. However, he denied contact with the government and expressed the hope that the nationalists and those involved in the intrigue might be removed from power.[84]

Argentina recognized the new Bolivian government early in January while the other American republics were withholding recognition: an action which served to confirm suspicions in the Department of State about both Argentina and the new government in Bolivia. Reading Hull's memoirs leaves little doubt of the impact of events in Bolivia on Washington's Argentine policy. He writes that "as evidence accumulated that Argentine officials had been implicated in the overthrow of the Bolivian government," Hull and other Department of State officials produced a memo which they sent to the President on January 8 suggesting a toughening of U.S. policy toward Argentina. The memo argued that Argentina might be planning to stir up similar revolutions elsewhere and that countries cooperating with the war effort should be helped—particularly Brazil. This would involve permitting Brazil to move ahead in her plans to send an expeditionary force overseas—an action which involved a major increase in arms and equipment assigned to Brazil.[85] The previous day Hull had also written Secretary of the Navy Frank Knox that the policy of allowing the export of maintenance items for the Argentine Navy should be reconsidered in view of events.[86]

Thus a major debate had been unleashed within the United States government centering in the Department of State. Laurance Duggan, in a memo of January 10 entitled "Argentine Policy," continued to argue for a policy designed to take the bloom off the war prosperity being enjoyed in Argentina. He warned against whipping up U.S. public opinion on the question of Argentina because there were distinct limits to what the United States could or could not do in regard to Argentina, and public opinion might not be able to comprehend these limits. He also suggested increased economic assistance for development projects in the other American republics as a means of rewarding their cooperation during the war. Duggan mentioned a possible foreign ministers meeting on the question of Argentina.[87]

According to the Hull memoirs, on January 12 Roosevelt sent the Secretary a memo approving increased military aid for Brazil and expressing the opinion that "the plot [of Argentina in the hemisphere] is more widespread than most people believe; that it has direct ramifications in Paraguay and that a great deal of preliminary work had been done in Uruguay, Chile, and Peru."[88] This raises the question of whether or not there was a serious plot underway. Argentina undoubtedly would have been comforted to have had changes in the governments in Uruguay, Chile and Peru but there is little evidence to suggest that actions in Buenos Aires presented a serious threat to the internal composition of those governments. What had happened in Bolivia may have been encouraged by Buenos Aires but it was much more a direct outgrowth of the ramifications of the Chaco War on Bolivian politics. Dissidents in other Latin American countries may have begun to feel a tie for the maverick government in Argentina and may have been encouraged by Argentina's refusal to cooperate with the United States; but effective, systematic Argentine governmental plotting in the affairs of other states is quite another matter.

Nonetheless, much of the planning in the Department of State was proceeding on the basis of possible successful subversions from Buenos Aires. On January 11 Hull sent a personal query to Armour listing several steps the United States was considering taking "preferably within the next week." These included a statement strongly critical of the Argentine government and concluding with the remark that, in view of the gravity of the situation, Armour was being recalled for consultation. The statement would have been coordinated with an Executive Order including Argentina in the list of countries subject to freezing by the Treasury. It also expressed the hope that Britain might be induced to cooperate.[89]

Ambassador Armour's answer[90] expressed agreement but said he felt that a United States–British embargo "on all articles essential to their [Argentina's] economy to the end that they will really feel the effects" should be initiated. He was reticent to predict the reaction of Argentine public opinion to such a measure, although he felt that opposition elements were hoping for such an act. Armour suggested that the indictment avoid legal arguments and concentrate on the increasingly totalitarian nature of the Argentine government.

The underlying theme of these discussions and others at the time were that the point of no return had been reached with Buenos Aires. Sanctions were now necessary. However, the limits of United States influence in Argentina were quickly clarified when discussions began with the British on the subject of sanctions against Argentina. Washington suggested a number of measures to London, the strongest being "a complete cessation of economic intercourse between Argentina and the United States, the United Kingdom, Brazil, and as many other American republics as possible."[91] The British were not eager. The economic needs of the island and Churchill's pragmatic approach to winning the war combined against Washington's efforts. It also seems likely that Britain felt as though it were to be called on in an attempt to bolster the inter-American system, an arrangement that it felt no particular desire to strengthen. Hull asked if London would be least agree to issue a strong statement simultaneously with a United States declaration critical of the government in Buenos Aires.[92] This was eventually done,[93] although the statement was not directly critical of Argentina.

The Department of State decided to release a statement strongly criticizing the new Bolivian government's ties with the Nazis and specifically mentioning Argentine machinations in the coup. With a joint United States–United Kingdom embargo impossible, this combined statement seemed to represent the outer limits of what the United States could do in view of the war situation and possible retaliation by Argentina.[94] It was finally decided to release the statement on January 24, 1944.

Meanwhile, the generals running the government in Buenos Aires managed to get themselves into an embarrassing and delicate situation as a result of an attempt to purchase arms from Germany.[95] In late August of 1942 Brazil had declared war on the Axis, thus placing itself in line for even larger quantities of weapons from the United States. After some initial contacts, in September of 1943 President Ramírez and a few of his advisers decided to send a special mission to Berlin in hopes of obtaining weapons. The man chosen was Osmar Alberto Helmuth, an Argentine naval reserve officer who apparently was affiliated with the German spy system in Argentina. When Helmuth's ship docked in Trinidad he was arrested, despite the fact that he had been assigned a diplomatic position in Spain by Buenos Aires. Presumably, the Allies had been informed of Helmuth's mission or they had intercepted and broken some coded messages.[96] In December the Argentine government was informed that Helmuth had confessed to being a German agent. Because Helmuth had his mission from President Ramírez and his advisers, the government in Buenos Aires was disturbed by the turn of events.

On the morning of the day the Department of State statement was to be released, Foreign Minister Gilbert called Ambassador Armour with the claim that he had an important announcement. He declared that the Helmuth spy case had led to the discovery of a serious Nazi espionage ring in Argentina.[97] Gilbert told Armour that the government had reached the definite decision to break relations with Germany within a week. The delay, he argued, was in order to gain the time needed to prepare the public and to advise Argentine ships to seek safe ports. Gilbert warned that there should be no action in Washington which would cause it to appear that Argentina had taken the action under pressure. In other words, the pressure of the United States would be effective only if it were kept below the surface so as to not arouse public opinion or bolster the position of the nationalists of the right. Armour, who had not threatened the government with the public statement on Bolivia, said that he understood that his government was going to release a declaration on the non-recognition of the Bolivian junta which would include references to Argentina. Gilbert asked if Washington could possibly stop the announcement. Armour said that he would immediately inform the Department of State of the Foreign Minister's call but reminded him that Argentina had promised previously to break relations and then had not done it. Gilbert assured the Ambassador that he was speaking with the authority of the President and gave his word that the action would be taken within five days. He also insisted that the breaking would be accompanied by strong measures against all Axis collaborators.

On this basis and because both Armour and the Argentine Ambassador to Washington recommended it, the Department of State decided at the last possible moment to omit Argentina from the statement on the Bolivian junta.[98] The statement confined itself to the comment that

> this government has been aware that subversive groups hostile to the Allied cause have been plotting disturbances against the American governments cooperating in defense of the hemisphere against Axis aggression.[99]

When Foreign Minister Gilbert was informed of the Department of State's decision he appeared to be "greatly relieved," according to Armour. The Ambassador again warned Gilbert against any break in relations not accompanied by stern action against Argentine nationalists collaborating with the Axis and involved in overthrowing neighboring governments. Gilbert gave these assurances to Armour and asked if the news that Argentina had decided to break

relations could be kept secret until the actual announcement was made in
Buenos Aires. This proved to be impossible since the Secretary of State had
already informed the foreign ministers of the other American republics
(except Bolivia) of the pending statement, and thus was forced to explain
why Argentina had been omitted from the statement at the last moment.[100]

On the morning of Wednesday, January 26, Ramírez broadcast his announcement to the nation. He referred to "the hospitality which the Argentine government and people" had extended to foreigners. He also spoke
in glowing terms of Argentina's efforts to maintain its neutrality. He referred
to hemispheric ties and then stated:

> We are faced with facts that have been verified by the Federal Police
> of the nation which reveal a secret and organized system of espionage
> and war information, attributable to the Axis countries.
> The national sovereignty has, then, been impaired under the protec-
> tion of the friendly hospitality guaranteed by the constitution of Argen-
> tina to all men who live within her territory.[101]

This, the President stated, had forced Argentina to break relations with
Germany and Japan.

There is a great deal of circumstantial evidence to suggest that the Ramírez group was fearful of repercussions growing from Washington's criticism
of Argentina's role in the Bolivian coup and therefore broke relations. When
Gilbert called Armour it seemingly was with the purpose of stopping Washington's announcement. Potash has suggested that actually it may have been
the fact that Helmuth had documents incriminating high-ranking Argentine
officials which made Buenos Aires anxious to hush up the case. And this
could be accomplished by doing what the United States wanted in this case.[102]

As the Department of State feared, the break in relations did not solve
the problem Washington perceived to exist in Argentina. This may have been
a self-fulfilling prophecy since for Buenos Aires to have continued taking
steps away from neutrality would have necessitated a strengthening of the
position of the pro-Allied elements. But striking the kind of bargain that
would have given Argentina some sort of visible reward was impossible:
On the one side there were the nationalists of the right who opposed such
bargaining and were willing to interpret concessions as infringements upon
Argentina's sovereignty; on the other side there was the Department of
State's crusade against fascism and all its sympathizers.

Secretary of State Hull was angered with Argentina by this point and
only commented that it was "gratifying" to hear of the break in relations
and then went on to say to a press conference that "it must be assumed
from her action that Argentina will now proceed energetically to adopt the
other measures which all of the American republics have concerted

for the security of the continent."[103] Thus a string of reciprocal concessions did not begin with Argentina's decision because Washington refused to recognize the Argentine action (which was, of course, largely symbolic in its immediate implications) as a meaningful one. But this is not to say that concessions from Washington would necessarily have de-escalated the tensions between the countries. It is only to suggest that the possibility existed.

Instead, the Department of State, upon receiving news of the promised break, began laying down guidelines regarding what was expected from Argentina in order to meet Washington's standards of hemispheric cooperation.[104] The Department included "full implementation of the Rio and Washington Resolutions with regard to economic and financial controls" and complete severance of "all telecommunications with Germany and Japan." Washington was also interested in full investigations of the spy rings in Argentina in the "belief that full disclosure of [these] data would implicate persons high in the Argentine government." The Department made a halt to Argentina's meddling in the politics of neighboring countries another requirement.

The Argentine Foreign Minister did inform Armour that Argentina intended to implement the break.[105] However, at the same time that the series of guidelines was being formulated, the Embassy was sending a despatch reporting that the government in Buenos Aires was increasingly assisting local Nazi firms by allowing cloaking operations. These involved the government's buying of materials which then went to blacklisted firms.[106] Although the report undoubtedly was based on information obtained prior to the promised break in relations, it did represent a trend that was to continue seemingly unabated.

On the day of Argentina's formal announcement of the break Armour met with Foreign Minister Gilbert to discuss the situation. The military officer turned diplomat assured Armour again that the government intended to act vigorously against anyone implicated in stirring up coups in other countries. He also promised a complete investigation of the Helmuth spyring case and assured the Ambassador that the government would press forward on other cases. The promise of publicity on the Helmuth case was particularly important to Armour because the failure of the government to publicize other cases seemed, from Washington's point of view, to have been a factor preventing the formation of anti-Nazi sentiment. Gilbert promised financial controls, although avoiding mention of the Rio commitments in this field, and a severing of telecommunications with Germany and Japan.[107] Armour, who had some hope for a better relationship stemming from the break,[108] suggested to Washington that perhaps there should be some selected relaxation of freezing measures then in effect in order to encourage the Argentine government. The Department of State declined pending further developments.[109]

The debate which now began to evolve over Argentina within the Department of State found Armour, and some other elements of the Embassy, advocating better treatment for the new government in hopes of encouraging it to take further pro-Allied steps. However, on February 12, 1944, Undersecretary of State Stettinius wired Armour that unless "further energetic action is forthcoming" from Argentina, "the break of relations can only be considered a subterfuge."[110] The note mentioned the failure to crack down on spies, failures to control the pro-Axis press, and the fact that firms with records of support for Axis activities were not being intervened. The Department did offer to reconsider the Argentine petroleum deal, to supply spare parts to the Navy, and to unfreeze the two major banking institutions if Buenos Aires did take action. Stettinius warned that there should be no bargaining.

What Armour apparently saw, and what was not seen in Washington, was the building pressure from the nationalists of the right against the Ramírez government. Never a particularly popular government, and one based on a tenuous compromise within the Army, a decisive action against the status quo was certain to shake the foundations of the alliance. The breaking of relations had this effect because a widespread belief arose that the Buenos Aires government had yielded to pressure from the United States in breaking relations. Armour suggested that the Helmuth case be widely publicized, but there was the feeling that the involvements of the case went so deep that it would be embarrassing to reveal the laxity surrounding the case.[111] Besides using the rumor that Ramírez had yielded to pressure, the nationalist elements were also encouraging the circulation of a rumor that the government was preparing to declare war.[112] There is nothing to suggest this was actually the intention of serious Argentine officials, and even less to suggest that the United States had any particular desire to have war declared at that point.

These rumors were the outcroppings of the bitter power struggle for control of the uncommitted group of military officers standing between the Ramírez, moderate wing and the nationalists of the right. The support of this group of officers was needed for any change in government, and it was also needed by the President in order to keep power. The break in relations and the relatively sympathetic viewpoint of the government toward the Allies had mobilized the nationalists against Ramírez. Also, there was the fact that the President had dissolved many of the nationalist organizations in January of 1944. The groups had not been well enough organized to provide much support for the government and were hampering the formulation of labor support.[113] The nationalists of the right then began to support the dissident military officers while the military men in the "middle" did not rally to support the existing power arrangement.

The climax of this process came on February 24, 1944, when Ramírez was forced from power. In this change of leadership the issues centered on the war, as opposed to the largely domestic issues which had brought the military men to power initially. The conflict also represented Ramírez's attempt to stand firm against the GOU, the lodge of young military officers of a nationalistic bent in which Perón was an important figure. Ramírez's account of the final meeting of his Cabinet as contained in a resignation statement of March 9,[114] told a confrontation at the Ministry of War the night of February 24 with a large number of important officers present. The officers claimed that the break in relations was due to pressure from the United States and therefore constituted an insult to Argentine national sovereignty. Of course, it is clear that there was pressure from the United States involved in the break. The officers at the meeting were also said to believe that Ramírez had already signed decrees calling for martial law, general mobilization, and a declaration of war against Germany and Japan.

Another aspect of the removal of Ramírez which clearly showed the degree to which international political questions had become a factor in Argentine politics was the form the action took. The new government was fearful of a refusal to recognize it by the other American republics such as had been applied to Bolivia. To avoid a similar situation it was announced that Ramírez was simply delegating his power to General Edelmiro Farrell and it was clearly implied that the action was temporary. The fiction that Ramírez was still President was initially retained and any statement inferring that he had been forced out under pressure was avoided.[115] On March 9 Ramírez wrote the above-mentioned letter of resignation which received wide distribution in Argentina via underground channels. The note was critical of the new government and the circumstances which led to his downfall.

From the beginning Ambassador Armour argued against treating the removal of Ramírez as a simple delegation of power. With Ramírez stepping down in the early morning hours of February 25, Armour's afternoon telegram to Washington said that "circumstantial evidence clearly points to another coup d'etat." He suggested that departmental consideration be given to a statement that "as in the case of the Bolivian coup, purely legalistic forms and tests cannot be followed with continential security . . . at stake" and proposing that, regardless of the question of the legality of the succession, collective consultation be held prior to any recognition. Armour made no secret that such a course of action was aimed at toppling the new government while it was still in its formative stage. He said that if the new Argentina ruling group were denied recognition, it would make the continuance in office of the Farrell government "difficult" and "would certainly encourage internal elements in opposition to it." Armour warned that if such ef-

forts failed, the Farrell government certainly would "redouble" its efforts
to bring down other governments in order to avoid remaining "completely
isolated."[116]

Washington agreed to Armour's suggestion. The Ambassador then began
a round of consultations with his colleagues in Buenos Aires. Initially, there
was some uncertainty about what had actually happened and it was suggested that Ramírez should be contacted in order to determine whether
or not his action actually was voluntary as claimed.[117] It soon became obvious that it had not been. The new ruling group was attempting to assure
the American diplomats that it was not pro-Axis. On February 28 General
Diego Mason, upon taking the post of Acting Minister of Foreign Affairs,
emphasized that the government would "always continue to pursue a foreign policy directed to the strict fulfillment of undertakings with respect
to continential security, solidarity and defense."[118] The statement assured
that "our foreign policy will not change" under Farrell. There were also
some further arrests of Axis spies, evidently as an attempt to soothe the
American republics. However, the intense patriotism of Farrell's public remarks caused Armour to compare the statements with the foreign policy
positions of Castillo and Ruiz-Guiñazú,[119] and he soon reached the conclusion that Colonel Perón was actually directing the new government.[120]

Unaware that the state of nonrecognition on which he was embarking
would extend for over a year and accomplish little, Stettinius made a
statement to his press conference of March 4 that the United States had
"reason to believe that groups not in sympathy with the declared Argentine
policy of joining the defense of the hemisphere" had been active in the
coup.[121] The Acting Secretary did not stress any legal aspects of the action but declared that "to deal with such grave issues on a purely technical
basis would be to close our eyes to the realities of the situation." The press
in the United States gave general approval to the decision.[122]

If there was some degree of immediate consensus on the question of
non-recognition of the new Argentine leadership within the Department of
State, this was not completely shared by the Latin American countries.
Thus Washington was forced to make continuing efforts to keep the other
American republics "in line." Early in March the government of Chile extended recognition. The Chilean Foreign Minister argued that legally there
had not been a change in government in Argentina.[123] Ambassador Bowers
wrote in his account of his years in Chile that the question of recognition
of the Farrell regime placed Chile "in a more delicate position than any of
her sister American states"[124] and referred to its need for Argentine meat
and its vulnerable border with Argentina. Bowers felt that in the final analysis the Chilean course of action had been wise because it provided a channel of communication with the Argentine regime. Paraguay, virtually a

satellite of Argentina and dependent on Buenos Aires for shipping, soon followed Chile. Then Bolivia extended recognition repaying Argentina's refusal to adhere to non-recognition when the Bolivian government had taken power months previously.[125] There was some worry that Peru, which had important trade links to Argentina, and Brazil might break the non-recognition front but they were persuaded to hold out. Uruguay, which had close economic ties with Argentina and had a history as a buffer state between Brazil and Argentina, was vulnerable but managed to resist Argentine pressure to recognize.

Although the United States did not recognize the new government, Ambassador Armour remained in Buenos Aires and was soon approached about a possible secret meeting with Perón.[126] The Ambassador was not pleased by the prospect since he was fearful that such an encounter might be used by the new government to claim that the United States did not really oppose it. Espil, the former Ambassador to Washington, argued in favor of the meeting. He said that the new regime was totally ignorant of what the United States wanted and what its position actually was. He claimed that the meeting would definitely be kept secret because if news of it leaked out it could be as embarrassing to Perón as to Armour.[127] The Ambassador queried the Department about the idea because he felt that some good might come from a clear explanation of the United States position to Perón. Overall, however, Armour was against the meeting, and the Department agreed, arguing that if it became known that the United States was having contact with the Argentine government, it could undermine the unified non-recognition policy of the American republics.[128]

Meanwhile, the Department of State was having problems reaching a consensus within itself on whether the policy of non-recognition should be continued and on the question of possibly strengthening the economic sanctions being applied against trade with Argentina. Bonsal of the American Republics Division opposed the break in relations with Argentina. [129] He argued that since Argentina was much stronger than Bolivia, it would be able to resist such pressures and, on the other hand, could in fact bring pressure to bear on her neighbors if they went along with the proposal to break relations. Knowing this, he argued, her neighbors were not anxious to participate in a non-recognition effort. Bonsal also feared that such an action would give fuel to the nationalist elements within the government and make them martyrs. He saw value in giving Armour free access to the officials since he might be able to change some attitudes or at least correctly state Washington's policy rather than allowing it to be distorted by rumors. Bonsal opposed the idea that had been mentioned by some officials of a meeting of diplomatic representatives of the American republics (presumably a foreign ministers conference) on the ground that there were so many differences of opinion between them. He did advocate reiterating the points made in the answer to Storni's message and making specific indictments against certain Argentina officials and activities. If this course of action failed, he argued, Argentina should be then treated as an unfriendly neutral, as was Spain, which would involve cutting off oil and the freezing of funds.

Armour was not advocating an immediate toughening of the existing policy unless the Department was willing to take "all-out measures."[130] The Embassy feared that measures which irritated, rather than actually harmed, would only furnish grounds for charges of "external pressure and infringement of sovereignty" which could cause "the various groups which are today at swords points being forced into a semblance of unity under the banner of nationalism." Armour also warned that there were dangers with a strong program in that it would have to be carefully implemented and designed to bolster the "better elements" while providing a face-saving solution that did not compromise Argentine dignity. The Embassy opposed freezing Argentine funds outside the country, but it did feel that a partial embargo on much of Argentina's international trade could be achieved simply by diverting Allied shipping away from Argentina. Emergency war requirements was the excuse the Embassy suggested for this maneuver.

The Department of State considered having the United States and England cut off imports, including beef, from Argentina. This plan was based on the prediction that there was sufficient beef on hand to supply England for six months.[131] The Embassy said that in the past it would have approved of the idea because it had always felt that "no government in Argentina could withstand more than a few weeks suspension of meat and other Allied purchases." Now, however, with a government "composed largely of undisciplined army officers, self-seeking army politicians and fanatic nationalists," the results of such an action were impossible to predict. The Embassy pointed out that large shipments of beef during February had opened up storage space—thereby giving Buenos Aires some ability to tolerate an embargo on beef. The Embassy also felt that Argentina's shipping for fuel supplies was abundant enough to allow its own ships to carry on a significant amount of trade without the benefit of Allied shipping.[132]

The not totally unspoken assumption behind the contemplated pressures was that the new regime could be toppled. The ultra-nationalist influence within the Argentine government turned overt attempts to pressure the government to alter its policies to the detriment of those applying the pressure—and some in the Department of State realized this. Within Argentina, the military was firmly in control. The civilian politicians, even confronted by an increasingly harsh dictatorship, could not bring themselves to heal past grievances. Armour reported that the Radical Party, which had formerly dominated politics, had "learned little from its trials and tribulations since the 1930 Revolution and is now [April 1944] little closer to unity than it was last June" at the time of the coup.[133] The oligarchy, which had ruled from 1930 until the Rawson-Ramírez coup, was also divided. Later, a strong element of the military would attempt to make an anti-Perón alliance with the oligarchy only to find the oligarchy so divided that it could not negotiate, thereby giving Perón the time he needed to rally support and return to power.[134]

The Department of State was becoming convinced that the new government was pro-Axis. Perón, who was becoming increasingly less a shadow figure behind the scenes, had visited the German-owned Bayer Company and had been honored by a luncheon during which he delivered a speech praising the firm.[135] Other Argentine Army officers were felt to have very close relations with German firms, and some of these companies, according to Department of State reports, had been favored in bidding on construction contracts.[136] The substance of these charges are difficult to dispute, but whether they in fact represented a favoritism toward Germany is doubtful. The government also acted as an intermediary to obtain materials for blacklisted companies having government contracts so they could complete contracted government projects. Finally, on March 24, 1944, the Secretary of State sent a telegram to the other American republics describing the pro-Axis activities of the Farrell regime during its first four weeks in office.[137] These included the censoring of American films in a pro-Axis manner, the halting of United Press services temporarily in Argentina, the appearance of *El Pampero* under a new name, the granting of contracts to German firms for the construction of barracks, and the control of the Secretariat of Press and Information by "notorious pro-Axis sympathizers."

Sir David Kelly, the British Ambassador to Buenos Aires during much of the war period, later wrote that he felt Perón was "not in the least interested in Nazi or any other ideology" but rather was seeking power.[138] Kelly's memoirs are extremely critical of United States policy during the period. He refers to a "sullen resentment" in Washington toward Argentina "which was manifested in turn against each succeeding regime in Argentina and became more and more violent after each disappointment."[139] He also described the United States actions against Argentina as a "continuous warfare of words and pinpricks," which led to the successive ousting of governments composed of more moderate elements until power fell into the hands of Perón.[140]

The process by which these decisions were made within the Department of State actually was considerably more complicated than it appears on the outside. In the case of Farrell's accession to power, the Department of State soon found itself at odds internally over how much pressure should, and could, be brought to bear on Argentina. England's dependence on Argentine beef made her reluctant toward pressuring Buenos Aires. Kelly's despatches to London indicating that he felt the policy of Washington to be ineffective probably also stiffened the English government against yielding to Washington's requests. One of the forms which the problem took within the Department of State was the question of deciding exactly what the minimum requirements for the extension of recognition would be. Basically, these seemed to include a crackdown on German espionage activities, which though flourishing were of little value this late in the war; appointment of Cabinet officers who were more pro-Allied (an intensely domestic question from Argentina's point of view), particularly in the Ministries of Foreign Relations and Interior; and perhaps some guarantee of free elections in the future.[141] There also was the question of stopping commercial dealings between the Argentine government and blacklisted firms.[142]

There were spokesmen both within the Department and outside who were not anxious for the United States to continue its policy of pressuring the Argentine government. On May 3, W. N. Walmsley, Jr., Chief of the Division of Brazilian Affairs in the Department, wrote a memorandum arguing that the morally repugnant aspects of the Argentine government had been overstressed, particularly since they had only a peripheral impact on the waging of the war.[143] He pointed out that Argentina was, perhaps in spite of itself, helping in the war effort by providing minerals, hides and agricultural products. He also pointed to Britain's dependence on Argentine meat and the fact that Argentine merchant marine ships were carrying a great deal of goods and the dry docks were functioning. Walmsley felt that Washington should be willing to make compromises since the other American republics had not been perfect in their execution of the agreements reached at Rio. He also argued that normal diplomatic relations be reopened so as to provide an avenue through which such pressure could be applied, although arguing that this pressure should remain hidden.

The major spokesman outside the government for a "soft" policy was Sumner Welles who had resigned in August 1943 as Undersecretary of State. One cannot know if his departure accounts for some of the later difficulties between the United States and Argentina; but it is clear that leaving was a personal tragedy for this gifted and knowledgeable diplomat. Apparently by mid-1942 it was widely rumored in Washington that Welles was a homosexual.[144] William C. Bullitt, a former Ambassador to Russia and France and an adviser to Roosevelt, took an interest in spreading the story[145] and finally confronted the President with evidence in a presumed attempt to take over Welles's position as Undersecretary.[146] At this point Welles was forced to resign.

The former Undersecretary, never a friend of Hull's, managed to retain many of his old contacts in Washington and was now in possession of a public forum for influencing public opinion through his newspaper columns. Particularly on the Argentine question Welles began to attack Hull and Morgenthau's developing efforts to crack down on the military government in Buenos Aires. He stated in his book *Where Are We Heading?* that the Farrell government had not been recognized because "Argentina had long been a 'pain in the neck' to three or four members of the Department of State who were . . . determining the hemispheric policy of the United States."[147] He was also critical of the fact that "a major part of the American press and many radio commentators" overlooked the fact that military governments dominated most Latin American countries while the United States public media was extraordinarily critical of the military government in Argentina. The Department of State, according to the former Undersecretary, was "peculiarly susceptible" to this type of pressure because of its sensitivity over its policy toward Spain and the Vichy government during World War II. This, according to his account, led the Department to pressure the other American republics not to recognize the new government "although relations with the Axis had been severed by the Ramírez government, and this decision had been maintained by the Farrell government."[148] Welles concluded that "the Good Neighbor Policy had suddenly undergone a woeful transformation. It had become unilateral and overbearing." Washington was operating under the assumption that its attitude "would bring about a rapid overturn of the Farrell government."[149]

Ambassador Armour, who was also critical of the actions of the new government, continued to favor sanctions only if they were clearly aimed and defined. On May 5 Hull wired Armour that the Secretary of the Treasury was again urging the freezing of Argentine gold in the United States and that the Department of State was seriously considering this course of action. Hull felt it should be accompanied by a tightening up on exports to Argentina and "diverting an occasional meat ship from the River Plate to the United States so that Argentina's position as a source of Britain's meat supply would be reduced," by reduction of the supply of oil at Caribbean ports being given to Argentine shipping, and by a reduction in the supply of coal. The freezing, according to the Department's suggestion, would be public but the other measures taken quietly. Armour, who had favored freezing at various times previously, this time opposed the freezing as a "dangerous and unwise step to take until our over-all policy" toward Argentina could be determined. He felt it would "humiliate without being strong enough to induce substantive changes." He argued that changes in the trade patterns should be supportable in terms of defense and not be obviously punitive.[150]

Meanwhile, the new Argentine government was sending intermediaries to the United States Embassy in an effort to open up contact with Washington. On May 15 Armour requested permission to talk privately with General Orlando Lorenzo Peluffo, the new Argentine Minister of Foreign Affairs.[151]

The Farrell government was beginning to pressure diplomats from nonrecogniz-ing countries to attend a number of ceremonies in connection with the up-coming May 25 Independence Day celebrations. Armour reported that some of the Latin American diplomats were "becoming increasingly restless" over the situation and were asking the United States to discuss the general prob-lems of recognition with their governments. Armour's request said that "if the conversation goes well, we may strengthen the hand of opponents of the Nationalists."[152] Evidently the Argentine approach suggesting the meeting with Peluffo also mentioned a possible conversation with Juan Perón, the shadowy military figure who was becoming more and more prominent in the Farrell administration. Armour felt that a conversation with Perón could be reserved for later, "depending on how things go" with Peluffo.

Washington approved the meeting with a long communication setting limits on Armour's course of action—although most of the boundaries were undoubt-edly already known to Armour. The Department particularly wanted it un-derstood that the meeting should discuss the "basic question of [the] Argen-tine attitude on implementation of [the] Axis break."[153] The Department warned that the meeting should be as secret as possible although it assumed "that despite every precaution to keep [the] meeting secret it will become known to your colleagues."[154] The meeting itself accomplished little. It was held in the apartment of Espil (who had been withdrawn from Washington) and lasted two hours.[155] The Argentine Foreign Minister Peluffo warned that the United States had to avoid giving any evidence that it was putting pres-sure on Argentina. He did, however, promise to carry out the break in rela-tions. Peluffo also assured Armour that attending the May 25 celebrations (religious and non-religious) would not be interpreted as recognition. Armour stated the position of Washington, and said that the United States was not planning to attend the independence celebrations, except for the religious services, despite the assurance that recognition would not be implied by the action. The Washington position was that not to take any action would imply formal recognition or informal support of the Argentine government.

There is evidence to suggest that an effort was made by some elements in the new Argentine government to have Armour declared persona non grata.[156] Judging from the version relayed by Espil, Foreign Minister Peluffo was par-ticularly offended by Armour and spoke in terms of sovereignty and pressure from Washington. However, he had opposed the idea that the United States be asked to withdraw Armour. Within a few days Peluffo was again speaking privately of a solution to the question of recognition.[157] This finally led to a meeting on June 3 between Armour and four Argentines: Espil, Peluffo, Perón, and Rear Admiral Alberto Teisaire, the Minister of the Marine.

Peluffo began the meeting by again reassuring the United States that Ar-gentina intended to implement the break in relations. He said he regretted the delay in the departure of the German diplomats, but blamed it on Germany's slowness in replying to communications. He felt that with recognition, it would be easier for the government to act on the matter since otherwise it appeared to be yielding to pressure from the United States. Of course, the opposite argument (which Armour did not mention) would have been that recognition followed by action against Germany would also have given the appearance of pressure from Washington. Since the new government had censorship over the news media, it seems difficult to believe that pressure could not have been brought to avoid stirring up public opinion, assuming that it would have been stirred up by such actions.

Perón supported Peluffo's idea that the revolutionary psychology made it difficult to move despite the fact that the government, according to the Colonel, had the support of the Army and the people. He astutely made the analogy with the war psychology in the United States which made the calm consideration of some subjects difficult. He recognized the dilemma: Argentina could not appear to act under pressure while Washington could not recognize without actions. Peluffo suggested that the matter be left to "our great ally Providence" which evidently was a reference to allowing events to solve the problem. It was suggested that both sides should do everything possible to create a better atmosphere in which to operate, and Perón agreed to discuss with Farrell possible restrictions against the Axis press. Armour was urged to try to have publicity given in the United States to those actions that had been taken by Buenos Aires, including the departure of German diplomats, measures to prevent smuggling, arrest of Axis agents, and so forth. Armour agreed to suggest this to Washington and asked if Peluffo could give him a full list of the acts taken and others they proposed to take to implement the break. At this the Foreign Minister balked, arguing that it would appear to be bargaining over the question of recognition. He did agree to provide a list of agents arrested.[158]

Meanwhile, the solid non-recognition front of the American republics seemed to be crumbling. The Ecuadorian government, with the return of José María Velasco Ibarra to office, was causing Washington problems.[159] Colombia was arguing that under present conditions Argentina apparently could get along perfectly well without recognition. The feeling was that with her independent position and her ties to Europe, Argentina could well end up a major power after the war, and therefore the existing policy should either be toughened or the government in Buenos Aires recognized. Bogotá placed the argument strictly in terms of power politics and the possible Argentine paramountcy in southern Latin America. The implication was that, in view of the impending recognition of Bolivia by the American republics as a result of concessions demanded by the United States which Bolivia made, perhaps Argentina should be recognized.[160]

Washington, however, was moving toward a toughening of policy. On June 23, 1944, Armour received word that he was being recalled for consultation and that he should proceed as soon as possible. The Department of State claimed that "the time has come for a comprehensive review of the entire situation" and cautioned against further talks with Foreign Minister Peluffo.[161] The Department of State was also requesting that other ambassadors, including the British representative to Buenos Aires, be recalled.[162] The United States made its case for this action in a long note sent to diplomatic missions in Latin America (excluding Argentina, Chile, and Bolivia).[163] Washington denied that non-recognition constituted intervention—despite the fact that it was privately viewed within the Department as an attempt to either change the composition of the government or to topple it. Events in Argentina were recounted in a light much more favorable to the Ramírez government than the United States had viewed them at the time. The note stated that members of the Farrell Cabinet had "repeatedly and candidly admitted" that Ramírez and his main supporters "were eliminated from the government by pro-Nazi, extremist elements because of the decision to break relations with the Axis." Although the new government had "occasionally protested a desire to see the break implemented," Washington charged Buenos Aires with a number of actions helpful to the Axis including obtaining newsprint for pro-Nazi papers, the release of "dangerous Axis spies and agents," and the giving of government contracts to German firms. The destruction of fundamental civil rights was also charged. The Department of State revealed that conversations between Armour and Foreign Minister Peluffo had failed on the question of whether recognition should come before or after implementation of the break and therefore the United States was satisfied that nothing could be gained from continuing the discussions. A separate approach was made to Chile, but after a friendly reception from Foreign Minister Fernández, Santiago refused to change its policy of recognizing the Farrell government.[164]

Although Paraguay felt itself unable to take action without substantial protection from the sizable economic and political pressure its neighbor Argentina could bring to bear,[165] most of the other countries, including Mexico, accepted the idea of withdrawing their representatives, although there is no sign of any great happiness over the policy. Argentina tried to thwart the action in a number of ways. The most novel was its approach to separate Latin American countries with requests to help mediate between Argentina and the United States. This was evidently done independently in each case with the hope of flattering the Latin American country involved and incidentally of embarrassing the United States. On the last day of July Acting Secretary of State Stettinius sent a circular letter to most of the United States diplomatic heads in Latin America warning against Argentina's course of action.[166]

The mid-1944 policy of persisting in non-recognition of the government in Buenos Aires "until there has been a fundamental re-orientation of that government's foreign policy"[167] was opposed by significant elements within the Department of State and the military.[168] Armour, upon his return to Washington, admitted that, due to a combination of prosperity and military control, he saw little chance of Farrell being ousted by force. He pointed out that even opposition elements in Argentina were divided as to what would be the most effective way of changing the government. One group of liberals was urging a continuation of the non-recognition policy until enough pressure had built up to cause the removal of Perón. Another group was urging that Washington take advantage of any small implementation of the break to re-establish diplomatic relations and thereby steer Buenos Aires toward the Allies. Armour professed some sympathy toward the latter view since he feared that the non-recognition front would crumble.[169]

Besides Armour, the Director of the Office of American Republic Affairs, Laurence Duggan—a protégé of Welles—also was uneasy with the policy of trying to pressure the Farrell government for policy changes. On June 24, 1944, he submitted a long memorandum which emphasized that enemy activity in Argentina was not an "actual" menace but only a "potential" danger. Thus, Duggan reasoned, the stamping out of this minor threat was "not worth risking damage to the Good Neighbor Policy." He mentioned that the Joint Chiefs of Staff statement had been made in late March and that the course of the war had improved significantly since that time, thereby making Argentina even less of a danger. Duggan then went into a long defense of the Good Neighbor Policy. He claimed that its success had led the Latin American nations to cast their lot with the United States during the war. "They acted not because Uncle Sam raised a menacing finger but because they thought it was the thing to do *in their own interests (which were identical with our interests)*."[170]

The memo then moved on to a discussion of the postwar world. He argued that the good feelings could be an enormous asset in "our main objective, namely, the creation of a decent postwar order." However, the United States had managed to create, beginning with the Rio Conference "an Argentine bogey which is now returning to haunt us." He advocated that the United States recognize that Argentina was no longer a threat and begin to consult with the other American republics regarding the postwar international organization. He also placed the blame for much of the restlessness among Latin American governments at the time on Washington's unwillingness to

consult with them on postwar problems, instead confining these discussions
to the big four. Duggan's solution was the calling of a foreign ministers meeting. This could not only break the impasse with Argentina, according to his
reasoning, but also "immeasurably improve the chances of the success of our
postwar plans." He suggested that the Department consider the idea of extending into postwar existence "those inter-American organizations which
have been so useful in meeting economic problems of general interest." Duggan felt this idea might ignite interest, particularly within the hemispheric
governments. The memorandum argued that the meeting should only consider the Argentine situation as a subordinate question, thereby keeping the
countries from taking rigid public positions. It claimed that "a reasonable
solution" could be found and "presented in such a way that Argentina
could not decline its acceptance." Duggan concluded the memo:

> The convocation of such a meeting is the type of bold, imaginative
> step necessary to break the Argentine impasse. It would definitely appeal
> to all the other governments. Its chances of successfully solving the Ar-
> gentine problem are believed infinitely greater than any other course
> yet suggested.[171]

It should be pointed out that Duggan's concept of the Good Neighbor
Policy was probably somewhat different from the general concept within
the Department of State. To a large extent the policy, according to Bryce
Wood's excellent study *The Making of the Good Neighbor Policy*,[172] was
shaped by the massive problems Sumner Welles found himself confronted
with when he was the President's representative to Cuba in 1933. At that
time Welles had managed to get himself into the position of dispensing
recognition on the basis of Washington's approval or disapproval of new
governments—in fact at one point he advocated landing the Marines but was
vetoed. The morass Welles found this to be was one of the fundamental
factors leading to the unilateral adoption of the non-interference policy
labeled the Good Neighbor Policy. Welles's distaste undoubtedly influenced
those around him directly concerned with Latin American policy and the
successes of the new policy reinforced this sentiment. However, many
others in the Department of State, such as Secretary Hull, had not been
through the entire process in quite the degree that those working with the
American republics had been. The others were aware of the extent of United
States power in Latin America and were aware that pressure continued to
be frequently used in day-to-day relations. What they seemed to be unaware
of was that the policy operated under a tacit set of complex rules and moods
which set limits on the extent to which the United States could exercise its
influence. Wood refers to the relations as being, "so amorphous yet so
real,"[173] and comments on the need for accurate reporting by diplomatic

missions along with "finesse and a sympathetic style of application, and a nice sense of timing."[174]

The measures taken by the Department of State in the case of Argentina from mid-1942 onward, even though reluctantly agreed to by the other American republics, were outside these boundaries in that they were public and forced the United States into a position from which it was embarrassing to make concessions. This was exactly the type of situation which the Good Neighbor Policy avoided. As for Argentina, Hull seemed unaware of the subtleties of the domestic political situation which was operating within a prosperous economic environment, as well as of that country's great ability to resist pressure. It is, of course, easy to use this line of reasoning to blame all the problems produced by the hard line toward Argentina on Hull and those close to him. This is to some extent the position Welles took in his writings after leaving the Department.[175] The former Undersecretary wrote that "it was at the 1936 Conference that Secretary Hull first developed that violent antipathy to Argentina which was later to become an obsession."[176] He also claimed that he discussed Hull's attitude with President Roosevelt prior to attending the Rio meeting.[177] Some have looked upon Welles's departure from the Department of State as fatal to the Good Neighbor Policy,[178] and Welles's remarks were frequently quoted in Latin America at the time in criticism of Washington's policy toward Buenos Aires.[179]

Certainly there is some truth in this characterization of Hull, but it should be remembered that the Secretary of State had opposed Welles's request to intervene militarily in Cuba in 1933 and had consistently held off the demand of Secretary of the Treasury Morgenthau for harsher action. It may also be, as Duggan suggested later, that the barrage of newspaper columns from Welles spurred Hull on in his efforts to vindicate his position.[180] Finally, it needs to be observed that the tension between Hull and Welles had been simmering for a long time, and, as the loser in the struggle for the upper hand in the Department of State, Welles may have been excessively committed to defending his policies toward Latin America.

John Kenneth Galbraith, in discussing the Cuban missile crisis of 1962, points to a kind of foreign policy "macho" factor which may well have applied to the decision making process during the tensions of the period in question. He has written of his worry over

> the peculiar dynamics of the Washington crisis meeting. This has the truly terrible tendency always to favor the most reckless position, for this is the position that requires the least moral courage. The man who says: "Let's move in with all we have and to hell with the consequences" will get applause and he knows it. He seems personally brave and also thinks he is. In fact, he is a coward who fears that in urging a more deliberate policy, he will invite the disapprobation of his colleagues or will later

be accused of advocating a policy of weakness. Normally, also, he is aided by his inability to foresee, or even to imagine, the consequences of the action he advocates. In contrast, the man who calls for caution, a close assessment of consequences, an effort to understand the opposing point of view, especially if Communist, and who proposes concessions must have great courage. He is a real hero and rare.[181]

The Galbraith comment is not universally operative but it does appear to have some validity when applied to the Department of State debate—and the debate outside the Department[182]—in that the memos discussing the alternatives seemed at times to indicate that a conciliatory position toward Argentina was somehow "appeasement," a word with a terrible connotation while American soldiers were dying in foreign lands as part of a war the United States saw as a struggle of good against evil.

Argentina did make some efforts in July to convince Washington that it actually was trying to implement the break in relations with the Axis. The Chilean Chargé d'Affaires in Buenos Aires was given an informal memorandum describing Argentine actions in connection with the break.[183] The memo, which was also designed for Washington's consumption, said that the German diplomats were leaving Argentina during July. It claimed that the Argentine government had tried to prevent German firms from doing anything drastic that might hamper hemispheric unity and that a system of supervision was being developed to enforce this. It denied any anti-Semitic stand by the Farrell government and claimed that *La Fronda* had been penalized for articles offensive to the United Nations.

Informed of the contents of the note, the United States Embassy in Buenos Aires was extremely critical.[184] The Embassy claimed that there were "no effective controls covering operations of Axis business and financial concerns with Argentina." It mentioned government contracts as late as mid-June which had gone to German firms on the proclaimed list. It also stated that newsprint from the National Penitentiary was finding its way to pro-German newspapers. However, by the end of July the Embassy was changing its emphasis somewhat in reporting that information available indicated that the Central Bank was enforcing decrees prohibiting financial transactions with Axis countries but that there were serious loopholes in the laws.[185] The Embassy continued to be hampered by the fact that it was never completely sure of its information. Without the cooperation of the Argentine government, or with that government attempting to plead its case, the Embassy did not have dependable sources of information.

Despite the continued opposition of the governmental agencies charged with responsibility for sustaining the war effort and domestic consumption,[186] in August Secretary Hull ordered a 40 to 65 percent cut in all U.S. imports from Argentina.[187] Although the Embassy in Buenos Aires felt that freezing Argentine funds in United States banks would have little positive effect and could lead to reprisals against the United States besides promoting "Great Britain's postwar trade position in Argentina" at the expense of the United States, in August these funds were frozen.[188]

In September of 1944, citing continued inaction against German interests in Argentina, the Department of State outlined an even stronger economic squeeze on the Farrell government.[189] It called for the prohibition of any exports to the Argentine armed services or armament industries. Railroad engines and cars, and automotive vehicles were also barred, along with the Fourdrinier phosphorous bronze screens necessary to continue the production of paper in Argentina. No Argentine development projects except those directly connected with the war effort were to be approved by Washington. Petroleum equipment was prohibited and several new restrictive devices were initiated.

This policy was also ineffective, and with rumors (and actual cases) of Germans fleeing to Argentina rising, the Department of State was becoming increasingly unhappy with events in Buenos Aires. By November the Department had decided that Argentina had "definite expansionist plans for the domination of South America and [was] working feverishly to develop a military machine strong enough to support arbitrary political and economic demands upon its neighbors."[190] In retrospect, there is little to support the idea that Argentina's attempts to strengthen itself were part of any plot to take over South America in late 1944. The actions can more easily be interpreted as efforts of the government to consolidate itself and to be prepared to resist pressure from the outside. This is not to argue that there were not individuals interested in an expansionist policy. The point is, Buenos Aires did not have the power to follow such a policy at the time.

THE ROLE OF ENGLAND

The intense nationalism of the new Argentine government, coupled with some control over the communications media, enabled the Farrell administration to interpret each effort by Washington to influence Argentine foreign policy as an affront to the national sovereignty. The level of Argentina's economic development and its distance from North America helped to increase the ability of Buenos Aires to resist Washington's policy. Still another factor influencing U.S.–Argentine relations deserves discussion: Argentina's close link with England. This link insulated Argentina because the health of England's economy was dependent during the war for supplies from Argentina, and London was continually reluctant to apply harsh sanctions. Hull's memoirs and Peterson's volume *Argentina and the United States 1810–1960*

both place much of the blame on England for the failure of United States
sanctions to be effective. Of course, if one wishes to blame the United
States for the failure, the statement can be turned around to say that the
policy failed because the Department of States was not astute enough to
realize that England was too dependent on Argentina to participate in
harsh sanctions.

England saw the problems in Argentina in terms of its need to keep open
the flow of various products, particularly beef. It also, as pointed out previously, did not find anything magical in the idea of hemispheric unity. In
fact, the idea frequently seemed to the British to be a mask behind which
the United States operated to dominate the hemisphere. If it was a mask,
it was certainly one the English envied since London was forced to operate through the colonial system, which meant that it was responsible
for the Empire's countries, whereas the United States could always turn
its back on the countries of Latin America. In the case of Argentina, London's
perception of the situation in Buenos Aires was particularly colored by the
fact that Argentina was more or less in London's economic sphere of influence and that the actions of the United States had a certain competitive
air about them. This shows especially in the recollections of England's Ambassador to Buenos Aires, and it probably influenced his reports to London.
Although Ambassador Kelly did not find it reprehensible, he says in his account of the situation in Argentina during World War II that the United
States was doing "everything possible to build up trade supremacy" while
the war was being waged.[191] A dissertation based on Washington diplomatic
records states:

> Indeed, the British had cause to be apprehensive over the conduct of
> Americans in Latin America during the war. As early as November 1940
> American government personnel had approached the British with a pro-
> posal to transfer British-held Argentine securities to American hands as
> part of an American loan for British purchases in Latin America. The
> British might not have been aware of an OCIAA [Office of the Coordi-
> nator of Inter-American Affairs] memo prepared in that month which
> states in regard to such a deal: "There are some good properties in the
> British portfolio and we might as well pick them up now. There is also
> a lot of trash which Britain should be allowed to keep." Nor were they
> perhaps aware of a memo which appears in President Roosevelt's files
> early in April 1944 proposing the acquisition by the United States of
> one billion dollars in such British-held Argentine securities in exchange
> for the equivalent sum being added to Britain's lend-lease credits.[192]

One can accept the postwar economic situation as a consideration in London and Washington without viewing it as the most important factor. The

Department of State was enough aware of this problem of economic competition in Argentina between London and Washington to assure the British that the United States would not try to make postwar trade agreements with Argentina.[193] Washington also felt that fascist infiltration into Buenos Aires would eventually threaten British investments.[194]

A classic study of British foreign policy based on classified records states that during late 1943 and early 1944

> the Foreign Office . . . thought that Mr. Hull was greatly exaggerating the damage done by the Argentine government to the Allies, and that anyhow his attempt to bring about the overthrow of the regime would fail. . . . The Foreign Office argued again and again that official gestures of disapproval, such as the withdrawal of ambassadors, were ineffective and that an attempt to apply economic sanctions would do more harm to the Allies than to the Argentine government.[195]

Contributing to this viewpoint was Ambassador Kelly, who felt that events in Buenos Aires, which the United States saw as a steady slippage to fascism, were nothing of the sort. Kelly later wrote:

> My own firm conviction, which I reported incessantly to London in the face of a sustained barrage by the American government and press (the latter faithfully echoed by the English press), was that in the overwhelming majority, the governing classes, the new military government, and Argentines of all classes, had no interest in Nazi or any other European ideology; that they felt they or their fathers had come from Europe precisely to say "goodbye to all that"; that they were first and last interested in themselves, in having a good time, and that their real desire was to carry on business as usual with both sides to a dispute in which they felt they had no personal or national interest.[196]

Ambassador Armour had returned to Argentina in October 1943, but in June 1944 he was again recalled to Washington "for consultations", effectively withdrawing the U.S. Ambassador from the country. Hull asked John Winant, U.S. Ambassador to Great Britain, to ask that Kelly also be brought home for consultation, "in order that there may be no appearance of division between" England and the United States.[197] The answer from England's Foreign Secretary Anthony Eden was that he opposed the idea, upon which London had not been consulted in advance, because the withdrawing of ambassadors during times of stress was not helpful and moreover the meat contract was coming up for settlement within three months. Hull pressed both Winant and Lord Halifax, England's Ambassador in Washington, to have Eden reconsider.[198] Roosevelt also sent a message to Prime Minister Churchill urging him to call home the British Ambassador in Buenos Aires for consultation "because of the importance of a common stand at this juncture."[199] Kelly was recalled. Churchill's position was best stated by a memo he sent to Eden:

> When you consider the formidable questions on which we have difficulty with the U.S., oil, dollar balances, shipping, policy to France, Italy, Spain, the Balkans, etc., I feel that we ought to try to make them feel we are friends and helpers in the American sphere.[200]

However, as the days in power of the Farrell government continued to mount, the remaining days of England's beef contract diminished. London was becoming increasingly restive in its partnership with the United States. On July 14, 1944, Churchill sent Roosevelt a message stating that England was willing "to do everything we can to help you and Mr. Hull with the South American countries" but pointing out England's dependence on imported meat. The message noted that "your people are eating per head more meat and poultry than before the war while ours are most sharply cut," and requested Roosevelt to ask Hull to do "nothing which would jeopardize" the chances of concluding a meat treaty with Argentina.[201] Roosevelt answered on July 22 with assurances that the United States would do nothing to hinder the meat treaty but reiterated the case against Argentina. He also stated that Argentina knew that to stop shipments of meat to England "would everywhere be considered a betrayal of the United Nations." Roosevelt pointed out that shipments from Argentina could continue, and had in the past, to supply the meat on the same basis without a contract. He closed with the statement "I know that we can continue to count on your help to liquidate this dangerous Nazi threat."[202] The note is slightly contradictory in that it seems to condemn Argentina as being pro-Axis and then indicates that to stop meat shipments would be a pro-Axis act. Of course, the United States was gambling that Argentina's economic dependence on meat exports would make it impossible for her to stop the shipments. The problem was that although the United States was willing to gamble, it was gambling with England's stakes and England was not pleased with the idea.

On August 2, 1944, Acting Secretary of State Stettinius wired instructions to Ambassador Winant to urge Eden to handle the meat negotiations in a manner designed "to reinforce our political position." The note warned that "unless they are so handled, the apparent divergence in our positions may be seriously accentuated." Stettinius suggested that the negotiations be prolonged and that "a firm stand" be taken on questions of price and other terms. He also urged that the English treat the meat negotiations "as an isolated commercial transaction dictated by special war needs" and "separate from fundamental political and economic policies."[203] The note suggested that England follow the United States in reducing its purchases from Buenos Aires to products absolutely essential to the war effort—a reduction of 40 to 65 percent of total purchases. On the same day Churchill was criticizing Argentina in the House of Commons. He referred to the traditional ties between London and Buenos Aires but lamented that the former friend had "chosen to dally with the evil, and not only with the evil but with the losing side." He then warned that all would not be forgotten after the war. Nations would have to be judged after the conflict by their role in the struggle. "Not only belligerents but neutrals will find that their position in the world cannot remain entirely unaffected by the part they have chosen to play in the crisis of the war," the Prime Minister said in closing his remarks on the Argentine situation.[204]

Despite these strong words, which constituted a final bluff by Churchill, London was deciding that the costs of sanctions or pressure against Argentina were simply too great. On August 4 the British Chargé d'Affaires delivered a written communication to the Secretary of State.[205] It pointed out that England had traditionally not attached any moral connotation to recognition and expressed doubts that recognition "can in fact be used to effect a change of government in Argentina"; it might, however, be valuable in extracting certain specific contributions "on the matters recommended by the Combined Chiefs of Staff." The British expressed some reservations regarding "the effect on the Latin-American temperament of the Argentine nation of ostracizing that country's government." The note claimed that London found it difficult to justify keeping its Ambassador away from Buenos Aires "for an indefinite period of time" since it could mean that British interests were "likely to suffer at the hands of an ultranationalist government" while the United States kept various missions there "advising the recalcitrant government." England warned that any decision should also be discussed with some of Argentina's neighbors since they were vulnerable to pressure from Buenos Aires. Evidently stung by the unilateral decision of Washington to withdraw Armour, which was then presented to England as a reason for its taking the same action with Kelly, this note, and a conversation between Winant and Eden, found London renewing its request that unilateral public statements on the question of Argentina be avoided.[206]

However, the United States continued to press its demand that England do nothing that could be interpreted as appeasement. The Department urged[207] that the meat negotiations be delayed or, if completed, be limited to a short-term contract. In mid-August 1944 Secretary Hull discussed the situation with Ambassador Halifax and Sir Alexander Cadogan, British Undersecretary for Foreign Affairs who was visiting Washington.[208] Hull stated, according to his account, that "the stamping out of nazism in Argentina is a major goal of London's policy." Once again the British were urged to go slow on the meat negotiations.

This problem of England's position was one of the factors contributing to dissent within the Department of State. Some officials were aware that even under wartime conditions, England was not a full-fledged satellite of the United States. Thus the Department was expending a significant amount of energy in trying to convince London of the danger Argentina presented and to convince the Foreign Office that cooperation in pressuring Argentina could produce favorable results.[209] Hull stated in a September 12 memo to Roosevelt that "it is no exaggeration to say that effective implementation of our Argentine policy depends on British cooperation in economic matters."[210] Rumors were persisting that England intended to sign a four-year contract with the Argentine government rather than operating on a month-by-month basis as recommended by Washington. The British had made it clear that they felt their primary obligation in the meat negotiations was to make sure that their people were adequately fed. Hull suggested to Roosevelt that perhaps the United States and the other Allied countries could help provide meat to England. The Secretary specifically mentioned that in view of the anticipated meat surplus in the United States it might be possible to send some of these stocks to England under lend-lease provided the United Kingdom reduced her purchases from Argentina.[211]

On September 16, 1944, Hull again approached the British Ambassador to Washington urging the English to use caution in making any agreement to purchase meat from Argentina.[212] Hull argued that the British meat supply was not in danger because the market was a buyer's market and not a seller's. According to the Hull memo, it seemed

> that the British officials were far more fearful about the risk than the President and myself and other members of this Government, and we based our views on the most elaborate and careful examination of all the facts and circumstances. This I reiterated to the Ambassador.

Of course the problem was that it was Britain's meat supply that was at stake. Therefore, British reluctance to endanger shipments from Argentina should not be surprising.

In an effort to cover up the fact that England was truly reluctant in its cooperation, Roosevelt issued a statement to the press late in September of 1944 which mentioned "the extraordinary paradox of the growth of Nazi-Fascist influence . . . and methods" at the same time the United Nations was winning. He quoted Churchill's remarks of August 2 warning that actions in the war would be held against countries afterwards. Roosevelt closed with the comment that the Nazi radio broadcasts to Latin America, the pro-Fascist press in Argentina, and "a few irresponsible individuals and groups in this and certain other Republics," were all attempting to undermine the American republics and the United Nations "by fabricating and circulating the vicious rumor that our counsels are divided on the course of our policy toward Argentina."[213] The Embassy in Buenos Aires reported back that the statement had been beneficial and heartening to democratic elements. It felt the statement served to emphasize the gravity of the Argentine international situation to those who had not realized the position into which Argentina had managed to work itself.[214] However, there were also claims in Argentina that the statement was an outgrowth of election politics in the United States (Roosevelt was running for his fourth term) and therefore should not be taken seriously.

Behind the facade of Washington-London unanimity, the Department of State showed particular irritation over a suggestion in the autumn of 1944 from the British Embassy that the Foreign Office in London wanted a clear statement of United States objectives to help guide it in its consideration of collaboration in economic sanctions against Argentina. Washington's note in answer to this request referred to those in control of the Argentine government as being pro-Nazi and anti-United Nations and said that Argentina's policy was to promote this type of government in other Latin American countries.[215] "No competent or well-informed person or authority denies this fact" Washington's note blithely proclaimed. It went on to state:

> The same military-Fascist group has definite expansionist plans for the domination of South America and is working feverishly to develop a military machine powerful enough to support arbitrary political and economic demands upon its neighbors. It is planning for and anticipates assitance from refugee Nazi technicians, economists and military personnel after the war. If this group is permitted to stabilize and solidify its position through the political tolerance and helpful trade of the principal United Nations it will threaten the peace of South America as soon as its strength permits.

The answer from Washington also flatly declared that the United States would never accredit an Ambassador to an Argentine government controlled by the same group. It closed by stating:

> It is our considered judgment that Great Britain in not following a similar course [of economic sanctions] and particularly by its actions in the economic field, is inevitably encouraging the present regime to believe that it can ultimately divide Great Britain from the United States.

Hull's explanatory memo to Ambassador Winant accompanying the messages to Eden lamented that despite the United States' frequently expressed complaints, the British Foreign Office had "manifested almost complete indifference to our views" and had given the Argentine diplomats "ample ground for the belief that a four-year contract is in ultimate certainty."[216] The Hull memo said there was no justification for even a two-year contract in the name of an emergency war situation. It pointed out that the United States Army had canceled an order for 43,000 tons of Argentine canned meat and that a British purchase of Argentina's exportable surplus could nullify the impact of this move. Hull reiterated his conviction that Britain had no reason to believe that Argentine would halt meat sales:

> All reports that we have with regard to the anxiety of the Argentines to conclude a meat contract with England, for psychological and political reasons, demonstrate that there is little danger that continuation of spot purchases would result in reprisals in the form of an embargo on meat.

The note reveals, once again, the willingness of Washington to gamble on breaking the back of the Argentina government with the British meat supply as the stakes. However, Hull went significantly further in his communication of October 10, 1944, in applying pressure to London. The instructions to Winant closed with the following:

> In presenting the foregoing views to Eden, please inform him that we cannot divorce our consideration of this matter from our consideration of British requests for our cooperation and assistance on a much more substantial scale in other areas. What we are asking could at worst involve only a minor sacrifice and no serious hazard to British interest.[217]

There is no other way to interpret this paragraph than as a threat to cut Washington's postwar assistance to Great Britain unless London cooperated in efforts to topple the government in Buenos Aires. The comment that this would involve "only a minor sacrifice" was not appreciated in the Foreign Office, where it was believed, contrary to the estimates of the United States, that if the supply of meat from Argentina was lost, the meat ration would be cut by two-thirds.[218]

On the same day Roosevelt was also protesting to Churchill via telegram the rumor that London might sign a four-year meat contract. The President said he felt that such a contract would undermine the united stand against Argentina and pointed out that the United States public was firmly behind the President on the question. Urging operation on a month-to-month basis, which the United States felt Argentina could not protest since it needed the export market, Roosevelt concluded "I feel that we can break this problem if we present a firm united stand during the weeks immediately ahead."[219] It was this type of thinking that the British Foreign Office found "absurdly optimistic."[220] The Prime Minister replied by pointing out London's fear that France, Belgium, and the Netherlands would come into the meat buying market with large stocks of gold and hurt British prices. Churchill agreed to temporarily accept the Washington month-to-month idea but warned that "later

on I must address you again" on the subject of the Argentine meat negotiations.[221]

London was not the only recalcitrant participant in this "united front"
against Argentina. Beginning in September Washington had increasing problems keeping the Latin American countries in line. On September 15, 1944,
the Secretary of State sent a warning to the United States diplomatic representatives in Latin America (except Peru, Uruguay and Argentina). It stated
that the Department viewed "as most serious" recent evidence indicating an
increase in legal and illicit re-exports from American republics to Argentina.[222]
It mentioned that while the trade was potentially profitable, it ran counter to
accepted hemispheric policy. Washington was also receiving complaints from
its Embassy in Buenos Aires that British and Canadian firms were selling goods
in Argentina that United States was not able to receive.[223] Early in October
the Deputy Foreign Economic Administrator sent a memo to Assistant Secretary of State Dean Acheson clarifying the commodities involved in the
shipments which violated the partial embargo instituted by Washington. Specifically mentioned were shipments of zinc, arsenate, fibres, and pig iron from
Mexico; shipments of iron, graphite and ultramarine blue from Brazil; iron,
steel, copper, coal, and calcium carbide from Chile.[224] Outside the American
republics, Canada, South Africa, Switzerland, and Spain were accused of
supplying products which substituted for items embargoed by the United
States. The memo also complained of "a large contraband traffic" between
American republics and Argentina which consisted of the re-exportation of
commodities obtained originally in the United States. The Deputy Foreign
Economic Administrator's memo questioned whether the limits on purchases
from Argentina were having a significant impact.

In mid-November of 1944 the question of British cooperation came to
another crisis as a result of a threat from Washington to cut off manufacturing materials Argentina needed to ship products to Britain (in this case a
sealing compound needed for shipping meat) until London's position was
clarified.[225] Churchill replied rather angrily, recounting the British decision
not to simply purchase on the basis of price and stating that Britain was
willing to continue meat purchases from Argentina on a month-by-month
basis until mid-1945 without a contract. The Prime Minister stated that he
"was of course very much hurt that this form of pressure should be applied
to us."[226] Roosevelt replied that no threat was intended and that he was
grateful for the English decision to continue meat purchases on a month-to-
month basis.[227]

London's agreement to buy meat on a monthly arrangement marked the
limits to which the English were willing to sacrifice. From their point of
view other imports from Argentina all fell into the necessity classification

and United States requests for reductions in imports of non-essential goods were irrelevant. They were already operating on the basis of imports limited to only essential goods. Certainly the British were not anxious to antagonize the Argentines and were well aware of the large sterling balances being accumulated in Argentine accounts for which London would be accountable after the war.[228] This accumulation also acted to limit London's purchases to the essential.

COLLAPSE OF NON-RECOGNITION

Relations between countries have an ebb and flow to them which makes the scholar's attempt to examine a particular event, or period of years, artificial. But there is some logic to stopping with the reversal of United States policy toward Argentina which took place early in 1945. The Argentine case study has shown a rising resistance on Argentina's part toward the foreign and domestic policy of the United States. By late 1944 Hull's efforts were clearly leading nowhere. The Farrell government was neither collapsing nor capitulating. The pressure from Washington, if anything, was given the military government a rallying point—Argentina was standing up to the Colossus of the North.

Four factors helped trigger the reversal of policy. First, when Hull was forced to leave in December of 1944 due to ill health, there were important changes in the personnel of the Department of State having Latin American responsibilities. Second, Argentina found a clever means to rally Latin American support for its cause by pressing for an inter-American meeting on the subject. Third, North American business interests saw the Argentine market moving away from United States companies and feared the nationalization of their interests.

Finally, it is in the previously discussed failure to obtain London's enthusiastic cooperation where one can see the first signs of the collapse of Hull's tough policy against the Farrell government. According to the United States Embassy in Buenos Aires,[229] by mid-December 1944 it was obvious that the British were disregarding cooperation in the limitation of exports to Argentina and, in fact, had been increasing the flow of goods besides signing a new petroleum supply contract. The Embassy also reported that "Mexican exports to Argentina . . . are higher today than in any previous period," that "Brazil is increasing exports to Argentina to a tremendous degree," and that "Chile is maintaining its export policy with Argentina."[230] Meanwhile, Argentine imports from the United States for the first ten months had fallen from 156,000,000 pesos in 1943 to a little more than 123,000,000 for the comparable period in 1944.

The Embassy's evaluation of the "tough" September economic policy called it "a failure" and suggested that its continuance would be "contrary to the best interests of the United States in Argentina." The reason for the lack of success, from the point of view of the Embassy, was primarily England's trade policy. The Embassy feared that British traders were moving in and profiting by the trade gaps left by United States withdrawals, and that this would have serious consequences after the war. Also, it was admitted, the policy had greatly harmed the popularity of the United States in Argentina while accomplishing nothing. A glance at the primary economic indicators for Argentina during this period show the ineffectiveness of the policy designed to slow down the Argentine economy.[231]

The Embassy recommended that "representations again be made to the British for complete and effective unity of policy toward Argentina." This should be buttressed, the note suggested, by two alternative courses of action in case England failed to cooperate. The first would be to cut off materials necessary for the continuation of British investments in Argentina. The other would be to open up the supply of goods from the United States in an effort to prevent further harm to United States interests in the country. Transportation of the items which would undermine the position of British and Latin American traders who were "sabotaging the September program" would strike at this group and also help the U.S. businessmen to regain their position.

The business interests who feared the loss of the Argentine market began to find a more friendly ear in Washington after Hull's departure in November 1944.[232] Edward R. Stettinius, Jr., a bureaucrat with limited expertise on Latin America, became Secretary of State. He made Nelson Rockefeller Assistant Secretary of State for Latin America in December of 1944. Rockefeller had been coordinator of the Office of Inter-American Affairs since 1940,[233] and, since part of his responsibilities in that position had been propaganda, he was sensitive to Latin American dissatisfaction over Washington's treatment of Argentina. Although Hull continued to oppose concessions toward Argentina even after he left office,[234] Stettinius allowed Rockefeller a free hand in guiding policy toward Latin America and this made compromise easier.

Aware that there was some sympathy in Latin America for its position, the Farrell administration in October of 1944 had asked the Governing Board of the Pan American Union for a meeting to discuss its position. Washington hoped to avoid a public hemispheric meeting on this topic and managed to get the meeting shifted so as to exclude Argentina on the ground that it had not participated in the war effort.[235] This became the Inter-American Conference on Problems of War and Peace held from February 21 to March 8, 1945 (popularly known as the Chapultepec Meeting).

Prior to that meeting talks did take place with Argentine officials, and on Feburary 3 the Embassy in Buenos Aires was notified of a new policy which would loosen restrictions on Argentina. It was hoped that this could be done without implying any change in the political position of non-recognition. The instructions commented:

> It is realized that the implications of adopting this policy are both delicate and possibly serious. This change has been approved even though it is realized that action taken under it will sooner or later lead to its being known in the Argentine and that this new economic policy may carry with it the implication of a change in our political policy, which we do not wish to revise.
>
> Part of the difficulties may be overcome by care in putting a new economic policy into effect. We hope to be able to modify the present arrangements by a gradual relaxation rather than take action so suddenly as to become unnecessarily conspicuous.[236]

The Argentine government did begin to take some steps before and after its acceptance of the Final Act of Mexico City, and these steps were interpreted in Washington as sufficient for recognition. The government

—declared a state of war with Japan and consequently Germany;

—made the *Graf Spee* crew members prisoners of war;

—promised internment of Japanese diplomatic and consular officials;

—blocked Axis funds in Argentina;

—issued a decree calling for the registration of all nationals of enemy countries over fourteen years old and the surrender of firearms and radios by these individuals; and

—ordered the takeover of several Axis firms.[237]

On this basis the non-recognizing American republics recognized the Farrell government on April 4. There were also some assurances that Argentina would move toward a return to democratic procedures. Perón went to great lengths to assure the United States Embassy that he was not interested in politics and would not be a candidate for President.[238] The decision to recognize was not approved by exiles, or by some opposition groups in Argentina who had hopes that continued non-recognition would bring down the Farrell government.[239]

Shortly thereafter, the policy toward Argentina reversed again, apparently due to changes in U.S. administration personnel,[240] but that particular situation is beyond the coverage of this analysis. The emphasis here has been on Washington's steadily increasing pressure on Argentina from late 1939 to late 1944 and the domestic changes in Buenos Aires that made this pressure ineffectual and possibly dysfunctional.

CONCLUSION

Perhaps after six chapters no conclusion is needed. The actions and results as presented in this study may speak for themselves. However, in the introduction three general areas of concern were mentioned: (1) the nature of the Pan-American relationship, (2) the operation of United States power, and (3) the effect this power has on domestic politics in Latin America. Therefore it seems proper to make a few comments on these questions as a conclusion.

PAN-AMERICANISM

At the heart of the Pan-American concept is the idea that the countries of the hemisphere stand in a special relationship to each other and share the same interests. This means that cooperation is therefore useful to advance these parallel interests. This is not to say that the Department of State continually spoke in terms of Pan-Americanism—although certainly the concept was mentioned at times. Nor did these officials believe in some mystical force called Pan-Americanism. It is only to suggest that these officials did see hemispheric relations in a special light which suggested that harmony was the rule and that interests were not in conflict.

The perception of Pan-Americanism varied within the hemisphere. The United States saw it as something benevolent—the father protecting his young. But how the United States defined it may have been reinforced by the fact that Pan-American rhetoric filled another purpose—it helped justify Washington's leadership in the hemisphere. The countries of Latin America were not supposed to go outside the Americas for assistance. Therefore they had to turn to the United States. If one wishes to look at the dark side, it justified domination; it was colonialism without colonies; it was imperialism without the stigma.

This is not unexpected. Larger and more powerful countries usually attempt to dominate their weaker neighbors. Thus Pan-Americanism becomes one of those ideologies which justifies the influence of one country over another—

at least in the eyes of the stronger country. There are other facets, other uses, of Pan-Americanism. But the argument developed here is that at least in some circumstances it served as a justification for a form of hegemony. One needs to go further, and observe that there is a dysfunctional aspect to the concept resulting from policymakers lacking a clear perception of what the idea was at its core. It is the difference between rhetoric and substance which exacerbated the difficulties in the cases under consideration. Some Department of State officials did not seem to realize that the good-father image was only part of the reality. This was shown most clearly (and rather quaintly) when the United States appealed to London in the name of Pan-Americanism for cooperation in punishing Argentina.

Other Department of State officials and most Latin American countries saw Pan-Americanism and the ties that operated in its name as channels of influence and cooperation. And this was undoubtedly how a country such as Chile viewed the concept: it was a means of influencing and restraining the United States. A father does not take advantage of his children. In the case of Argentina, however, the fact that the country was not so weak as to be vulnerable to the United States provided the flexibility to take Pan-Americanism or leave it. The role of Argentine nationalism, the influence of England, and the relationship with Brazil, all combined to influence Buenos Aires to reject Pan-American cooperation after mid-1940, when it began to regard Washington's proposals with a suspicion born of a nationalistic sensitivity.

U.S. POWER

What do the preceding chapters suggest about the forms and utilization of United States power?

In the case of Chile, it seems that Santiago continually realized that it was a satellite of (i.e., dependent on) the United States. Particularly regarding markets for its goods, with the European trade severed by the war, Chile recognized the importance of the United States to Chile's economy and did everything it could to deepen those economic ties (thereby increasing its dependency).[1] Relations between President Ríos and Washington sometimes moved slowly as the Chileans misunderstood, avoided, and hesitated, but there was little doubt that they recognized Washington's power and therefore its leadership.

The same is not necessarily true of situations that potentially or actually involved the Congress in Santiago and its counterpart in Washington. These bodies seem to have been more nationalistic than the executives. Sometimes the presence of patriotic congressmen on both sides was used as a threat in the bargaining process. There were periods of exception to this dichotomy between nationalistic congressmen and more pragmatic executives in the case of Argentina, but these stemmed from domestic political conflicts in that country.

Washington hoped the rhetoric of Pan-Americanism would be helpful in obtaining cooperation from Latin America during World War II. As long as winning the war was the top priority, it was obviously impossible to spare military forces for influencing Latin America; and, furthermore, Chile and Argentina were too developed and too far from the United States for their effective use. The problem with economic pressure was that the two countries were providing significant services to the Allied war machine. They were not unrewarded for this. If one can generalize about such a situation, on balance the South American countries needed the United States market during the war more than the United States needed their goods. But Washington nevertheless desperately wanted the copper and the many other supplies coming from Chile and Argentina; and England's dependence on Argentina's beef is also clear. This made economic sanctions difficult for Washington to justify during the heat of the war. Thus it was only when the world struggle was almost over that the United States began to think in terms of an effective economic punishment for Argentina, and the agencies in Washington primarily charged with the war effort or the economic well-being of the United States were the most reluctant to pay the price for pressuring Argentina.

Also slowing the use of economic sanctions were the lingering concepts of the Good Neighbor Policy. This was a symbol which those in Washington opposed to sanctions were sometimes able to manipulate. For example, Roosevelt apparently responded to it in his initial refusal to follow Secretary of the Treasury Morgenthau's recommendation that Argentine financial reserves in the United States be frozen.

Previously it was noted that for the United States not to have tried to dominate Latin America would have violated the rules of the international game (i.e., would have run counter to the operation of the system). Obviously such a comment at one level represents acceptance of spheres of influence and power politics as an accurate description of world politics— in other words, the traditionalist power approach to international relations.[2] On the other hand, the discussion has been critical of Washington's attempts to dominate the government in Buenos Aires. Is there not, then, a contradiction between a willingness to speak of spheres of influence and domination as natural, and a critical attitude toward efforts to dominate?

The point is that Washington overextended its influence by trying to dictate Argentina's foreign policy, particularly under the conditions prevailing in Buenos Aires during the war. Why did it overextend itself?

One mistake was to perceive Argentina as somehow lumped in with the other Latin American countries. The Pan-American concept suggested to individuals not knowledgeable about Latin America that the same policy be applied to all countries. This is not to say that Cordell Hull believed Argentina and El Salvador to be of the same size or strength. But the problem is that Argentina's position was closer to a Spain or a Sweden than to a Haiti. When one begins with a perception that includes Argentina with a group of other countries, such as Pan-Americanism does, the uniqueness of its situation is obscured. It should have been obvious that Argentina had an ability to resist U.S. initiatives.

The case of Brazil has been referred to only peripherally. But the Brazilian situation is important because it served to confuse Washington's wartime understanding of the Argentine problem. Brazil was powerful and yet was cooperating. Why couldn't Argentina? There have been two excellent books dealing with the Brazilian case.[3] Both suggest that, besides the traditional Argentine-Brazilian rivalry for South American leadership, Brazil was simply more astute at placating (perhaps deceiving may be a better word) the United States. Stanley Hilton states it most clearly when he writes:

> In reality, when it perceived its interests as different from Washington's, as in trade matters [involving Germany], Rio de Janeiro followed essentially the same independent policy as Buenos Aires. The difference seems to be that Brazil publicly and privately at every turn assured the United States of its solidarity, whereas Argentina seemed to take pride in open confrontations with Washington. Once Brazilian policymakers learned how prized the rhetoric of good-neighborliness was in Washington, they skillfully used their protestations in conjunction with hints about what Berlin was doing, or was willing to do, for Brazil in order to ward off American pressure or secure further concessions from the United States.
>
> The Good Neighbor Policy was probably the most potent weapon in Brazil's diplomatic arsenal, as Brazilian officials masterfully exploited Washington's unwillingness to adopt sanctions against Brazil for infringements of the American-Brazilian treaty and its readiness to be satisfied with rhetoric in pursuing its commercial aims.[4]

It should be added that Brazil was in a better position to play this game because Vargas had been largely successful in stifling dissent.

The fact that the war was straining Washington's foreign policy decision-making process should not be overlooked in our understanding of the ineffectiveness (and counterproductivity) of the policy toward Argentina. Clearly the government was consumed with the need to win the war. Events in Asia and Europe were determining the policy toward Latin America. What Washington wanted was a Latin American policy that coordinated with its struggle against the Axis. Due to its size and location, the United States felt it had major geopolitical responsibilities outside the hemisphere. These responsibilities were not shared by the Latin American countries, who saw their role in the international system much differently than the United States saw its role. But in most cases it was either beneficial to share the responsibilities (the United States paid strong prices for goods that could not be sold elsewhere) and/or the societies were so penetrated that it was impossible to resist Washington's initiatives. Ambassador Armour frequently warned the State Department of the distinctive qualities of Argentina and of the peculiar evolution of its political process; but reading the replies to his despatches one gets the feeling that his warnings were not treated seriously, or at least not fully grasped, especially by Hull.

This narrative has not emphasized the problems of getting the other Latin American countries to cooperate in such matters as enforcing the proclaimed list and the rationing of supplies. Argentina and Chile's refusal to break diplomatic relations immediately after the Rio meeting focused attention on their cases, but several of the other countries had dismal records in cracking down on the businesses of local Axis sympathizers, and it is difficult to find any country that was outstanding in this. The reason is threefold. First, the bureaucracies of these countries were not set up to handle such matters. Second, the actions intruded into domestic political relationships and balances that were frequently based on personal favors and tacit understandings. Finally, as always there was the fact that the Latin American perception of the sacrifices demanded by the war was different from Washington's simply because they did not share the same sense of global responsibility.

DOMESTIC POLITICS AND INTERNATIONAL PRESSURES

The final question concerns the impact of United States pressure on the domestic politics of the countries involved and the effect the domestic political systems of Argentina and Chile had on their ability or determination to resist the leadership of Washington.

It is in examining this subject that one begins to see the complexities of the concept of penetration or of dependency's clientele elite. Clearly the controlling upper classes in Chile were tied to the export of copper and nitrates and realized the need for their purchase by the United States. Thus we have an almost classic case of the clientele elite. Whatever profits were accruing to the elite by the stimulus the war was giving local industries, it still saw its prosperity tied to the export of primary products. And it believed that the country's level of prosperity also depended on the export market—a conclusion even the most fervent *dependentista* would admit to in the short run.

The political situation in Chile at the time included powerful leftist parties that had supported the winning presidential candidates in the 1938 and 1942 elections. Since the Allies stood against fascist totalitarianism, to the extent that the parties of the left saw the global conflict as a holy war, they were pro-Allied. The rightist elements in Chile had developed close ties to the United States—particularly during the second Alessandri administration. Here was the heart of the clientele elite. It was not that they necessarily agreed with Washington's political ideology; but it was from this group that the United States corporations drew their lawyers, and it was with these individuals that social activities took place.

The situation in Argentina was far different. In the first place, to the extent the exporters were dependent, it was on the purchases of England. But the right wing in Argentina was far more complicated. In part due to the frustration which developed between 1930 and 1943 over Argentina's hope for a future as a world leader, the Franco version of *Hispanidad* attracted many followers. And Argentine politics produced the rise of that unusual military ideology that Perón came to represent. Although the war had heightened political tensions in Buenos Aires, the June 4, 1943, coup largely resulted from domestic political factors.

The war and United States pressure did enter into the negotiations among the military leaders after the coup. Within this group—composed of novices at diplomatic bargaining—masculinity was threatened by the slightest sign of United States pressure. And those who opposed the United States position were quick to emphasize the real and imagined pressures. If the conservative political parties in Argentina had realized what would follow the overthrow of Castillo, they might well have made a coalition with the moderate political parties in order to impede the rise of the military government. The well of Argentine politics was too poisoned by that time, however, and when the corporate ideology and power interests of the military led to its cultivation of labor, the military's position was solidified.

There are other influential factors, but when one tries to select a basic factor for interpreting the unfolding of events discussed in this study, it is the differences in domestic political balances which explain best how Washington's suggestions and pressures were received. By 1943 the Argentine political system had worked itself into a position in which the amount of coercion the United States could generate (which was limited by geography, the necessity of winning the war, the need to protect U.S. business interests, and England's precarious economic situation) could only accomplish the opposite of what the United States wanted. So a "soft line" toward Buenos Aires might have been more productive, but it would have accomplished little more than preventing increased tension between the two countries.

It must be noted that it would be incorrect to assume that the involvement of the United States in the politics of Argentina and Chile was always at the initiative of the Colossus of the North. Chilean Foreign Minister Rosetti staked his political future on warm relations with the United States. There were forces in Argentine politics that actively sought the support of the United States in order to advance their own interests. One case of this was the April-May 1940 neutrality proposal of President Ortiz and Foreign Minister Cantilo in which they suggested a pro-Allied position far ahead of what Roosevelt was trying to pursue at the time. The move is probably best explained as an attempt by the Ortiz group to combat the ultra-nationalist and pro-Axis elements by projecting the image that Argentina was taking the lead in inter-American affairs and to develop a supporting coalition including the Radicals and the Socialists.

This study suggests one additional general lesson. Foreign policy decisionmakers in a country which attempts to convince another country (the influencee) to adopt a particular policy commonly consider (1) whether or not the influencee can be convinced, and (2) the price to be paid by the decisionmaker's government. But there is another important determination to be made: What will be the effect on the domestic politics of the influencee if it refuses to be pressured into action as the influencer wishes? These are evaluations of great delicacy, and a good ambassador, continually observing the intricacies of his host country's domestic politics, may be in the best position to judge the possible effects. Certainly blanket policy suggestions which the decisionmaker's country applies to several countries are potentially dangerous. For example, it can be argued that the Ramírez government's breaking of diplomatic relations with the Axis caused its collapse, which led to a less cooperative government. The United States might have fared better had it not demanded the break in relations (which was made into a larger-than-life symbol of public capitulation by those who opposed it) and instead simply have asked Ramírez's people—when they were ready to cooperate—to quietly crack down on Axis activities. Or, with the benefit of hindsight, it can be suggested that the Department of State should have been ready to make more concessions in return for the break in order to bolster pro-Allied elements.

NOTES

INTRODUCTION

1. Arthur P. Whitaker, *The Western Hemisphere Idea* (Ithaca, N.Y., 1954).
2. *The Inter-American System* (London, 1966), p. 323.
3. James N. Rosenau, "Pre-theories and Theories of Foreign Policy," *Approaches to Comparative and International Politics*, ed. R. Barry Farrell (Evanston, Ill., 1966), p. 65.
4. *Latin America in World Affairs* (New York, 1967), p. 16.
5. Ibid., pp. 4–5.
6. Probably as good a general statement of the theory as is available is the introduction to Ronald H. Chilcote and Joel Edelstein, eds., *Latin America: The Struggle with Dependency and Beyond* (New York, 1974), pp. 1–87.
7. Michael J. Francis, "Dependency as a Theory of International Relations," (Paper, International Studies Association Annual Meeting, Washington, 1975).
8. Theodore Lowi, "American Business, Public Policy, Case Studies and Political Theory," *World Politics* 16 (July 1964); James N. Rosenau, ed., "Foreign Policy as an Issue-Area," *Domestic Sources of Foreign Policy* (New York, 1967).
9. James N. Rosenau, "Comparative Foreign Policy: Fad, Fantasy, or Field?" *International Studies Quarterly* 12 (September 1968); Rosenau, ed., *Comparing Foreign Policies: Theories, Findings and Methods* (New York, 1974).
10. E.g., George Modelski, *A Theory of Foreign Policy* (New York, 1962).
11. Rosenau, "Pre-theories and Theories of Foreign Policy," p. 40.
12. David Green, *The Containment of Latin America* (Chicago, 1971).
13. James Petras, ed., *Latin America: From Dependence to Revolution* (New York, 1973).
14. Randall Bennett Woods "United States Policy Toward Argentina: From Pearl Harbor to San Francisco" (University of Texas, Dissertation, 1972), pp. 190–93, 220–22, 342–43.
15. Graham T. Allison, *Essence of Decision: Explaining the Cuban Missile Crisis* (Boston, 1971).
16. " 'The Bureaucratic Politics' Approach: U.S.–Argentine Relations, 1942–47," *Latin America and the United States: The Changing Political Realities*, eds. Julio Cotler and Richard R. Fagen (Stanford, Cal., 1974).
17. Robert J. Art, "Bureaucratic Politics and American Foreign Policy: A Critique," *Policy Sciences* 4 (Dec. 1973):486.
18. Morton Halperin, *Bureaucratic Politics and Foreign Policy* (Washington, 1974), pp. 11–25.

19. One begins to see the benefit of cognitive maps when confronted by such a problem. See Jeffery Hart, "Geopolitics and Dependency: Cognitive Maps of Latin American Foreign Policy Elites" (Paper, Annual Meeting of the American Political Science Association, Chicago, 1976).

20. M. Halperin, *Bureaucratic Politics and Foreign Policy*, pp. 11–12.

21. Guillermo O'Donnell, "Commentary on May" in Cotler and Fagen, *Latin America and the United States*, pp. 170–72.

22. *The Containment of Latin America*.

23. Dick Steward, *Trade and Hemisphere: The Good Neighbor Policy and Reciprocal Trade* (Columbia, Mo., 1975), p. viii.

24. Ibid.

25. James Petras, "U.S.–Latin American Studies: A Critical Assessment," *Science and Society* 32 (Spring 1968).

26. The position is well stated in Werner Levi, "Ideology, Interests, and Foreign Policy," *International Studies Quarterly* 14 (Mar. 1970).

CHAPTER 1

Prewar Chile

1. Federico Gil, *The Political System of Chile* (Boston, 1966), p. 2.

2. John Reese Stevenson, *The Chilean Popular Front* (Philadelphia, Pa., 1942), p. 1.

3. Merwin L. Bohan and Morton Pomeranz, *Investment in Chile* (Washington, 1960), p. 43.

4. Ibid., p. 49.

5. An excellent example of this is Alejandro Venegas, *Sinceridad: Chile ultimo en 1910* (Santiago, 1910).

6. This generalization is illustrated by Maurice Zeitlin and Richard Earl Ratcliff, "Research Methods for the Analysis of the Internal Structure of Dominant Classes: The Case of Landlords and Capitalists in Chile," *Latin American Research Review* 10 (Fall 1975).

7. For an interesting analysis of the political party system in Chile at the time, see United States National Archives, 825.00/997, Embassy in Santiago to Secretary of State, June 16, 1937. Hereafter, documents from the National Archives are cited by the call number, type, and date of the document. Secretary of State is shortened to S/S and Undersecretary to U/S. The author believes that a longer citation form may be misleading and therefore has tried to provide only enough information to help the researcher find the document. For example, with a few exceptions, documents or despatches from an embassy are cited as such even though signed by the Ambassador. Almost everything was addressed to the Secretary of State (standard procedure) but this does not necessarily mean that the Secretary saw the document.

8. The proportional representation system (D'Hondt) worked strongly to the benefit of the conservative rural interests as opposed to the urban representation, R. Cruz Coke, *Geografía Electoral de Chile* (Santiago, 1952), pp. 61-62.

9. For a balanced discussion of this period see Orville Grant Cope, III, "Politics in Chile: A Study of Political Factions and Parties and Election

Procedures" (Claremont Graduate School, Dissertation, 1963), pp. 277–99.

10. Stevenson, *The Chilean Popular Front*, p. 62.

11. The reader should not be confused by the fact that the Liberal Party was not liberal in terms of current usage of the word.

12. Stevenson, *The Chilean Popular Front*, pp. 89–90.

13. The figures that follow are drawn from Comisión Económica para América Latina de las Naciones Unidas, *Antecedents Sobre El Desarrolo Chilena 1925–1952* (Santiago, 1955), 1:103.

14. Bohan and Pomeranz, *Investment in Chile*, p. 12.

15. Ibid., p. 42.

16. Department of State, *Foreign Relations of the United States, 1936*, 5: 149. Hereafter this series is cited as FRs. Since the author also considers the specific citations of the documents to be frequently misleading, and because the volumes are readily available, the specific situations of the footnoted document are not included.

17. Bohan and Pomeranz, *Investment in Chile*, p. 216.

18. Ibid.

19. 825.00/1029, Embassy in Santiago to S/S, Apr. 20, 1938.

20. 825.51/968, Embassy in Santiago to S/S, Mar. 24, 1938.

21. 825.51/961, Statement from Foreign Bondholders Protective Association Council, Jan. 11, 1938.

22. 825.51/948, Memo, Gustavo Ross to Sumner Welles, Oct. 4, 1937.

23. 825.51/986, Memo, Mar. 15, 1938.

24. Bohan and Pomeranz, *Investment in Chile*, p. 232.

25. Clark W. Reynolds, "Development Problems of an Export Economy," in Markos Mamalakis and Reynolds, *Essays on the Chilean Economy* (Homewood, Ill., 1965), p. 236.

26. FRs, 1938, 5:433.

27. Ibid., p. 442.

28. Ibid., pp. 446–47.

29. Stevenson, *The Chilean Popular Front*, pp. 79–80.

30. Ibid., p. 80. See also Michael Potashnik, "Nacismo: National Socialism in Chile, 1932–1938" (University of California at Los Angeles, Dissertation, 1974).

31. Ibid., pp. 68–69.

32. (Cambridge, Mass., 1965), pp. 47–48.

33. Alan Angell, *Politics and the Labour Movement in Chile* (London, 1972), pp. 103–120.

34. E. Halperin, *Nationalism and Communism in Chile*, p. 126.

35. Ibid.

36. Stevenson, *The Chilean Popular Front*, p. 73.

37. Arturo Valenzuela, "The Scope of the Chilean Party System," *Comparative Politics* 4 (Jan. 1972).

38. 825.00/1030, Embassy in Santiago to S/S, Apr. 26, 1938.

39. Ibid.

40. Jack Ray Thomas, "The Evolution of a Chilean Socialist: Marmaduke Grove," *Hispanic American Historical Review* 47 (Feb. 1967).

41. Stevenson, *The Chilean Popular Front*, p. 76.

42. Ibid., p. 71.
43. "Ibáñez Returns to Chile," *New York Times,* May 11, 1937, p. 20.
44. Stevenson, *The Chilean Popular Front,* p. 77.
45. E. Halperin, *Nationalism and Communism in Chile,* p. 45.
46. Stevenson, *The Chilean Popular Front,* p. 87.
47. 825.48 Earthquake, 1939/40, Memo, Jan. 31, 1939.
48. 825.48 Earthquake, 1939/94, Memo, Feb. 16, 1939.
49. Ibid.
50. This account is drawn from FRs, 1939, 5:439–43.
51. Ibid., p. 441.
52. 825.51/1058, Embassy in Santiago to S/S, Mar. 8, 1938.
53. FRs, 1939, 5:444.
54. 825.00/1162, Embassy in Santiago to S/S, July 28, 1939.
55. FRs, 1939, 5:447–49.
56. Ibid., p. 447.
57. Ibid., p. 450.
58. Ibid., p. 452.
59. 825.51/1151, Embassy in Santiago to S/S, Sep. 23, 1939.
60. 825.51/1162, Embassy in Santiago to S/S, Oct. 18, 1939.
61. 825.6352/117, Memo, Apr. 18, 1940.
62. 825.75/15, Telegram, Embassy in Santiago to U/S, June 21, 1940.
63. *Chile Through Embassy Windows: 1939–1953* (New York, 1958).
64. This same situation can be found in a reading of most memoirs written by former ambassadors. It is particularly obvious, and at times is discussed, in John Kenneth Galbraith's *Ambassador's Journal* (New York, 1969), which deals with Galbraith's two years as Washington's representative to India. See also Sheldon Appleton, "Systematic Bias in U.S. Foreign Affairs Reporting: A Critique and a Proposal," *International Studies Quarterly* 16 (June 1972).
65. FRs, 1939, 5:432.
66. Ibid., pp. 438–39.
67. 825.00/1217, Embassy in Santiago to S/S, May 25, 1940.
68. For general accounts of the meeting see Adolf Berle, "After Lima," *Yale Review* 28 (1939), 449–71; Charles A. Thomson, "Results of the Lima Conference," *Foreign Policy Reports* 15 (Mar. 15, 1939); Edward Tomlinson, "The Meaning of Lima," *Current History* 49 (Feb. 1939), 37–40; Department of State, *Report of the Delegation of the United States of America to the Eighth International Conference of American States* (Washington, 1941).
69. FRs, 1938, 5:42; 710.H Continental Solidarity/74, Telegram, S/S in Lima to U/S, Dec. 15, 1939.
70. 710.H/338, Memo, Dec. 20, 1938. The proceedings can be found in the Archives listed under 710.H/436 and 710.H/538.
71. *The Time for Decision* (New York: 1944), p. 212.
72. Ibid.
73. For a copy of the map and an explanation, plus the Declaration itself, see FRs, 1939, 5:35–37.
74. J. Lloyd Mecham, *The United States and Inter-American Security* (Austin, Tex., 1961), p. 183.
75. FRs, 1939, 5:38. For more detail of Chile's small role in the conference see "Se está creando en América una atmósfera de solidaridad más efectiva, despojadad de lirismo y con vista hacia la realidad," *La Nación* (Santiago), Oct. 11, 1939.

76. C. Neale Ronning, *Law and Politics in Inter-American Diplomacy* (New York, 1963), pp. 108–9.

77. Cordell Hull, *The Memoirs of Cordell Hull* (New York, 1948), p. 690. Hereafter cited as *Memoirs*.

78. Stevenson, *The Chilean Popular Front*, p. 102.

79. See Frederick M. Nunn, *Chilean Politics, 1920–1931: The Honorable Mission of the Armed Forces* (Albuquerque, N.M., 1970); and Liisa North, *Civil-Military Relations in Argentina, Chile and Peru* (Berkeley, Cal., 1966).

80. H. E. Bicheno, "Anti-Parliamentary Themes in Chilean History: 1920–1970," *Allende's Chile*, ed., Kenneth Medhurst (New York, 1972).

81. Fritz Epstein, "European Military Influence in Latin America," (Microfilm of unbound typescript in Library of Congress, 1942? , reproduced in 1961 at the University of Chicago), p. 99.

82. Stetson Conn and Byron Fairchild, *The Western Hemisphere: The Framework of Hemisphere Defense* (Washington, 1960), p. 173.

83. Ibid.

84. Ibid., pp. 173–74.

85. 825.248/150A, Telegram, S/S to Embassy in Santiago, Sep. 8, 1939.

86. 825.248/156, Embassy in Santiago to S/S, Jan. 10, 1940.

87. 825.248/152, Embassy in Santiago to S/S, Nov. 13, 1939.

88. 825.248/152, Letter, S/S to Secretary of War, Dec. 28, 1939.

89. 825.248/174, Telegram, Embassy in Santiago to S/S, May 14, 1940.

90. Conn and Fairchild, *The Western Hemisphere*, pp. 1–29.

91. Ibid., pp. 8–9.

92. Ibid., pp. 9–10.

93. Ibid., p. 26.

94. Ibid., p. 27.

95. Ibid., p. 28.

96. Memo, G–2 for Chief of Staff, 9 July 1940, AF 380 (5–24–40), italics in original, quoted in Conn and Fairchild, *The Western Hemisphere*, p. 179.

97. Unless otherwise indicated, this discussion follows Conn and Fairchild, *The Western Hemisphere*, pp. 207–237.

98. U.S. Department of State, Division of American Republics, "Nazi Activity in the American Republics," 1938, National Archives, pp. 6–9.

99. See FRs, 1939, 5:1–14.

100. Memo of Conversation, 21 Feb. 1940, WPD 4228, quoted in Conn and Fairchild, *The Western Hemisphere*, p. 208.

101. 810.24/97, Memo, Mar. 26, 1940; and FRs, 1940, 5:5–6.

102. FRs, 1940, 5:12–13.

103. 825.00/1213 1/2, President to Embassy in Santiago, May 24, 1940.

104. FRS, 1940, 5:52.

105. Bowers, *Chile Through Embassy Windows*, p. 61.

106. FRs, 1940, 5:55.

107. FRs, 1939, 5:100–21.

108. Ibid., p. 123.

109. The shock was particularly great because Chilean society liked to view itself as an outpost of French culture.

110. See 740.0011 European War 1939/2253, Embassy in Santiago to S/S, Apr. 10, 1940; and 710.11/2489, Embassy in Santiago to S/S, Apr. 30, 1940.

111. 740.00111 A.R./1104, Embassy in Santiago to S/S, May 15, 1940.

112. 825.00/1224, Embassy in Santiago to S/S, June 28, 1940.

113. 825.00/1224, Telegram, Embassy in Santiago to S/S, June 30, 1940.
114. U.S. State Department, "Nazi Activity in the American Republics," pp. 59–60.
115. 825.00 N/61, Embassy in Santiago to S/S, June 12, 1940.
116. Ibid.
117. For an example of this type of support, see "Sentido del concepto de neutralidad,"*El Mercurio,* Oct. 5, 1940.
118. 825.00/1266, Embassy in Santiago to S/S, Oct. 17, 1940.
119. Miriam Ruth Hochwald, "Imagery in Politics: A Study of the Ideology of the Chilean Socialist Party" (University of California at Los Angeles, Dissertation, 1971), pp. 127–31.
120. Stevenson, *The Chilean Popular Front,* p. 108.
121. 825.00/1291, Telegram, Embassy in Santiago to S/S, Jan. 7, 1941.
122. Stevenson, *The Chilean Popular Front,* pp. 109–10; see also Richard R. Super, "The Chilean Popular Front Presidency of Pedro Aguirre Cerda, 1938–1941" (Arizona State University, Dissertation, 1975).
123. Stevenson, *The Chilean Popular Front,* p. 110.
124. Ibid., p. 105.
125. E. Halperin, *Nationalism and Communism in Chile,* pp. 126–27.
126. Stevenson, *The Chilean Popular Front,* pp. 122–37.
127. These figures are based on ibid., pp. 114–15, and 825.00/1217, Embassy in Santiago to S/S, Nov. 20, 1940. There are some discrepancies between the figures and at least one typographical error in the Stevenson figures.
128. 825.00/1318, Telegram, Embassy in Santiago to S/S, Mar. 19, 1941.
129. 825.00/1337, Embassy in Santiago to S/S, Apr. 24, 1941.
130. 825.00/1364, Telegram, Embassy in Santiago to S/S, June 11, 1941.
131. For an excellent study of the copper industry in Chile, see Theodore H. Moran, *Multinational Corporations and the Politics of Dependence: Copper in Chile* (Princeton, N.J., 1974).
132. 825.5151/633, Telegram, Embassy in Santiago to S/S, Aug. 5, 1941.
133. Most of the major documents connected with this exchange are in FRs, 1941, 6:578–96.
134. 811.20 Defense (M) Chile/67, Memo, Dec. 1, 1941.
135. FRs, 1941, 6:594.
136. Ibid., p. 595.
137. Reynolds, "Development Problems of an Export Economy," p. 239.
138. Ibid., pp. 239–240.
139. Ibid., p. 240. James Petras in his provocative article "U.S. Business and Foreign Policy," *New Politics* 6 (Fall 1967), takes this figure seriously but does not discuss the totally artificial nature of the world market during the war.
140. 825.6374/1456, Memo, Sep. 24, 1941.
141. 825.6374/1392, Memo, Sep. 18, 1940.
142. 825.24/171, Telegram, Embassy in Santiago to U/S, July 15, 1940.
143. 825.51/1310, Memo, Jan. 21, 1941.
144. 825.24/183, Bowers to Welles, Mar. 7, 1941.
145. FRs, 1941, 6:552–54.
146. Ibid., p. 571.
147. Ibid., p. 137.
148. "Chile no cedera bases militares a los Estados Unidos."

149. "Declaración alentadora del Embajador norteamericano," *La Opinion,* June 4, 1941.

150. 862.20225/262, Embassy in Santiago to U/S, July 31, 1941.

151. FRs, 1941, 6:573–75.

152. 825.00/1426, Embassy in Santiago to S/S, Oct. 9, 1941.

153. 862.20225/304, Memo, Oct. 9, 1941.

154. In 1891, 17 U.S. sailors were injured and two were killed while on shore leave from the U.S.S. *Baltimore* in an incident that began in the True Blue Saloon in Valparaíso. The United States claimed the men received inadequate police protection. Chile initially refused to apologize, but after feelings had become agitated, did apologize and paid $75,000 in damages. Generally speaking, Chile sees the incident as an example of U.S. belligerence.

155. "Proyecto de Ley contra instituciones o partidos políticos que obedecen a inspiraciones doctrinarias extranjeras," *El Mercurio,* Sep. 5, 1941.

156. Bowers, *Chile Through Embassy Windows,* pp. 63–64.

157. 825.00/1427, Telegram, Embassy in Santiago to S/S, Oct. 16, 1941.

158. 825.00/1599, Bowers to President Roosevelt, Nov. 24, 1941.

159. Lawrence Littwin, "An Integrated View of Chilean Foreign Policy," (New York University, Dissertation, 1967), p. 203.

160. Much of this is drawn from 825.00/1367, Embassy in Santiago to S/S, June 11, 1941.

161. 825.458/37, Bowers to Hull, Sep. 22, 1941.

162. "El 165° aniversario de la Independencia de Estados Unidos fue celebrado brillantemente," *El Mercurio,* July 5, 1941; and 123 Bowers, Claude G./262, Embassy in Santiago to S/S, July 7, 1941.

163. FRs, 1941, 6:39–45.

164. 825.00/1474, Embassy in Santiago to U/S, Oct. 22, 1941.

165. FRs, 1941, 6:74.

166. Ibid., p. 75.

167. Ibid., pp. 119–20.

168. Ibid., p. 120.

CHAPTER 2

Prewar Argentina

1. Center for Latin American Studies, University of California at Los Angeles, *Statistical Abstract of Latin America, 1962* (Los Angeles, Cal., 1963), p. 10.

2. Bailey, *Latin America in World Affairs,* p. 44.

3. Hubert Herring, *A History of Latin America* (New York, 1955), p. 634.

4. Peter H. Smith, *Argentina and the Failure of Democracy: Conflict among the Political Elites, 1904–1955* (Madison, Wis., 1974), p. 93.

5. Marvin Goldwert, "The Rise of Modern Militarism in Argentina," *Hispanic American Historical Review* 48 (May 1968).

6. Smith, *Argentina and the Failure of Democracy,* pp. 94, 97.

7. David Rock, *Politics in Argentina, 1890–1930: The Rise and Fall of Radicalism* (London, 1975), p. 263.

8. Herring, *A History of Latin America,* p. 635.

9. Peter G. Snow, *Argentine Radicalism* (Iowa City, Iowa, 1965), pp. 46–58.

10. Herring, *A History of Latin America*, p. 636.

11. Ibid., p. 215.

12. Tomás Roberto Fillol, *Social Factors in Economic Development: The Argentine Case* (Cambridge, Mass., 1961), p. 43.

13. Peter H. Smith, *Politics and Beef in Argentina* (New York, 1969), p. 252.

14. Arthur P. Whitaker, *The United States and Argentina* (Cambridge, Mass., 1954), p. 103.

15. Harold F. Peterson, *Argentina and the United States, 1810–1960* (Buffalo, N.Y., 1964), p. 342.

16. The Socialist opposition to the pact is outlined in Jorge Abelando Ramos, *Revolución y contra-revolución en la Argentina*, vol. 2 (Buenos Aires, 1965), pp. 412–414. For a good discussion of the question see chapter one of Alberto A. Conil Paz and Gustavo E. Ferrari, *Argentina's Foreign Policy, 1930–1962*, trans. John J. Kennedy (Notre Dame, Indiana, 1966). See also Richard Setaro, "The Argentine Fly in the Ointment," *Harpers* (August 1949), pp. 205–6.

17. Peterson, *Argentina and the United States*, p. 342, 358.

18. Fillol, *Social Factors in Economic Development*, p. 44.

19. Ibid., p. 49.

20. Javier Villanueva, "Economic Development" in *Prologue to Perón: Argentina in Depression and War, 1930–1943*, ed. Mark Falcoff and Ronald H. Dolkart (Berkeley, Cal., 1975), p. 74.

21. Ysabel F. Rennie, *The Argentine Republic* (New York, 1945), pp. 259–61.

22. Fillol, *Social Factors in Economic Development*, p. 46.

23. Carlos Díaz-Alejandro, *Essays on the Economic History of the Argentine Republic* (New Haven, Conn., 1971), pp. 189–205.

24. Villanueva, "Economic Development," p. 80.

25. Rennie, *The Argentine Republic*, p. 249.

26. 711.359 Sanitary/113, Off-record Comments, Hull, Press Conference, Aug. 16, 1935.

27. 711.359 Sanitary/250, Memo, Jan. 12, 1937.

28. "Entendimento Commercial con Los Estados Unidos," *La Prensa*, Jan. 25, 1937.

29. 611.355/256, Memo, Mar. 31, 1941.

30. 600.1115/1117, Memo, Mar. 21, 1939.

31. Manuel A. Machado, Jr., *Aftosa: A Historical Survey of Hoof-and-Mouth Disease and Inter-American Relations* (Albany, N.Y., 1969), p. 28.

32. 711.359 Sanitary/409, Memo, Nov. 15, 1937.

33. 711.359 Sanitary/497, Embassy in Buenos Aires to S/S, Sep. 10, 1940; and RG:59, Division of Latin American Republics, Box 2, bound volume of conversations, Nov. 11, 1938.

34. "The Department of State and the Non-National Interests: The Cases of Argentine Meat and Paraguayan Tea," *Inter-American Economic Affairs* 15 (Autumn 1961), p. 23.

35. Ibid., pp. 23–24.

36. Steward, *Trade and Hemisphere*, pp. 186–97; FRs, 1939, 5:294–302.

37. William Simonson, "Nazi Infiltration in South America, 1933–1945" (Tufts University, Dissertation, 1964), pp. 303–4.

38. Steward Edward Sutin, "The Impact of Nazism on the Germans in Argentina" (University of Texas at Austin, Dissertation, 1975), pp. 69–73.

39. 810.00 F/32, "Memorandum on Italian Fascist and German Nazi Activity in the American Republics," by S. Chapin, Feb. 17, 1938; hereafter cited as Chapin Memo.

40. P. W. Bidwell, *Economic Defense of Latin America* (Boston, 1941), pp. 45–46.

41. Simonson, "Nazi Infiltration in South America," p. 529. On the German influence in the military see Marvin Goldwert, *Democracy, Militarism and Nationalism in Argentina, 1930–1966* (Austin, Tex., 1972), pp. 60–74; George Pope Atkins and Larry V. Thompson, "German Military Influence in Argentina, 1921–1940," *Journal of Latin American Studies* 4 (Nov. 1972).

42. Simonson, "Nazi Infiltration in South America," p. 529.

43. Ibid.; and see Darío Canton, "Military Interventions in Argentina: 1900–1966" (paper, International Sociological Association, London, 1967), pp. 10–12.

44. FRs, 1938, 4:217–18, 320.

45. Ibid., p. 318.

46. Chapin Memo; and Canton, "Military Interventions in Argentina."

47. 711.35/106, Memo, Aug. 9, 1935.

48. (Stanford, Cal.; 1969), p. 119.

49. Chapin Memo.

50. *Documents on German Foreign Policy, 1918–1945*, C, (Washington: 1953), 5:866–67. Hereafter this series of volumes is cited as *DGFP*.

51. 835.001 Ortiz, Roberto/88, Embassy in Buenos Aires to S/S, Mar. 5, 1938. This condescending, semi-racist remark was not totally untypical of some of the U.S. diplomats to Latin America at the time; although generally Argentina, due to its large immigrant population, was less subject to this type of comment.

52. Ibid.

53. Rennie, *The Argentine Republic*, p. 262.

54. Ibid.

55. Jorge Aberlando Ramos, *Revolución y contra-revolución en la Argentina, nueva historia de los Argentinos* (Buenos Aires, 1961), p. 123.

56. Simonson, "Nazi Infiltration in South America," p. 531.

57. Ibid., p. 534.

58. *DGFP*, D, 5:845–52.

59. Ibid., p. 849; Simonson, "Nazi Infiltration in South America," p. 537.

60. Simonson, "Nazi Infiltration in South America," pp. 559–60.

61. Sutin, "The Impact of Nazism on the Germans in Argentina."

62. Hull, *Memoirs*, p. 605.

63. Donald Dozer, *Are We Good Neighbors?* (Gainesville, Fla., 1959), p. 49.

64. FRs, 1938, 5:33–36.

65. See "Address of Dr. José María Cantilo," Department of State,

Report of the Delegation of the United States of America to the Eighth International Conference of American States (Washington, 1941), p. 92. See also Daniel A. Holly, "The United States and the Inter-American System, 1939–1945" (University of Denver, Dissertation, 1966), pp. 107–8.
66. See above, ch. 1, n. 68.
67. 735.00/24, Embassy in Buenos Aires to S/S, Apr. 28, 1939.
68. *DGFP*, D, 8:157.
69. Simonson, "Nazi Infiltration in South America," pp. 566–67.
70. "Argentina Recognizes Poland," *New York Times*, Oct. 21, 1939, p. 3.
71. *DGFP*, D, 9:292–93.
72. Stanley E. Hilton, "Argentine Neutrality, September 1939–June 1940: A Re-Examination," *The Americas* 22 (Jan. 1966); Joseph S. Tulchin, "The Argentine Proposal for Non-Belligerency, April 1940," *Journal of Inter-American Studies* 11 (Oct. 1969).
73. FRs, 1940, 1:743–44.
74. Ibid., pp. 752–55.
75. Ibid., pp. 755–56.
76. Stanley E. Hilton, *Brazil and the Great Powers, 1930–1939* (Austin, Tex., 1975), ch. 6.
77. Robert A. Divine, *The Illusion of Neutrality* (Chicago, 1962).
78. Tulchin, "The Argentine Proposal for Non-Belligerency," pp. 576–77.
79. 720.00111 A.R./1178, Embassy in Buenos Aires to S/S, May 24, 1940.
80. 835.857/20, Memo, May 31, 1940.
81. 835.857/11, Telegram, Embassy in Buenos Aires to S/S, June 3, 1940.
82. *DGFP*, D, 9:494–95.
83. Simonson, "Nazi Infiltration in South America," p. 572.
84. *DGFP*, D, 9:495, 545.
85. Ibid., p. 495.
86. Ibid., p. 660.
87. Ibid., p. 661.
88. Potash, *The Army & Politics in Argentina*, pp. 122–26.
89. Goldwert, *Democracy, Militarism and Nationalism in Argentina*, p. 51. See also Falcoff and Dolkart, "Political Developments," *Prologue to Perón*, pp. 39–40.
90. Alberto Ciria, *Partidos y poder en la Argentina moderna, 1930–1946* (Buenos Aires, 1964), pp. 89–91.
91. 835.857/24, Embassy in Buenos Aires to S/S, Oct. 3, 1941. See also Rodolfo E. Modern, "La neutralidad de la Republica Argentina en las dos guerras mundiales," *Revista Juridica de Buenos Aires* 2 (May–Aug. 1966): 198–200.
92. Simonson, "Nazi Infiltration in South America," p. 579.
93. Richard A. Leopold, *The Growth of American Foreign Policy* (New York, 1962), p. 561.
94. Hilton in his "Argentine Neutrality, September 1939–June 1940" emphasizes the impact of the fall of France.
95. Simonson, "Nazi Infiltration in South America," p. 581.
96. Rennie, *The Argentine Republic*, p. 279.

97. *DGFP*, C, 9:529-31.

98. Ibid., p. 615.

99. Peterson, *Argentina and the United States*, p. 410.

100. 740.00111 A.R./425, Telegram, U/S to S/S, Oct. 3, 1939.

101. Hull, *Memoirs*, p. 690.

102. 710. Consultation (2)/98, Embassy in Buenos Aires to S/S, June 21, 1940.

103. FRs, 1940, 5:240; See also Connell-Smith, *The Inter-American System*, pp. 112-117.

104. FRs, 1940, 5:235-37.

105. Ibid., pp. 353-67, 240; and "Twenty Nations and One," *Fortune*, 22 (Sep. 1940), pp. 74ff.

106. William G. Cooper, "New Light on the Good Neighbor Policy: The United States and Argentina, 1933-1939" (University of Pennsylvania, Dissertation, 1972), p. 231.

107. FRs, 1940, 5:484.

108. Ibid., pp. 492-94.

109. Ibid., pp. 495-504.

110. Technical questions were involved in the talks, but these could have been overcome if the more basic problems had been solved.

111. FRs, 1940, 5:460-63.

112. Ibid., p. 464.

113. Ibid., pp. 465-66.

114. Ibid., p. 481.

115. Ibid., p. 482. See also "$50,000,000 U.S. Loan Granted Argentina," *New York Times*, Dec. 6, 1940, p. 1; "Dollars for Argentina," *New York Times*, Dec. 7, 1940, p. 16; and "$60,000,000 Loan Goes To Argentina," *New York Times*, Dec. 12, 1940, p. 7.

116. FRs, 1940, 5:460-63.

117. Ibid., p. 22.

118. Ibid., pp. 22-23.

119. Ibid., p. 23.

120. Ibid., p. 27.

121. Ibid., p. 29.

122. Ibid., pp. 31-32.

123. Ibid., pp. 33-34, contains a summary of the reply.

124. Conn and Fairchild, *The Western Hemisphere*, p. 37.

125. FRs, 1940, 5:36-38.

126. Simonson, "Nazi Infiltration in South America," pp. 597-606.

127. Ibid., pp. 600-601.

128. Ibid., pp. 601-2.

129. *DGFP*, D, 12:228-29.

130. Potash, *The Army & Politics in Argentina*, pp. 128-29.

131. 862.20235/434, Embassy in Buenos Aires to S/S, Apr. 23, 1941.

132. 811.20235/1, Embassy in Buenos Aires to S/S, Feb. 10, 1941.

133. Alton Frye, *Nazi Germany and the American Hemisphere, 1933-1941* (New Haven, Conn., 1967), p. 119.

134. 811.20235/1, Feb. 10, 1941.

135. 862.20235/434, Embassy in Buenos Aires to S/S, Apr. 23, 1941.

136. 710. Consultation 3/711, Embassy in Buenos Aires to S/S, Feb. 19, 1942. For a sophisticated discussion of the internal political competition for control of Castillo or his favors see Potash, *The Army and Politics in Argentina*, pp. 126-81.

137. 862.20235/434, Apr. 23, 1941.

138. 835.00/994, Embassy in Buenos Aires to S/S, Mar. 26, 1941.

139. Potash, *The Army & Politics in Argentina*, p. 152.

140. For information on the airlines in South America the best sources are William Burden, *The Struggle for the Airways in Latin America* (New York, 1943); David Bushnell, *Eduardo Santos and the Good Neighbor* (Gainesville, Fla., 1967); Melvin Hall and Walter Peck, "Wings for the Trojan Horse," *Foreign Affairs* 19 (Jan. 1941), pp. 347-69; and see FRs, 1941, pp. 334-57 regarding Argentina.

141. 835.24/157, Memo, June 24, 1941; and 810.20 Defense/1052A, Embassy in Buenos Aires to U/S, July 5, 1941.

142. 810.20 Defense/1094, Armour to U/S, May 21, 1941.

143. FRs, 1941, 6:323-24.

144. 835.24/170, Memo of Conversation, July 31, 1941.

145. FRs, 1941, 6:324.

146. 835.24/170, July 31, 1941.

147. 810.20 Defense/1255, Memo, July 12, 1941.

148. FRs, 1941, 6:325.

149. Conil Paz and Ferrari, *Argentina's Foreign Policy*, p. 83.

150. FRs, 1941, 6:326.

151. Ibid., pp. 332-33.

152. For example, compare the Argentine draft, ibid., pp. 332-34, with the Bolivian agreement signed Dec. 6, 1941, pp. 428-31, and the Brazilian agreement signed Oct. 1, 1941, pp. 534-39.

153. 835.24/241, Memo, Nov. 28, 1941.

154. 835.24/242, Memo, Dec. 5, 1941.

155. 835.24/243, Memo, Dec. 10, 1941.

156. FRs, 1941, 6:387-88.

157. Ibid., p. 399.

158. Steward, *Trade and Hemisphere*, pp. 195-96, and Peterson, *Argentina and the United States*, p. 412.

159. 611.3531/1948, Embassy in Buenos Aires to S/S, Oct. 15, 1941; and 611.3531/1969, Embassy in Buenos Aires to S/S, Oct. 18, 1941.

160. Steward, *Trade and Hemisphere*, p. 196.

161. Smith, *Argentina and the Failure of Democracy*, pp. 50-56, 71-87.

162. 862.20234/526, Embassy in Buenos Aires to S/S, July 16, 1941.

163. 862.20235/526, July 16, 1941.

164. Simonson, "Nazi Infiltration in South America," p. 626.

165. Cámara de Diputados de la Nación, COMISION INVESTIGADORA DE ACTIVIDADES ANTIARGENTINAS, Informe No. 1 (Buenos Aires, 1941).

166. Cámara de Diputados de la Nación, COMISION INVESTIGADORA DE ACTIVIDADES ANTIARGENTINAS, Informe No. 2 (Buenos Aires, 1941).

167. Quoted in 862.20235/578, Telegram, Embassy in Buenos Aires to S/S, Sep. 6, 1941.

168. Arthur P. Whitaker, *Inter-American Affairs, 1941* (New York, 1942), p. 218.

169. Cámara de Diputados de la Nación, COMISION INVESTIGADORA DE ACTIVIDADES ANTIARGENTINAS, Informe No. 3 (Buenos Aires, 1941).
170. Cámara de Diputados de la Nación, COMISION INVESTIGADORA DE ACTIVIDADES ANTIARGENTINAS, Informe No. 4 (Buenos Aires, 1941).
171. Cámara de Diputados de la Nación, COMISION INVESTIGADORA DE ACTIVIDADES ANTIARGENTINAS, Informe No. 5 (Buenos Aires, 1941).
172. *DGFP,* D, 13:401-2.
173. Ibid.
174. Ibid., pp. 443-44.
175. Ibid., p. 469.
176. Ibid., p. 470.
177. Simonson, "Nazi Infiltration in South America," p. 642.
178. 835.24/214, Memo attached to Embassy in Buenos Aires to S/S, Nov. 26, 1941.
179. Simonson, "Nazi Infiltration in South America," p. 646.
180. Whitaker, *Inter-American Affairs,* pp. 226-27.
181. *DGFP,* C, 13:913.
182. Ibid., p. 914.
183. Hilton, "Argentine Neutrality, September 1939-June 1940," pp. 244-45.
184. This type of information was taken very seriously in some of the scare literature at the time. See H. Fernández Artucio, *The Nazi Underground in South America* (New York, 1942) and Saxtone E. Bradford, *The Battle for Buenos Aires* (New York, 1943). For a more balanced discussion see Sutin, "The Impact of Nazism on the Germans in Argentina."
185. Potash, *The Army & Politics in Argentina,* pp. 154-55.

CHAPTER 3

Compromise at Rio

1. 710. Consultation (3)/8, Memo, Feb. 17, 1941.
2. 710. Consultation (3)/9, Memo, Mar. 14, 1941.
3. 710. Consultation (3)/9 1/7, Memo, Mar. 16, 1941.
4. 710. Consultation (3)/9 2/7, Memo, Mar. 24, 1941.
5. Ibid.
6. 710. Consultation (3)/9 4/7, Memo, May 22, 1941.
7. 710. Consultation (3)/9 4/7, Memo, May 22, 1941.
8. 710. Consultation (3)/11, Telegram, Embassy in Rio to S/S, June 10, 1941.
9. 710. Consultation 3/73, Memo, Dec. 13, 1941; and 710. Consultation 3/95, Embassy in Santiago to S/S, Dec. 16, 1941.
10. E.g., 710. Consultation 3/267, Memo, Dec. 15, 1941; and 710. Consultation 3/112 2/11, Memo, Dec. 18, 1941.
11. 710. Consultation 3/112 4/11, Memo, Dec. 27, 1941.
12. 710. Consultation (3)/6 1/2, Memo, Jan. 6, 1941.
13. FRs, 1942, 5:10-11; and 710. Consultation 3/132, Telegram, Embassy in Rio to U/S, Dec. 29, 1941.
14. 740.0011 Pacific War/1512, Embassy in Buenos Aires to S/S, Dec. 24, 1941.

15. FRs, 1942, 5:16 22.

16. 710. Consultation (3)/116, Telegram, Embassy in Asuncion to S/S, Dec. 26, 1941.

17. 710. Consultation (3)/118, Telegram, Legation in La Paz to S/S, Dec. 26, 1941.

18. 710. Consultation (3)/118, Telegram, S/S to Legation in LaPaz, Dec. 29, 1941.

19. FRs, 1942, 5:24–25.

20. Ibid., p. 7.

21. Ibid., p. 8.

22. 710. Consultation 3/605, Memo, Dec. 30, 1941.

23. 740.0011 European War 1939/18259, Telegram, Embassy in Buenos Aires to S/S, Jan. 7, 1942.

24. Ibid.

25. 710. Consultation (3)/254B, Telegram, Jan. 7, 1942.

26. FRs, 1942, 5:27.

27. 740.0011 European War 1939/18260, Telegram, from Embassy in Buenos Aires to S/S, Jan. 7, 1942.

28. FRs, 1942, 5:27.

29. Ibid., p. 28.

30. Ibid.

31. This is also the interpretation of Lawrence Duggan in his *The Americas: The Search for Hemispheric Security* (New York, 1949).

32. 710. Consultation (3)/598, Miscellaneous Bound Telegrams, U/S to Embassy in Santiago, Jan. 19, 1942.

33. 710. Consultation (3)/261, Memo, Dec. 23, 1941.

34. Frye, *Nazi Germany and the American Hemisphere*, p. 166. For an excellent background on the Brazilian position see Hilton, *Brazil and the Great Powers.*

35. 710. Consultation (3)/302:telegram, U/S to S/S, Jan. 13, 1942.

36. Bryce Wood, *The United States and the Latin American Wars* (New York, 1965).

37. 710. Consultation 3/629, Embassy in Buenos Aires to S/S, Feb. 5, 1942.

38. 710. Consultation (3)/148, Telegram, Embassy in Rio to S/S, Dec. 31, 1941.

39. 710. Consultation (3)/302, Telegram, Embassy in Rio to S/S, Jan. 13, 1942.

40. 710. Consultation (3)/508A, Telegram, S/S to American Delegation in Rio, Jan. 25, 1942.

41. 710. Consultation 3/477, Telegram, Embassy in Rio to S/S, Jan. 25, 1942.

42. A good discussion of this question is to be found in Francis Daniel McCann, Jr., "Brazil and the United States and the Coming of World War II, 1937–1942" (University of Indiana, Dissertation, 1967), pp. 161–78.

43. 710. Consultation (3)/428A, Telegram, S/S to Embassy in Buenos Aires, Jan. 21, 1941.

44. Rosetti's instructions based on Conversation between Acting Foreign Minister Pedregal, U.S. Ambassador Bowers, and Cecil Lyon of the U.S. Embassy, 710. Consultation (3)/605, Memo, Jan. 22, 1942.

45. Ibid.; and FRs, 1942, 5:301.

46. 710. Consultation (3)/598, Miscellaneous Bound Telegrams, Embassy in Rio to Embassy in Santiago, Jan. 23, 1942.

47. 710. Consultation (3)/408, Telegram, Embassy in Santiago to S/S, Jan. 19, 1942.

48. FRs, 1942, 5:30.

49. Ibid., p. 31.

50. Ibid., p. 33.

51. 710. Consultation (3)/450, Memo, Jan. 22, 1942.

52. 710. Consultation 3/605, Memo, Jan. 23, 1942.

53. 710. Consultation (3)/458, Telegram, U/S to S/S, Jan. 23, 1942.

54. Ibid.

55. This account of approval of the formula is primarily based on Conversation between Ambassador Armour and officials of the Argentine Foreign Ministry, 710. Consultation (3)/598, Miscellaneous Bound Telegrams, Embassy in Buenos Aires to U/S in Rio, Jan. 22, 1942.

56. 710. Consultation (3)/458, Telegram, U/S to S/S, Jan. 23, 1942.

57. FRs, 1942, 5:34.

58. Ibid.

59. Ibid., p. 39.

60. Ibid.

61. Ibid.

62. Ibid., p. 42.

63. The best articles on the Rio agreements at the time were David H. Popper, "The Rio de Janeiro Conference of 1942," *Foreign Policy Reports* 18 (Apr. 15, 1942); and Charles Fenwick, "The Third Meeting of Ministers of Foreign Affairs at Rio de Janeiro," *American Journal of International Law* 36 (1942): 169–203.

64. 710. Consultation (3)/629, Embassy in Buenos Aires to S/S, Feb. 5, 1942.

65. 710. Consultation (3)/718, Telegram, Embassy in Buenos Aires to S/S, Mar. 13, 1942.

66. 825.00/1609, Bowers to Welles, Feb. 4, 1942.

67. 710. Consultation (3)/552, Telegram, Embassy in Santiago to S/S, Jan. 31, 1942.

68. 710. Consultation (3)/562, Telegram, Embassy in Santiago to S/S, Feb. 2, 1942.

69. 710. Consultation (3)/650, Telegram, Embassy in Santiago to S/S, Feb. 17, 1942.

70. Consultation (3)/708, Telegram, Embassy in Santiago to S/S, Mar. 6, 1942.

71. 710. Consultation (3)/723, Memo, Mar. 5, 1942.

72. 710. Consultation (3)/712, Telegram, Embassy in Santiago to S/S, Mar. 11, 1942.

73. 710. Consultation (3)/722, Telegram, Embassy in Santiago to S/S, Mar. 14, 1942.

74. 710. Consultation (3)/746, Memo, Mar. 16, 1942.

75. 740.0011 European War 1939/21679, Telegram, Embassy in Santiago to S/S, May 19, 1942.

76. 710. Consultation (3)/811, Telegram, Embassy in Santiago to S/S, July 13, 1942; 740.0011 European War 1939/26072, Telegram, Embassy in Santiago to S/S, Nov. 27, 1942.

77. Hull, *Memoirs,* pp. 1148–49.

78. Ibid., p. 1149.

79. Ibid.

80. *Seven Decisions That Shaped History* (New York, 1950), p. 117.

81. FRs, 1942, 5:37; Welles, *Seven Decisions That Shaped History,* pp. 114–21; Welles, *The Time for Decision,* pp. 220–34.

82. Hull, *Memoirs,* pp. 1147–48.

83. Ibid., p. 1150.

84. Ibid., p. 1144.

85. Fred L. Israel, ed., *The War Diary of Breckinridge Long* (Lincoln, Neb., 1966), p. 67.

86. 710. Consultation (3)/254C, Telegram, U/S to Embassy in Buenos Aires, Jan. 7, 1942.

87. McCann, "Brazil and the United States and the Coming of World War II," pp. 172–78.

88. p. 111.

89. Ibid., p. 120.

90. Hull, *Memoirs,* pp. 1227–31, gives more detail of Hull's side of the general problem.

91. Welles's departure from the State Department is discussed below, ch. 6.

CHAPTER 4

Chile Temporizes

1. FRs, 1941, 6:77.

2. Ibid., p. 78.

3. Ibid.

4. 894.20210/134, Telegram, to S/S, Jan. 6, 1942.

5. FRs, 1941, 6:147.

6. FRs, 1942, 6:3,

7. 825.248/246, Telegram, Embassy in Santiago to S/S, Jan. 20, 1942.

8. Ibid.

9. FRs, 1942, 6:4.

10. Ibid.

11. 825.25/339, Memo, Jan. 21, 1942.

12. FRs, 1942, 6:5.

13. Ibid., pp. 5–6.

14. Ibid., pp. 6–7.

15. FRs, 1942, 5:307–8.

16. Stevenson, *The Chilean Popular Front,* pp. 117–18.

17. Ibid., p. 118.

18. 825.00/1528, Letter, Bowers to Roosevelt, Dec. 15, 1941.

19. "El General Ibáñez y los Estados Unidos," *El Mercurio,* Dec. 17, 1941.

20. 825.00/1525, Letter, Bowers to Duggan, Dec. 21, 1941.

21. 825.00/1467, Telegram, Embassy in Santiago to U/S, Dec. 7, 1941; and, same call number, S/S to Embassy in Santiago, Dec. 8, 1941.

22. Bowers, *Chile Through Embassy Windows,* p. 299.

23. 825.00/1594, Memo, Jan., 1942.

24. FRs, 1942, 6:9–10.

25. Ibid., p. 12.

26. Ibid., p. 8.

27. Ibid., p. 12.

28. Ibid., p. 13.

29. 825.24/428, Memo, Feb. 17, 1942; and 825.24/406, Memo, Mar. 6, 1942.

30. 825.24/395, Telegram, Embassy in Santiago to U/S, Mar. 17, 1942; and 825.24/395, Telegram, S/S to Embassy in Santiago, Mar. 18, 1942.

31. 810.20 Defense/3172, Memo, Aug. 12, 1942.

32. This account of the sinking of the *Tolten* is based on newspaper accounts and 825.857/15A, Telegram, U/S to Embassy in Santiago, Mar. 16, 1942; and 825.857/15, Telegram, Embassy in Santiago to S/S, Mar. 19, 1942.

33. 825.857/15, Telegram, Mar. 19, 1942.

34. 825.857/15, Memo, no date.

35. 825.857/18, Telegram, Embassy in Santiago to S/S, Mar. 23, 1942.

36. 825.857/23, Telegram, Embassy in Santiago to U/S, Mar. 24, 1942.

37. 825.857/24C, Memo, Mar. 26, 1942.

38. 825.857/25, Telegram, Embassy in Santiago to S/S, Apr. 3, 1942.

39. FRs, 1942, 6:19.

40. 825.00/1602, Telegram, Embassy in Santiago to S/S, Feb. 25, 1942; and 710. Consultation (3)/722, Telegram, Embassy in Santiago to S/S, Mar. 14, 1942.

41. 825.00/1602.

42. 710. Consultation (3)/722.

43. Spruille Braden, *Diplomats and Demagogues: The Memoirs of Spruille Braden* (New Rochelle, N.Y., 1971), p. 91.

44. 825.00/1640, Memo, Mar. 5, 1942.

45. 825.00/2003, Letter, Bowers to Welles, Apr. 15, 1942.

46. "Clientele-elite" is a term from the dependence literature; the concept is best treated by Susanne Bodenheimer, "Dependency and Development: The Roots of Latin American Underdevelopment," *Politics and Society,* 1 (May 1971).

47. Bowers, *Chile Through Embassy Windows,* pp. 98–99.

48. 825.00/1605, U/S to Embassy in Santiago, February 28, 1942.

49. Bowers, *Chile Through Embassy Windows,* p. 100.

50. 825.00/1607, Telegram, Embassy in Santiago to S/S, Mar. 2, 1942.

51. Bowers, *Chile Through Embassy Windows,* pp. 78–79 825.00/1736, Bowers to Welles, Aug. 11, 1942.

52. 825.24/706, Embassy in Santiago to S/S, Nov. 24, 1942.

53. 825.00/1641, Memo, Mar. 16, 1942.

54. 740.0011 European War 1939/21299, Letter, Donald Heath to Duggan, Apr. 9, 1942.

55. 825.00/1655, Roosevelt to Bowers, Apr. 24, 1942.

56. 825.01/178, Memo, July 13, 1942.

57. 825.24/569, Memo, May 5, 1942; see also Minutes, Meeting of Liaison Committee, June 3, 1942 (National Archives).

58. 825.248/287, Memo, June 30, 1942.

59. 825.00/1714, Letter, Heath to Duggan, July 20, 1942.

60. FRs, 1942, 6:29.

61. Ibid.

62. 825.24/582 1/2, Memo, July 29, 1942.

63. FRs, 1942, 6:29–31.

64 825.24/614, Memo, Aug. 7, 1942.
65. FRs, 1942, 6:31–32.
66. 810.20 Defense/3172, Memo, Aug. 12, 1942.
67. FRs, 1942, 6:35.
68. 740.0011 European War 1939/25746 7/8, Memo, Nov. 13, 1942.
69. FRs, 1942, 6:39.
70. Ibid., p. 38.
71. Ibid.
72. 825.796/140, Memo, Dec. 3, 1942; and 825.796/140, Memo, Dec. 5, 1942.
73. FRs, 1942, 6:41–42.
74. Ibid., p. 43.
75. 825.24/767, Memo, Dec. 19, 1942.
76. 825.24732 1/2, Memo, Dec. 19, 1942.
77. FRs, 1942, 6:45–46.
78. FRs, 1943, 6:796; and 824.24/732 1/2, Memo, Dec. 26, 1942.
79. 825.24/493, Embassy in Santiago to S/S, June 12, 1942.
80. 825.24/745 2/5, Memo, Dec. 16, 1942.
81. 825.00/1650, Embassy in Santiago to S/S, Apr. 25, 1942.
82. FRs, 1942, 6:28–29.
83. E.g., 740.0011 European War 1939/23467, Roosevelt to Bowers, Aug. 10, 1942.
84. 825.00/1650, Embassy in Santiago to S/S, Apr. 25, 1942.
85. E.g., 711.25/214, Memo, Oct. 16, 1942.
86. 825.00/2094, Embassy in Santiago to S/S, Feb. 12, 1944.
87. FRs, 1942, 6:28–29.
88. 825.01/178, Memo, July 13, 1942.
89. Leopold, *The Growth of American Foreign Policy*, p. 604.
90. 740.0011 European War 1939/21968, Telegram, Embassy in Santiago to S/S and U/S, June 2, 1942.
91. 825.00/1650, Embassy in Santiago to S/S, Apr. 25, 1942.
92. 825.51/1450, Embassy in Santiago to S/S, May 18, 1942.
93. FRs, 1942, 6:22–23.
94. Ibid., p. 23.
95. Ibid., p. 24.
96. Ibid.
97. Ibid., pp. 24–25.
98. 825.51/1453, Embassy in Santiago to S/S, June 20, 1942.
99. FRs, 1942, 6:95. Such comments are particularly ironic in view of Washington's firm refusal to help formulate any kind of hemispheric economic organization after the war.
100. 835.001 Rios, Juan Antonio/91, Memo, Sep. 19, 1942.
101. 825.85/131, Embassy in Santiago to S/S, May 30, 1942; 825.00/1687, Embassy in Santiago to S/S, June 12, 1942; and 810.20 Defense/3172, Memo, August 12, 1942.
102. 825.85/131, Embassy in Santiago to S/S, May 30, 1942; and 825.00/1687, Embassy in Santiago to S/S, June 12, 1942.
103. 825.00/1650, Embassy in Santiago to S/S, Apr. 25, 1942.
104. Bowers, *Chile Through Embassy Windows,* p. 99.
105. Ibid.

106. 825.911/91, Telegram, Embassy in Santiago to S/S, July 26, 1942.

107. 825.911/91, Telegram, S/S to Embassy in Santiago, Aug. 1, 1942.

108. 825.911/107, Memo, Dec. 26, 1942.

109. FRs, 1943, 5:797.

110. 711.25/277, Embassy in Santiago to S/S, Nov. 11, 1942.

111. 123 Bowers, Claude G/292 1/2, Memo, Feb. 6, 1943.

112. 825.00/1689, Bowers to President, April 29, 1942.

113. 711.25/120, Telegram, Embassy in Santiago to U/S, May 20, 1942.

114. FRs, 1942, 6:24–25.

115. 825.24/499, Memos, Apr. 11, 1942, Apr. 13, 1942; also, Minutes, Meeting of Liaison Committee, June 22, 1942.

116. 825.00/1691, Embassy in Santiago to U/S, May 31, 1942; 825.00/1687, Telegram, U/S to Embassy in Santiago, June 20, 1942; and 825.00/1736, Embassy in Santiago to U/S, Aug. 11, 1942.

117. 725.00/18, Telegram, Embassy in Santiago to S/S, July 8, 1942.

118. 825.00/1691, Embassy in Santiago to U/S, May 31, 1942; and 825.00/1736, Embassy in Santiago to U/S, Aug. 11, 1942. Welles seemed ready to accept, as a partial explanation, the idea that Ríos did not understand U.S. policy. See Minutes, Meeting of Liaison Committee, June 22, 1942.

119. 825.00/1727, Embassy in Santiago to S/S, Aug. 19, 1942.

120. FRs, 1942, 6:34.

121. Ibid., p. 27.

122. Claude Bowers, *My Life* (New York, 1962), p. 304.

123. 825.00/1598, Philip W. Bonsal to Welles, Nov. 10, 1941.

124. 825.00/1736, Bowers to Welles, Aug. 11, 1942.

125. Appleton, "Systematic Bias in U.S. Foreign Affairs Reporting."

126. 825.24/614, Memo, Aug. 7, 1942.

127. 825.001 Ríos, Juan Antonio/66, Embassy in Santiago to S/S, Aug. 27, 1942.

128. 825.00/1738, Welles to Bowers, Aug. 29, 1942.

129. 825.001 Ríos, Juan Antonio/59, Telegram, Embassy in Santiago to S/S Aug. 27, 1942.

130. FRs, 1942, 6:33; and 825.001, Ríos, Juan Antonio/84, Memo, Sep. 10, 1942.

131. FRs, 1942, 6:33.

132. 810.74/485, Telegram, Embassy in Santiago to S/S, Sep. 24, 1942.

133. FRs, 1942, 6:93.

134. Ibid., pp. 35–36.

135. "Welles Pledges All Aid to Russia," *New York Times*, Oct. 9, 1942, p. 7; Hull, *Memoirs*, p. 1383.

136. "Twenty-Ninth National Foreign Trade Convention," *Department of State Bulletin*, Oct. 10, 1942, p. 810.

137. 825.00/1759 1/2, Bowers to Roosevelt, Oct. 10, 1942; and 825.001 Ríos, Juan Antonio/113, Embassy in Santiago to S/S, Oct. 10, 1942.

138. *Chile Through Embassy Windows*, p. 110.

139. 825.001 Ríos, Juan Antonio/111, Telegram, Embassy in Santiago to S/S, Oct. 9, 1942.

140. 825.001, Ríos, Juan Antonio/113, Telegram U/S to Embassy in Santiago, Oct. 10, 1942.

141. Ibid.

142. "Exchange of Messages Between . . . ," *Department of State Bulletin,*
Oct. 17, 1942, p. 838.
143. Ibid.
144. FRs, 1942, 5:198.
145. 825.00/1684, Bowers to Welles, May 14, 1942.
146. For a summary of the Bowers–Barras Jarpa memo see FRs, 1942,
5:225–28. It is difficult to evaluate this and other pieces of information in
this category because almost none of the documents relating to the gathering
of intelligence (and no FBI reports) are public. Chile rather consistently
doubted U.S. reports of Axis intelligence efforts and it may have been that
the United States exaggerated the danger. The author feels that most of the
specific information produced by United States intelligence gatherers was
reasonably accurate although its evaluations may have been less than per-
ceptive. Evidently, U.S. businessmen were a prime source of intelligence.
147. Ibid., p. 226.
148. Ibid., pp. 108–85.
149. Ibid., p. 122.
150. Ibid.
151. Ibid., pp. 129–32.
152. Ibid., pp. 135–37.
153. Ibid., p. 138.
154. Ibid.
155. Ibid.
156. Ibid., p. 161.
157. Bowers, *Chile Through Embassy Windows.*, pp. 115–16.
158. FRs, 1942, 6:99–100.
159. Ibid., p. 104.
160. Ibid., p. 105.
161. Ibid.
162. Ibid., p. 108.
163. Ibid., p. 109.
164. Ibid., pp. 108–9.
165. Ibid., p. 110.
166. Ibid.
167. Ibid., p. 111.
168. Ibid.
169. Ibid., p. 113.
170. Ibid.
171. 825.6363, Memo, Sep. 14, 1942.
172. 825.6363/276, Bowers to Roosevelt, Sep. 24, 1942.
173. 810.74/485, Telegram, Embassy in Santiago to S/S, Sep. 24, 1942.
174. FRs, 1942, 6:116.
175. Ibid., pp. 120–23.
176. Ibid., p. 132.
177. 840.51 Frozen Credits/11006, Memo, Aug. 21, 1943.
178. FRs, 1942, 6:28.
179. 862.20225/747A, Telegram, U/S to Embassy in Santiago, Oct. 29, 1942.
180. 862.20225/748, Telegram, Embassy in Santiago to U/S, Oct. 30, 1942.
181. FRs, 1942, 5:100–101.
182. The Emergency Advisory Committee for Political Defense was formulated

by the Rio Declarations with the purpose of coordinating hemispheric actions against subversion.

183. FRs, 1942, 5:103–5.
184. 862.20225/814A 1/2, Telegram, Embassy in Santiago to S/S, Nov. 6, 1942.
185. Unlike the United States, the post of Minister of the Interior in Latin American countries deals with internal order.
186. FRs, 1942, 5:237–39.
187. Luis Palma Zúñiga y Julio Iglesias Meléndez, *Presencia de Juan Antonio Ríos* (Santiago, 1957), p. 169.
188. 740.0011 European War 1939/25883, Telegram, Embassy in Santiago to S/S, Nov. 20, 1942.
189. FRs, 1942, 6:42–43.
190. 740.0011 European War 1939/27116, Memo, Dec. 17, 1942.
191. FRs, 1942, 6:42–43.
192. 825.24/767, Memo, Dec. 19, 1942.
193. FRs, 1942, 6:44.
194. Ibid., p. 45.
195. FRs, 1943, 5:795; see also Oscar Bermúdez Miral, *El Drama Politico de Chile* (Santiago, 1947), pp. 145–46.
196. Ibid., p. 799.
197. Ibid., p. 800.
198. Ibid., pp. 102–3.
199. (Notre Dame, Indiana, 1963). See especially his chapter "The Chilean Right and the United States," pp. 243–56.
200. Ríos did make the trip after the war.
201. FRs, 1943, 5:800.
202. Ibid., p. 805.
203. Ibid., pp. 809–10.
204. 862.20210/2422, Telegram, Embassy in Santiago to S/S, June 30, 1943.
205. 840.51 Frozen Credits/11006, Embassy in Santiago to S/S, July 3, 1943.
206. 840.51 Frozen Credits/11006, Embassy in Santiago to S/S, July 6, 1943.
207. FRs, 1944, 7:788.
208. Ibid., pp. 788–89.
209. Ibid., pp. 789–90.
210. Ibid., p. 798.
211. Ibid., p. 799.
212. Ibid., p. 800.
213. FRs, 1943, 5:900.
214. Ibid., p. 901.
215. Ibid., pp. 902–4.
216. Ibid., pp. 904–5.
217. Ibid., p. 907.
218. 710. Consultation 3/855A, Memo, no date.
219. The decrees are summarized in FRs, 1944, 7:753–54.
220. Ibid., pp. 762–66.
221. Ibid., p. 779.
222. FRs, 1943, 5:812.
223. 723.25/73, Embassy in Santiago to S/S, Mar. 1, 1943.
224. FRs, 1943, 5:825.

225. Ibid., pp. 819-20.
226. 810.24/373, Memo, Sep. 25, 1943.
227. Conn and Fairchild, *The Western Hemisphere*, p. 235.
228. Ibid., pp. 235-36.
229. 825.24/1670, Memo, Dec. 27, 1943.
230. FRs, 1944, 7:673-79.
231. Ibid., p. 676.
232. Ibid., pp. 680-81.
233. Ibid., p. 684.
234. Conn and Fairchild, *The Western Hemisphere*, p. 236.
235. This statement is based on a comparison of figures in FRs, 1944, 7:684, 687.
236. 825.24/9 – 1544, Memo by Heath, Sep. 15, 1944.
237. FRs, 1944, 7:684.
238. 825.6374/1473, Memo, Mar. 22, 1943.
239. 825.6374, Memo, Apr. 21, 1943.
240. 825.6374/1480, Memo, May 7, 1943.
241. FRs, 1943, 5:844-48.
242. 825.6374/1490, Memo, July 15, 1943.
243. Ibid.
244. Same call number, Memo, July 16, 1943.
245. Same call number, Memo, July 17, 1943.
246. 825.6374/1506, Memo, Aug. 26, 1943.
247. 825.6374/6 – 2244, Memo War Production Board, June 20, 1944.
248. FRs, 1943, V, p. 854-57.
249. 825.6374/1515, Memo, Sep. 9, 1943.
250. 825.6374/1520, Embassy in Santiago to S/S, Sep. 25, 1943.
251. Reynolds, "Development Problems of an Export Economy," p. 237.
252. Moran, *Multinational Corporations and the Politics of Independence*, p. 68.
253. 825.6363/407, Memo, June 15, 1944.
254. FRs, 1943, 5:63.
255. Ibid., p. 66.
256. U.S. Department of State, Division of Latin American Republics "Chile and Its Relations with the United States," Feb. 13, 1943, National Archives, Box 5, RG:59.
257. Comisión Económica para América Latina de las Naciones Unidas, *Antecedentes Sobre El Desarrollo de la Economía Chilean, 1925-1952*, 1:103.
258. Ibid., p. 53.
259. 825.00/1972, Embassy in Santiago to S/S, Aug. 27, 1943.
260. 825.00/2155, Hull to Bowers, May 3, 1944.
261. This account of Chile and the prerequisites of the San Francisco Conference is based on FRs, 1944, 7:691, 700.
262. Ibid., p. 695.
263. FRs, 1945, 9:756-57.
264. Ibid., p. 757.
265. Ibid., p. 759.
266. Ibid., p. 760.
267. Ibid., pp. 760-61.
268. Ibid., p. 761.

269. Ibid., p. 764.

270. Ibid., p. 767.

271. Ibid., p. 769.

272. Although the election results showed a minor increase for the right, foreign policy was not the major issue. For the results see Germán Urzúa Valenzuela, *Los Partidos Políticos Chilenos* (Santiago, 1968), p. 87.

CHAPTER 5

The Last Days of Civilian Government in Argentina

1. This paragraph based on FRs, 1941, 6:57–58.

2. Ibid., p. 60.

3. Ibid., p. 36.

4. Ibid., p. 61.

5. Welles, Memo, sub: War Situation: Attitude of Argentina, Dec. 10, 1941, State Department, Division of Latin American Republics, Welles Conversations, bound volumes, RG:59, box 3. Potash, *The Army & Politics in Argentina,* p. 164, suggests Germany had not agreed to this.

6. FRs, 1941, 6:63.

7. Ibid., p. 65.

8. Article 23. See also Article 86, paragraph 19.

9. FRs, 1941, 6:62.

10. 835.00/1108 1/2, Memo, Dec. 12, 1941.

11. FRs, 1941, 6:68.

12. Ibid., p. 63.

13. 835.00/1108 1/2, Memo, Dec. 12, 1941.

14. 835.20/67, Memo, Dec. 22, 1941.

15. 862.20235/727, Telegram, Embassy in Buenos Aires, Jan. 17, 1942; and 862.20235/742, Telegram, Embassy in Buenos Aires to S/S, Jan. 23, 1942.

16. 800.20235/63, Embassy in Buenos Aires to S/S, February 4, 1942.

17. Potash, *The Army & Politics in Argentina,* p. 163. This is based on documents from the German diplomatic archives.

18. Ibid., p. 164.

19. *Argentina en el mundo* (Buenos Aires, 1961), p. 91.

20. 835.00/1176, Embassy in Buenos Aires to S/S, Mar. 27, 1942. These figures conflict with some others but seem to be fairly representative.

21. FRs, 1942, 5:307–8.

22. FRs, 1942, 6:6–7.

23. FRs, 1942, 5:329.

24. Ibid., p. 334.

25. Ibid., p. 335.

26. Ibid.

27. Ibid., pp. 371–72.

28. Ibid., p. 376.

29. Ibid., pp. 373–75.

30. Conil Paz and Ferrari, *Argentina's Foreign Policy,* p. 83.

31. Ibid., pp. 84–85.

32. Ibid., p. 91; and FRs, 1942, 5:377–78.

33. FRs, 1942, 5:355, 385.
34. Ibid., p. 378.
35. Ibid., p. 379.
36. 835.24/301, Telegram, S/S to Embassy in Buenos Aires, Feb. 12, 1942.
37. 835.34/578, Telegram, Embassy in Rio to S/S, Mar. 11, 1942; 810.20 Defense/2344, Telegram, Embassy in Buenos Aires to S/S, Apr. 2, 1942.
38. FRs, 1942, 5:383–384.
39. Ibid., p. 384.
40. 835.24/384, Suggested Press Release, Mar. 20, 1942.
41. FRs, 1942, 5:383.
42. Ibid., p. 385.
43. Ibid., pp. 385–86.
44. Ibid., p. 386.
45. Ibid., pp. 386–87.
46. Ibid., pp. 387–90.
47. Ibid., p. 392.
48. Ibid., pp. 393–94; and 835.34/603, Memo, Apr. 23, 1942.
49. FRs, 1942, 5:395.
50. Ibid., pp. 396–99.
51. Ibid., p. 399.
52. Ibid., p. 400.
53. p. 97.
54. FRs, 1942, 5:398.
55. 835.032/175, Telegram, Embassy in Buenos Aires to S/S July 27, 1942; and 810.20 Defense/3193, Embassy in Buenos Aires to S/S, Aug. 22, 1942.
56. Potash, *The Army & Politics in Argentina*, p. 172.
57. United States Government, *Consultation among the American Republics with Respect to the Argentine Situation* (Washington, 1946), pp. 8–15 (hereafter cited as *Argentine Consultation*); and Simonson, "Nazi Infiltration in South America," pp. 669–73, although Simonson's account is drawn primarily from the former source.
58. Potash, *The Army & Politics in Argentina*, pp. 173–74.
59. 835.857/28, Telegram, Embassy in Buenos Aires to S/S, Apr. 23, 1942; and 835.857/30, Telegram, Embassy in Buenos Aires to S/S, Apr. 25, 1942.
60. 835.857/31, Telegram, S/S to Embassy in Buenos Aires, Apr. 29, 1942.
61. 835.857/31, Telegram, S/S to Embassy in Buenos Aires, Apr. 30, 1942.
62. 835.857/40, Administrator of War Shipping Administration to S/S, May 20, 1942.
63. 835.857/39, Embassy in Buenos Aires to S/S, May 11, 1942.
64. "Según el Jefe de la Armada de la Unión el 'Victoria' fué Torpedeado," *La Prensa*, May 26, 1942; "El Commandante del Victoria Volvió en el Río San Juan," *La Nacion*, May 26, 1942; and "El torpedeamiento del 'Victoria,'" *El Mundo*, May 26, 1942.
65. 835.857/57, Telegram, Embassy in Buenos Aires to S/S, June 17, 1942; also see Modern, "La neutralidad de la Republica Argentina en las dos guerras mundiales," pp. 200–201.
66. 835.857/81, Embassy in Buenos Aires to S/S, July 7, 1942.
67. Ibid.; also see Modern, "La neutralidad de la Republica Argentina en las dos guerras mundiales," pp. 201–3.
68. Peterson, *Argentina and the United States*, p. 422.

69. 611.355/262, Draft Memo, U/S to Secretary of Agriculture, Jan. 5, 1942.
70. 611.355/303, Duggan to U/S, Feb. 18, 1942. See also Felix Weil, *Argentine Riddle* (New York, 1944), pp. 200–209, for a clear statement against the ban.
71. 611.355/307, Duggan to U/S, Mar. 10, 1942; and 611.355/306, Duggan to U/S, Mar. 20, 1942.
72. 611.355/317, Duggan to U/S, Mar. 30, 1942.
73. 611.355/308, Telegram, Embassy in Buenos Aires to U/S, Apr. 15, 1942.
74. 611.355/316, Memo, Apr. 16, 1942.
75. 611.355/310, Duggan to U/S, Apr. 17, 1942.
76. 611.355/319, May 11, 1942.
77. 611.355/319, Acting S/S to Ambassador Espil, May 22, 1942.
78. 611.355/319, Duggan to Hawkins, May 15, 1942. There is also some information to suggest that at the time Argentina was interested in the United States market because it was hoped that the United States would pay premium prices for quick-frozen Tierra del Fuego mutton for which the British had refused to pay the premium prices.
79. 800.20235/103, Embassy in Buenos Aires to S/S, Apr. 14, 1942.
80. 800.20235/96, Welles to Armour, Apr. 3, 1942.
81. Potash, *The Army & Politics in Argentina,* p. 167.
82. Simonson, "Nazi Infiltration in South America," p. 650.
83. U.S. Government, *Argentine Consultation,* pp. 72–73.
84. 810.20 Defense/2709, Telegram, Embassy in Buenos Aires to U/S, May 23, 1942.
85. Ibid.
86. 735.00/34, Accounts of Acting President's Message to Congress, May 28, 1942.
87. FRs, 1942, 5:201–2.
88. 740.0011 European War 1939/22790, Telegram, Embassy in Buenos Aires to S/S, July 8, 1942.
89. 835.032/170, Telegram, Embassy in Buenos Aires to S/S, July 20, 1942. See also Rennie, *The Argentine Republic,* p. 298.
90. 835.032/175, Telegram, Embassy in Buenos Aires to S/S, July 27, 1942.
91. FRs, 1942, 5:202–3.
92. Ibid., p. 204.
93. Ibid., p. 205.
94. Ibid.
95. Ibid., pp. 208–9.
96. Ibid., pp. 210–11.
97. Ibid., p. 212.
98. Ibid., p. 224.
99. Ibid., pp. 218–24.
100. Snow, *Argentine Radicalism,* p. 58.
101. 740.0011 European War 1939/24861, Embassy in Buenos Aires to S/S, Oct. 3, 1942.
102. Conil Paz and Ferrari, *Argentina's Foreign Policy,* p. 71; Simonson, "Nazi Infiltration in South America," p. 657.
103. Article 86, paragraph 14. See also Modern, "La neutralidad de la Republica Argentina en las dos guerras mundiales," pp. 204–5.

104. Simonson, "Nazi Infiltration in South America," p. 658.

105. Ibid., pp. 658–59.

106. FRs, 1942, 5:230.

107. Ibid.

108. 800.20235/206, Memo, Oct. 28, 1942.

109. FRs, 1942, 5:233–34.

110. Ibid., p. 239.

111. Ibid., pp. 240–41.

112. Ibid., pp. 242–45.

113. Ibid., p. 247.

114. Ibid., p. 248; Hull, *Memoirs,* p. 1382; and Simonson, "Nazi Infiltration in South America," p. 666.

115. FRs, 1942, 5:250.

116. Ibid., pp. 252–54.

117. Ibid., p. 259.

118. Ibid., p. 258.

119. 862.20210/2104 1/2, Memo, Dec. 24, 1942.

120. FRs, 1943, 5:4–5.

121. Ibid., pp. 8–9.

122. 862.20210/2189, Telegram, Embassy in Buenos Aires to S/S, Jan. 23, 1943.

123. Ibid.

124. 862.20210/2252, Memo, Embassy in Buenos Aires to S/S, Feb. 1, 1943.

125. FRs, 1942, 5:110. An interesting account from the point of view of the companies involved is in Anthony Sampson, *The Sovereign State of ITT* (New York, 1973), pp. 33–38.

126. FRs, 1942, 5:114.

127. Ibid., p. 119.

128. Western Telegraph, a British subsidiary, refused to provide information.

129. FRs, 1942, 5:123.

130. Ibid., p. 129.

131. Ibid., p. 132.

132. Ibid., pp. 460–61.

133. E.g., ibid., p. 148.

134. Ibid., pp. 154–55.

135. Ibid., pp. 172–73.

136. Ibid., p. 174.

137. Ibid., pp. 175–76.

138. Ibid., p. 176.

139. Ibid., pp. 177–78.

140. 835.741/13, Telegram, Embassy in Buenos Aires to S/S, Dec. 2, 1942.

141. FRs, 1942, 5:178–79.

142. 800.20235/236 1/2, Memo, Dec. 8, 1942.

143. FRs, 1942, 5:179–80.

144. Ibid., p. 182.

145. FRs, 1943, 5:514–15.

146. Ibid., p. 516.

147. Ibid., p. 517.

148. Ibid., p. 518.

149. Ibid., p. 515..

150. Ibid., p. 516.

151. E.g., ibid., pp. 520, 522.

152. Ibid., pp. 522–23.

153. Ibid., p. 519.

154. Ibid., p. 520.

155. "Enrique Ruiz-Guiñazú, 86, Dies; Ex-Argentine Foreign Minister," Nov. 15, 1967, p. 46.

156. *La Política Argentina y el Futuro de America* (Buenos Aires).

157. 740.0011 European War 1939/11290, Memos, May 14, May 15, 1941.

158. Welles, *Seven Decisions That Changed the World,* p. 100.

159. Ibid.

160. *The Time for Decision,* p. 229.

161. Ibid.

162. 835.00/1210, Speech, May 14, 1942.

163. E.g., 835.032/170, Telegram, Embassy in Buenos Aires to S/S, July 20, 1942.

164. *DGFP,* D, 13:86–87.

165. E.g., see 835.00/1291, Memo, Oct. 6, 1942. The quotations which follow are based on his "The Necessary Revolution" which is an excerpt from "How to Effect the Revolution We Need," *La Argentina ante si misma* (Buenos Aires, 1942), pp. 173–85, *passim,* which is included in Joseph R. Barager's *Why Perón Came to Power* (New York, 1968), pp. 161–73.

166. 810.20 Defense/2695A, Telegram, S/S to Embassy in Buenos Aires, May 15, 1942.

167. 735.00/37, Memo, Aug. 14, 1942.

168. 800.20235/206, Memo, Oct. 28, 1942.

169. Welles, Memo, sub: Conversation between Espil and Welles, Subject Waldo Frank, Aug. 4, 1942, State Department, Division of Latin American Republics, Welles Conversations, bound volumes, RG:59, box 3. The observation regarding Espil should not be taken to mean that he was actively changing the policy in his presentations to Washington. It is only that he encouraged a belief in Washington that the policy of Buenos Aires was malleable and that sometimes Espil underestimated the points of disagreement.

170. 835.00/1145, Telegram, Acting S/S to Embassy in Buenos Aires, Feb. 24, 1942.

171. 835.00/1145, Telegram, Embassy in Buenos Aires to U/S, Feb. 23, 1942.

172. 835.00/1179, Memo, Mar. 23, 1942.

173. 835.032/180, Memo, Aug. 1, 1942.

174. 735.41/8, Memo, Oct. 9, 1942.

175. 835.00/1358, Embassy in Buenos Aires to S/S, Feb. 5, 1943.

176. Ibid.

177. 810.20 Defense/2709, Telegram, Embassy in Buenos Aires to U/S, May 23, 1942.

178. 835.00/1374, Memo, Feb. 8, 1943.

179. A good memo on these questions is 710. Consultation (3)/835, Argentine Balance Sheet, Sep. 25, 1942.

180. 835.24/790, Memo, Sep. 23, 1942.

181. Ibid. The monthly schedule in this memo called for the following:
coal, 16,000 tons; newsprint, 7,500 tons; paper and manufactures, 5,000; iron,
and steel, 5,000; tin plate, 4,000; wood and manufacturers, 1,500; chemicals,
1,000 tons. A total of 40,000 tons.

182. 835.00/1358, Embassy in Buenos Aires to S/S, Feb. 4, 1943.

183. 835.00/1374, Memo, Feb. 8, 1943.

184. 835.24/1313, Memo, Feb. 24, 1943.

185. Extracts from Memo, FRs, 1943, 5:471-72.

186. Ibid., p. 468.

187. 835.24/1879, Armour to Assistant S/S Acheson, June 11, 1943;
835.24/1563, Memo, May 11, 1943. Later, the BEW reverses its position.

188. 835.24/2077, Memo, Aug. 6, 1943.

189. An article that argues effectively in favor of harsher sanctions against
Argentina is Norman MacKenzie, "Argentina and Britain," *Political Quarterly*
(London) (April-June, 1945).

190. 835.24/1980, Memo, Aug. 9, 1943.

191. 740.00112A European War 1939/1187, Embassy in Buenos Aires to
S/S, May 14, 1942.

192. 740.00112A European War 1939/21092, Embassy in Buenos Aires to
S/S, Nov. 18, 1942.

193. FRs, 1943, 5:411.

194. 740.00112A European War 1939/21092, S/S to Embassy in Buenos
Aires, Feb. 23, 1943.

195. 740.00112A European War 1939/35517, Memo, Aug. 28, 1943.

196. FRs, 1943, 5:403, 415.

197. Ibid., p. 409.

198. Ibid., p. 413.

199. Ibid., p. 475. The author is using the question of complexity as an
excuse for not going into detail on the matter.

200. 710. Consultation (3)/835, Memo, Embassy in Buenos Aires to S/S,
Dec. 9, 1942.

201. FRs, 1942, 5:460-61.

202. E.g., ibid., pp. 463-71.

203. Ibid., pp. 471-74.

204. John Morton Blum, *From the Morgenthau Diaries: Years of War, 1941-
1945* (Boston, 1967), p. 196.

205. See ibid., pp. 194-96.

206. FRs, 1942, 5:471-74.

207. Blum, *From the Morgenthau Diaries*, p. 196.

208. FRs, 1942, 5:471.

209. Ibid., pp. 58-73. This is a memo summing up the results of the meeting.

210. 710. Consultation (3)/835, Memo, Dec. 9, 1942.

211. FRs, 1943, 5:468.

212. Ibid., pp. 313-14.

213. Ibid., pp. 314-25.

214. Ibid., p. 480.

CHAPTER 6

Sanctions Against Argentina

1. 835.00/1579, Memo, June 21, 1943; Francis Herron, *Letters from the Argentine* (New York, 1943), p. 295.
2. Jose L. de Imaz, *Los que mandan* (Buenos Aires, 1964), p. 20.
3. Martin Needler, "Political Development and Military Intervention in Latin America," *American Political Science Review* 60 (Sep. 1966), 618.
4. Frederick A. Hollander, "Oligarchy and the Politics of Petroleum in Argentina: The Case of the Saltra Oligarchy and Standard Oil, 1918–1933" (University of California at Los Angeles, Dissertation, 1976).
5. See Snow, *Argentine Radicalism*, p. 58; Peterson, *Argentina and the United States* p. 429; Ciria, *Partidos y Poder en la Argentina Moderna*, pp. 87–88; de Imaz, *Los que mandan*, pp. 20–25.
6. Potash, *The Army & Politics in Argentina*, pp. 191–93.
7. These observations are expanded upon in Whitaker, *The United States and Argentina*, pp. 39–46.
8. Peter G. Snow offers some interesting observations regarding the class basis of the Radicals in "The Class Basis of Argentine Political Parties," *American Political Science Review* 63 (Mar. 1969), 618. See also Smith, *Argentina and the Failure of Democracy*, ch. 2.
9. Falcoff and Dolkart, *Prologue to Perón*, p. 111.
10. *Nationalism in Contemporary Latin America* (New York, 1966), p. 53.
11. The other two types—"populist," which perhaps Irigoyen at his most radical represented, and "nasserist," which one can stretch to Perónism—need not enter the discussion at this point.
12. Whitaker and Jordan, *Nationalism in Contemporary Latin America*, p. 57.
13. David C. Jordan, "Argentina's Nationalist Movements and the Political Parties (1930–1963): A Study of Conflict" (University of Pennsylvania, Dissertation, 1964), pp. 65–66.
14. Marysa Gerassi, "Argentine Nationalism of the Right: The History of an Ideological Development, 1930–1946" (Columbia University, Dissertation, 1964).
15. Jordan, "Argentina's Nationalist Movements and the Political Parties," p. 85.
16. Gerassi, "Argentine Nationalism of the Right," p. 1–2.
17. Jordan, "Argentina's Nationalist Movements and the Political Parties," pp. 65–66.
18. Fredrick B. Pike and Thomas Stritch, eds., *The New Corporatism* (Notre Dame, Ind., 1975) has an interesting set of essays on this topic.
19. Gerassi, "Argentine Nationalism of the Right," p. 145.
20. See Gerassi, "Argentine Nationalism of the Right"; also, Weil, *Argentine Riddle*, pp. 49–52.
21. Gerassi, "Argentine Nationalism of the Right," p. 153.
22. 835.00/1280, Embassy in Buenos Aires to S/S, Sep. 29, 1942; 835.01/63, Embassy in Buenos Aires to S/S, Mar. 12, 1943.

23. *Nationalism in Latin America* (New York, 1966), p. 160.

24. *Catholicism, Nationalism, and Democracy in Argentina* (Notre Dame, Ind., 1958).

25. *DGFP*, C, 5:848.

26. Weil, *Argentine Riddle*, pp. 7–9; Paul E. Brown, "Ideological Origins of Modern Argentine Nationalism" (Claremont Graduate School, Dissertation, 1965), pp. 132–33; 835.414/43, Embassy in Buenos Aires to S/S, May 16, 1944; 835.00/1130, Report, Central Information Office of Embassy in Buenos Aires, Jan. 16, 1942; 711.35/169, Memo, Jan. 12, 1943; J. J. Hernández Arregui, *La formación de la conciencia nacional, 1930–1960* (Buenos Aires, 1960).

27. Brown, "Ideological Origins of Modern Nationalism," pp. 132–133.

28. Samuel L. Baily, *Labor, Nationalism and Politics in Argentina* (New Brunswick, N.J., 1967), p. 72.

29. The Darío Canton paper "Military Interventions in Argentina," is interesting on this topic.

30. Whitaker and Jordan, *Nationalism in Contemporary Latin America*, p. 66.

31. Much of the writing on this topic, including the reports of the United States Embassy in Buenos Aires at the time, puts great emphasis on this point. However, Potash, *The Army & Politics in Argentina* (particularly in chapter seven) does not seem to take the problem as seriously as domestic political questions.

32. (New York, 1944), pp. 3–39, *passim.* See also the account in Ruth L. Greenup and Leonard Greenup, *Revolution before Breakfast* (Chapel Hill, N.C., 1947).

33. See FRs, 1943, 5:365–78, for a sample of these despatches.

34. Ciria, *Partidos y Poder en la Argentina Moderna,* p. 99; Goldwert, *Democracy, Militarism, and Nationalism in Argentina,* p. 80.

35. FRs, 1943, 5:368.

36. 835.00/1511, Telegram, Embassy in Rio to U/S, June 9, 1943; and 835.00/1525, Telegram, Embassy in Rio to U/S, June 10, 1943.

37. 835/00/1525, Telegram, June 10, 1943.

38. 835.00/1582, Memo, June 24, 1943.

39. FRs, 1943, 5:385.

40. Ibid., p. 387.

41. Ibid., p. 388.

42. Ibid., p. 391.

43. Ibid., pp. 395–96.

44. Ibid., pp. 419–424.

45. Ibid., p. 424.

46. Ibid., p. 428.

47. 835.00/1651, Armour Memo, July 5, 1943.

48. FRs, 1943, 5:429–30; and 835.00/1651, Armour Memo, July 6, 1943.

49. FRs, 1943, 5:429–30.

50. Josephs, *Argentina Diary*, pp. 84–90.

51. FRs, 1943, 5:436.

52. 835.00/1582, Duggan to Welles, June 24, 1943.

53. FRs, 1943, 5:444.

54. Ibid., pp. 444–47.

55. Ibid., pp. 446–47; 835.00/1716, Armour Memo, July 30, 1943.

56. FRs, 1943, 5:447–51.

57. 835.00/1762, Memo, Aug. 9, 1943.

58. FRs, 1943, 5:451–52.

59. 840.51 Frozen Credits 35/234, Memo, Aug. 7, 1943.

60. FRs, 1943, 5:454–60.

61. 835.00/1911, Memo, Sep. 7, 1943.

62. FRs, 1943, 5:460; Josephs, *Argentina Diary*, p. 148.

63. Josephs, *Argentina Diary*, pp. 148–49; and 835.00/1901, Memo, Sep. 14, 1943.

64. "Statement Assails Hull," *New York Times*, Sep. 12, 1943, p. 46.

65. *The Ruling Few* (London, 1952), p. 297.

66. Potash, *The Army & Politics in Argentina*, p. 222.

67. Conil Paz and Ferrari, *Argentina's Foreign Policy*, p. 111.

68. Ramos, *Revolución y contra-revolución en Argentina*, 2:572.

69. Greenup and Greenup, *Revolution before Breakfast*, pp. 243–44.

70. This is the interpretation of David Rudgers, "Challenge to the Hemisphere: Argentina Confronts the United States, 1938–1947" (George Washington University, Dissertation, 1972), p. 351.

71. 835.00/2162, Memo, Oct. 16, 1943.

72. FRs, 1943, 5:462–63.

73. Josephs discusses these closings, *Argentina Diary*, pp. 190–91.

74. 840.51 Frozen Credits 35/155, Memo, Oct. 30, 1943; FRs, 1943, 5:496–99.

75. 840.51 Frozen Credits 35/155, Memo, Oct. 30, 1943.

76. FRs, 1943, 5:495.

77. Ibid., p. 496.

78. Hull, *Memoirs*, pp. 1379, 1388. See also Acheson's account of this Hull-Morgenthau rivalry in Dean Acheson, *Present at the Creation* (New York, 1969), pp. 9–11; and see Blum, *From the Morgenthau Diaries*, pp. 194–206.

79. 835.00/2184, Memo, Nov. 13, 1943.

80. FRs, 1943, 5:506–7.

81. This tactic of the coordinated, selective placement of advertising in Latin American papers evidently had success in influencing editorial policies in some countries during the war. See Bushnell, *Eduardo Santos and the Good Neighbor.*

82. Josephs, *Argentina Diary*, p. 320.

83. 835.918/117, Telegram, Embassy in Buenos Aires to S/S, Jan. 7, 1944.

84. 835.00/2274, Telegram, Embassy in Buenos Aires to U/S, Jan. 24, 1944.

85. Hull, *Memoirs*, p. 1390. For a much different interpretation of events in Bolivia and the United States reaction, see Green, *The Containment of Latin America*, pp. 142–52.

86. 835.34/832, Memo, Jan. 7, 1944.

87. 711.35/212, Memo, Jan. 10, 1944.

88. Hull, *Memoirs*, pp. 1390–91.

89. FRs, 1944, 7:228–29.

90. Ibid., pp. 229–31.

91. Ibid., p. 228.

92. 835.50/150, Memo, Jan. 19, 1944.

93. FRs, 1944, 7:441.

94. 835.51/159, Memo, Jan. 19, 1944.

95. This account of the Helmuth case is drawn primarily from Potash, *The Army & Politics in Argentina,* pp. 172-73, 222-23, and 230-33.

96. The degree to which the Allies were reading coded messages from spies in Buenos Aires is difficult to ascertain. Knowledge that this was going on would be carefully protected, but such "accidents" as Helmuth's arrest seem to be best understood through either broken codes or double agents. See David Kahn, *The Codebreakers* (New York, 1967), chs. 14-16.

97. FRs, 1944, 7:231.

98. 835.00/2899, Memo, Jan. 27, 1944.

99. FRs, 1944, 7:440.

100. Ibid., pp. 232-33.

101. Ibid., p. 378.

102. Potash, *The Army & Politics in Argentina,* pp. 231-32.

103. FRs, 1944, 7:240.

104. Ibid., pp. 238-40.

105. Ibid., p. 9.

106. Ibid., pp. 236-37.

107. Ibid., pp. 242-43.

108. Woods, "United States Policy Toward Argentina," p. 183.

109. FRs, 1944, 7:247.

110. Ibid., p. 250.

111. Ibid., pp. 246-47.

112. 835.00/2351, Telegram, Embassy in Santiago to S/S, Feb. 15, 1944; 835.00/2357, Memo, Feb. 15, 1944; and 835.00/2372, Telegram, Embassy in Buenos Aires to S/S, Feb. 19, 1944.

113. Brown, "Ideological Origins of Modern Argentine Nationalism," pp. 171-73.

114. FRs, 1944, 7:263-64.

115. Ibid., p. 257.

116. Ibid., pp. 252-54.

117. Ibid., p. 254.

118. Ibid., p. 255.

119. Ibid., pp. 258-59.

120. Ibid., p. 257.

121. Ibid., pp. 259-60.

122. Irving S. Lewis, "American Press Opinion of Argentina, 1939-1949" (Georgetown University, Thesis, 1959), ch. 6, pp. 1-5.

123. FRs, 1944, 7:294-95.

124. Bowers, *Chile Through Embassy Windows,* p. 123.

125. Ibid., p. 260.

126. Ibid.

127. Ibid., pp. 260-62.

128. Ibid., p. 262.

129. 835.00/2692, Memo, Mar. 1, 1944; 835.00/2620, Memo, Mar. 4, 1944.

130. FRs, 1944, 7:413.

131. Ibid.

132. Ibid., p. 416.

133. 835.00/2814, Embassy in Buenos Aires to S/S, Apr. 20, 1944.

134. Kelly, *The Ruling Few,* pp. 113, 308-10.

135. FRs, 1944, 7:302.
136. Ibid., p. 303.
137. Ibid., pp. 264–65.
138. *The Ruling Few*, p. 310.
139. Ibid., p. 288.
140. Ibid., p. 297.
141. FRs, 1944, 7:265–66.
142. Ibid., pp. 267–68.
143. 835.00/2824, Memo, May 3, 1944.
144. Israel, *The War Diary of Breckinridge Long*, p. 281.
145. Ibid., p. 324.
146. May, "The Bureaucratic Politics Approach," p. 150.
147. (New York, 1946), p. 197.
148. Ibid., p. 198.
149. Ibid., p. 199.
150. FRs, 1944, 7:269–70.
151. Ibid., p. 271.
152. Ibid.
153. Ibid.
154. Ibid., pp. 271–73.
155. 835.01/420, Telegram, Embassy in Buenos Aires to S/S, May 22, 1944.
156. FRs, 1944, 7:275.
157. Ibid., p. 274.
158. Ibid., pp. 276–77.
159. 835.01/6-2644, Telegram, Embassy in Quito to S/S, no. 657, June 26, 1944.
160. FRs, 1944, 7:314–15; 835.01/5-2444, Memo, Wendelin to Raynor, May 24, 1944.
161. FRs, 1944, 7:278.
162. Ibid., pp. 279, 320.
163. Ibid., pp. 315–20.
164. Ibid., pp. 321–24.
165. Ibid., pp. 328–29.
166. Ibid., p. 335.
167. 835.24/7-1744, Memo, Spaeth, July 17, 1944.
168. FRs, 1944, 7:324, 326.
169. 835.00/7-2444, Excerpts of Minutes, Meeting of the Policy Committee of the Department of State, July 10, 1944.
170. FRs, 1944, 7:324-27. Emphasis is Duggan's.
171. Ibid., p. 327.
172. (New York, 1961).
173. Ibid., p. 328.
174. Ibid., p. 337.
175. E.g., *The Time for Decision*, p. 236.
176. Welles, *Seven Decisions That Shaped History*, p. 104.
177. Ibid., p. 105.
178. E.g., Francisco Cuevas Cancino, *Roosevelt y la Buena Vecindad* (Mexico City, 1954), p. 438; for an intensely anti-Hull account of the Argentine crisis see pp. 436–50.

179. Woods, "United States Policy Toward Argentina," pp. 220–22.

180. Duggan, *The Americas*, p. 105.

181. "Storm Over Havana: Who Were the Real Heroes? ," *Chicago Tribune Book World,* Jan. 19, 1969, p. 1.

182. For an example of this type of approach see Robert Bendiner, *The Riddle of the State Department* (New York, 1942).

183. FRs, 1944, 7:280, is the summary on which this account is based.

184. Ibid., pp. 280–83.

185. Ibid., pp. 283–84.

186. Woods, "United States Policy Toward Argentina," p. 227.

187. FRs, 1944, 7:337.

188. Ibid., p. 284.

189. Ibid., p. 348–49.

190. 835.01/11-2144, Memo for President, "Our Policy Toward Argentina," Nov. 21, 1944.

191. *The Ruling Few,* p. 293.

192. David Eric Green, "Security and Development: The United States' Approach to Latin America, 1940-1948" (Cornell University, Dissertation, 1967), p. 127. This is the work on which Green based *The Containment of Latin America*; a similar quote is found there on page 140. The dissertation quotation is a bit more to the point and therefore is cited here.

193. 710. Consultation (4)/8-544, Memo by Gray, Aug. 5, 1944.

194. 835.01/8-744, Memo from Gray, Aug. 7, 1944.

195. Sir Llewellyn Woodward, *British Foreign Policy in the Second World War* (London, 1962), p. 412.

196. *The Ruling Few,* p. 114.

197. FRs, 1944, 7:321.

198. Ibid., p. 330.

199. Ibid., p. 332.

200. Woodward, *British Foreign Policy in the Second World War*, pp. 413, 414–16.

201. FRs, 1944, 7:333.

202. Ibid., p. 334.

203. Ibid., p. 337.

204. Ibid., p. 338.

205. Ibid., pp. 338–40.

206. Ibid., pp. 340, 341.

207. Ibid., pp. 342–43.

208. Ibid., p. 343.

209. Ibid., pp. 345–48.

210. Ibid., p. 349.

211. Ibid., p. 350.

212. Ibid., pp. 351–52.

213. Ibid., pp. 356–57.

214. Ibid., pp. 357–58.

215. Ibid., pp. 361–62.

216. Ibid., p. 362.

217. Ibid., p. 363.

218. Woodward, *British Foreign Policy in the Second World War*, p. 417.

219. FRs, 1944, 7:363.

220. Woodward, *British Foreign Policy in the Second World War,* p. 415.
221. FRs, 1944, 7:364.
222. Ibid., p. 350.
223. Ibid., pp. 355–56.
224. Ibid., p. 358.
225. Ibid., pp. 366–67.
226. Ibid.
227. Ibid., p. 371.
228. Kelly, *The Ruling Few,* p. 293.
229. FRs, 1944, 7:371–77.
230. Ibid., p. 373.
231. E.g., Leopoldo Portnoy, *Análisis crítico de la economía Argentina* (Mexico City, 1961), p. 8; United Nations Secretariat of the Economic Commission for Latin America, *Economic Survey of Latin America, 1948* (Lake Success, N.Y., 1949), pp. 2, 4. Also note the almost total lack of comment regarding the impact of the war on the Argentine economy (except on the point of accumulated reserves and as a stimulus to industrialization) in Aldo Ferrer, *The Argentine Economy* (Berkeley, Calif., 1967) translated from *La Economía Argentina* (Mexico City, 1963) and Villaneuva "Economic Development" in Falcoff and Dolkart, *Prologue to Perón.*
232. Woods, "United States Policy Toward Argentina," summarizes this well, pp. 251–58.
233. Peter Collier and David Horowitz, *The Rockefellers: An American Dynasty* (New York, 1976), pp. 228–34.
234. Hull, *Memoirs,* p. 1405–7.
235. FRs, 1945 9:1–153. See also Michael Francis, "The United States and the Act of Chapultepec," *Southwestern Social Science Quarterly* 45 (Dec. 1964).
236. FRs, 1945, 9:528.
237. Ibid., pp. 374–75.
238. Ibid., p. 380.
239. 835.00/4–545, Memo, J. E. Brown, Apr. 19, 1945; 835.00/2-845, Enclosure to Despatch 5432, Embassy in Montevideo to S/S, Feb. 8, 1945; 835.00/10-744, Despatch 16319, Embassy in Buenos Aires to S/S, Oct. 7, 1944.
240. On this see Thomas F. McGann, "The Ambassador and the Dictator: The Braden Mission to Argentina and Its Significance for United States Relations with Latin America," *The Centennial Review* 6 (Summer 1962); Rudolph Reeder, "The United States and Argentina, 1943–1948: An Ethical Case Study" (American University, Dissertation, 1969); Braden, *Diplomats and Demagogues,* chs. 30–33; Rudgers, "Challenge to the Hemisphere."

CONCLUSION

1. Anthony O'Brien "The Politics of Dependency: A Case Study of Chile, 1938–1945" (University of Notre Dame, Dissertation, 1976).
2. Hans Morgenthau, *Politics Among Nations: The Struggle for Power and Peace* (New York, any edition).
3. Hilton, *Brazil and the Great Powers;* Frank D. McCann, *The Brazilian-*

American Alliance, 1937–1945 (Princeton, N.I., 1973); see also John D. Wirth, *The Politics of Brazilian Development, 1930–1954* (Stanford, Cal., 1969).
    4. Hilton, *Brazil and the Great Powers,* p. 227.

INDEX

Declaration of Lima *(continued)*,
55, 142, 145
Declaration of Panama (1939), 26,
57, 63, 65, 67, 79, 142, 145
del Pedregal, Guillermo, 21, 38, 85,
94
Democrats (Chile), 15, 123
Denmark, 32
Dependency, 2–3, 60, 181, 220, 230,
232, 242–43, 245
Díaz-Alejandro, Carlos, 256n
Divine, Robert A., 258n
Dolkart, Ronald H., 256n, 258n,
277n, 283n
Dominican Republic, 80, 119
Dozer, Donald, 257n
Duggan, Laurence, 37, 104–5, 107,
134, 139, 152, 159, 179–83,
199, 203, 207, 209, 225–27,
262n, 282n
Duran Bernales, Florencio, 34

Earthquake, 7, 17–20
Ecuador, 31, 84, 90, 121, 143, 223
Edelstein, Joel, 249n
Eden, Anthony, 231-33, 235
Eighth International Conference of
American States (Lima, 1938),
24–25, 54–56, 78, 148
El Pampero, 67, 74–75, 147, 160,
188, 196, 219
El Salvador, 244
Emergency Advisory Committee for
Political Defense, 123, 127,
166–68, 268–69n
England, 9–10, 12, 29, 32, 38, 43–
44, 46–48, 51–52, 54, 56, 58–
59, 64–68, 72, 74, 78, 132,
145, 159, 169–70, 172–73,
192–93, 203
reluctance to cooperate with U.S.,
102, 150, 178–79, 181–82,
207, 210, 218–20, 229–39,
242–43, 246
Epstein, Fritz, 253n
Escobar, Adrian Cesar, 205
Escudero, Oscar, 135
Espil, Felipe, 58, 70–71, 82, 149–50,

153–54, 159, 166–67, 177,
199, 204, 217, 222
Export-Import Bank, 18–21, 65,
181, 186–87

Fagen, Richard, 249n
Fairchild, Byron, 253n, 259n, 270n
Falcoff, Mark, 192, 256n, 258n,
277n, 283n
Farrell, Edelmiro, 215–16, 219, 221–
22, 224–25, 228–29, 232, 238–
40
Farrell, R. Barry, 249n
Fascism, 5, 28, 40, 45, 56, 72, 176,
206, 231, 234, 246
Fenwick, Charles, 263n
Fernández Artucio, Hugo, 260n
Fernández y Fernández, Joaquín,
123, 128, 130, 141–43, 224
Ferrari, Gustavo E., 156, 256n, 260n,
271n, 273n, 279n
Ferrer, Aldo, 283n
Fillol, Tomás Roberto, 256n
FOMENTO (Chilean Development
Corporation), 20–21, 38
Foreign Bondholders Protective
Association (FBHPA), 10–13
France, 14, 26, 32, 38–39, 42, 56,
59, 62, 65, 67, 169, 176, 221,
236
Francis, Michael, 249n, 283n
Franco, Francisco, 22, 24, 176, 194,
246
Frye, Alton, 259n, 262n

Gache, Roberto, 171, 173–74
Galbraith, John Kenneth, 227–28,
252n
Gerassi, Marysa, 193, 277n
German
airlines in Latin America, efforts
to control, 69, 147, 204
military advisers in Latin America,
27–28, 52
propaganda in Argentina, 52, 57,
59, 63, 67–68, 73–76, 83, 148,
160–62